BESTSELLING
BOOK SERIES

eBay® For Dummies,® 4th Edition

Cheat Sheet

eBay Time and Updates

eBay's clocks are set to military time in the Pacific Time zone. Look at the table on my Web site, which has a printable conversion chart of eBay times. Also keep abreast of changes at eBay by visiting my Web site and get a free subscription to my newsletter. Here's the Web address:

www.coolebaytools.com

Know Your Auction Terms

- **Reserve price:** The minimum price a seller is willing to accept for an item up for auction. Setting a reserve is optional, and only the seller knows the reserve price. If the bidding doesn't exceed the reserve, the seller has the option to keep the item. eBay charges the seller a small fee for this option.

- **Minimum bid:** The lowest acceptable bid for an item, set by the seller. This amount must be determined by the seller and is not kept secret. Minimum bid amounts are often different from reserve prices.

- **Multiple Item (Dutch) auction:** An auction that allows a seller to put multiple identical items up for sale instead of holding multiple separate auctions. The seller must sell all items at the *lowest winning price.* You can bid on one, some, or all of the items.

- **BIN (Buy It Now):** You have the option of purchasing an item with the BIN option. If you feel the BIN price is a bit more than you want to pay, place a bid at the minimum bid level (or the most you'd like to pay). That way, the BIN option disappears, and you may just win the item at the lower price.

- **Proxy bid:** You can decide the most you're willing to pay for an item and allow eBay's bidding program to place bids for you while you go on with your life. The proxy bidder ups the ante incrementally to beat out your competition until you're outbid or win the auction.

Tips for Sellers

- Find out as much as you can about the item's value, history, and condition.

- Answer all questions posed by prospective bidders via e-mail within several hours. Don't let too much time pass by, lest you appear uninterested in their queries.

- Check out your eBay competition. If a ton of other auctions are taking place at the same time for the same kind of item and the bidding is competitive, wait until the competition is fierce for a few select items.

- Make sure your item isn't prohibited or considered questionable by eBay. If you're not sure, read eBay's guidelines and check your local laws.

- Be sure to add a picture to spruce up your auction, and make sure that your title highlights the item's keywords — but don't gloss over its flaws in the description. Being direct, informative, and concise shows potential buyers that you're honest and easy to work with.

For Dummies: Bestselling Book Series for Beginners

eBay® For Dummies, 4th Edition

Cheat Sheet

Tips for Buyers

Before you bid on an item in an auction, follow these tips:

- Research the item before you bid, and search completed auctions to see what price similar items have sold for in the past. If the item is new and can be bought in a store, do some online research to find out what the stores are selling the item for. Don't overbid!

- Make a mental note of the cost of shipping prior to bidding on an item. Add the shipping cost to your total bid to get a clear idea of the total amount you will be paying.

- Check the seller's feedback. No matter how high the feedback rating is, be sure the latest feedback isn't negative.

- Bid in odd increments. Bidders often bid in round numbers (like 25-cent increments). If you bid in 27-cent increments, you can win by just 2 cents!

- Have fun and be prepared to pay for whatever you bid on. **Remember:** In many states, placing a bid is a binding contract.

Feedback Stuff You Need to Know

Before you send feedback to another eBay member or read feedback eBay members have sent you, make sure you do the following:

- Before you bid on an item on eBay, **do** check the seller's feedback rating by clicking the number that appears next to the seller's User ID.

- Even if you see a large amount of positive feedback, **do** check to be sure that the seller doesn't also have a growing number of negative feedback responses — especially recently. In the eyes of other eBay members, you're only as good as your last few transactions, so beware.

- **Do** take a breather before you leave negative feedback for another eBay member. eBay won't remove feedback if you change your mind or overreact to a situation.

- The seller is **not** required to leave you feedback when you pay for the item. Feedback is based on the entire transaction, so the buyer may not post any feedback until the item arrives and you're both happy.

- If someone gives you positive feedback, **do** reciprocate by giving him or her positive feedback, too.

- If you receive negative feedback and feel your side of the transaction is worth telling, **do** be sure to give your reply in a neutral tone. You may also add a line responding to feedback you've received, to explain the situation to those who read the comment.

For Dummies: Bestselling Book Series for Beginners

eBay®
FOR
DUMMIES®
4TH EDITION

by Marsha Collier

WILEY

Wiley Publishing, Inc.

eBay® For Dummies, 4th Edition

Published by
Wiley Publishing, Inc.
111 River Street
Hoboken, NJ 07030-5774

Copyright © 2004 by Wiley Publishing, Inc., Indianapolis, Indiana

Published by Wiley Publishing, Inc., Indianapolis, Indiana

Published simultaneously in Canada

For general information on our other products and services or to obtain technical support, please contact our Customer Care Department within the U.S. at 800-762-2974, outside the U.S. at 317-572-3993, or fax 317-572-4002.

Wiley also publishes its books in a variety of electronic formats. Some content that appears in print may not be available in electronic books.

Library of Congress Control Number: 2003116372

ISBN: 0-7645-5654-1

Manufactured in the United States of America

10 9 8 7 6 5 4 3 2

4B/RU/QR/QU/IN

WILEY   Is a trademark of Wiley Publishing, Inc.

About the Author

Marsha Collier spends a good deal of time on eBay. She loves buying and selling (she's a PowerSeller) as well as meeting eBay users from around the world. As columnist, author of three best-selling books on eBay, and guest lecturer at eBay University, she shares her knowledge of eBay with millions of online shoppers. Thousands of eBay fans also read her monthly newsletter, *Cool eBay Tools,* to keep up with changes on the site.

Out of college, Marsha worked in Fashion Advertising for the *Miami Herald* and then as Special Projects Manager for the *Los Angeles Daily News.* Upon the birth of her daughter in 1984, she founded a home-based advertising and marketing business. Her successful business, the Collier Company, Inc., was featured by *Entrepreneur* magazine in 1985, and in 1990, Marsha's company received the Small Business of the Year award from her California State Assemblyman and the Northridge Chamber of Commerce.

Most of all, Marsha loves a great deal — that's what drew her to eBay in 1996, and that's what keeps her busy on the site now. She buys everything from replacement toothbrush heads to parts for pool equipment to designer dresses. Marsha knows how to *work* eBay, and in this book, she shares that knowledge with you.

Dedication

To all the future eBay buyers and sellers who have purchased this book to get a taste of how much fun online buying and selling can be. I look forward to seeing your auctions and hearing your stories.

I also dedicate this book to all the employees at eBay, who work very hard and don't always get noticed or appreciated by the community. I want to thank all of you for your endeavors; you make eBay a fun and profitable site to visit for millions of people. Keep on doing what you're doing.

Author's Acknowledgments

This book couldn't have been written without the input from thousands of eBay sellers and buyers that I've spoken to from all over the country. You inspire me to work harder and do my best to help all of you.

I've made so many friends along my eBay travels. My original coauthor on the first book, Roland Woerner: If it wasn't for you, this book wouldn't be here. There's also my close friend and eBay buddy, Jillian Cline: Thanks for trying out all my wacky eBay ideas; I'm glad they've helped both of us! Thanks to the rest of my eBay buddies — who always seem to have a moment when I call.

I particularly want to thank my editors at Wiley Publishing, Inc.: project editor Becky Huehls; my super tech editor Louise (aunt*patti) Ruby (who, by the way, was one of the very first eBay employees); Steven Hayes, who amazes me all the time with new ideas; and Andy Cummings, my publisher, who's never been too big to inspire a little guy like me.

Thank you all!

Publisher's Acknowledgments

We're proud of this book; please send us your comments through our online registration form located at www.dummies.com/register/.

Some of the people who helped bring this book to market include the following:

Acquisitions, Editorial, and Media Development

Associate Project Editor: Rebecca Huehls

Senior Acquisitions Editor: Steve Hayes

Senior Copy Editors: Kim Darosett, Barry Childs-Helton

Copy Editor: Virginia Sanders

Technical Editor: Patti Louise Ruby

Editorial Manager: Leah Cameron

Permissions Editor: Carmen Krikorian

Media Development Manager: Laura VanWinkle

Media Development Supervisor: Richard Graves

Editorial Assistant: Amanda Foxworth

Cartoons: Rich Tennant (www.the5thwave.com)

Production

Project Coordinator: Courtney MacIntyre

Layout and Graphics: Andrea Dahl, Stephanie D. Jumper, Lynsey Osborn, Heather Ryan, Jacque Schneider

Proofreaders: Andy Hollandbeck, TECHBOOKS Publishing Services

Indexer: TECHBOOKS Publishing Services

Publishing and Editorial for Technology Dummies

Richard Swadley, Vice President and Executive Group Publisher

Andy Cummings, Vice President and Publisher

Mary C. Corder, Editorial Director

Publishing for Consumer Dummies

Diane Graves Steele, Vice President and Publisher

Joyce Pepple, Acquisitions Director

Composition Services

Gerry Fahey, Vice President of Production Services

Debbie Stailey, Director of Composition Services

Contents at a Glance

Table of Contents

Introduction

*T*hank you for joining the thousands of people interested in learning the no-nonsense facts about eBay from an active user. I'm a longtime eBay shopper and PowerSeller. My "real" career was in retail marketing (now it's full-time eBay — teaching and writing). I work from home and apply my background successfully to all facets of the site.

Welcome to *eBay For Dummies,* 4th Edition! I can't begin to tell you how excited I am that my enthusiasm and excitement for shopping and selling on eBay has spread to so many corners of the world. eBay users (like you and I) total over 78 million — that's quite a community. It's a community of buyers who don't see the need to pay retail price for items they buy, and of sellers who forage out wholesale bargains to sell online and make a few dollars. This makes eBay the new international marketplace, and the best part is that eBay is available to anyone who wants to take the time to figure out how it works.

eBay isn't hard to master, but just like with any tool, if you know the ins and outs, you're ahead of the game. You can get the bargains, and when you sell, you can make the most money. You've come to the right place to find out all about eBay. This book is designed to help you understand everything you need to know about buying and selling at eBay, the most successful person-to-person trading community Web site. You get all the tools you need to get moving at eBay, whether you're new to the Internet or a Webaholic. You see how to turn your everyday household clutter into cold, hard cash — and how to look for items that you can sell at eBay. If you're a collector (or you'd like to be), I show you how to figure out how much you should spend, how to make smart bids, and how to win the auctions. How much money you earn (or spend) depends entirely on how *often* and how *smartly* you conduct your eBay transactions. You decide how often you want to run auctions and place bids; I'm here to help with the *smart* part by sharing tips I've learned along the way.

A Web site as complex as eBay has many nooks and crannies that may confuse the first-time user. Think of this book as a detailed road map that can help you navigate eBay, getting just as much or as little as you want from it. Unlike an actual road map, you won't get frustrated folding it back to its original shape. Just close the book and come back anytime you need a question answered.

After you figure out the nuts and bolts of eBay, you can start buying and selling stuff. I have a ton of terrific buying and selling strategies that help you get the most out of your auctions. With this book and a little elbow grease, you can join the ranks of the millions of people who use their home computers to make friends, become part of the eBay community, have a lot of fun, and make a profit. When you've got the hang of eBay and feel that it's time to graduate from this book, look for my other book, *Starting an eBay Business For Dummies* — it'll take you to the highest plateau.

About This Book

Remember those open-book tests that teachers sprang on you in high school? Well, sometimes you may feel like eBay pop-quizzes you while you're online. Think of *eBay For Dummies,* 4th Edition, as your open-book-test resource with all the answers. You don't have to memorize anything; just keep this book handy to help you get over the confusing parts of eBay.

With that in mind, this book is divided into pertinent sections to help you find your answers fast. I'll show you how to

- ✔ Get online and register at eBay.
- ✔ Navigate eBay to do just about anything you can think of — search for items for sale, set up auctions, monitor your transactions, and join the chat room circuit.
- ✔ Bid on and win eBay auctions.
- ✔ Choose an item to sell, pick the right time for your auction, market it so that a ton of bidders see it, and make a profit.
- ✔ Communicate well and close deals without problems, whether you're a buyer or a seller.
- ✔ Become a part of a really unique community of people who like to collect, buy, and sell items of just about every type.

Do not adjust your eyes. To protect the privacy of eBay users, screen images (commonly called *screen shots*) in this book blur User IDs.

Foolish Assumptions

You may have picked up this book because you heard that people are making big bucks trading at eBay and you want to find out what's going on. Or you heard about the bargains and wacky stuff you can find in the world's largest garage sale. If either of these assumptions is true, this is the right book for you.

Here are some other foolish assumptions I've made about you:

- ✔ You have, or would like to have, access to a computer, a modem, and the Internet so that you can do business at eBay.

- ✔ You have an interest in collecting stuff, selling stuff, and buying stuff, and you want to find out more about doing that stuff online.

- ✔ You want tips and strategies that can save you money when you bid and make you money when you sell. (You too? I can relate. Talk about all things to all people!)

- ✔ You're concerned about maintaining your privacy and staying away from people who try to ruin everyone's good time with negligent (and sometimes illegal) activity.

If you think the expression *surfing the Web* has something to do with spiders and boogie boards, then this book can get you started, but you may want to browse through *The Internet For Dummies,* 9th Edition, by John R. Levine, Margaret Levine Young, and Carol Baroudi, for a crash course in Internet confidence. The book comes from Wiley Publishing, Inc., just like the book you're reading now. From time to time (and by astounding coincidence), I mention other titles in the *For Dummies* series that you may find helpful.

How This Book Is Organized

This book has five parts. The parts stand on their own, which means that you can read Chapter 5 after you read Chapter 10 or skip Chapter 3 altogether. It's all up to you. I do think that you should at least dip into Chapter 1 and Chapter 2 to get an overview on what eBay is all about and find out how to become a registered user.

If you're already conducting transactions at eBay, you certainly can jump ahead to get good tips on advanced strategies to enhance your auctions. Don't wait for permission from me — just go for it. I won't argue with you that jazzy auctions equal higher profits!

Part I: Forget the Mall: Getting a Feel for eBay

In this part, I tell you what eBay is and how you use it. I take you through the registration process, help you organize your eBay transactions and interactions using the My eBay page, and get you comfortable navigating the site from the home page.

Part II: Are You Buying What They're Selling?

If you're pretty sure you want to start making bids on items, this part gives you the lowdown on searching, grading an item's value, researching, bidding, and winning auctions.

That old cliché, "Let the buyer beware," became a cliché because even today (maybe especially today) it's sound advice. Use my friendly, fat-free tips to help you decide when to bid and when to take a pass.

Part III: Are You Selling What They're Buying?

This part gets you up to speed on how to sell your items at eBay. Think of it as an eBay course in marketing. Here you find important information on how to conduct your auctions, what to do after you sell an item, how to ship the item, and how to keep track of all the money you make. Even Uncle Sam gets to chime in on his favorite topic: taxes. Know the rules so your friendly local tax office doesn't invite you over for a snack and a little audit.

I also show you how to jazz up your auctions by adding pictures and how to use basic HTML to link your auctions to your own home page. (If you don't have a home page, don't freak out: Links are optional.) You can make your digital images look like high art with my tips, hints, and strategies.

Part IV: Oy Vay, More eBay! Special Features

Check out this part to discover how to handle privacy issues relating to eBay and how you can resolve buying and selling issues with the help of Rules & Safety (SafeHarbor), eBay's problem-solving clearinghouse. Also included are ways of having fun with the eBay community and using charity auctions to bid on great items for a good cause.

Part V: The Part of Tens

In keeping with a long *For Dummies* tradition, this part is a compendium of short chapters that give you ready references and useful facts. I share more terrific tips for buying and selling items, as well as descriptions of my favorite software programs that can help lighten your auction load.

In addition to all these parts, you also get two appendixes. Appendix A gives some insider information on how to spot a trend before the rest of the world catches on and how to acquire items cheaply that others may spend a bundle on. Appendix B is an introduction to starting your own part- or full-time business on eBay. It's part inspiration and part hard-learned facts. After you've read that and you're ready to go to the next level, take a look at my other book, *Starting an eBay Business For Dummies*. It takes off where this book ends.

Icons Used in This Book

These are facts that you just *have* to know! Time is money at eBay. When you see this shortcut or timesaver come your way, read the information and think about all the moola you just saved.

Think of this icon as a sticky note for your brain. If you forget one of the pearls of wisdom revealed to you, you can go back and reread it. If you *still* can't remember something here, go ahead, dog-ear the page — I won't tell. Even better: Use a yellow highlighter.

Don't feel my pain. I've done things wrong at eBay before and want to save you from my mistakes. I put these warnings out there bright and bold so that you don't have a bad experience. Don't skip these warnings unless you're enthusiastic about masochism.

When you see this icon, you know you're in for the real deal. I created this icon especially for you to give you war stories (and success stories) from eBay veterans (*learn from their experiences* is my motto) that can help you strategize, make money, and spare you from the perils of a poorly written auction item description. You can skip over these icons if you want to, but you may get burned if you do.

What Now?

Like everything else in the world, eBay constantly evolves. Some of the eBay screens in this book may look slightly different than the ones you see on your home computer monitor. That's just eBay tweaking and changing. My job is to arm you with everything you need to know to join the eBay community and begin conducting transactions. If you hit rough waters, just look up the problem in the table of contents or index in this book. I either help you solve it or let you know where to go at eBay for some expert advice.

Although eBay makes its complex Web site as easy to navigate as possible, you may still need to refer back to this book for help. Don't get frustrated if you have to keep reviewing topics before you feel completely comfortable trading at eBay.

After all, Albert Einstein once said, "Don't commit to memory something you can look up." (I forget when he said that. . . .)

Feedback, Please

Communication makes the world go round, and I'd love to hear from you. Contact me at `talk2marsha@coolebaytools.com`. Please know that I can't answer every question you send. There isn't enough time in the day — between writing, teaching, and oh yes, my family! Do know that I'll read each e-mail. The best questions will be answered in my newsletter.

My free newsletter comes out almost every month, full of new facts to ease your way on eBay! You can sign up for it at my Web site `www.coolebay tools.com`.

Caution: Information highway roadwork next three miles

You'd think that with millions of people accessing the eBay Web site every day, those Silicon Valley guys would have enough to keep them busy. As if! But hey, everybody's sprucing up now that it's the new millennium, and eBay wants to make the site even more new and exciting — that means switching things around to see if you notice. For example, you may see a *link* (an image or group of words that takes you to a different part of the site after you click it) on the home page that's there today and gone tomorrow, replaced with something else. Don't have a cow — the *main navigation bar* is like your own personal breadcrumb trail. It can get you into eBay, around the block, and out of the woods with nearly no hassles.

Part I
Forget the Mall: Getting a Feel for eBay

The 5th Wave   By Rich Tennant

"Guess who found a KISS Merchandise blowout at eBay while you were gone?"

In this part . . .

New technology can be intimidating for anyone. You've wanted to visit eBay, maybe buy something, but eBay feels kind of big and scary. What you need is someone to point out the most useful tools you need to get around, help you find out how eBay works, and start showing you how to do your own transactions. That's what I do in Part I.

In this part, I give you the information you want to know about how eBay works and what it offers its members. Find out how to become a registered user, maneuver the eBay Home page, and customize your very own private My eBay page. You can also find out about the all-important feedback profile that follows every eBay user around like a shadow.

Chapter 1

Why eBay Is a Terrific Place to Buy and Sell

*e*Bay has emerged as *the* marketplace of the twenty-first century. In July 2003, *Wired* magazine predicted that eBay's promise is that "retailing will become the national pastime." The founders had a pretty great idea back in 1995 (read about some eBay history in the "eBay's humble beginnings" sidebar later, in this chapter), and the world has taken to shopping and selling online. eBay is a safe and fun place to shop for everything from collectibles to clothing, all from the comfort of your home.

eBay is now also a marketplace for new merchandise. It's no longer just the destination for collectibles and old china patterns. These days you can purchase new and useful items, such as alarm systems, fancy electronic toothbrushes, light bulbs, clothing, cars, homes — just about anything you can think of.

Take a look around your house. Nice toaster. Great-looking clock. Spiffy microwave. Not to mention all the other cool stuff you own. All these household appliances and collectibles are fabulous to own, but when was the last time your toaster turned a profit? When you connect to eBay, your PC or Mac magically turns into a money machine. Just visit eBay and marvel at all the items that are just a few mouse clicks away from being bought and sold.

In this chapter, I tell you what eBay is and how it works. eBay is the perfect alternative to spending hours wandering through antique shops or swap meets looking for the perfect doohickey. It can also be your personal shopper for gifts and day-to-day items. Not only can you buy and sell stuff in the privacy of your home, but you can also meet people who share your interests. The folks who use the eBay site are a friendly bunch, and soon you'll be buying, selling, swapping stories, and trading advice with the best of them.

To get to eBay, you need to access the Internet. To access the Internet, you need a computer — either a personal computer (PC) or Macintosh (Mac) — with an Internet connection, or you can get MSN TV (née WebTV). If you're not ready to take the high-tech plunge, this book shows you how to start operating at eBay (and earning money) without owning a single cyber thing.

What Is eBay, and How Does It Work?

The Internet is spawning all kinds of new businesses (known as *e-commerce* to Wall Street types), and eBay is one of its few superstars. The reason is simple: It's the place where buyers and sellers can meet, do business, share stories and tips, and have fun. It's like one giant online potluck party — but instead of bringing a dish, you sell it!

eBay *doesn't* sell a thing. Instead, the site does what all good hosts do: It creates a comfy environment that brings people with common interests together. You can think of eBay like you think of the person who set you up on your last blind date — except the results are often a lot better. Your matchmaking friend doesn't perform a marriage ceremony but does get you in the same room with your potential soul mate. eBay puts buyers and sellers in a virtual store and lets them conduct their business safely within the rules that eBay has established.

All you need to do to join eBay is fill out a few forms online and click. Congratulations — you're a member with no big fees or secret handshakes. After you register, you can buy and sell anything that falls within the eBay rules and regulations. (Chapter 2 eases you through the registration process.)

The eBay home page, shown in Figure 1-1, is your first step to finding all the cool stuff you can see and do at eBay. You can conduct searches, find out what's happening, and get an instant link to the My eBay page, which helps you keep track of every auction item you have up for sale or have a bid on. You can read more about the eBay home page in Chapter 3 and find out more about My eBay in Chapter 4.

Yikes! What happened? The eBay home page on your computer looks nothing like the one in Figure 1-1? Don't rub your eyes — even squinting hard won't help; eBay has a different version of the home page for those who have never registered on eBay. Even if *you* have never registered, someone else who uses the computer may already have. Take a look at Figure 1-2 and see if it's a closer match.

Figure 1-1:
The eBay
home page,
your starting
point for
bargains
and for
making
some
serious
cash.

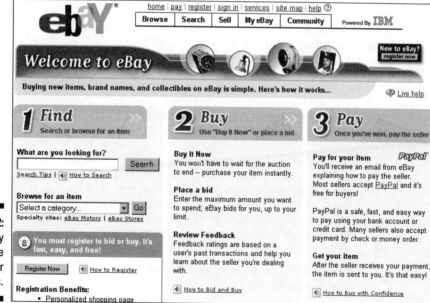

Figure 1-2:
The "eBay
Lite" home
page for
new users.

eBay's humble beginnings

The long-standing urban legend says eBay all started with a Pez dispenser. But as romantic as the story is (of the young man who designed the site for his fiancée to trade Pez dispensers), it sadly was public relations spin. The founder, Pierre Omidyar, had the right vision at the right time, and the first item he sold on the site was a broken laser pointer. Day by day, new people (including me in 1996) were drawn to the site from Internet chatter. The site eventually grew to the point where it began to strain Pierre's ISP. The ISP charged him more, so he started charging a small listing fee for sellers, just so he could break even. Legend has it that the day $10,000 in fees arrived in Pierre's mailbox, he quit his day job. (I hope that's not apocryphal too!)

eBay was born on Labor Day, 1995. The name eBay is taken from Echo Bay, the name Pierre originally wanted for his company. Upon checking with the State of California, he found that the name was taken by another company, so he shortened the name to eBay — and the rest, as they say, is history.

All About Auctions

The value of an item is determined by how much someone is willing to spend to buy it. That's what makes auctions exciting. eBay offers several kinds of auctions, but for the most part, they all work the same way. An *auction* is a unique sales event where the exact value of the item for sale is not known. As a result, there's an element of surprise involved — not only for the bidder (who may end up with a great deal) but also for the seller (who may end up making a killing). Here's how an auction works from a seller's and a bidder's perspective:

- **Seller:** A seller pays a fee, fills out an electronic form, and sets up the auction, listing a *minimum bid* he or she is willing to accept for the item. Think of an auctioneer at Sotheby's saying, "The bidding for this diamond necklace begins at $5,000." You might *want* to bid $4,000, but the bid won't be accepted. Sellers can also set a *reserve price* — sort of a financial safety net that protects them from losing money on the deal. I explain how this stuff works later in this section.

- **Bidder:** Bidders in auctions duke it out over a period of time (the minimum is one day, but most auctions last a week or even longer) until one comes out victorious. Usually, the highest bidder wins. The tricky thing about participating in an auction (and the most exciting aspect) is that no one knows the final price an item goes for until the last second of the auction.

eBay auctions

Unlike "traditional" live auctions that end with the familiar phrase "Going once, going twice, sold!" eBay auctions are controlled by the clock. The seller pays a fee and lists the item on the site for a predetermined period of time; the highest bidder when the clock runs out takes home the prize.

Reserve-price auctions

Unlike a minimum bid, which is required in any eBay auction, a *reserve price* protects sellers from having to sell an item for less than the minimum amount they want for it. You may be surprised to see a 1968 Jaguar XKE sports car up for auction at eBay with a minimum bid of only a dollar. It's a fair bet that the seller has put a reserve price on this car to protect himself from losing money. The reserve price allows sellers to set lower minimum bids, and lower minimum bids attract bidders. Unfortunately, if a seller makes the reserve price too high and it isn't met by the end of the auction, no one wins.

eBay charges a fee for sellers to run these auctions. Nobody knows (except the seller and the eBay computer system) what the reserve price is until the auction is over, but you can tell from the auction page whether you're dealing with a reserve-price auction. Reserve-price auctions are in the listings alongside the other items, so you have to click and option an auction to find out whether it has a reserve. If bids have been made on an item, a message also appears on the page saying whether the reserve price has been met. You can find out more about bidding on reserve-price auctions in Chapter 6 and setting up a reserve-price auction in Chapter 9.

Live Auctions

If you yearn for that traditional, "going-going-gone" (highest bidder wins) sort of auction, you can participate in auctions that are running live at a gallery in real time. In *eBay Live Auctions,* you can bid via eBay's Internet hook-up just as if you were sitting in a chair at the auction house. These auctions are usually for unique and interesting items that you're not likely to find in your locality. For more on these sales, see Chapter 6. Figure 1-3 shows the Live Auctions home page located at www.ebay.com/liveauctions.

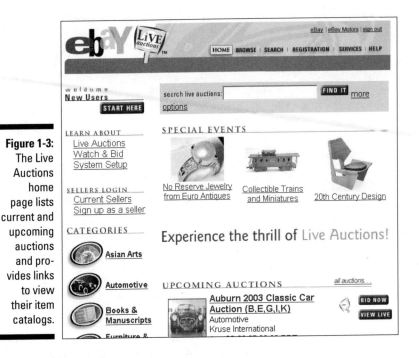

Figure 1-3: The Live Auctions home page lists current and upcoming auctions and provides links to view their item catalogs.

Restricted-access auctions

If you're over 18 years of age and interested in bidding on items of an adult nature, eBay has an adults only *(Mature Audiences)* category, which has restricted access. Although you can peruse the other eBay categories without having to submit credit card information, you must have a credit card number on file at eBay to view and bid on items in this category. Restricted-access auctions are run like the typical timed auctions. To bid on adult items, you first need to agree to a terms of use page after entering your User ID and password. This page pops up automatically when you attempt to access this category.

If you aren't interested in seeing or bidding on items of an adult nature, or if you're worried that your children may be able to gain access to graphic adult material, eBay has solved that problem by excluding adult-content items from easily accessible areas like the Featured Items page. And children under the age of 18 aren't allowed to register at eBay and should be under an adult's supervision if they do wander onto the site.

Charity auctions: All for a good cause

A *charity auction* is a high-profile fundraising auction where the proceeds go to a selected charity. Most people don't wake up in the morning wanting to own the shoes that Ron Howard wore when he put his footprints in cement at Mann's Chinese Theater in Hollywood, but one-of-a-kind items like that are often auctioned off in charity auctions. (In fact, someone did want those shoes badly enough to buy them for a lot of money at eBay.) Charity auctions became popular after the NBC *Today Show* sold an autographed jacket at eBay for over $11,000 with the proceeds going to Toys for Tots. Charity auctions are run like most other auctions at eBay, but because they're immensely popular, bidding can be fierce, and the dollar amounts can go sky high. Many famous celebrities use eBay to help out their favorite charities. I suggest that you visit these auctions and bid whenever you can. Charity auctions are a win-win situation for everyone. You can read more about celebrity auctions in Chapter 18.

Private (shhh-it's-a-secret) auctions

Some sellers choose to hold private auctions because they know that some bidders may be embarrassed to be seen bidding on a box of racy neckties in front of the rest of the eBay community. Others may go the private route because they are selling big-ticket items and don't want to disclose their bidder's financial status.

Private auctions are run like the typical timed auctions except that each bidder's identity is kept secret. At the end of the auction, eBay provides contact info to the seller and to the high bidder, and that's it.

You can send e-mail questions to the seller in a private auction, but you can't check out your competition because the auction item page shows the current bid price but not the high bidder's User ID.

Multiple Item (Dutch) auctions

Multiple Item — Dutch — auctions have nothing to do with windmills, wooden shoes, or sharing the check on a date. A *Multiple Item auction* allows a seller to put multiple, identical items up for sale. Instead of holding 100 separate auctions for 100 pairs of wooden shoes, for example, a seller can sell them all in one listing. As a buyer, you can elect to bid for 1, 3, or all 100 pairs. But unless you're running an alternative boutique (or know a giant centipede who needs all those clogs), you probably want to bid on just one pair. For more on Multiple Item auctions, see Chapter 6.

A Multiple Item auction can't be conducted as a private auction.

Buying It Now at eBay

You don't have to participate in an auction at eBay to buy something. If you want to make a purchase — if it's something you *must* have — you can usually find the item and buy it immediately. Of course, using Buy It Now (*BIN* in eBay speak) doesn't come with the thrill of an auction, but purchasing an item at a fraction of the retail price without leaving your chair or waiting for an auction to end has its own warm and fuzzy kind of excitement. If you seek this kind of instant gratification on eBay, visit the eBay stores. Or you can isolate these items by clicking the Buy It Now tab when browsing categories or performing searches.

eBay Stores

Visiting eBay Stores is as easy as clicking the eBay Stores link from the home page. Thousands of eBay sellers have set up stores with merchandise meant for you to Buy It Now. eBay Stores are classified just like eBay, and you can buy anything from socks to jewelry to appliances.

Sellers who open an eBay store have to meet a certain level of experience on eBay, and when you buy from eBay Stores, you're protected by the same fraud protection policy that you are covered with in eBay auctions. Figure 1-4 shows the eBay Stores hub page.

Buy It Now and fixed-price sales

More and more sellers are selling items with a *Buy It Now* option or at a fixed price. This enables you to buy an item as soon as you see one at a price that suits you. For more on how these sales work, check out Chapter 6.

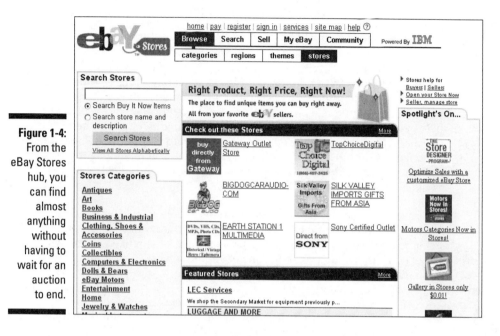

Figure 1-4:
From the
eBay Stores
hub, you
can find
almost
anything
without
having to
wait for an
auction
to end.

So You Wanna Sell Stuff

If you're a seller, creating an auction page at eBay is as simple as filling out an online form. You type in the name of your item and a short description, add a crisp digital picture, set your price, and voilà — it's auction time. (Okay, it's a tad more involved than that — but not much.) eBay charges a small fee ($0.30 to $3.30) for the privilege. When you list your item, millions of people (eBay has close to 80 million registered users) from all over the world can take a gander at it and place bids. With a little luck, a bidding war may break out and drive the bids up high enough for you to turn a nice profit. After the auction, you deal directly with the buyer, who sends you the payment either through a payment service or through the mail. Then you ship the item. Abracadabra — you just turned your item (everyday clutter, perhaps) into cash.

You can run as many auctions as you want, all at the same time. To get info on deciding what to sell, leaf through Chapter 9; to find out how to set up an auction, jump to Chapter 10; and to get the scoop on advanced selling, visit Chapter 14. When it's time to go pro, check the appendixes in the back of this book.

So You Wanna Buy Stuff

If you're a collector or you just like to shop for bargains, you can browse 24 hours a day through the items up for auction in eBay's tens of thousands of categories, which range from Antiques to Writing Instruments. Find the item you want, do a little research on what you're buying and who's selling it, place your bid, and keep an eye on it until the auction closes. When I wrote my last book, *eBay Bargain Shopping For Dummies* (Wiley Publishing, Inc.), I had a great time visiting the different categories and buying a little something here and there — it's amazing just how varied the selection is. I even bought some tires!

Take a look at Chapter 5 for info on searching for items to bid on. When you see an item you like, you can set up a bidding strategy and let the games begin. Chapter 6 gives you bidding strategies that can make you the winner. When you win the auction, you can get expert advice about completing the transaction from Chapter 8.

You can bid as many times as you want on an item, and you can bid on as many auctions as you want. Just keep in mind that each bid is a binding contract that you'll be required to pay for should you win.

Research for Fun and Profit

eBay's awesome search engine allows you to browse through countless *categories* of items up for sale. As a buyer, you can do lots of comparison shopping on that special something you just can't live without or just browse around until something catches your eye. If you're a seller, the search engine allows you to keep your eye on the competition and get an idea of how hot your item is. That way, you can set a competitive price. To find out more about using search options and categories, check out Chapters 3 and 5.

The search engine also lets you find out what other people are bidding on. From there, you can read up on their *feedback ratings* (eBay's ingenious honor system) to get a sense of how good their reputations are — *before* you deal with them.

eBay's Role in the Action

Throughout the auction process, eBay's computers keep tabs on what's going on. When the auction or sale is over, eBay takes a small percentage of the final selling price and instructs the seller and buyer to contact each other through e-mail. At this point, eBay's job is pretty much over, and eBay steps aside.

Most of the time, everything works great, everybody's happy, and eBay never has to step back into the picture. But if you happen to run into trouble in paradise, eBay can help you settle the problem, whether you're the buyer or the seller.

eBay regulates members with a detailed system of checks and balances known as *feedback,* which is described in Chapter 4. The grand plan is that the community polices itself. Don't get me wrong — eBay does jump in when sketchy activity comes to light. But the people who keep eBay most safe are the community members, the buyers and sellers who have a common stake in conducting business honestly and fairly. Every time you sell something or win an auction, eBay members have a chance to leave a comment about you. You should do the same for them. If they're happy, the feedback is positive; otherwise, the feedback is negative. Either way, your feedback sticks to you like glue.

Building a great reputation with positive feedback ensures a long and profitable eBay career. Negative feedback, like multiple convictions for grand-theft auto, is a real turnoff to most folks and can make it hard to do future business at eBay.

If your feedback rating becomes a –4 (negative 4), eBay suspends your buying and selling privileges. You can find out more about how eBay protects you as a buyer or a seller in Chapters 16 and 17.

Features and Fun Stuff

So eBay is all about making money, right? Not exactly. The folks at eBay aren't kidding when they call it a community — a place where people with similar interests can compare notes, argue, buy and sell, and meet each other. Yes, people have gotten married after meeting at eBay. (Take a guess how friends bought them wedding gifts!)

Chatting it up

eBay has dozens of specific chat rooms and discussion boards (even a Night Owl's Nest — for those who can't sleep) whose topics range from advertising to trading cards. So if you have no idea what that old Mobil gas station sign you found in your grandfather's barn is worth, just post a message on the Advertising chat board. Somewhere out there is an expert with an answer for you. Your biggest problem is deciding whether to keep the sign or put it up for auction. Those are good problems to have!

One of my favorite chat rooms is The eBay Q&A chat room. If something is happening on eBay, here's where you'll hear about it first. The folks on this board stay abreast of happenings and are always happy to help or at least lend an ear. For more about posting messages and chat rooms, visit Chapters 5 and 17.

Rules & Safety (SafeHarbor)

Rules & Safety (SafeHarbor) is the catchall resource for information and services about making deals at eBay safer — and for information on what to do if deals go sour. I don't like to think about it, but sometimes — despite your best efforts to be a good eBay user — buyers or sellers don't keep their word. In a small percentage of cases, unscrupulous louts sometimes do invade the site and try to pull scams. You may buy an item that isn't as it was described, or the winner of your auction doesn't send the payment. Sometimes even honest members get into disputes. Rules & Safety is an excellent resource when you need questions answered or you need a professional to come in and handle an out-of-hand situation. Chapter 16 tells you all about Rules & Safety.

Extra Gizmos You're Gonna Want

At some point in your eBay career, you'll become comfortable with all the computer-related hoops you have to jump through to make the eBay magic happen. At that time, you may be ready to invest in a few extra devices that can make your eBay experiences even better. Digital cameras and scanners can help make your time at eBay a more lucrative and fun adventure. You find out how to use digital technology in your auctions in more detail in Chapter 14.

Chapter 2

The Bucks Start Here: Signing Up at eBay

. . . .

In This Chapter

▶ Using eBay's easy forms (the shape of things to come)

▶ Getting up close and personal about privacy

▶ Identifying with User IDs and passwords

▶ Learning the ropes (eBay rules and regs)

. . . .

*Y*ou've probably figured out that you sign on to eBay electronically, which means you don't *really* sign on the proverbial dotted line as folks did in days of old before computers ran the world. Nowadays, the art of scribbling your signature has become as outdated as vinyl records (although you can still get vinyl records at eBay if you're feeling nostalgic).

Compared to finding a prime parking space at the mall during the holidays, signing up at eBay is a breeze. About the toughest thing you have to do is type in your e-mail address correctly.

In this chapter, you find out everything you need to know about registering at eBay. You get tips on what information you have to disclose and what you should keep to yourself. Don't worry — this is an open-book test. You don't need to memorize state capitals, the periodic table, or multiplication tables.

Registering at eBay

You don't have to wear one of those tacky "Hello, My Name Is" stickers on your shirt after you sign in, but eBay needs to know some things about you before it grants you membership. You and several million other folks will be roaming around eBay's online treasure trove; eBay needs to know who's who. So, keeping that in mind, sign in, please!

---

eBay internationale!

eBay has Web sites in the United States, Argentina, Australia, Austria, Brazil, Belgium, Canada, China, France, Germany, Ireland, Italy, Korea, Mexico, The Netherlands, New Zealand, Singapore, Spain, Sweden, Switzerland, Taiwan, and (whew) the United Kingdom. The vast majority of eBay users that you trade with are from the United States, but the international membership is growing.

You don't have to be a rocket scientist to register at eBay, but you can buy a model rocket or something bigger after you do. The only hard-and-fast rule at eBay is that you have to be 18 years of age or older. Don't worry, the Age Police won't come to your house to card you; they have other ways to discreetly ensure that you're at least 18 years old. (**Hint:** Credit cards do more than satisfy account charges.) If you're having a momentary brain cramp and you've forgotten your age, just think back to the premiere of *The Cosby Show*. If you can remember watching the original episodes of that favorite show of the early '80s, you're in. Head to the eBay home page and register. The entire process takes only a few minutes.

Registering Is Free and Fun (And Fast)

Before you can sign up at eBay, you have to be connected to the Web. This is the time to fire up your computer and connect to the Internet. After you open your Internet browser, you're ready to sign up.

Just type **www.ebay.com** in the address box of your browser and press Enter. Your next stop is the eBay home page. Right there, where you can't miss it, is the registration Register Now link shown in Figure 2-1. Click the link and let the sign-up process begin. You can also get to the Registration form by clicking eBay's welcome mat links; see Chapter 3 for details.

eBay's home page changes regularly. Alternatively, it may be the home page pictured in Figure 1-2 in Chapter 1. If you don't see a Register Now button, look around the page — there will be an obvious Register button somewhere.

Figure 2-1:
Click this
link to
register, and
soon you'll
be trading
online like
a pro!

When you're at the Registration form, you go through a four-step process. Here's an overview:

1. Enter the basic required info.

2. Read and accept the user agreement.

3. Confirm your e-mail address.

4. Breeze through (or past) the optional information.

The following sections fill you in on all the details.

The Registration pages on eBay are through a secure SSL connection. *SSL* (Secure Sockets Layer) enables you to have an encrypted connection to eBay because a bunch of really smart techie types made it that way. You can tell because the normal *http* at the beginning of the Web address (also called the URL) is now *https*. Also, you'll see a small closed lock at the bottom-left (or bottom-right) corner of your screen. I could tell you how SSL works, but instead I'll just give you the bottom line: It *does* work, so trust me and use it. The more precautions eBay (and you) take, the harder it is for some hyper-caffeinated high-school kid to get into your files.

So, what's your sign? Filling in your required information

After you click the Register button links, you're taken to the heart of the eBay Registration pages. To get started follow these steps:

1. **At the top of the first registration page, eBay shows the steps of the registration process and asks you to fill in some required information (see Figure 2-2).**

   Here's what eBay wants to know about you:

   - Your full name, address, and primary telephone number. eBay keeps this information on file in case the company (or a member who is a transaction partner) needs to contact you.

   - You can also include, if you want, a secondary phone number and a fax number.

   - Your e-mail address (`yourname@myISP.com`).

   If you register with an *anonymous e-mail service* such as Yahoo! Mail or Hotmail, you're taken to a page that requires additional information for authentication. You must provide valid credit card information for identification purposes. Your information is protected by eBay's privacy policy, and your credit card won't be charged.

Figure 2-2:
Some of the required information for your eBay registration.

eb**Y**   Register for eBay and Half.com   h**a**lf.com

Registration: Enter Information   ⑦ Need Help?
① **Enter Information**   2 Agree to Terms   3 Confirm Your Email

First name   **Last name**
Marsha   Collier

Street address
12345 Anywhere St

City
Los Angeles

State   **Zip code**   **Country**
California   ▼   91210   United States
                                           Change country
Primary telephone   **Extension**
(310) 555-1212

Secondary telephone **Extension**
(   )

Important: To complete registration, enter a valid email address that you can check

After yo input your personal information, you're ready to create your eBay persona.

2. **Scroll down the page to select your new eBay User ID.**

   See "Choosing a User ID," later in this chapter, for some tips on selecting your User ID.

3. **Choose a permanent password, enter it in the Create Password box, and then type it a second time in the Re-enter Password box to confirm it.**

   For more information on choosing a password, see "A Quick Word about Passwords," later in this chapter.

4. **Create your unique secret question and input the answer.**

   The secret question you select here is used by eBay to identify you if you ever have problems signing in.

   If you're registering with an anonymous e-mail address, this is where you enter your credit card information.

5. **Type in your date of birth.**

6. **Make sure all the info you entered is correct.**

   Think back to your second-grade teacher, who kept saying, "Class, check your work." Remember that? She's still right! Review your answers.

   If eBay finds a glitch in your registration, such as an incorrect area or zip code, you see a warning message. This is part of eBay's security system to ward off fraudulent registrations. Use the Back button to correct the information — if you put in a wrong e-mail address, for example, eBay has no way of contacting you. So you don't hear a peep from eBay regarding your registration until you go through the entire process all over again.

7. **Click the Continue button to move onto the next screen.**

If you've made a mistake, eBay gives you the opportunity to correct the information by using the Edit Information button.

If you registered with an anonymous e-mail service, such as Yahoo! Mail or Hotmail, you must enter your credit card information, as I mentioned earlier, before you see the license agreement, which I cover in the next section. If, when you look at it, your eyes start glazing over at all the legalese, the next section can help you make sense of it.

Do you solemnly swear to . . . ?

After you click Continue, you're taken to a page that has the eBay User Agreement and Privacy Policy. At this page, you take an oath to keep eBay safe for democracy and commerce. You promise to play well with others, not to cheat, and to follow the golden rule. No, you're not auditioning for a super-hero club, but don't ever forget that eBay takes this stuff very seriously. You can be kicked off eBay or worse. (Can you say "federal investigation"?)

Be sure to read the User Agreement thoroughly when you register. So that you don't have to put down this riveting book to read the legalese right this minute, I provide the nuts and bolts here:

- ✔ You understand that every transaction is a legally binding contract. (Click the User Agreement link at the bottom of any eBay page for the current eBay Rules and Regulations.)

- ✔ You agree that you can pay for the items you buy and the eBay fees that you incur. (Chapter 8 fills you in on how eBay takes its cut of the auction action.)

- ✔ You understand that you're responsible for paying any taxes.

- ✔ You're aware that if you sell prohibited items, eBay can forward your personal information to law enforcement for further investigation. (Chapter 9 explains what you can and can't sell at eBay — and what eBay does to sellers of prohibited items.)

- ✔ eBay makes clear that it is just a *venue,* which means it's a place where people with similar interests can meet, greet, and do business.

When everything goes well, the eBay Web site is like a school gym that opens for Saturday swap meets. At the gym, if you don't play by the rules, you can get tossed out. But if you don't play by the rules at eBay, the venue gets un-gymlike in a hurry. eBay has the right to get state and federal officials to track you down and prosecute you. But fair's fair; if you click the appropriate box on this page, eBay keeps you posted by e-mail of any updates in the User Agreement.

If you're a stickler for fine print, head to these Internet addresses for all the *Ps* and *Qs* of the latest policies:

```
pages.ebay.com/help/community/png-user.html
pages.ebay.com/help/policies/privacy-policy.html
```

Before you can proceed, you must click the two check boxes shown in Figure 2-3, which indicates that you really, really understand what it means to be an eBay user. Because I know that you, as a law-abiding eBay member, will have no problem following the rules, go ahead and click the I Agree to These Terms button at the bottom of the page, which takes you to a screen stating that eBay is sending you an e-mail. You're almost done.

The next step is confirming your e-mail address, which I cover in the next section.

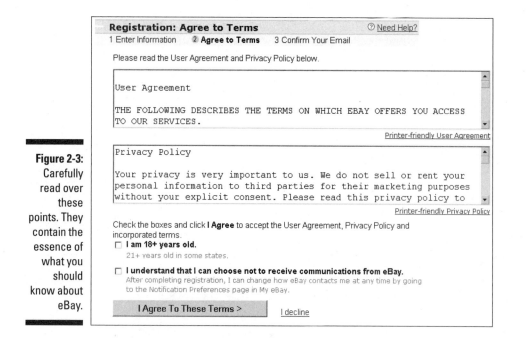

Figure 2-3:
Carefully
read over
these
points. They
contain the
essence of
what you
should
know about
eBay.

It must be true if you have it in writing

After you accept the User Agreement, it takes eBay less than a minute to
e-mail you a confirmation notice, as shown in Figure 2-4. When you receive
the eBay registration confirmation e-mail, print it out. What's most important
is the confirmation code. If you lose that number, go back to the initial eBay
registration page and follow Step 2. You can also click the link in your e-mail
to get the confirmation number.

With your confirmation number in hand, head back to the eBay Registration
page by clicking the link supplied in your e-mail. If your e-mail doesn't support links, go to this address:

```
pages.ebay.com/register
```

After you reconnect with eBay and it knows your e-mail address is active,
you'll be heartily congratulated, as shown in Figure 2-5.

If you don't receive your eBay registration confirmation e-mail within 24
hours, there was most likely an error in your e-mail address. At this point, the
customer-support folks can help you complete the registration process. Go to
the following address:

```
pages.ebay.com/help/contact_inline/index.html
```

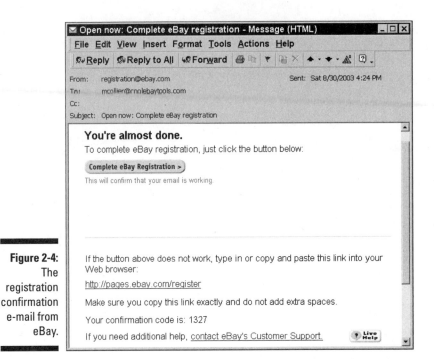

Figure 2-4:
The
registration
confirmation
e-mail from
eBay.

Figure 2-5:
It's time
to start
shopping!

If for some reason (brain cramp is a perfectly acceptable excuse) you incorrectly type in the wrong e-mail address, you have to start the registration process all over again with a different User ID (eBay holds the previous ID for 30 days). If you run into a snag, you can click the Live Help button that appears on many pages. See Figure 2-6 for my Live Help discussion.

Getting to know you: Optional information

Now that you're a full-fledged, officially registered member of the eBay community, you may see an eBay pop-up window, giving you the option to provide more information on yourself. These optional questions allow you to fill in your self-portrait for your new pals at eBay.

Figure 2-6:
I clicked
Live Help to
inquire
about a
registration
problem.
Within a
couple of
minutes, I
was online
with a real
person.

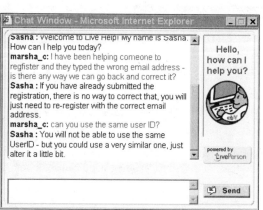

Figure 2-6: I clicked Live Help to inquire about a registration problem. Within a couple of minutes, I was online with a real person.

Although eBay doesn't share member information with anyone, you don't have to answer the optional questions if you don't want to.

The following points show you the optional questions eBay asks. You decide what you feel comfortable divulging and what you want to keep personal. eBay asks for this information because the company wants a better picture of who is using its Web site. In marketing mumbo-jumbo, this stuff is called *demographics* — statistics that characterize a group of people who make up a community. In this case, it's the eBay community. Here is the optional information you can provide:

- ✔ **Annual household income:** Fill this in if you want to (eBay states that this info is kept anonymous), but I think this information is too personal. If you're not comfortable with it, skip it.

- ✔ **Your highest completed education level:** Again if this is too personal, leave this area blank.

After selecting your responses from the drop-down box, you can click Submit. If you're not in the mood right now, you can click the Answer Later link. (This pop-up box will reappear for your response later in your eBay dealings.) If you don't want to answer any of the demographic queries, click the Please Don't Ask Me Again link at the bottom of the pop-up window.

A Quick Word about Passwords

Picking a good password is not as easy (but is twice as important) as it may seem. Whoever has your password can (in effect) "be you" at eBay — running auctions, bidding on auctions, and leaving possibly litigious feedback for others. Basically, such an impostor can ruin your eBay career — and possibly cause you serious financial grief.

Don't tell anyone, but your info is safe at eBay

eBay keeps most personal information secret. The basics (your name, phone number, city, and state) go out only to answer the specific request of another registered eBay user (if you're involved in a transaction with that person), law enforcement, or members of the eBay Verified Rights Owner Program (eBay's copyright-watchdog program). Other users may need your basic access info for several reasons — a seller may want to verify your location, get your phone number to call you regarding your auction, or double-check who you really are. If somebody does request your info, you get an e-mail from eBay giving you the name, phone number, city, and state of the person making the request. You need to keep your information up-to-date. If you don't, you risk being banished from the site.

As with any online password, you should follow these common-sense **rules** to protect your privacy:

- ✔ Don't pick anything too obvious, such as your birthday, your first name, or your Social Security number. (***Hint:*** If it's too easy to remember, it's probably too easy to crack.)

- ✔ Make things tough on the bad guys — combine numbers and letters (use upper- AND lowercase) or create nonsensical words.

- ✔ Don't give out your password to anyone — it's like giving away the keys to the front door of your house.

- ✔ If you ever suspect someone has your password, immediately change it by going to the following address:

    `pages.ebay.com/services/myebay/selectpass.html`

- ✔ Change your password every few months just to be on the safe side.

A Not-So-Quick Word about Choosing a User ID

eBay gives you the option of picking your User ID. Making up a User ID is my favorite part. If you've never liked your real name (or never had a nickname), here's your chance to correct that situation. Have fun. Consider choosing an ID that tells a little about you. Of course, if your interests change, you may regret too narrow a User ID.

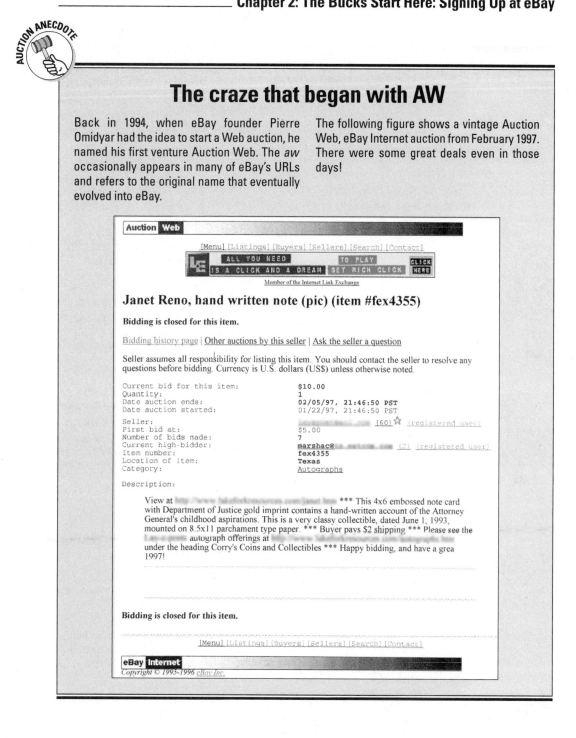

The craze that began with AW

Back in 1994, when eBay founder Pierre Omidyar had the idea to start a Web auction, he named his first venture Auction Web. The *aw* occasionally appears in many of eBay's URLs and refers to the original name that eventually evolved into eBay.

The following figure shows a vintage Auction Web, eBay Internet auction from February 1997. There were some great deals even in those days!

Auction **Web**

[Menu] [Listings] [Buyers] [Sellers] [Search] [Contact]

ALL YOU NEED   TO PLAY   CLICK HERE
IS A CLICK AND A DREAM   GET RICH CLICK

Member of the Internet Link Exchange

Janet Reno, hand written note (pic) (item #fex4355)

Bidding is closed for this item.

Bidding history page | Other auctions by this seller | Ask the seller a question

Seller assumes all responsibility for listing this item. You should contact the seller to resolve any questions before bidding. Currency is U.S. dollars (US$) unless otherwise noted.

Current bid for this item:	$10.00
Quantity:	1
Date auction ends:	02/05/97, 21:46:50 PST
Date auction started:	01/22/97, 21:46:50 PST
Seller:	(60) (registered user)
First bid at:	$5.00
Number of bids made:	7
Current high-bidder:	marshac@ (2) (registered user)
Item number:	fex4355
Location of item:	Texas
Category:	Autographs

Description:

    View at *** This 4x6 embossed note card with Department of Justice gold imprint contains a hand-written account of the Attorney General's childhood aspirations. This is a very classy collectible, dated June 1, 1993, mounted on 8.5x11 parchament type paper. *** Buyer pays $2 shipping *** Please see the autograph offerings at under the heading Corry's Coins and Collectibles *** Happy bidding, and have a grea 1997!

Bidding is closed for this item.

[Menu] [Listings] [Buyers] [Sellers] [Search] [Contact]

eBay **Internet**
Copyright © 1995-1996 eBay Inc.

You can call yourself just about anything; you can be silly or creative or boring. But remember, this ID is how other eBay users will know you. So here are some common-sense rules:

- ✔ Don't use a name that would embarrass your mother.
- ✔ Don't use a name with a negative connotation, such as *scam-guy*.
- ✔ Don't use a name that's too weird. If people don't trust you, they won't buy from you.
- ✔ eBay doesn't allow spaces in User IDs, so make sure that the ID makes sense when putting two or more words together.

If you're dying to have several short words as your User ID, you can use underscores or hyphens to separate them, as in *super-shop-a-holic*. If you permanently sign in to eBay on your computer, typing underscores or dashes won't slow you down.

You can change your User ID once every 30 days if you want to, but I don't recommend it. People come to know you by your User ID. If you change your ID, your past does play tagalong and attaches itself to the new ID. But if you change your User ID too many times, people may think you're trying to hide something.

Nevertheless, to change your User ID, click the My eBay link at the top of most eBay pages. From your My eBay login page, click the Preferences/Set-up tab and scroll to the Change My User ID link, fill in the boxes, and click the Change User ID button. You now have a new eBay identity.

eBay also has some User ID rules to live by:

- ✔ No offensive names (like &*#@@guy).
- ✔ No names with *eBay* in them. (It makes you look like you work for eBay, and eBay takes a dim view of that.)
- ✔ No names with & (even if you *do* have both looks&brains).
- ✔ No names with @ (like @Aboy).
- ✔ No symbols such as the greater than or less than symbols (> <) or consecutive underscores __.
- ✔ No IDs that begin with an *e* followed by numbers, an underscore, a dash, a period, or a dot.
- ✔ No names of one letter (like Q).

When you pick your User ID, make sure that it isn't a good clue for your password. For example, if you use *Natasha* as your User ID, don't pick *Boris* as your password. Even Bullwinkle could figure that one out.

Hey, AOL users, this one's for you: Make sure that your Mail Controls are set to receive e-mails from eBay. If you have Internet e-mail blocked, you need to update your AOL Mail Controls. To do so, enter the AOL keyword **Mail Controls**.

Your License to Deal (Almost)

You are now officially a *newbie,* or eBay rookie. The only problem is that you're still at the window-shopping level. If you're ready to go from window-shopper to item seller, just zip through a few more forms, and before you know it, you can start running your own auctions at eBay.

Until you've been a member of eBay for 30 days, a picture of a beaming golden cartoonlike icon is next to your User ID wherever it appears on the site. This doesn't mean that you have been converted into a golden robot; the icon merely indicates to other eBay users that you are new to eBay.

Chapter 3

There's No Place Like the Home Page

In This Chapter

▶ Getting the lay of the land
▶ Using the eBay home page's links and icons
▶ Getting the first word on searches
▶ Checking out featured auctions and other fun stuff

*T*he writer Thomas Wolfe was wrong: You *can* go home again — and again. At least at eBay you can! Month after month, millions of people land at eBay's home page without wearing out the welcome mat. The eBay home page is the front door to the most popular auction site on the Internet.

Everything you need to know about navigating eBay begins right here. In this chapter, I give you the grand tour of the areas you can reach right from the home page with the help of links.

What Is the Home Page?

The eBay home page is shown in Figure 3-1 and includes the following key areas:

- ✔ A navigation bar at the top of the page with five eBay links that can zip you straight to any of the many eBay areas, as well as seven additional — and powerful — links right above the navigation bar

- ✔ A search box that — like the Search link in the navigation bar — helps you find items by title keywords

- ✔ A list of links to auction categories

- ✔ Links to eBay's specialty sites, featured auctions, fun stuff like charity auctions, and information about what else is happening at eBay

Figure 3-1:
The home
page, your
jumping-off
point for fun
and values.

Do not adjust your computer monitor. You're not going crazy. You may notice that a link was on the eBay home page yesterday and is gone the next day. The links on the eBay home page change often to reflect what's going on — not just on the site, but in the world as well. Figure 3-2 gives you a look at an alternate eBay home page, which is only shown to new, unregistered visitors to the site.

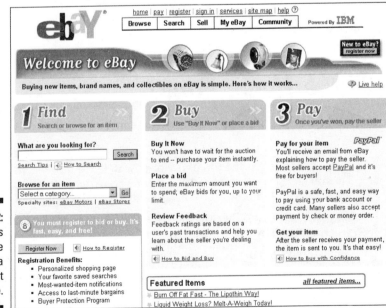

Figure 3-2:
New visitors
to the site
see a
different
home page.

Sign In, Please

Sign In is possibly the most powerful of all the links on the eBay pages, and it should be your first stop if you plan on doing any business at eBay (see Figure 3-3).

By going to the Sign In page and signing in, you don't have to enter your User ID when you bid or post items for sale. The Sign In page also takes you to a link that allows you to change your sign in or My eBay preferences. (See Chapter 4 for info on My eBay.)

If you're the only one who uses your computer, be sure to check the box that says "Keep me signed in on this computer unless I sign out." This way, you're always signed in to eBay every time you go to the site. The Sign In process places a *cookie* (a techno-related thingy — see Chapter 15 for details) on your computer that remains a part of your browser until you sign out. If you don't check the box, you will only be signed in while you're on the site. If there's no activity for 40 minutes — or if you close your browser — the cookie expires, and you have to sign in again.

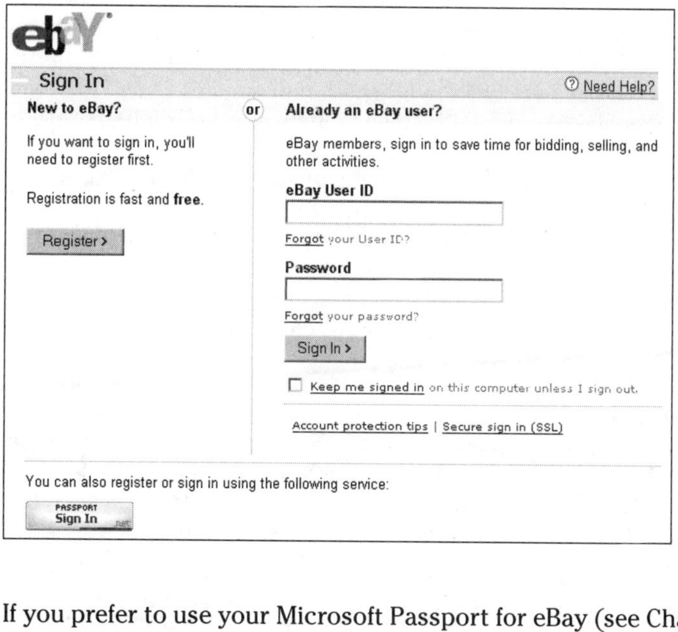

Figure 3-3:
The eBay
Sign In
page.

If you prefer to use your Microsoft Passport for eBay (see Chapter 2), click the Passport Sign In box and then enter your Passport e-mail address and password. When you're prompted, enter your eBay User ID and password. Your Passport is then activated for use on eBay until you sign out.

Here's how to get to the eBay Sign In page and sign in:

1. **Click the Sign In link above the navigation bar on any eBay page.**

2. **At the bottom of the new page that appears, click the Secure Sign In SSL link.**

   Using SSL keeps your personal information even more secure than usual. (See Chapter 2 for details about SSL.)

3. **Enter your User ID and password.**

4. **Click the Secure Sign In box.**

You're now signed in to eBay and can travel the site with ease. You can enter your My eBay page by clicking the My eBay link that appears in the upper-right corner. (See Chapter 4 for more on My eBay.) You may also click the link under the eBay Welcome to change your sign in or display preferences.

This Bar Never Closes

The *navigation bar* is at the top of the eBay home page and lists five eBay links that take you directly to any of the different eBay areas. Using the navigation bar is kind of like doing one-stop clicking. You can find this bar at the top of every page you visit at eBay. When you click one of the five links, you get a subnavigation bar with specific links to other related important places.

Think of links as expressways to specific destinations. Click a link just once, and the next thing you know, you're right where you want to be. You don't even have to answer that annoying old question, "When are we gonna get there?" from the kids in the backseat.

Here, without further ado, are the five navigation bar links and where they take you:

- **Browse:** Takes you to the page that lists Featured Items (see Chapter 6), all the main eBay categories, and Spotlights On (links to charity auctions and eBay promotions that vary from time to time). You also find Cool Features — eBay promotions and several mystery auctions (random items chosen from the millions up for bidding). From this page, you can link to any one of the millions of items up for auction at eBay.

  Under the Browse tab, you find links to browse by categories, geographic regions, themes, or stores. Click the browse regions link to be swept to the local trading area of your choice (see Figure 3-4). eBay has divvied up over 60 U.S. regions into mini-eBays. Although these items are found at the regular eBay site, you can find items that would cost too much to ship from a distance. You can also narrow down your search to items near you. Just select the closest major metropolitan area to your home and click it.

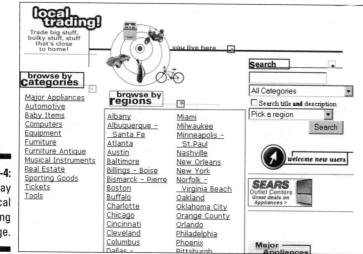

Figure 3-4:
The eBay
Local
Trading
hub page.

When you click to browse a category (for example, Books: Antiquarian & Collectible: First Editions), you see some boxes to the left of the auction listings. These boxes offer you ways to search, and the Display box gives you a different viewing option to browse:

- **All Items** is the default setting for the page. This option delivers on its promise — you see all items, including those in the Gallery. Gallery thumbnail previews appear in the status column to the left of the item's title. If your Internet connection can handle it, this is the way to go.

- Click **Gallery View** in the Display box to be taken to eBay's version of an auction catalog, the Gallery.

  The Gallery features pictures, also called *thumbnails,* of auction items. The sellers paid extra for them to appear here, so scan the thumbnails until you find an item that interests you. Click the thumbnail, and you're taken to that item's auction page.

  Note that not all sellers list their items in the Gallery View area, so by not browsing All Items, you may be missing out on some special items or deals.

You bid on Gallery items the same way as you do traditional auctions. The only difference is that eBay charges the seller an extra $0.25 to hang up an item in the Gallery or $19.95 to have a featured auction in the Gallery. (Jump over to Chapter 10 to find out how to get your item in the door of this exclusive club.)

- **Search:** Takes you to the eBay main Search page. Because over 10 million items are up for auction at any given time, finding just one (say, an antique Vermont milk can) is no easy task. The main Search page includes five specific searches (see "Exploring Your Home Page Search

Options" later in this chapter). From the subnavigation bar, you can click Find Members to search for other members and get information about their feedback (more on that stuff in Chapter 6). In addition, the subnavigation bar links you to Favorite Searches, a resident area of your My eBay page. It's eBay's way of helping you find what you're looking for (more about that in Chapter 17).

✔ **Sell:** Takes you to the Sell Your Item form that you fill out to start your auctions. I explain how to navigate this form in Chapter 9. The subnavigation bar directs you to a Seller Guide, your Seller account (links to access seller account-related information), and eBay's seller tools links page.

✔ **My eBay:** Takes you to your personal My eBay page, where you keep track of all your buying and selling activities, account information, and favorite categories (more about My eBay in Chapter 4).

✔ **Community:** Takes you to a page where you can find the latest news and announcements, chat with fellow traders in the eBay community, find charity auctions, and find out more about eBay. Chapters 17 and 18 tell you how to use these resources.

At the top of almost every eBay page, you find six small (but powerful) links that are just as important as the links on the navigation bar:

✔ **Home:** Takes you right back the home page. Use this link from any other page when you need to get back to the home page right away.

✔ **Pay:** When you click Pay, you go to a page that shows the last few items you've won and haven't paid for. Figure 3-5 shows how items that I've won but haven't yet paid for appear when I click the Pay link.

✔ **Sign In / Sign Out:** This link, which toggles between Sign In and Sign Out depending on your sign-in status, is important, and I remind you about it throughout this book.

✔ **Services:** Takes you to the eBay Services Overview page. Here, you can find links to pages that tell you all about buying and selling, registration pages, the Feedback Forum, SafeHarbor, the My eBay page, the About Me page, and other eBay programs.

✔ **Site Map:** Provides you with a bird's-eye view of the eBay world. Every *top-level* (or main) link available at eBay is listed here. If you're ever confused about finding a specific area, try the Site Map first. If a top-level link isn't listed here, it's not at eBay — yet.

✔ **Help:** Opens the pop-up eBay Help Center. The eBay Help Center overview page consists of a search box, in which you can type your query, tabs for help topics, an A-Z index, and a link to Ask an eBay Member (which links you to member-populated question-and-answer boards). The page offers links to the answers to the most frequently asked questions by eBay users and the Security Center.

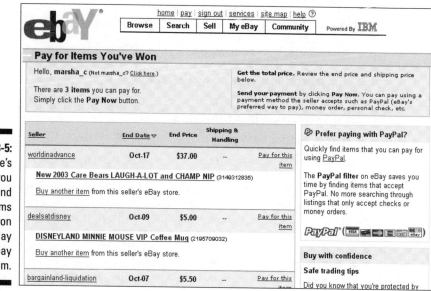

Figure 3-5:
Here's
where you
can find
the items
you've won
on eBay
and pay
for them.

If you get turned around, confused, or just can't find the answer to your question, you can find eBay's old Help Center at `pages.ebay.com/help/index.html` (for now). It may be of help in a pinch.

Exploring Your Home Page Search Options

There's an old Chinese expression that says, "Every journey begins with the first eBay search." Okay, the quote's a bit updated. Very wise words nonetheless. You can start a search from the home page in one of two ways:

- ✔ **Use the search box.** It's right there at the top of the home page next to the phrase "What are you looking for?" and it's a fast way of finding item listings.

- ✔ **Use the Search button on the navigation bar or the Smart Search link below the search box on the home page.** These links take you to the Basic Search page, where you can do all kinds of specialized searches.

Both options give you the same results. The instructions I offer in the next two sections about using these search methods are just the tip of the eBay iceberg. For the inside track on how to finesse the eBay search engine to root out just what you're looking for, visit Chapter 5.

Peering through the home page search box

To launch a title search from the home page, follow these steps:

1. **In the search box, type no more than a few keywords that describe the item you're looking for.**

   Refer to Figure 3-1 to see the search box.

2. **Click the Find It button.**

   The results of your search appear on-screen in a matter of seconds.

You can type just about anything in this box and get some information. Say you're looking for *Star Trek* memorabilia. If so, you're not alone. The television show premiered on September 8, 1966, and even though it was canceled in 1969 because of low ratings, *Star Trek* has become one of the most successful science-fiction franchises in history. If you like *Star Trek* as much as I do, you can use the search box on the eBay home page to find all sorts of *Star Trek* stuff. I just ran a search and found 20,329 items in 1,263 categories on eBay with *Star Trek* in their titles.

Try the Smart Search link under the search box to narrow down your search. This link takes you to the Basic Search page, which is explained in the following section.

When you search for popular items at eBay (and a classic example is *Star Trek* memorabilia), you may get inundated with thousands of auctions that match your search criteria. Even if you're traveling at warp speed, you could spend hours checking each auction individually. ("Scotty, we need more power *now!*") If you're pressed for time like the rest of us, eBay has not-so-mysterious ways for you to narrow down your search so that finding a specific item is much more manageable. Turn to Chapter 5 for insider techniques that can help you slim down those searches and beef up those results.

Going where the Search button takes you

One of the most important buttons on the navigation bar is the Search button. When you click this button, you're whisked away to the main Search page, which promptly presents you with five search options. Each option enables you to search for information in a different way. Here's how the search options on the menu can work for you:

✔ **Basic Search:** Search by keywords or item number. Type in the keywords that describe an item (for example, **Superman lunchbox** or **antique pocket watch**) and click Search, and you can see how many are available at eBay.

You can also search by item number. Every item that's up for auction at eBay is assigned an item number, which is displayed next to the item name on its page. To find an item by number, just type the number and click Search, and away you go. To find out more about how individual auction pages work at eBay, spin through Chapter 6.

You can also find items by number if you type the item number into any of the small search boxes that appear on eBay pages.

🖝 **Advanced Search:** This feature enables you to define your search without using a bunch of code. It works pretty much the same as the Basic Search method, but you can exclude more features from your search. You can also take advantage of eBay's regional trading and find items for sale in your neighborhood. Figure 3-6 shows the Advanced Search options.

The search by category filter is a snappy new search function that helps you figure out which subcategories have the item you want or, if you want to sell, helps you decide where to list your item for sale. It produces a regular search in a selected category, but also has a column on the left side of the page that lets you know which subcategories your item is listed in and how many of the item are listed in each category.

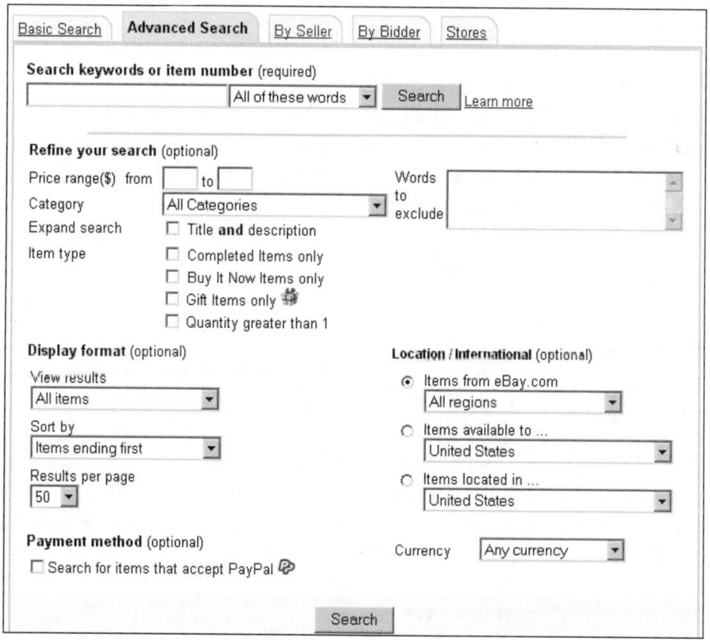

Basic Search   **Advanced Search**   By Seller   By Bidder   Stores

Search keywords or item number (required)

[_____] [All of these words ▾] [Search] Learn more

Refine your search (optional)

Price range($) from [___] to [___]
Category [All Categories ▾]
Expand search ☐ Title **and** description
Item type ☐ Completed Items only
    ☐ Buy It Now Items only
    ☐ Gift Items only 🎁
    ☐ Quantity greater than 1

Words to exclude [_____]

Display format (optional)

View results
[All items ▾]
Sort by
[Items ending first ▾]
Results per page
[50 ▾]

Location / International (optional)

⦿ Items from eBay.com
  [All regions ▾]
○ Items available to ...
  [United States ▾]
○ Items located in ...
  [United States ▾]

Payment method (optional)
☐ Search for items that accept PayPal 🅿

Currency [Any currency ▾]

[Search]

Figure 3-6: The Advanced Search page and its options.

To find an item that sold at eBay in the past, indicate that you want to use the Completed Items Only search. Type in the keywords of an item, and you get a list of items of this type that have been sold in the last 14 (or so) days, as well as what they sold for. You can use this type of search to strategize your asking price before you put an item up for auction (or to determine how much you will have to bid to win an item).

Although Chapter 5 tells you all you need to know about searching eBay, the following list explains some other searches that you can perform from the Search page. In a nutshell, here's what they do:

- **By Seller:** Every person at eBay has a personal User ID (the name you use to conduct transactions). Use a By Seller search if you liked the merchandise from a seller's auction and want to see what else the seller has for sale. Type the seller's User ID, and you get a list of every auction that person is running.

- **By Bidder:** For the sake of practicality and convenience, User IDs help eBay keep track of every move a user makes at eBay. If you want to see what a particular user (say, a fellow *Star Trek* fan) is bidding on, use the By Bidder search. Type in a User ID in the By Bidder search box, and you get a list of everything the user is currently bidding on, as well as how much he or she is bidding. I show you how to use the By Bidder search option as a strategic buying tool in Chapter 6.

- **Store Search:** Here's something I bet you didn't know: When you use eBay's search engine, it doesn't search eBay stores for matching items. I think that's a bunch of malarkey, but who am I? By searching for your item here, you'll see if any matching items are available in eBay stores (perhaps even at lower prices).

If you're looking for a particular eBay store, eBay provides a search box that allows you to search for a store by name (or part of the name).

Using eBay's "Welcome Mat"

eBay welcomes new users to its home page with a blue welcome mat. I'm talking about the three buttons on the eBay home page that are next to the words *Welcome New Users*. Clicking one of these links takes you to some of the most important places at eBay. (Of course, if you happen to be looking for a new welcome mat, you've come to the right Web site — generally, you can find around 180 of them up for sale.)

After you log onto the eBay site several times and sold a thing or two, you may not see the "Welcome Mat." It's not that eBay doesn't welcome you. It's just that eBay wants you to have new information in its place when you're familiar with the site.

eBay features three buttons on the map: Learn To Buy, Safety Tips, and Register Now. Actually, if you see this page, you've probably registered, unless another registered eBay user uses that computer. If you haven't registered, turn to Chapter 2 to get the quick and painless facts about the easy eBay registration process.

You may also see a Live Help button on the home page. This is the most useful of all. By using this link, you can get into a direct conversation with an eBay customer service representative. He or she can answer any of your basic questions about the site. I show you how Live Help works in Chapter 2.

Home Links, the Next Generation

If you look carefully, you can see several other links on the home page, which give you express service to several key parts of the site. Here are the highlights:

- **Specialty Sites:** Here's where clicking a link gets you to eBay's new specialty sites. A click on eBay Motors brings you to ebaymotors.com, an area dedicated to the sale of almost everything with a motor and wheels. eBay Stores (stores.ebay.com) takes you to a separate area of eBay that is loaded with thousands of stores from eBay sellers. eBay stores are filled with items you can purchase without bidding.

- **Featured Items:** Visit the featured items. (Translation: Sellers paid more to have them featured in this section.)

- **Charity:** This link takes you to the many charity auctions that benefit worthwhile organizations.

- **Live Auctions:** This link takes you to incredibly fun live auctions. Chapter 18 is the place to go for more info on live auctions.

- **Professional Services:** This link takes you to an area with freelance people who are looking for jobs, where professionals bid for your work.

- **Global Sites:** This links to eBay's international auction sites.

You may notice that the graphic links on the home page change from day to day — even hour to hour. If you're interested in the featured areas of the site, visit this page several times a day to see the entire array of special happenings at eBay.

Maneuvering through Categories

So how does eBay keep track of the millions of items that are up for auction at any given moment? The brilliant minds at eBay decided to group items into a nice, neat little storage system called *categories*. The home page lists most of the main categories, but currently eBay lists tens of thousands of subcategories, ranging from Antiques to Writing Instruments. And don't ask how many sub-subcategories (categories within categories) eBay's got — I can't count that high.

Well, okay, I *could* list all the categories and subcategories currently available at eBay — if you wouldn't mind squinting at a dozen pages of really small, eye-burning text. But a category browse is an adventure that's unique for each individual, and I wouldn't think of depriving you of it. Suffice it to say that if you like to hunt around for that perfect something, you're in browsing heaven now.

Here's how to navigate around the categories:

1. **Click the category that interests you, such as Books or DVDs & Movies.**

   You're transported to the category's page. You see categories and subcategories listed next to each heading. Happy hunting.

   If you don't find a category that interests you among those on the home page, simply click the Browse button on the navigation bar, and you're off to the main categories page. Not only do you get a pretty impressive page of main categories and subcategories, but you also get a short list of featured auctions and a link to them all.

   If you really and truly want to see a list of all the categories and subcategories, click the See All Categories in the Category Overview link on the main category page. Alternatively you can go to `listings.ebay.com/pool1/listings/list/overview.html`.

2. **After the category page appears, find a subcategory underneath the main category title that interests you. Click the subcategory, and keep digging through the sub-subcategories until you find what you want.**

   For example, if you're looking for items honoring your favorite television show, click the Entertainment category. The page that comes up includes subcategories of DVDs & Movies, Memorabilia, Music, and Video Games. You will notice that the Memorabilia category has many links, including the Television Memorabilia subcategory. If you click TV Memorabilia, you're off to a listing page that lists the subcategories (on the left column of the page) Ads, Flyers, Apparel, Clippings, Photos, Pins, Buttons, Posters, Press Kits, Props, Scripts, Wardrobe, and Other. At the top of that page, you also find featured auctions and, under them, the current Television auctions. Little *icons* (pictures) next to the listings tell you more about each item — whether it's pictured (the camera) and whether it's a new item (the sunrise). You can also click the tabs to isolate Auctions only or Buy It Now items.

   By the way, I have lots more to say about featured items in Chapter 10.

3. **When you find an item that interests you, click the item and the full Auction page pops up on your screen.**

Congratulations — you've just navigated through several million items to find that one TV-collectible item that caught your attention. (Pardon me while I bid on that Lily Munster — Yvonne DeCarlo signed picture.) You can instantly return to the home page by clicking its link at the top of the page (or return to the Listings page by repeatedly clicking the Back button at the top of your browser).

Near the bottom of every subcategory page, you can see a link list of numbers. The numbers are page numbers, and you can use them to fast-forward through all the items in that subcategory. So, if you feel like browsing around page 8, without going through 8 pages individually, just click number 8; you're presented with the items on that page (their listings, actually). Happy browsing.

If you're a bargain hunter by habit, you may find some pretty weird stuff while browsing the categories and subcategories of items at eBay — some of it super-cheap and some of it (maybe) just cheap. (There's even a Weird Stuff category — no kidding!) Remember that (as with any marketplace) you're responsible for finding out as much as possible about an item before you buy — and definitely before you bid. So, if you're the type who sometimes can't resist a good deal, ask yourself what you plan to *do* with the pile of garbage you can get for 15 cents — and ask yourself *now,* before it arrives on your doorstep. Chapters 6 and 7 offer more information on savvy bidding.

Going Global

Listed below the Categories list are links to eBay's international auction sites. You may enter eBay Argentina, Australia, Austria, Belgium, Brazil, Canada, China, France, Germany, Ireland, Italy, Korea, Mexico, The Netherlands, New Zealand, Singapore, Spain, Sweden, Switzerland, Taiwan, and (whew) the United Kingdom. Click one of these links, and you jet off to eBay sites in these countries. The international sites are in the countries' native languages. It might be a good place to practice your third-year French — or maybe not! Remember that after you leave eBay USA, you're subject to the contractual and privacy laws of the country you're visiting.

Using the Featured Items Link

Here at eBay, money talks pretty loudly. In the center of the home page, you see a list of the auctions eBay is featuring at the moment. eBay usually posts six featured items at any given time and rotates items throughout the day so that as many sellers as possible get a shot at being in the spotlight. When you click the featured auction's All Featured Items link, you're instantly beamed to eBay's Home Page Featured Items section.

AUCTION ANECDOTE

Excuse me, do you have any Don Ho cocktail glasses?

As a matter of fact, yes! eBay adds new categories all the time to meet the needs of its users. For example, some specialized categories have popped up — with some interesting items:

✔ **Cultural:** Tribal masks, Kenyan drums, a Mexican turtle planter, an ebony walking cane, and a Persian camel seat. (Found under Collectibles: Cultures and Religions: Cultures)

✔ **Firefighting:** A fire hose nozzle, an antique leather fireman's helmet (sorry, no antique leather firemen — yet), a West Virginia Fire Department badge, and a German fireman-shaped beer stein. (Found under Collectibles: Historical Memorabilia: Firefighting)

✔ **Vanity Items:** An Art Deco nail buffer, a child's hairbrush from the 1950s, a set of

vintage hat pins, an antique curling iron, and a lady's compact made by Hudnut. (Found under Collectibles: Vintage Clothing and Accessories: Vanity Items)

✔ **Weird Stuff:** Gag lotto tickets, an antique artificial arm, a skeleton wedding cake couple, a genuine hummingbird's nest, a 1960s lava lamp, and a stuffed chicken collection. (Found under: Everything Else: Weird Stuff)

✔ **Hawaiiana:** A coconut monkey bank, a hula-girl table lamp, a set of Don Ho cocktail glasses (See? They do exist!), an antique Hawaiian wedding shirt, and a Diamond Head surfing trivet. (Found under: Collectibles: Cultures: Hawaiiana)

You can find everything from Las Vegas vacations to Model-T Fords to diet products in the Home Page Featured Items. Home Page Featured Items are not for mere mortals with small wallets. They've been lifted to the exalted *featured* status because sellers shelled out lots of money to get them noticed. All you need to get your auction featured is $99.95 ($199.95 for Multiple Item listings), plus a second or two to click Home Page Featured Item on the Sell Your Item form. (See Chapter 10 if you have an item that all eyes must see.)

Note that bidding on these items works the same way as bidding on regular items.

The Home Page Featured Items page contains many expensive items. Sellers who put up high-priced items have been around the block a few times and make it clear that they will verify each bid on the item. That means if you place a bid on Jay Leno's autographed Harley Davidson (recently up for auction to benefit the Auction for America), be prepared to get a phone call from the seller. The seller may ask you to prove that you can actually pay for the motorcycle. Nothing personal; it's strictly business.

Charities

Click the Charity link on the home page, and you see links to eBay charity auctions. Charity auctions are a great way for memorabilia collectors to find one-of-a-kind (and authentic) items. Winning bids contribute to programs that help charities. (Chapter 18 tells you more about what charity items you can bid on — and the good you can do with your checkbook.)

Promotion du jour

The eBay community is constantly changing. To help you get into the swing of things right away, eBay provides a special box with links that take you right to the current word on the latest eBay special events.

 Even if the main promotion box doesn't appeal to you, usually you can find some interesting links dotted around the home page without a headline. You can find a standing home for the Spotlights On (eBay's special promotions, big-ticket items, and keywords) by clicking the See All eBay Categories link from the home page.

You *can* get there from here — lots of places, in fact:

✔ A rotating list of special-interest links changes at least once a day. (Half the fun is getting a closer look at pages you haven't seen.)

✔ Special money-saving offers from third-party vendors can be a boon if you're on the lookout for a bargain.

Bottoming Out

At the very bottom of the home page is an unassuming group of links that provide more ways to get to some seriously handy pages:

✔ **Announcements:** Visit the General Announcements Board when you want to know about any late-breaking news.

✔ **Register:** This is another link to the eBay registration page.

✔ **Shop eBay-o-rama:** This link enables you to browse and buy eBay merchandise from the eBay company store.

✔ **Security Center:** This link takes you to a page where concerns about fraud and safety are addressed. It's such an important eBay tool that I dedicate an entire chapter to this program. Before buying or selling, it's a good idea to check out Chapter 15.

- ✔ **Policies:** This is a good place to visit to brush up on the site's policies and guidelines.

- ✔ **PayPal:** This link takes you to the home page of PayPal, the eBay online payment service.

- ✔ **Feedback Forum:** This link takes you to one of the most important spots at eBay. The Feedback Forum is where you can find out if you've forgotten to place feedback on a transaction, place feedback, and respond to feedback left for you, all in one friendly location.

- ✔ **About eBay:** Click this link to find out about eBay the company and to get its press releases, company overview, and stock information. You can also find out about eBay community activities and charities — and even apply for a job at eBay.

- ✔ **Jobs:** Click here if you want to work *for* eBay instead of *through* eBay.

- ✔ **Affiliates Program:** If you have your own Web site and want to make a few bucks, click this link. If you sign up for the program and put a link to eBay on your Web page, eBay pays you $5 for any new user that signs up directly from your Web site (plus other bonuses).

- ✔ **eBay Downloads:** A link to eBay-supplied selling-assistance software. See Chapter 20 for more on these programs.

- ✔ **eBay Gift Certificates:** Send anyone an eBay gift certificate for any special occasion. You can print it out yourself, or eBay will send it to any e-mail address you provide. The gift certificate is good for any item on the site, and you can pay for it immediately with PayPal.

Below these links, you'll also find a little link area that mimics the links on the top-of-the page navigation bar.

On other eBay pages, the bottom navigation bar looks a little different. It often includes even more links so that you can cruise the site quickly without necessarily having to use the navigation bar.

Chapter 4

My Own Private eBay

I know eBay is a sensitive kind of company because it gives all users plenty of personal space. This space is called the My eBay page, and it's your private listing of all your activities on eBay — sort of a "This is your eBay life." I think it's the greatest organizational tool around, and I want to talk to somebody about getting one for organizing my life outside of eBay.

In this chapter, you find out how you can use the My eBay page to keep tabs on what you're buying and selling, find out how much money you've spent, and add categories to your own personalized list so that you can get to any favorite eBay place with just a click of your mouse. You gain knowledge of the ins and outs of feedback — what it is, why it can give you that warm, fuzzy feeling, and how to manage it so all that cyber-positive reinforcement doesn't go to your head.

Getting to Your My eBay Page

Using your My eBay page makes keeping track of your eBay life a whole lot easier. And getting there is easy enough. After you register at eBay, you have two easy ways to get to your My eBay page. The most practical way to enter eBay is always through the Sign In link (described in Chapter 3). If you haven't signed in, you can access your My eBay page by following these steps:

1. **On the top of any eBay page, click the My eBay button in the eBay navigation bar.**

    You're sent to the My eBay Sign In page, shown in Figure 4-1.

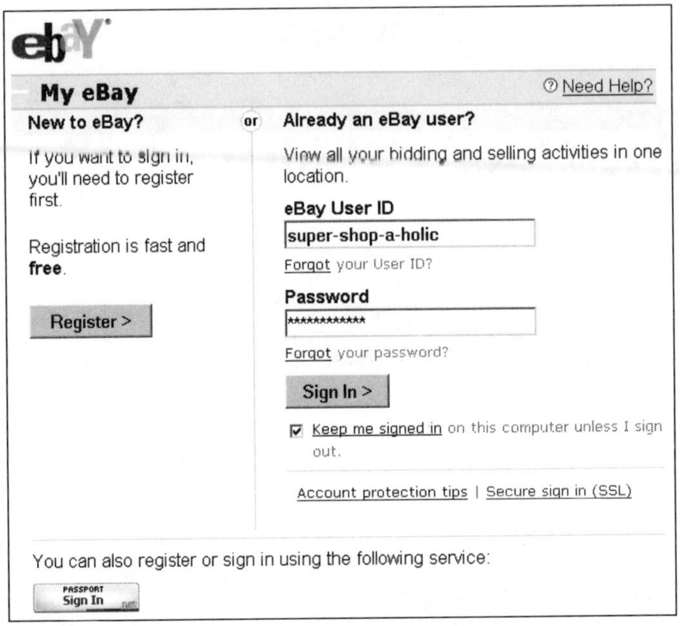

eBay

My eBay   ⑦ Need Help?

New to eBay?   **or**   **Already an eBay user?**

If you want to sign in,   View all your bidding and selling activities in one
you'll need to register   location.
first.
                                 eBay User ID
Registration is fast and | super-shop-a-holic |
free.
                                 Forgot your User ID?

| Register > | **Password**
                                 | ************ |

                                 Forgot your password?

                                 | Sign In > |

                                 ☑ Keep me signed in on this computer unless I sign
                                   out.

                                 Account protection tips | Secure sign in (SSL)

Figure 4-1:   You can also register or sign in using the following service:
The My
eBay Sign | PASSPORT
In page. | Sign In net |

You don't have to be on the eBay home page to find My eBay or Sign In.
As you maneuver around the Web site, the links follow you like Mona
Lisa's eyes.

 2. **Decide if you want to sign in with Microsoft Passport (see Chapter 3)
    or with your eBay User ID.**

    If you sign in with Microsoft Passport, you are taken to the My eBay page
    for your eBay User ID. If your MSN e-mail address is different from the
    one you use at eBay, you're prompted to input your eBay User ID and
    password.

 3. **Type in your User ID and password.**

    If you've forgotten your eBay User ID or password, click the Forgot Your
    User ID or Forgot Your Password link. For your User ID, you can then
    type in your e-mail address, and eBay will send you an e-mail with your
    User ID. Your User ID appears in any search results, posts, or pages. For
    the password, you have to answer your "secret" question (the one you
    filled in when you registered). If you don't remember that, eBay will send
    you a password-reset e-mail if you input your correct contact informa-
    tion with telephone number.

 4. **Click the Sign In button to enter My eBay.**

    You've arrived at your My eBay Welcome page. You find some handy
    links on this page. You can go to any of the following places:

- **My eBay Preferences tab:** Click this link to get to the Preferences tab of your My eBay page. For more on what you'll find there, see Table 4-1.

- **Item I Last Looked At:** If you realized you weren't signed in while you were looking at an item, this link takes you back to that item with a click of your mouse.

- **My eBay:** This is probably the link you're looking for. This takes you to your My eBay area.

- **Sell Your Item:** If you've signed in to sell an item, click here.

- **Check Out the Announcement Board for Site Updates:** This link brings you to the System Announcement page. This is where you go to see if there have been any interruptions in the eBay system or upcoming changes.

5. **Click the My eBay link to go to (finally) the My eBay page (see Figure 4-2).**

My eBay - Hello queen-of-shopping (0)

| Bidding/Watching | Selling | Favorites | Accounts | Feedback | Preferences | All |

Go to: Items I'm Bidding On | Items I've Won | Items I'm Watching | Items I Didn't Win   ⑦Need Help?

Items I'm Bidding On (3 Items)   ▸See totals | All item details

Items that you are currently winning are green and bold, those that you are **not** currently winning are red.

Item #	Start Price	Current Price	My Max Bid	Qty	# of Bids	Start Date	(PST) End Date	Time Left
Mary Frances Suede Cream Clutch Embroidered (reserve price not yet met)								
3427748848	$49.99	$76.89	$75.89	1	5	Aug-23	Sep-02 12:15:00	1d 0h 57m
Queen Mother Red Hat Club Rhinestone Pin NEW								
2654261650	$9.99	$9.99	$10.58	1	1	Aug-24	Sep-03 17:56:26	2d 6h 39m
Porcelain figural box KITTEN AND YARN								
3240305299	$4.99	$4.99	$5.78	1	1	Aug-31	Sep-07 17:17:00	6d 5h 59m
Totals	Start Price	Current Price	My Max Bid	Total Qty	# of Bids			
All items	$64.97	$91.87	$92.25	3	7			
Items that I'm winning	$14.98	$14.98	$16.36	2	2			

Figure 4-2:
Your My eBay page, the hub for your eBay activities.

Houston, we don't have a problem

Here's an item I wish I'd bought: a Neil Armstrong signed NASA portrait w/COA (Certificate of Authenticity). It was a very clean 8-x-10-inch color NASA portrait signed by Neil Armstrong, the first human on the moon. In recent years, Armstrong has been very reclusive, and his autographs are difficult to obtain in any form. Many forgeries are being offered, so buyer beware. This portrait came with a lifetime COA. The starting price was $10, and the portrait sold on eBay in 1999 for $520!

Many believe that Neil Armstrong's autograph will be among the most important of the twentieth century. Just think about it. He was the first human to step onto another celestial body. This feat may never happen again, and certainly not in our lifetimes. When I updated this book for the third edition, this same portrait was selling for $650. A quick scan on eBay today says that such a signed picture just closed at $1,925. Why didn't I follow my own advice and buy one?

The My eBay page consists of seven tabs, where you may view different areas of your eBay business: Bidding/Watching, Selling, Favorites, Accounts, Feedback, Preferences, and All. Table 4-1 gives you the scoop on these tabs.

Table 4-1	The Display Tabs on Your My eBay Page
Click Here	*To See This on Your My eBay Page*
Bidding/ Watching	Every auction you're currently bidding on and items you've won. Further down the page, you find every auction that you've marked to watch.
Selling	Every auction in which you're currently selling items. You also have a list of the items you've sold.
Favorites	Links to your favorite categories, searches, sellers, and stores.
Accounts	What you currently owe eBay and links to locations where you can get information on payment terms, fees and credits, and refunds. It also links to your PayPal account.
Feedback	The most recent feedback comments about you and links that send you to all your feedback, all the feedback you've left, and an area where you can respond to feedback.
Preferences	Lets you select the activities in which you want eBay to remember your password so that you don't have to type it in every time (like when selling, bidding, managing items, and so on). It also gives you the option to change your personal information on eBay.
All	All the tab items from your My eBay page seen in one scrollable page.

At the bottom of each tabbed page are important links to activities and information that relate to the My eBay activity tab that you're on.

Don't confuse the My eBay page with the About Me page. The About Me page is a personal Web page that you can create to let the world know about you and your eBay dealings. (You don't have to have an About Me page if you don't want to — but they are free for the taking and are fun to share.) I tell you how to get your own About Me page in Chapter 14.

Choosing Your My eBay Preferences

One of the tabs at the top of your My eBay page is Preferences. eBay created this feature to help you avoid having to type your password every time you do certain activities, such as bid, check your account balance, and participate in auctions. The only catch is that you have to sign in before you can set your preferences.

The first time you enter your My eBay page (by clicking the My eBay link on the top of every page), you see that eBay requires you to sign in before going any further. So, click the link and sign in. After you do so with your User ID and password, you're presented with the Sign In and Display Preferences page. The options have check boxes. You can customize these options by checking the boxes (one click per box does it).

You have to decide which activities you want activated when you sign in to eBay (you can always change these later). The most convenient thing to do is check all the options. If you do, you won't waste much time inputting your user ID and password as you participate in auctions and sales on the site.

After you've signed in and set up your my eBay page, you can change any of your preferences by going to the Preferences tab, shown in Figure 4-3. As you scroll down the page, you can make changes in the following areas:

- **Personal Information:** You can change registration information, update your e-mail address, add wireless e-mail, create an About Me page, and more.

- **My eBay Preferences:** You can customize how your My eBay page appears in your browser.

- **Sign In Activities:** You can change the initial setting you've set up for your Sign In activities.

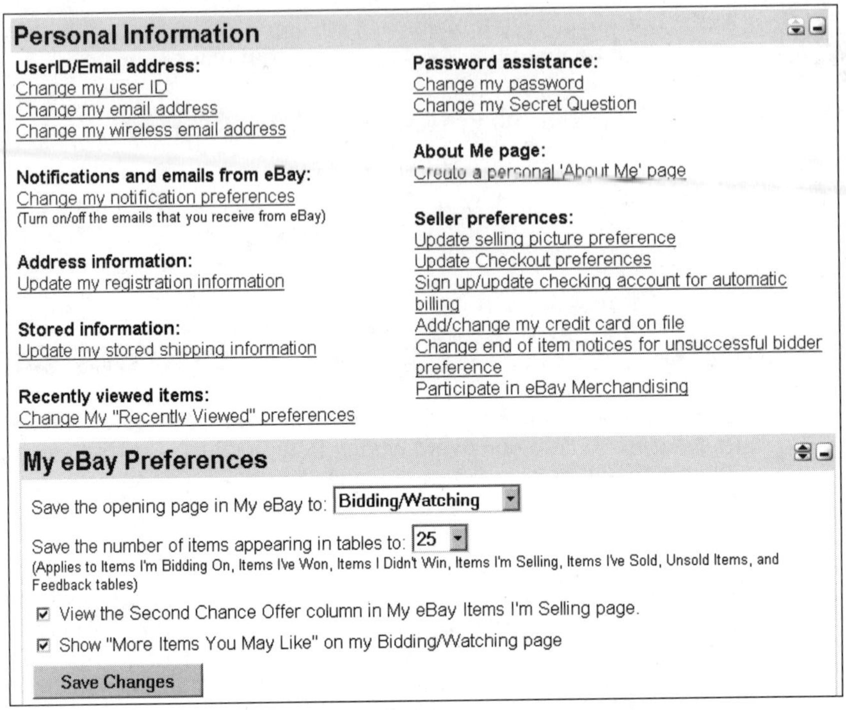

Personal Information

UserID/Email address:
Change my user ID
Change my email address
Change my wireless email address

Notifications and emails from eBay:
Change my notification preferences
(Turn on/off the emails that you receive from eBay)

Address information:
Update my registration information

Stored information:
Update my stored shipping information

Recently viewed items:
Change My "Recently Viewed" preferences

Password assistance:
Change my password
Change my Secret Question

About Me page:
Create a personal 'About Me' page

Seller preferences:
Update selling picture preference
Update Checkout preferences
Sign up/update checking account for automatic billing
Add/change my credit card on file
Change end of item notices for unsuccessful bidder preference
Participate in eBay Merchandising

My eBay Preferences

Save the opening page in My eBay to: [Bidding/Watching ▼]

Save the number of items appearing in tables to: [25 ▼]
(Applies to Items I'm Bidding On, Items I've Won, Items I Didn't Win, Items I'm Selling, Items I've Sold, Unsold Items, and Feedback tables)

☑ View the Second Chance Offer column in My eBay Items I'm Selling page.

☑ Show "More Items You May Like" on my Bidding/Watching page

[**Save Changes**]

Figure 4-3:
Even more eBay activities that you can control from your My eBay Preferences page.

When you finally get to your My eBay page, save yourself a lot of work and time by using your browser to bookmark your My eBay page as a favorite. Doing so saves you a lot of keystrokes later on. If you want to send a shortcut to your desktop, in Internet Explorer choose File⇨Send⇨Shortcut to Desktop. This way, you can open your browser directly onto your My eBay page. Some folks also make their My eBay page their browser home page so that their My eBay page appears the minute they log on. That's dedication.

Setting Up Your Account

When you first explore your My eBay page, you'll see that your eBay Accounts tab has not been activated. The eBay folks set up an account for you when you list something to sell. That way, they can keep track of the fees charged for listing items on the site. Even if the items don't sell, eBay keeps the fee. It doesn't cost you a nickel in fees to look around or sign up — or even to buy. (For details on how eBay charges you for its services, see Chapter 9.)

eBay account status

Even though you've already become a registered eBay user (if you haven't registered, see Chapter 2), you don't have to submit your credit card information until you list an item for auction or until you bid in an auction that has special rules requiring a credit card. You can provide eBay with this credit card information right from your My eBay Accounts page, which you access by clicking the Accounts tab.

After you start selling, your Accounts page becomes very powerful. Figure 4-4 shows you what the Accounts section of the My eBay page is all about. You can look up every detail of your account history, as well as make changes to your personal preferences (such as how and when you want to pay fees). If you think eBay owes you money, you can submit a refund request from here as well. Before you jump into the money game, you may want to review the links that eBay gives you to manage your money:

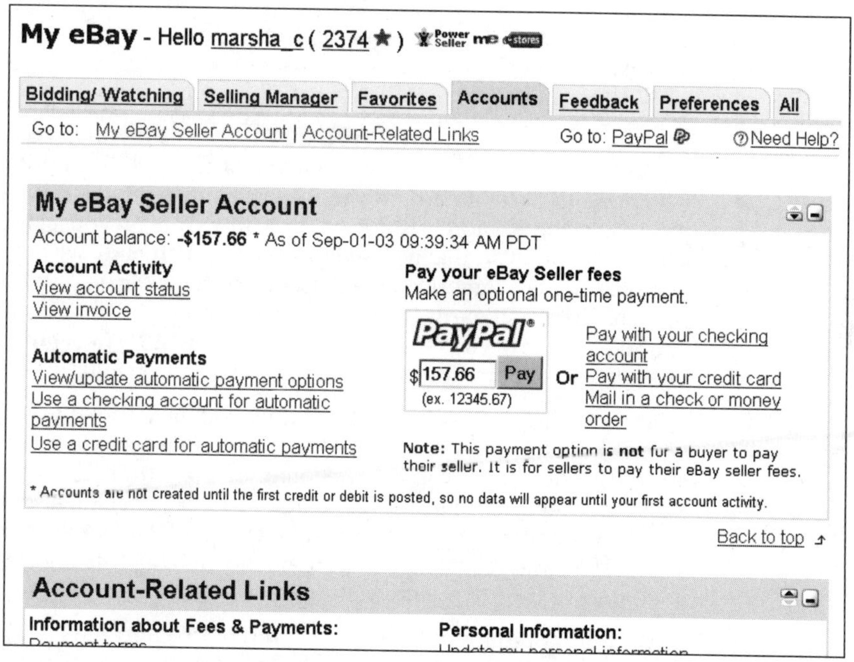

My eBay - Hello marsha_c (2374 ★) 💰Power Seller me estores

| Bidding/ Watching | Selling Manager | Favorites | **Accounts** | Feedback | Preferences | All |

Go to: My eBay Seller Account | Account-Related Links   Go to: PayPal 🅿   ⑦ Need Help?

My eBay Seller Account

Account balance: **-$157.66** * As of Sep-01-03 09:39:34 AM PDT

Account Activity
View account status
View invoice

Automatic Payments
View/update automatic payment options
Use a checking account for automatic payments
Use a credit card for automatic payments

Pay your eBay Seller fees
Make an optional one-time payment.

PayPal®
$ 157.66 [Pay] Or
(ex. 12345.67)

Pay with your checking account
Pay with your credit card
Mail in a check or money order

Note: This payment option is **not** for a buyer to pay their seller. It is for sellers to pay their eBay seller fees.

* Accounts are not created until the first credit or debit is posted, so no data will appear until your first account activity.

Back to top ↗

Account-Related Links

Information about Fees & Payments:
Payment terms

Personal Information:
Update my personal information

Figure 4-4:
The Accounts section of your My eBay page.

What's that thingy?

For the first 30 days after you register or change your User ID (which you can do anytime, as Chapter 2 explains) — eBay gives you an icon that stays next to your User ID every time it appears on eBay (when you bid, run an auction, or post a message on any of the chat boards).

So why the icon? eBay calls the graphic of a beaming robot-like critter the "new ID" icon. It's

sort of a friendly heads-up to others that you are a new user. (If you've changed your User ID, the icon consists of two of the little guys with an arrow connecting them.) You still have all the privileges that everybody else has on eBay while you're breaking in your new identity. The icons are nothing personal, just business as usual.

✔ **View Account Status:** Click here to get a complete explanation of your eBay account — charges, credits, and your current balance (see Figure 4-5).

✔ **View Invoice:** Click here to see your most recent invoice and details of the transactions.

✔ **View/Update Automatic Payment Options:** Although all sellers must provide a credit card, you don't have to use this credit card to pay your monthly fees — unless you're using one of eBay's international sites, which require credit card payments. On a single-payment basis, you may pay with a check, money order, or even directly from your PayPal account. Click here and fill in the information. Even though eBay welcomes Visa, you may also use American Express, Discover, or MasterCard. You can also change credit cards here at any time. Every month, eBay charges your card for fees you incurred the previous month. You can see these charges on your credit card statement as well as on your eBay account.

When you click to View Account Status, you have the option to view your account activity by date range. You can also see your account status by clicking View Entire Account. Clicking there shows your entire account — every transaction — since you began selling at eBay. I checked my account. I've sold on eBay since 1997, and it's a truly impressive statement. I don't recommend clicking this unless you have a good deal of time to spend waiting for it to load.

✔ **PayPal link:** A quick click here, and you're taken to the PayPal home page. Check out Chapter 6 for more on the PayPal payment service.

When you give eBay your credit card information, eBay attempts to authorize your card immediately. Your credit card company's response, either Declined or Approved, appears on your View Account Status page.

1568237545	Nov-25-01 20:43:14 PST	Final Auction Value fee	1034174035	-	-$1.36
		Final price $29.50.			
1568344664	Nov-25-01 20:43:14 PST	Final Auction Value fee	1664622902	-	-$1.23
		Final price $24.50.			
1568344689	Nov-25-01 20:43:14 PST	Final Auction Value fee	1664622907	-	-$0.25
		Final price $4.99.			
1568913211	Nov-26-01 13:01:07 PST	Insertion fee	1669513617	-	-$0.30
1568913214	Nov-26-01 13:01:07 PST	Gallery fee	1669513617	-	-$0.25
1568916437	Nov-26-01 13:02:36 PST	Insertion fee	1669514209	-	-$0.30
1568916438	Nov-26-01 13:02:36 PST	Gallery fee	1669514209	-	-$0.25
1576983219	Nov-28-01 20:18:08 PST	Final Auction Value fee	1300773372	-	-$0.77
		Final price $15.50.			
1576984679	Nov-28-01 20:21:41 PST	Final Auction Value fee	1488635942	-	-$1.40
		Final price $31.00.			
1576930942	Nov-28-01 20:22:08 PST	Final Auction Value fee	1037165799	-	-$2.09
		Final price $58.77.			

Figure 4-5:
Here's a look at how eBay invoices and account statuses appear when you request them.

Account-related links

The account-related links at the bottom of the Accounts page are among the most useful links in your My eBay page if you're selling at eBay. These are the links relating to your financial dealings with eBay:

✓ **Payment Terms:** Although you need to post a credit card for ID purposes to sell at eBay, you can pay your eBay bill in one of three ways. You can change your method of payment at any time. See Table 4-2 to find out when the different payments are charged to your account.

- **Credit Card on File:** You can place your credit card on file with eBay so that each month eBay can place your selling charges on your credit card. I've been using this format since I became an eBay user and find that it works out very well.

- **PayPal:** You can make single payments directly through your PayPal account. If you have a cash balance in your account, you can have it applied to your eBay bill; if not, you can pay the amount through the credit card you've registered on PayPal.

- **eBay Direct Pay:** This form of payment allows eBay to swoop into your personal checking account once a month and remove the money you owe. When you sign up for this option, your bank account is automatically debited on a predetermined day, based on your billing cycle. Can you tell I'm not a big fan of this payment type? I just don't like anyone removing funds from my account without my authorizing the withdrawal each time.

- **Check or Money Order Payment:** This can be a bit dodgy if you plan to do any volume of selling on eBay. Your payment must arrive at eBay on time. No kidding. eBay can charge you 1.5 percent interest a month on the unpaid balance or just suspend your account — not a pretty picture.

The downside of paying eBay fees by check or money order is that you're charged if you bounce a check, miss a payment, or use Canadian dollars instead of U.S. dollars. You're supposed to get an e-mail invoice at the end of the month, but even if you don't, eBay expects to be paid on time. A word to the wise: Keep close tabs on your account status if you choose to pay this way.

✔ **Make a One-Time Payment:** If you're about to hit your credit limit or you don't want eBay making monthly charges on your credit card, you can make a one-time payment. Check out the Pay Your eBay Seller Fees area to make a one-time payment. To pay by check, you need an eBay payment coupon, which you can get by clicking the Mail in a Check or Money Order link, printing out the coupon page, and following the directions. If you want to make a one-time credit card payment, click the Pay with Your Credit Card link; or to write a virtual e-check from your bank account, click the Pay with Your Checking Account link. You'll arrive at an SSL-secured area to type in your information. Click Submit, and the stuff is sent to eBay for processing. It's just that easy.

✔ **Refunds:** If your eBay seller account has a credit balance of $1 or more that you're not planning to use, you can get it back by clicking the Refund link. If you've used the Sign In feature, you merely click the Print a Refund Request box to get to a printable refund request coupon. If you haven't used the Sign In feature, you have to type your User ID and password to access the personalized form. Print out the form on the page, fill it out, and then either fax it or send it by mail to eBay.

Table 4-2		eBay's Automatic Payments	
Billing Cycle	*Invoice*	*Deducted from Checking Account*	*Credit Card Charged*
15th of month	Between 16th and 20th	5th of the next month	5–7 days after receipt of invoice
Last day of month	Between 1st and 5th of next month	20th of next month	5–7 days after receipt of invoice

Requesting a Final Value Fee credit

If you sell an item and the buyer backs out (a rare but disheartening situation), you can at least get a refund on some of the fees that eBay charges you as a seller. These are the *Final Value Fees,* and they're based on the selling price of the item. The Credit Request link takes you to the Non Paying Bidder/Buyer policy overview page.

Before you can collect a Final Value Fee refund, the following conditions must apply:

- ✔ After your auction, you have to allow bidders at least three business days to respond to you. If they don't respond, you can send them an optional Payment Reminder from your My eBay Selling page. Don't dilly-dally; you have up to 30 days to send this eBay-generated e-mail.

- ✔ If at least seven days have elapsed since the end of the transaction and you have the feeling that you're not going to see your money, you *must* file a Non-Paying Bidder Alert. After you file this notice, eBay sends you (a copy) and the bidder an ominous e-mail reminding the bidder to complete the transaction.

   You have up to 45 days from the end of the auction to file a Non-Paying Bidder Alert — and you can't get a Final Value Fee credit without filing this alert.

- ✔ The next ten days after you file the Non-Paying Bidder Alert are your "work out" period — the period where you and the bidder hopefully complete your transaction. You may try to give the bidder a call to resolve the situation during this time.

- ✔ After the ten days have passed but no more than 60 days have elapsed since the end of the auction, you may file for a Final Value Fee credit.

If you have begun the process and filed for a Final Value Fee credit and manage to work things out with the buyer, eBay etiquette says you should have the Non-Paying Bidder Alert removed from the buyer's account. Buyers with too many of these warnings can be suspended from using the eBay site. You can find this form at the following address:

```
cgi3.ebay.com/aw-cgi/eBayISAPI.dll?RemoveNPBWarning
```

Getting Your Favorites Area Together

Part of the fun of eBay is searching around for stuff that you'd never in a million years think of looking for. Wacky stuff aside, most eBay users spend their time hunting for specific items — say, Barbie dolls, Elvis memorabilia, or U.S. stamps. That's why eBay came up with the Favorites area of your My eBay page. Whenever you view your My eBay Favorites page, you see a list of your favorite searches, four of your favorite categories, and a list of your favorite sellers and stores. But because eBay isn't psychic, you have to tell it what you want listed.

Choosing your favorite categories

You can choose only four categories to be your favorites, and with over 30,000 categories to choose from, you need to make your choices count. If you're having a hard time narrowing down your category picks, don't worry: Your choices aren't set in stone. You can change your Favorites list whenever you want. (Chapter 3 offers details on eBay categories.)

To choose your favorite categories and list them on your My eBay Favorites page, follow these steps:

1. **Click the Favorites tab and scroll to the My Favorite Categories area.**

2. **Click the Add/Change Categories link (next to the My Favorite Categories head).**

   You see four windows, each containing category listings for four of your category favorites. These windows contain all of eBay's categories and subcategories and sub-subcategories and sub-sub-subcategories.

3. **In the far-left column, click the category you want.**

   The column to the right automatically changes to reflect more choices based on the main category you selected. Be sure to highlight the categories and subcategories you want, as shown in Figure 4-6.

4. **Continue across from left to right.**

   Depending on your choices, you may have to scroll through each window to find the subcategory you're looking for. After you've completed your choice, a number appears in the window at the top. That's your category number.

5. **Repeat this process for Favorites Category 2 through Category 4.**

   If you don't want to use all four choices, just delete any numbers in the chosen category window.

6. **Click the Submit button at the bottom of the page.**

   You get an acknowledgment that your changes have been made. Click the My eBay link at the top of the page to see your new favorite categories.

How specific you get when choosing your favorites depends on how many items you want to see. The narrower your focus, the fewer items you have to wade through. The more general your favorites, the broader the range of items you have to view. Just below each of your favorites are four options for screening your favorites. Which link you choose to view auctions depends on what kind of information you're looking for. Whether you're doing some preliminary searching on a category or monitoring the last few days (or minutes) of an auction, you'll find a sorting link that best meets your needs.

Here's a list of the sorting options in your Favorite Categories area and when to use them. You can also use these options to browse eBay categories when you're in a shopping mood:

- ✔ **Current:** Shows you every item currently being auctioned in the category, with the newest items shown first. If you want to look at all the current auctions for a category, you end up with a gazillion pages of items awaiting sale in a particular category for the next week.

- ✔ **New Today:** Shows you every item that was put up for auction during the past 24 hours. The little rising sun icon next to the item tells you that the item was listed today.

- ✔ **Ending Today:** Shows you every auction that is closing in the next 24 hours. The ending time is printed in red if the auction closes within the next hour.

If you're pressed for time, I suggest that you use the New Today link or the Ending Today link. Both links narrow down the number of listed auctions to a manageable number. For more information on narrowing down searches at eBay, see Chapter 5.

- ✔ **Going, Going, Gone:** Shows you every auction that's ending in the next five hours, all the way down to the last few seconds. This link offers a great way to find items you can bid on down to the wire.

When you view auctions from the Going, Going, Gone link, remember that eBay updates this page only every hour or so, so be sure to read the Auction End time. (Use the eBay time conversion chart on my Web site, www.coolebaytools.com, to decipher time differences.) Due to this same hourly update, sometimes the Going, Going, Gone items actually *are* gone — the auctions have ended.

Figure 4-6: Choosing your favorite categories.

Category required   You have chosen category # 3461

Just click in the boxes below from left to right until you have found the appropriate category for your item. The chosen category number will appear in the small box to indicate that you have made a valid selection.

Antiques & Art ->	Coins: US ->	United States ->	General
Books, Movies, Music ->	Coins: World ->	Australia ->	19th Century:Unused
Coins & Stamps ->	Currency: US ->	Canada ->	19th Century:Used
Collectibles ->	Currency: World ->	Br. Comm. Other	1901 to 1940: Unused
Computers ->	Exonumia ->	UK (Great Britain) ->	1941 to Date: Unused
Dolls, Doll Houses ->	Scripophily ->	Europe ->	20th Century:Used
Jewelry, Gemstones ->	Stamps ->	Latin America ->	Air Mail
Photo & Electronics ->		Other World ->	Back of Book
Pottery & Glass ->		Philately ->	Booklets
Sports ->		Topical ->	Collections, Mixture
Toys, Bean Bag Plush ->			Confederate States
Everything Else ->			Covers, Event

Your favorite searches and sellers

If you shop eBay anything like I do, you'll be looking for similar things and sellers over and over again. The My eBay Favorites area allows you to make note of your favorite searches and sellers. You can perform these searches and visit these stores with a click of your mouse.

Favorite searches

You have the opportunity to list a maximum of 100 searches on the page. When you want to repeat one of these searches, just click the Search name to search for the items. eBay will even e-mail you up to 30 of your searches when new items are listed. (For more on that advanced function, check out Chapter 18.)

To add a search to your favorites, perform a search. (For details on how to perform a search, see Chapter 5.) When the search appears on your screen, click the Add to My Favorite Searches link, shown in the top-right corner of Figure 4-7.

The search is now transported to your My eBay Favorite Searches preferences area for that particular search, as shown in Figure 4-8. If you want to be notified by e-mail when new items are listed, select the check box and the time frame next to Email Preferences.

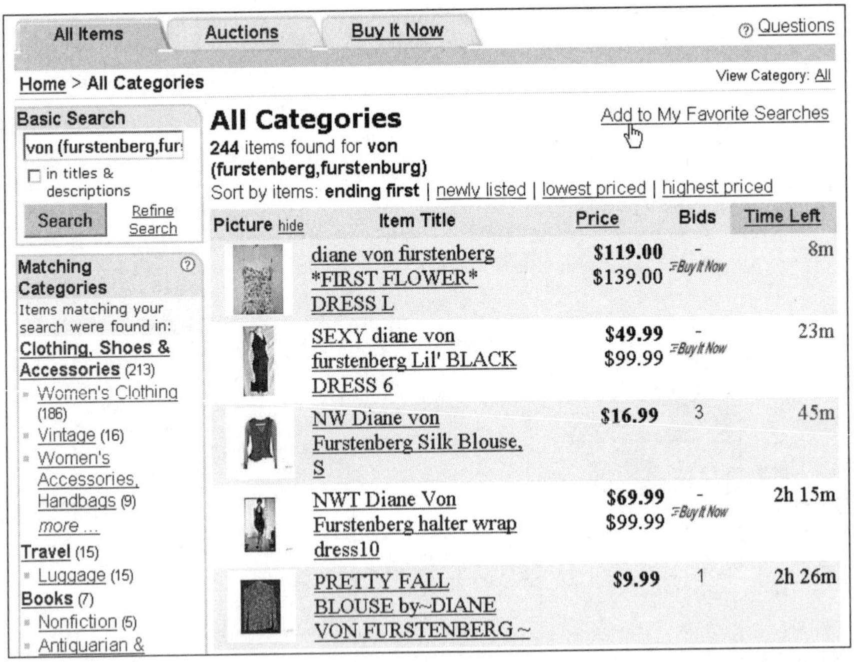

Figure 4-7: Click the Add to My Favorite Searches link to send a search to your My eBay Favorites page.

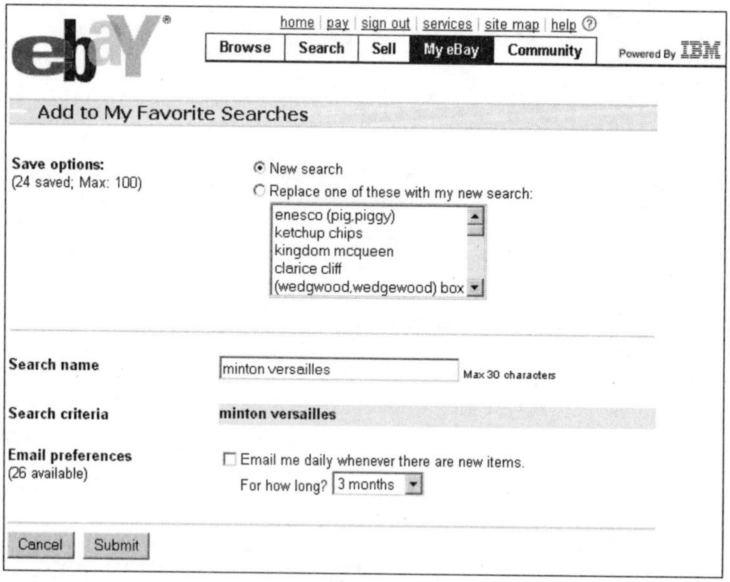

home | pay | sign out | services | site map | help
Browse
Search
Sell
My eBay
Community
Powered By IBM
Add to My Favorite Searches
Save options:
(24 saved; Max: 100)
New search
Replace one of these with my new search:
enesco (pig,piggy)
ketchup chips
kingdom mcqueen
clarice cliff
(wedgwood,wedgewood) box
Search name
minton versailles
Max 30 characters
Search criteria
minton versailles
Email preferences
(26 available)
Email me daily whenever there are new items.
For how long?
3 months
Cancel
Submit

Figure 4-8: The Adding a Favorite Search details page.

Favorite sellers

When you find a seller whose merchandise and prices are right up your alley and you'd like to occasionally check out the seller's auctions, you can list the seller in the My Favorite Sellers/Stores area:

1. **When you've shopped eBay and found a seller that you're happy with, make note of the seller's name or User ID.**
2. **Go to your My eBay Favorite Sellers/Stores area and click the Add New Seller/Store link.**
3. **Type in the seller's User ID or store name and click the Save Favorite button.**

   The seller or store now appears on your My Favorite Sellers/Stores area. To view the seller's current auctions or visit his or her store, click the link to the right of the seller's name.

Got the time? eBay does. Click eBay Official Time (you can find it on the far-left column of the Site Map or on any search results page). The eBay clock is so accurate that you can set your watch to it. And you may want to, especially if you want to place a last-second bid before an auction closes. After all, eBay's official time is, um, *official.* Here's a quick link to the eBay current date and time:

```
cgi3.ebay.com/aw-cgi/eBayISAPI.dll?TimeShow
```

All Sorts of Sorting: Keeping Track of Your Auction Items

If you want to keep tabs on the items you're selling and bidding on (and why wouldn't you?), start thinking about how to sort them *before* you start looking for the first item you want to bid on. That's also pretty good advice for planning your first auction.

From the My eBay page, you can sort the items you're selling and bidding on several ways. That gives you a lot of options to think about, dwell on, and ponder. Each sorting method does pretty much the same thing, so pick the one that catches your eye and don't lose any sleep over your choice. After all, life's too short — and here you can change anything by clicking the option titles. (Wish the rest of life were like that?) Table 4-3 goes into more detail about sorting methods.

Table 4-3	Sorting Methods and What They Do
Sort By	*Does This*
Item #	Lists items in numerical order by item number.
Start Price	Lists items by their opening prices (only for items you're selling).
Current Price	Lists items by current highest bid. This listing changes often.
Reserve Price	Lists items by the secret reserve price you set when you started the auction (only for items you're selling). For more on reserve auctions, turn to Chapter 10.
Qty	Lists items according to how many are available. For example, if you're bidding on an item in a Multiple Item (Dutch) auction, 2, 10, 100, or even more of the same item may be auctioned at the same time. (See Chapters 7 and 10 to find out how Multiple Item auctions work.)
# of Bids	Lists items by the number of bids they've received.
Start Date	Lists items based on when the auction began.
Time Left	Lists items by the time left in the sales period (only sortable in the Items I'm Watching tab).
End Date PDT	Lists items based on when the auction ends. This is one option that eBay automatically chooses for you if you don't select one on your own. This is the way most people view their lists.

All auctions at eBay are based on Pacific Daylight or Pacific Standard Time, depending on the time of year.

You need to decide how long you want eBay to show the information about the items you're buying and selling on your My eBay page. You can show an item's history for as long as 30 days. In a check box on the My eBay page, you can type in how many days of eBay history you want to show on your pages (see Figure 4-9). Just type in the number of days you want to display information and click the Go button. You can also select that period of time to be your default (what you will see every time you go to the page). Select the Save This Setting check box and click Go, and you're set!

Figure 4-9:
My eBay
time
settings.

Following the Action on Your Bidding/Watching Area

I have the most fun at eBay when I'm shopping. Shopping at eBay is exciting, and I can find a zillion great bargains. Fortunately, eBay gives us a place to keep all our shopping information together: on the My eBay Bidding/Watching page (refer to Figure 4-2).

Seeing the Items I'm Bidding On

When you bid on an item, eBay automatically lists the item in the Items I'm Bidding On area of your My eBay Page. If you're winning the auction, the price appears in green; if you're losing, it appears in red. Dutch and completed auctions appear in black. You can watch the progress of the auction from here and see the number of bids on the item, the high bid, and how much time is left until the end of the auction. All this information can help you decide whether you want to jump back in and make a bid. eBay also keeps a total of all your active bids at the bottom of this area in the Current Totals: Items I'm Winning section — which should hopefully help you stay within your spending limits.

Keeping track of Items I've Won

When you've won an auction or purchased an item in a store, it appears in the Items I've Won area. From here, you can visit the auction to print out the auction page or double-check it. You can also pay for your item through PayPal direct from here; if you've already paid, you can check the current status in Next Step/Status. You can also click a Leave Feedback link here — after you've received the item and are satisfied with your purchase — to leave feedback.

Sleuthing with Items I'm Watching

Items I'm Watching is my most active area of my My eBay page (see Figure 4-10). This is the place for you to work on your strategy for getting bargains without showing your hand by bidding. In this area, you can watch the auction evolve and decide if you want to bid on it. You can list several auctions for the same item and watch them all develop and then bid on the one that you can get the best deal. You can track the progress of up to 30 auctions in your Items I'm Watching area.

Moving auctions into this area is easy. When you've found an auction that you want to keep track of, look for the Watch This Item (Track It in My eBay) link next to the item title (on the right). If you click this link, the item is transported to your Items I'm Watching area.

Figure 4-10: The Items I'm Watching area of the My eBay page.

Select (all)	Item #	Current Price	# of Bids	Time Left	Seller	Bid on this item
	Sony Clie PEG-NR70V Palm Handheld $582 NR					
☐	3043319007	$92.00	11	0d 3h 27m		Bid Now!
	New Womens BANDOLINO Boots size 8 M					
☐	2852223081	$19.99	1	0d 4h 17m		Bid Now!
	STUNNING 8.0 CARATS DIAMOND BRACELET *FANCY*					
☐	2653925367	$364.00	23	0d 4h 33m		Bid Now!
	Cosmopolitan Martini Rhinestone Anklet NEW					
☐	2654694526	$9.99	1	4d 7h 1m		Bid Now!
	Vintage LISNER blue rhinestone CORONET brooch					
☐	2655390010	$22.50	--	5d 2h 54m		Bid Now!
	CALLAWAY STEELHEAD PLUS DRIVER WOMENS MINT					
☐	3624443288	$65.05	6	6d 0h 24m		Bid Now!
	NEW eBay Bargain Shopping for Dummies SIGNED ◄stores					
☐	2946682895	$14.99	Buy It Now	n/a	marsha_c	Buy It Now

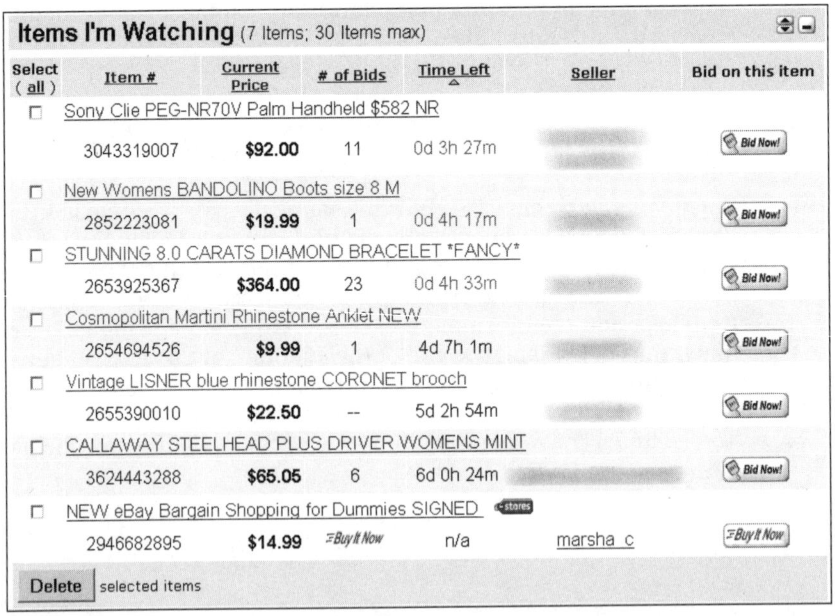

Items I'm Watching (7 Items; 30 Items max)

Delete selected items

Surveying Your Sales on Your My eBay Selling Page

Your My eBay page supplies you with the tools to keep track of items you're selling on eBay. The My eBay Selling page works very much the same as the Bidding page, but this time you're making the money — not spending it! Your current auction sales are listed in the Items I'm Selling area. The items with bids on them appear in green, and the ones without bids are in red. At the bottom, you have a dollar total of the current bids on your auctions.

Items I'm Selling

Very much like the Items I'm Bidding On section of the Bidding/Watching page, the Items I'm Selling area keeps track of your ongoing auctions at eBay. You can observe the auction action in real time (or at least every time you refresh the page). You can see how many bids have been placed, when the auction closes, and the time left in the auction. If you want more information about what's going on, click the handy All Item Details link, which gives you a mini-version of each auction (without the description).

Items I've Sold

When the sale is final, the items go into the Items I've Sold area (shown in Figure 4-11). Here's where you can keep track of the sale. You can check whether the buyer has paid with PayPal and what the transaction status is. If the buyer has completed checkout, you can get his or her information by clicking the Next Steps/Status link. If the buyer hasn't completed checkout, you can click the Send Invoice button to send the buyer an invoice. Very handy!

If you haven't heard from the buyer after three days (the prescribed eBay deadline for contact), you can click the Payment Reminder link. After selecting what information you want eBay to send, eBay sends a firm nudge to your winner, reminding him or her that transactions at eBay are binding contracts.

After the transaction is complete (which means the item has arrived and the buyer is happy with his or her purchase), you can click the handy Leave Feedback link to leave feedback about the buyer.

You can also relist the item from a quick link or place a Second Chance offer to an underbidder if you have more than one of the item. See the nearby sidebar for more on the Second Chance feature.

Select (all)	Item #	Last Sale	End Price	Reserve Price	Qty	High Bidder (s)/Buyer (s)	Next Steps/Status	Payment Reminder	Feedback	Relist	Second Chance hide
		End Date									

Items I've Sold (4 Items) — ►See totals · ►Show items for past `2` days `Go` (30 days max) ☐ Save this setting — ✓ = Relisted item — (PST)

CLOUD DOME KIT for Digital Macro Image Photos «stores»
☐ 2921845275 Oct-02 Aug-05 $168.90 n/a 9 | See Buyers | Purchase Information | | Leave Feedback | Relist |

Starting an eBay Business for Dummies SIGNED «stores»
☐ 2944149042 Oct-02 Sep-01 $22.50 n/a 3 | See Buyers | Purchase Information | | Leave Feedback | Relist |

eBay Live 2003 TIPS for Dummies AUTHOR SIGNED
☐ 3624444916 Sep-04 -- $5.74 n/a 1 | | Pending | Available in 3 days | Leave Feedback | Relist | Send |

2 Photography Photo Light NIB Lighting Kit
☐ 2948061302 Sep-02 -- $113.50 n/a 1 | | `Send Invoice` | Available in 3 days | Leave Feedback | Relist | Send |

`Delete` selected items

Totals	End Price	Reserve Price	Total Qty
Items I've Sold	$1,706.84	$0.00	14

Figure 4-11: The Items I've Sold area and all its options.

eBay's Selling Manager/Selling Manager Pro

If you're at the point where you're selling bunches of items on the site, you may want to subscribe to one of eBay's Selling Manager tools. These tools make your Selling area look completely different. The tools give you the opportunity to handle more sales in a compact and convenient design. See Chapter 20 for detailed information.

Your secret seller tool — Second Chance!

Those cagey great minds at eBay have come up with another great selling implement. Say that you have multiples of a single item (you *did* sell that set of Minton china one piece at a time, didn't you?) or the winning bidder backs out of the transaction without paying. Second Chance offer gives you the opportunity to offer the item to one of the underbidders (okay, the losers) at their high bid price. The Second Chance opportunity is available for up to 60 days after the sale ends.

You can offer the item to only one of the under-bidders at a time and make this personal offer good for one to seven days. The bidder receives an e-mail regarding the offer and can access it on the site through a special link. It is visible only to you and the other bidder for the duration of the offer.

The best part is that eBay doesn't charge any additional listing fees for this feature, but you are charged the Final Value Fee after the transaction is complete.

Keeping Track of Your Transactions

Yes, I bug you about printing stuff out — not because I'm in cahoots with the paper industry but because I care. The best way to protect yourself is to keep good records on your own. Don't depend on eBay to cover you — not that eBay doesn't care. But this is your money, so keep a close eye on it.

Now don't become a pack rat and overdo it. To help point you in the right direction, here's a list of important documents I think you should print and file whether you're a buyer or a seller:

- ✔ Auction pages as they appear when they close
- ✔ Bank statements indicating any payment you receive that doesn't clear
- ✔ Insurance or escrow forms
- ✔ Refund and credit requests
- ✔ Receipts from purchases you make for items to sell on eBay

Always, always, *always* save every e-mail message you receive about a transaction, whether you buy or sell. Also save your *EOAs* (End of Auction e-mails) that eBay sends. For more information about EOAs and correspondence etiquette after the auction is over, see Chapters 8 and 12.

Why should you save all this stuff? Here are some reasons:

- ✔ Even if you're buying and selling just a couple of items a month on eBay, you need to keep track of who you owe and who owes you money.
- ✔ Good e-mail correspondence is a learned art, but if you reference item numbers, your e-mail is an instant record. If you put your dates in writing — and follow up — you have a nice, neat paper trail.
- ✔ Documenting the transaction through e-mail will come in handy if you ever end up in a dispute over the terms of the sale.
- ✔ If you sell specialized items, you can keep track of trends and who your frequent buyers are.
- ✔ Someday the IRS may come knocking on your door, especially if you buy stuff for the purpose of selling it on eBay. Scary, but true. For more on where you can get tax information, take a look at Chapter 9.

When it comes to keeping records via e-mail and documents about transactions, I say that after you've received your feedback (positive, of course), you can dump it. If you get negative feedback (how could you?), hang on to your paperwork for a little longer. Use your discretion, but generally you can toss the paperwork from a bad transaction after it has reached some sort of resolution. (You can find out more about feedback in the next section.)

Once a month, do a seller search on yourself and print out your latest eBay history. Chapter 5 tells you more about doing seller searches, organizing your searches, and starting files on items you want to track.

Getting and Giving Feedback

You know how they say you are what you eat? At eBay, you are only as good as your feedback says you are. Your feedback is made up of comments — good, bad, or neutral — that people leave about you (and you leave about others). In effect, people are commenting on your overall professionalism. (Even if you're an eBay hobbyist with no thought of using it professionally, a little businesslike courtesy can ease your transactions with everyone.) These comments are the basis for your eBay reputation.

Because feedback is so important to your reputation on eBay, you don't want others leaving feedback or making bad transactions under your name. The only way to ensure this doesn't happen is to always keep your password a secret. If you suspect somebody may know your password, change it before that person has a chance to sign in as you and ruin your reputation. (For more on selecting and protecting your level of privacy, see Chapters 1 and 15.)

When you get your first feedback, the number that appears next to your User ID is your feedback rating, which follows you everywhere you go at eBay, even if you change your User ID or e-mail address. It sticks to you like glue. Click the number next to any User ID and get a complete look at the user's feedback profile. The thinking behind the feedback concept is that you wouldn't be caught dead in a store that has a lousy reputation, so why on Earth would you want to do business on the Internet with someone who has a lousy reputation?

You're not required to leave feedback, but because it's the benchmark by which all eBay users are judged, whether you're buying or selling, you should *always* leave feedback comments. Get in the frame of mind that every time you complete a transaction — the minute the package arrives safely if you're a seller or an item you've bid on and won arrives — you should go to eBay and post your feedback.

Every time you get a positive comment from a user who hasn't commented on you before, you get a point. Every time you get a negative rating, this negative cancels out one of your positives. Neutral comments rate a zero — they have no impact either way. eBay even has what it calls the Star Chart, shown in Figure 4-12, which rewards those with good-and-getting-higher feedback ratings.

Figure 4-12:
The eBay
feedback
achievement
Star rating.

eBay awards Stars to our members when they achieve a certain Feedback Rating.

- A "Yellow Star" (☆) represents a Feedback Profile of 10 to 99.
- A "Turquoise Star" (★) represents a Feedback Profile of 100 to 499.
- A "Purple Star" (★) represents a Feedback Profile of 500 to 999.
- A "Red Star" (★) represents a Feedback Profile of 1,000 to 4,999.
- A "Green Star" (☆) represents a Feedback Profile of 5,000 to 9,999.
- A "Yellow Shooting Star" (✦) represents a Feedback Profile of 10,000 to 24,999.
- A "Turquoise Shooting Star" (✦) represents a Feedback Profile of 25,000 to 49,999.
- A "Purple Shooting Star" (✦) represents a Feedback Profile of 50,000 to 99,999.
- A "Red Shooting Star" (✦) represents a Feedback Profile of 100,000 or higher.

The flip side (or Dark Side to you *Star Wars* fans) of the star system is negative numbers. Negative comments deduct from your total of positive comments, thereby lowering the number beside your User ID. *eBay riddle:* When is more than one still one? Gotcha, huh? The answer is, when you get more than one feedback message from the same person. Confused? This should help: You can sell one person 100 different items, but even if the buyer gives you a glowing review 100 times, your feedback rating doesn't increase by 100. In this case, the other 99 feedback comments appear in your feedback profile, but your rating increases only by one. There's one other thing: Say you sell to the same eBay user twice. The user can give you positive feedback in one case and negative feedback in another case — neutralizing your feedback by netting you a 0 feedback rating from this person. eBay set up the system this way to keep things honest.

Anyone with a –4 rating has his or her eBay membership terminated. Remember, just because a user may have a 750 feedback rating, it doesn't hurt to click the number after the name to double-check the person's eBay ID card. Even if someone has a total of 1,000 feedback messages, 250 of them *could* be negative.

You can get to your personal feedback profile page right from your My eBay page by clicking the Feedback tab.

Feedback comes in three exciting flavors:

- ✔ **Positive feedback:** Someone once said, "All you have is your reputa-tion." Reputation is what makes eBay function. If the transaction works well, you get positive feedback; whenever it's warranted, you should give it right back.

- ✔ **Negative feedback:** If there's a glitch (for instance, it takes six months to get your *Charlie's Angels* lunchbox or the seller substitutes a rusty ther-mos for the one you bid on or you never get the item), you have the right — some would say *obligation* — to leave negative feedback.

✓ **Neutral feedback:** You can leave neutral feedback if you feel so-so about a specific transaction. It's the middle-of-the-road comment. Say you bought an item that had a little more wear and tear on it than the seller indicated, but you still like it and want to keep it.

How to get positive feedback

If you're selling, here's how to get a good reputation:

✓ Establish contact with the buyer (pronto!) after the auction ends (see Chapter 12).

✓ After you've received payment, send out the item quickly (see Chapter 12).

✓ Make sure that your item is exactly the way you described it (see Chapter 10).

✓ Package the item well and ship it with care (see Chapter 12).

✓ React quickly and appropriately to problems — for example, the item's lost or damaged in the mail or the buyer is slow in paying (see Chapter 12).

If you're buying, try these good-rep tips:

✓ Send your payment fast (see Chapter 8).

✓ Keep in touch via e-mail with the seller (see Chapter 8).

✓ Work with the seller to resolve any problems in a courteous manner (see Chapters 8 and 12).

How to get negative feedback

If you're selling, here's what to do to tarnish your name big time:

✓ Tell a major fib in the item description. (Defend truth, justice, and legitimate creative writing — see Chapter 10.)

✓ Take the money but "forget" to ship the item. (Who did you say you are? See Chapter 17.)

✓ Package the item poorly so that it ends up smashed, squashed, or vaporized during shipping. (To avoid this pathetic fate, see Chapter 12.)

If you're buying, here's how to make your status a serious mess:

✓ Bid on an item, win the auction, and never respond to the seller. (Remember your manners and see Chapter 6.)

✔ Send a personal check that bounces and never make good on the payment. (See Chapter 17 — and don't pass Go.)

✔ Ask the seller for a refund because you just don't like the item. (Remember how to play fair and see Chapter 8.)

The Feedback page

When you click the Feedback section of your My eBay page, you'll see all the tools you need for feedback. Think of your feedback profile as your eBay report card. Your goal is to get straight *As* — in this case, all positive feedback. Unlike a real report card, you don't have to bring it home to be signed.

When someone clicks the feedback number next to your User ID, they see the following information (see Figure 4-13):

✔ **Your User ID:** Your eBay nickname appears, followed by a number in parentheses — the net number of the positive feedback comments you've received, minus any negative feedback comments you may have gotten (but that wouldn't happen to you . . .).

✔ **Your membership information:** Listed here is the date you first signed up as a member of the eBay community. Beneath that is the country from which you're registered, your star rating (refer to Figure 4-12), and any icons leading to more areas related to you on eBay, like your About Me page (see Chapter 14). This area also notes whether you are a PowerSeller (see Chapter 20) and whether you have an eBay Store.

✔ **Your overall profile makeup:** This area sums up the positive, negative, and neutral feedback comments people have left for you.

✔ **Your eBay ID card with a summary of most recent comments:** This area is a scorecard of your feedback for the last six months. At the bottom of the feedback tote board is a summary of your bid retractions — the times you have retracted bids during an auction.

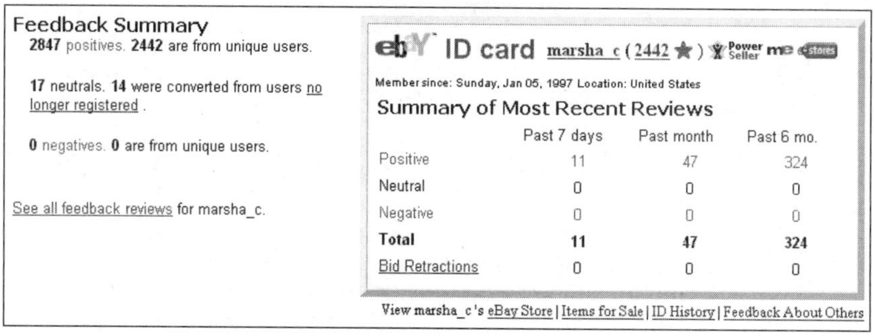

Figure 4-13:
The feedback profile report card — there's one on every member.

Feedback Summary
2847 positives. **2442** are from unique users.

17 neutrals. **14** were converted from users <u>no longer registered</u>.

0 negatives. **0** are from unique users.

<u>See all feedback reviews</u> for marsha_c.

ebY ID card <u>marsha_c</u> (<u>2442</u> ★) ⓦ Power Seller me stores

Member since: Sunday, Jan 05, 1997 Location: United States

Summary of Most Recent Reviews

	Past 7 days	Past month	Past 6 mo.
Positive	11	47	324
Neutral	0	0	0
Negative	0	0	0
Total	**11**	**47**	**324**
<u>Bid Retractions</u>	0	0	0

View marsha_c 's <u>eBay Store</u> | <u>Items for Sale</u> | <u>ID History</u> | <u>Feedback About Others</u>

Extra, extra, read all about it

Normally, I believe in the adage, "Keep your business private." But not when it comes to feedback. The default setting is for public viewing of your feedback. This way, everyone at eBay can read all about you.

If you want to make your feedback a private matter, you need to go to the Feedback Forum (click the Services link on the navigation bar and then click the Go Directly to the Feedback Forum link), click the Make Your Feedback Profile Public or Private link, and reset it to Private.

Hiding your feedback is a bad idea. You want people to know that you're trustworthy; being honest and upfront is the way to go. If you hide your feedback profile, people may suspect that you're covering up bad things. It's in your best interest to let the spotlight shine on your feedback history.

It's your reputation, your money, and your experience as an eBay member. Keep in mind that all three are always linked.

Be careful when you retract a bid. All bids on eBay are binding, but under what eBay calls "exceptional circumstances," you may retract bids — very sparingly. Here are the circumstances in which it's okay to retract a bid:

- ✔ If you've mistakenly put in the wrong bid amount — say, $100 instead of $10

- ✔ If the seller adds to his or her description after you've placed your bid, and the change considerably affects the item

- ✔ If you can't authenticate the seller's identity

You can't retract a bid just because you found the item elsewhere cheaper or you changed your mind or you decided that you really can't afford the item. See Chapter 6 for more information on retracting bids.

Reading your feedback

Your eBay reputation is at the mercy of the one-liners that buyers and sellers leave for you in the form of feedback comments.

Each feedback box contains these reputation-building (or -trashing) ingredients:

- ✔ The User ID of the person who sent it. The number in parentheses next to the person's name is his or her own feedback rating.

- ✔ The date and time the feedback was posted.

✔ The item number of the transaction that the feedback refers to. If the item has closed in the past 30 days, you can click the transaction number to see what the buyer purchased.

✔ S or B — *S* if you were the seller, and *B* if you were the buyer in the transaction.

✔ Feedback comes in different colors: praise (in green), negative (in red), or neutral (in black).

✔ The feedback the person left about you.

You have the last word — responding to feedback

After reading feedback you've received from others, you may feel compelled to respond. If the feedback is negative, you may want to defend yourself. If it's positive, you may want to say *thank you*.

To respond to feedback, follow these steps:

1. **In the Feedback section of your My eBay page, click the Review and Respond to Feedback about Me link.**

   You're transported to the Review and Respond to Feedback Comments Left for You page.

2. **When you find the feedback you want to respond to, click the Respond link.**

3. **Type in your response.**

Do not confuse *responding* to feedback with *leaving* feedback. Responding does not change the other user's feedback rating; it merely adds a line below the feedback with your response.

Leaving feedback with finesse

Writing feedback well takes some practice. It isn't a matter of saying things; it's a matter of saying *only the appropriate things*. Think carefully about what you want to say because once you submit feedback, it stays with the person for the duration of his or her eBay career. I think you should always leave feedback, especially at the end of a transaction, although doing so isn't mandatory. Think of leaving feedback as voting in an election: If you don't leave feedback, you can't complain about lousy service.

Mincing words: The at-a-glance guide to keeping feedback short

eBay likes to keep things simple. If you want to compliment, complain, or take the middle road, you have to do it in 80 characters or less. That means your comment needs to be short and sweet (or short and sour if it's negative, or sweet and sour if you're mixing drinks or ordering Chinese food). If you have a lot to say but you're stumped about how to say it, here are a few examples for any occasion. String them together or mix and match!

Positive feedback:

- Very professional
- Quick e-mail response
- Fast service
- A+++
- Good communication
- Exactly as described
- Highly recommended
- Smooth transaction
- Would deal with again
- An asset to eBay
- I'll be back!

Negative feedback:

- Never responded
- Never paid for item
- Check bounced, never made good
- Beware track record
- Not as described
- Watch out — you won't get paid

Neutral feedback:

- Slow to ship but item as described
- Item not as described but seller made good
- Paid w/MO (money order) after check bounced
- Poor communication but item came OK

eBay says to make feedback "factual and emotionless." You won't go wrong if you comment on the details (either good or bad) of the transaction. If you have any questions about what eBay says about feedback, click the Services link on the navigation bar and then click the Go Directly to the Feedback Forum link on the next page.

In the Feedback Forum, you can perform six feedback-related tasks:

- **See feedback about an eBay user.**
- **Leave feedback for many auctions at once.** Here, you see all pending feedback for all transactions within the past 90 days. You are presented with a page of all your transactions for which you haven't left feedback. Fill them in, one at a time, and with one click, you can leave as many as 25 feedback comments at once.

- ✔ **Review and respond to existing feedback about you.**

- ✔ **Review the feedback you have left for others.** Here, you may also leave follow-up feedback after the initial feedback should situations change.

- ✔ **Make your feedback profile public or private.** Remember, if you make your feedback profile private, you may hinder your future business on eBay. See the sidebar "Extra, extra, read all about it," elsewhere in this chapter.

- ✔ **Check the Feedback FAQ to review any changes in the feedback system.**

In the real world (at least in the modern American version of it), anybody can sue anybody else for slander or libel; this fact holds true on the Internet, too. It's a good idea to be careful not to make any comments that could be libelous or slanderous. eBay is not responsible for your actions, so if you're sued because of negative feedback (or anything else you've written), you're on your own. The best way to keep yourself safe is to stick to the facts and don't get personal.

If you're angry, take a breather *before* you type out your complaints and click the Leave Comment button. If you're convinced that negative feedback is necessary, try a cooling-off period before you send comments. Wait an hour or a day and then see whether you feel the same. Nasty feedback based on emotion can make you look vindictive (even if what you're saying is true).

Safety tips for giving feedback

And speaking of safety features you should know about feedback, you may want to study up on these:

- ✔ Remember that feedback, whether good or bad, is *sticky*. eBay won't remove your feedback comment if you change your mind later. Be sure of your facts and carefully consider what you want to say.

- ✔ Before you leave feedback, see what other people had to say about that person. See whether what you're thinking is in line with the comments others have left.

- ✔ Your feedback comment can be left as long as the transaction remains on the eBay server. This is usually within 90 days of the end of the auction. After 90 days have passed, you must have the transaction number to leave feedback.

- ✔ Your comment can only be a maximum of 80 letters long, which is really short when you have a lot to say. Before you start typing, organize your thoughts and use common abbreviations to save precious space.

- ✔ Before posting negative feedback, try to resolve the problem by e-mail or telephone. You may discover that your reaction to the transaction is based on a misunderstanding that can be easily resolved.

✔ eBay users generally want to make each other happy, so use negative feedback *only as a last resort.* See Chapters 8 and 10 for more details on how to avoid negative feedback.

If you do leave a negative comment that you later regret, you can't remove it. You can go back to follow up and leave an explanation or a more positive comment (but it won't change the initial feedback or rating), so think twice before you blast.

The ways to leave feedback

Several ways are available to leave feedback comments:

✔ If you're on the user's Feedback page, click the Leave Feedback link; the Leave Feedback page appears.

✔ In the Items I've Won area of your My eBay page, click the Leave Feedback link next to the auction.

✔ Go to your auction and click the Leave Feedback icon.

✔ In the Feedback Forum, click the Leave Feedback about an eBay User — See All Pending Comments at Once link to see a list of all your completed auctions from the last 90 days for which you haven't yet left feedback.

✔ Click the Services link in the main navigation bar and then click Feedback Forum. On the next page that appears, click the Go Directly to the Feedback Forum link.

To leave feedback, follow these steps:

1. **Enter the required information.**

   Note that your item number is usually filled in, but if you're placing feedback from the user's Feedback page, you need to have the number at hand.

2. **Choose whether you want your feedback to be positive, negative, or neutral.**

3. **Click the Leave Feedback button.**

eBay will consider removing feedback if . . .

✔ eBay is served with a court order stating that the feedback in question is slanderous, libelous, defamatory, or otherwise illegal. eBay will also accept a settlement agreement from a resolved lawsuit submitted by both attorneys and signed by both parties.

✔ Negative feedback can be expunged by a ruling by a certified arbitrator where both parties agreed to submit the issue for binding arbitration. You can find this service on SquareTrade; see Chapter 16 for details.

✔ The feedback in question has no relation to eBay — such as comments about transactions outside of eBay or personal comments about users.

✔ The feedback contains a link to another page, picture, or JavaScript.

✔ The feedback is comprised of profane or vulgar language.

✔ The feedback contains any personal identifying information about a user.

✔ The feedback refers to any investigation, whether by eBay or a law-enforcement organization.

✔ The feedback is left by a user who supplied fraudulent information when registering at eBay.

✔ The feedback is left by a person who can be identified as a minor.

✔ The feedback is left by a user as a part of harassment.

✔ The feedback is intended for another user, when eBay has been informed of the situation and the same feedback has been left for the appropriate user.

Part II

Are You Buying What They're Selling?

The 5th Wave   By Rich Tennant

"Oh, that there's just something I picked up as a grab bag special from the 'Everything Else' category."

In this part . . .

After you have an idea how to get around the eBay site, you'll probably want to get started. You've come to the right place. Here you can find all the information you need to start bidding and winning auctions.

Although eBay is a lot more fun than school, you still have to do your homework. After you've registered to become an eBay member (in Part I), you can place a bid on any item you see. But first you have to find the item that's right for you . . . and then maybe find out what it's worth. And what happens when you win?!

In this part, I show you how to find the items you want without sifting through every single one of eBay's millions of auctions. I also give you an insider's look at determining the value of a collectible, determining how much you're willing to spend, and using the right strategy to win the item at just the right price. When the auction is over, follow my advice to make closing the deal go smooth as silk. Watch the positive feedback come pouring in.

Chapter 5

Seek and You Shall Find: Research

. . . .

In This Chapter

▶ Getting sound real-world buying advice on collectibles

▶ Getting solid online buying advice

▶ Checking out information sources for savvy buyers

▶ Conducting a special item search at eBay

. . . .

Think of walking into a store and seeing thousands of aisles of shelves with millions of items on them. Browsing the categories of auctions at eBay can be just as pleasantly boggling, without the prospect of sore feet. Start surfing around the site and you instantly understand the size and scope of what's for sale there. You may feel overwhelmed at first, but the clever eBay folks have come up with lots of ways to help you find exactly what you're looking for. As soon as you figure out how to find the items you want to bid on at eBay, you can protect your investment-to-be by making sure that what you find is actually what you seek.

Of course, searching is easier if you have an idea of what you're looking for. In this chapter, I offer first-time buyers some expert collecting tips and tell you how to get expert advice from eBay and other sources. I also give you tips for using the eBay turbo search engine from a buyer's perspective.

The best advice you can follow as you explore any free-market system is *caveat emptor* — let the buyer beware. Although nobody can guarantee that every one of your transactions will be perfect, research items thoroughly before you bid so that you don't lose too much of your hard-earned money — or too much sleep.

General Online Tips for Collectors

If you're just starting out at eBay, chances are you like to shop and you also collect items that interest you. You'll find out pretty early in your eBay adventures that a lot of people online know as much about collecting as they do about bidding — and some are serious contenders.

The ultimate family station wagon for sale

Need a lift? Drive in style in a 1977 Cadillac Fleetwood Hearse. Only 91K miles! Fully loaded: V8, P/S, P/B, P/W. Gray & Black w/Black interior. Good engine, good brakes, five extra tires, and a stereo system. Buyer must pick up after check clears.

This hearse sold in 1999 at eBay for $600. It seems the value of these old hearses just goes up. When updating this book to the third edition, I found a 1971 Cadillac hearse, fully loaded, but with untold miles, selling for over $2,500. Now, in 2003, I found a gleaming 1972 Cadillac Superior Crown Sovereign hearse — with only 57,000 miles! Retired in 2002, this baby sold for $7,400! Wow, whoda thunk it? Maybe I should be investing in hearses.

How can you compete? Well, in addition to having a well-planned bidding strategy (covered in Chapter 7), knowing your stuff gives you a winning edge. I've gathered the opinions of two collecting experts to get the info you need about online collecting basics. (If you're already an expert collector but want some help finding that perfect something at eBay so you can get ready to bid, you've got it. See "Looking to Find an Item? Start Your eBay Search Engine," later in this chapter.) I also show you how one of those experts puts the information into practice, and I give you a crash course on how items for sale are (or should be) graded.

The experts speak out

Bill Swoger closed his collectibles store in Burbank, California, and sold the balance of his G.I. JOEs and Superman items at eBay. And Lee Bernstein, a columnist and collectibles dealer who operates Lee Bernstein Books and Collectibles from her home base in Schererville, Indiana, not only frequents eBay but also has her own Web site (www.eLee.com). Bill and Lee offer these tips to collectors new to eBay:

- ✔ **Get all the facts before you put your money down.** Study the description carefully. It's your job to analyze the description and make your bidding decisions accordingly. Find out whether all original parts are included and whether the item has any flaws. If the description says that the Fred Flintstone figurine has a cracked back, e-mail the seller for more information.

- ✔ **Don't get caught up in the emotional thrill of bidding.** First-time buyers (known as *Under-10s* or newbies because they have fewer than ten transactions under their belts) tend to bid wildly, using emotions instead of brains. If you're new to eBay, you can get burned if you just bid for the thrill of victory without thinking about what you're doing.

I can't stress how important it is to determine an item's value. But because values are such flighty things (values depend on supply and demand, market trends, and all sorts of other cool stuff), I recommend that you get a general idea of the item's value and use this ballpark figure to set a maximum amount of money you're willing to bid for that item. Then *stick* to your maximum and don't even think about bidding past it. If the bidding gets too hot, there's always another auction. To find out more about bidding strategies, Chapter 7 is just the ticket.

✔ **Know what the item should cost.** Buyers used to depend on *price guides* — books on collectibles and their values — to help them bid. Bill says that price guides are becoming a thing of the past. Sure, you can find a guide that says a *Lion King* Broadway poster in excellent condition has a book price of $75, but if you do a search at eBay, you'll see that they're actually selling for $20 to $30.

When your search at eBay turns up what you're looking for, average out the current prices that you find. Doing so gives you a much better idea of what you need to spend than any price guide can.

✔ **Timing is everything, and being first costs.** In the movie-poster business, if you can wait three to six months after a movie is released, you get the poster for 40 to 50 percent less. The same goes for many new releases of collectibles. Sometimes you're wiser to wait and save money.

✔ **Be careful of presell items.** Sometimes you may run across vendors selling items that they don't have in stock at the moment but that they'll ship to you later. For example, before *Star Wars Episode I: The Phantom Menace* came out, some vendors ran auctions on movie posters they didn't have yet. If you had bid and won, and for some reason the vendor had a problem getting the poster, you'd have been out of luck. Don't bid on anything that can't be delivered as soon as your check clears. See some of eBay's presale rules later in this chapter.

✔ **Being too late can also cost.** Many collectibles become more difficult to find as time goes by. Generally, as scarcity increases, so does desirability and value. Common sense tells you that if two original and identical collectibles are offered side by side, with one in like-new condition and the other in used condition, the like-new item will have the higher value.

✔ **Check out the seller.** Check the feedback rating (the number in parentheses next to the person's User ID) a seller has before you buy. If the seller has many comments with very few negative ones, chances are good that this is a reputable seller. For more on feedback, check out Chapter 4.

Although eBay forbids side deals, an unsuccessful bidder may (at his or her own risk) contact a seller after an auction is over to see if the seller has more of the item in stock. If the seller is an experienced eBay user (a high feedback rating is usually a tip-off) and is interested in the bidder's proposition, he or she may consider selling directly to a buyer. See Chapter 7 for more details, but don't forget that eBay strictly prohibits this behavior. If you conduct a side deal and are reported to eBay, you can be suspended. Not only that, but buyers who are ripped off by sellers in away-from-eBay transactions shouldn't look to eBay to bail them out. You're on your own. The eBay-legal way to purchase these items is by asking the seller to post another of the item for you — or if you were an underbidder in the auction, send you a Second Chance offer.

✔ **If an item comes to you broken in the mail, contact the seller to work it out.** The best bet is to request insurance (you pay for it) before the seller ships the item. But if you didn't ask for insurance, it never hurts to ask for a refund (or a replacement item, if available) if you're not satisfied. Chapter 12 offers the lowdown on buying shipping insurance, and Chapter 16 provides pointers on dealing with transactions that go sour.

Go, Joe: Following an expert on the hunt

Bill looks for specific traits when he buys G.I. JOE action figures. Although his checklist is specific to the G.I. JOE from 1964 to 1969, the information here can help you determine your maximum bid on other collectibles (or whether an item is even *worth* bidding on) before an auction begins. As you find out in Chapter 7, the more you know before you place a bid, the happier you're likely to be when you win. Bill's checklist can save you considerable hassle:

✔ **Find out the item's overall condition.** For G.I. JOE, look at the painted hair and eyebrows. Expect some wear, but overall, a collectible worth bidding on should look good.

✔ **Be sure the item's working parts are indeed working.** Most G.I. JOE action figures from this period have cracks on the legs and arms, but the joints should move, and any cracks should not be so deep that the legs and arms fall apart easily.

✔ **Ask if the item has its original parts.** Because you can't really examine actual items in detail before buying, e-mail the seller with specific questions relating to original or replacement parts. Many G.I. JOE action figures are rebuilt from parts that are not from 1964 to 1969. Sometimes the figures even have two left or right hands or feet! If you make it clear with the seller before you buy that you want a toy with only original parts, you'll be able to make a good case for a refund if the item arrives rebuilt as the Six Million Dollar Man. Chapter 7 has plenty of tips on how to protect yourself before you bid, and Chapter 16 has tips on what to do if the deal goes bad.

> ✔ **Ask if the item has original accessories.** A G.I. JOE from 1964 to 1969 should have his original dog tags, boots, and uniform. If any of these items are missing, you will have to pay around $25 to replace each missing item. If you're looking to bid on any other collectible, know in advance what accessories came as standard equipment with the item, or you'll be paying extra just to bring it back to its original version.
>
> ✔ **Know an item's value before you bid.** A 1964 to 1969 vintage G.I. JOE in decent shape, with all its parts, sells for $125 to $150 without its original box. If you're bidding on a G.I. JOE action figure at eBay and you're in this price range, you're okay. If you get the item for less than $125, congratulations — you've nabbed a bargain.
>
> ✔ **If you have any questions, ask them *before* you bid.** Check collectors' guides, research similar auctions at eBay, and visit one of eBay's category chat rooms.

Making the grade

Welcome to my version of grade school without the bad lunch. One of the keys to establishing value is knowing an item's condition, typically referred to as an item's *grade*. Table 5-1 lists the most common grading categories that collectors use. The information in this table is used with permission from (and appreciation to) Lee Bernstein (www.elee.com) and can also be found at the eBay Web site.

Table 5-1	Grading Categories	
Category (Also Known As)	*Description*	*Example*
Mint (M, Fine, Mint-In-Box [MIB], 10)	A never-used collectible in perfect condition with complete packaging (including instructions, original attachments, tags, and so on) identical to how it appeared on the shelf in the original box.	Grandma got a soup tureen as a wedding present, never opened it, and stuck it in her closet for the next 50 years.
Near Mint (NM, Near Fine, Like-New, 9)	The collectible is perfect but no longer has the original packaging, or the original packaging is less than perfect. Possibly used but must appear to be new.	Grandma used the soup tureen on her 25th anniversary, washed it gently, and then put it back in the closet.

(continued)

Table 5-1 *(continued)*

Category (Also Known As)	Description	Example
Excellent (EX, 8)	Excellent: (EX, 8): Used, but barely. Excellent is just a small step under Near Mint, and many sellers mistakenly interchange the two, but "excellent" can have very minor signs of wear. The wear must be a normal, desirable part of aging or so minor that it's barely noticeable and visible only upon close inspection. Damage of any sort is not "very minor." Wear or minor, normal factory flaws should be noted. (Factory flaws are small blemishes common at the time of manufacture — a tiny air bubble under paint, for example.)	Grandma liked to ring in the New Year with a cup of soup for everyone.
Very Good (VG, 7)	Looks very good but has defects, such as a minor chip or light color fading.	If you weren't looking for it, you might miss that Grandma's tureen survived the '64 earthquake, as well as Uncle Bob's infamous ladle episode.
Good (G, 6)	Used with defects. More than a small amount of color loss, chips, cracks, tears, dents, abrasions, missing parts, and so on.	Grandma had the ladies in the neighborhood over for soup and bingo every month.
Poor (P or G-, 5)	Barely collectible, if at all. Severe damage or heavy use. Beyond repair.	Grandma ran a soup kitchen.

Grading is subjective. Mint to one person may be Very Good to another. Always ask a seller to define the meaning of the terms used. Also, be aware that many amateur sellers may not really know the different definitions of grading and may arbitrarily add Mint or Excellent to their item descriptions.

Finding More Research Information

Hey, the experts have been buying, selling, and trading collectible items for years. But just because you're new to eBay doesn't mean you have to be a newbie for decades before you can start bartering with the collecting gods.

I wouldn't leave you in the cold like that — and neither would eBay. You can get information on items you're interested in, as well as good collecting tips, right at the eBay Web site. Visit the Category-Specific Discussion Boards in the Community area. You can also search the rest of the Web or go the old-fashioned route and check the library (yes, libraries are still around).

Keep in mind that there are truly several prices for an item. The retail (or manufacturer's suggested retail price — MSRP) price, the "book" value, the secondary market price (the price charged by resellers when an item is unavailable on the primary retail market), and the eBay selling price. The only way to ascertain the price an item will go for on eBay is to research completed auctions. Later in this chapter, I give you the skinny on how to research a completed auction.

Searching sites online

If you don't find the information you need at eBay, don't go ballistic — just go elsewhere. Even a site as vast as eBay doesn't have a monopoly on information. The Internet is filled with Web sites and Internet auction sites that can give you price comparisons and information about cyberclubs.

Your home computer can connect to powerful outside servers (really big computers on the Internet) that have their own fast-searching systems called *search engines.* Remember, if something is out there and you need it, you can find it right from your home PC in just a matter of seconds. Here are the addresses of some of the Web's most highly regarded search engines or multi-search-engine sites:

- AltaVista (www.altavista.com)
- Dogpile (www.dogpile.com)
- Excite (www.excite.com)
- Google (www.google.com)
- Yahoo! (www.yahoo.com)

The basic process of getting information from an Internet search engine is pretty simple:

1. **Type the address of the search-engine site in the Address box of your Web browser.**

   You're taken to the Web site's home page.

2. **Find the text box next to the button labeled Search or something similar.**

3. **In the text box, type a few words indicating what interests you.**

Be specific when typing in search text. The more precise your entry, the better your chances of finding what you want. Look for tips, an advanced search option, or help pages on your search engine of choice for more information about how to narrow your search.

4. **Click the Search (or similar) button or press Enter on your keyboard.**

The search engine presents you with a list of how many Internet pages have the requested information. The list includes brief descriptions and links to the first group of pages. You'll find links to additional listings at the bottom if your search finds more listings than can fit on one page (and if you ask for something popular, like *Harry Potter,* don't be surprised to get millions of hits).

Always approach information on the Web with caution. Not everyone is the expert he or she would like to be. Your best bet is to get lots of different opinions and then boil 'em down to what makes sense to you. And remember — *caveat emptor.* (Is there an echo in here?)

For more on using Internet search engines, try *Researching Online For Dummies,* by Reva Basch and Mary Ellen Bates (Wiley Publishing, Inc.).

If you're researching prices to buy a car on eBay, look in your local newspaper to get a good idea of prices in your community. Several good sites are on the Internet. My personal favorite is `www.nadaguides.com`. I've had many of my friends (and editors) visit the various sites, and we've settled on this one because it seems to give the most accurate and unbiased information.

Finding other sources of information

If you're interested in collecting a particular item, you can get a lot of insider collecting information without digging too deep:

- ✔ **Go to other places at eBay.** eBay's chat rooms and message boards (covered in detail in Chapter 17) are full of insider info. The eBay community is always willing to educate a newbie.

- ✔ **Go to the library.** Books and magazines are great sources of info. At least one book or one magazine probably specializes in your chosen item. For example, if old furniture is your thing, *Antiquing For Dummies,* by Ron Zoglin and Deborah Shouse (Wiley Publishing, Inc.), can clue you in to what antiques collectors look for.

If you find an interesting specialty magazine at the library, try entering the title in your search engine of choice. You may just find that the magazine has also gone paperless: You can read it online.

- ✔ **Go to someone else in the know.** Friends, clubs, and organizations in your area can give you a lot of info. Ask your local antiques dealer about clubs you can join and see how much info you end up with.

Looking to Find an Item? Start Your eBay Search Engine

The best part about shopping on eBay is that, aside from collectibles, you can find just about everything from that esoteric lithium battery to new designer dresses (with matching shoes) to pneumatic jackhammers. New or used, it's all here — hiding in the over 13 million daily listings.

Finding the nuggets (deals) can be like searching for the proverbial needle in the haystack. The search secrets in this chapter will put you head and shoulders above your competition for the deals.

eBay has lots of cool ways for you to search for items (sample 'em in Chapter 3). These are the four main options:

- ✔ Search Title (Basic or Advanced Search)
- ✔ Search by Seller
- ✔ Search by Bidder
- ✔ eBay Stores

AUCTION ANECDOTE

Testing, testing . . . how long does a search take at eBay?

Having a massive search engine is a matter of necessity at eBay — millions of items are up for auction at any given time — and often, an easy, fast search makes all the difference between getting and not getting. After all, time is money, and eBay members tend to be movers and shakers who don't like standing still.

So how long do searches really take at eBay? I put it to the test. In the Search window of the eBay home page, I typed in **1933 Chicago World's Fair Pennant** and let 'er rip.

The search engine went through about 10 million general items and World's Fair items (860 of them in 1999 and close to 1,200 items in 2003!) and gave me my one specific item in just four seconds. (Now, if the wizards at eBay could only figure out a way to find that sock that always escapes from clothes dryers, they'd really be on to something.)

By the way, in 1999 that slightly wrinkled felt pennant got four bids and sold for $17.50; in 2003, the aging pennant sold for $43.88 with eight bids.

You can access the four search options by clicking the Search link on the navigation bar at the top of any eBay page where you can customize your search. Each search option can provide a different piece of information to help you find the right item from the right seller at the right price.

If you want to be thorough in your eBay searches, I recommend that you conduct searches often by saving them in your My eBay Favorite Searches area (see Chapter 2 to find out how). And when you find a particularly juicy item or subcategory, bookmark it, or if it's an item, click Watch This Item (a link on the auction page just under the item number), or use your My eBay page. (See Chapter 18 for more on eBay's personal shopper.)

Using the eBay Search Page

When you click Search on the navigation bar, the Basic search page appears. It's the most basic of searches (with a few options) and the one you'll be using the most.

When you use any of the Search options on eBay, the search engine looks for every listing (auction or fixed price) that has the words you're looking for in the title or the description (if you specify so). The title (as you may expect) is just another word or group of words for what you call the item. For example, if you're looking for an antique sterling iced-tea spoon, just type **sterling iced tea spoon** into the search window (see Figure 5-1). If someone is selling a sterling iced-tea spoon and used exactly those words in his or her title or description, you're in Fat City.

Before you click the Search button, narrow down your search further. When you type in your search title, you have the option of choosing how you want the search engine to interpret your search entry. You can have the search engine search the title and description for

- ✔ All the words you type
- ✔ Some of the words you type
- ✔ The exact phrase in the order you've written it

When you're familiar with the tricks listed later in this chapter, you'll be able to get most of these fancy Search results in one of the many search boxes you see littered around the eBay site.

In addition, you can choose other criteria:

- ✔ **What price range you want to see:** Type in the price range you're looking for, and eBay searches the specific range between that low and high price. If money is no object, leave this box blank.

✔ **Words to exclude:** If you want to find a sterling iced-tea spoon, but you don't want it to be plated silver, exclude the word *plated*.

✔ **The payment:** You may restrict your search to items that accept PayPal.

✔ **Within a category:** Use this option if you want to limit your search to a particular main (or *top-level*) category, for example, instead of searching all eBay categories.

✔ **The item location:** You can narrow your search into over 50 eBay Local Trading regions.

✔ **The order in which you want your results to appear:** If you indicate Items Ending First, the search engine gives you the results so that auctions closing soon appear first on the list. Newly Listed Items First lists all the newly listed auctions. Lowest Prices First and Highest Prices First list them just that way.

✔ **Whether you want the search engine to check through item titles alone or check both item titles *and* item descriptions:** You will get more hits on your search if you select the Search Title and Description check box, but you may also get too many items that are out of your search range. See "Narrowing down your eBay search," later in this chapter, for some solid advice.

Okay, *now* click the Search button. In a few seconds, you see the fruits of all the work you've been doing. (Wow, you're not even perspiring.)

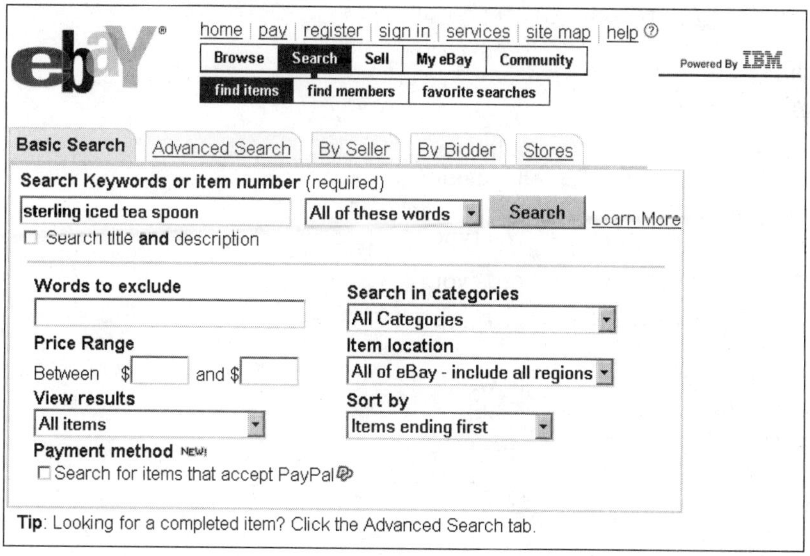

Figure 5-1: Using Search to find a sterling iced-tea spoon.

When running the search for sterling iced-tea spoon, I came up with 29 items. But some people may call them *ice tea spoon*. So, using one of the search tricks I show you in Table 5-2 (later in this chapter), I changed my search to *sterling (ice,iced) tea spoon* and got 50 items. See Figure 5-2 for those results.

Next to item listings you often see pictures, or *icons.* A golden yellow rising sun picture means the listing is brand new (this icon stays on for the first 24 hours an item is listed), a small camera means the seller has included a digital picture along with the item description, and a picture frame indicates that the item is listed with a photo in the Gallery.

Here are some tips for interpreting and working with your search results:

- ✔ If you ever see a mysterious icon in a listing (eBay makes up new icons from time to time), just click the picture with your mouse, and you'll be taken to a help page, which describes the icon's meaning.

- ✔ All items put up for auction at eBay are assigned item numbers. Using an item number is extremely handy if you don't want to wade through a title search again as you follow an auction or find out about auctions that have closed. Sure, you can type in **large tanzanite pave diamond ring** into the title search over and over, but after you find one, all you have to do is enter the item number in the Search box. This is a lot simpler; trust me.

- ✔ An easy way to keep track of an auction you're interested in is to click the Watch This Item link at the top right of the auction page. The auction is then listed on your My eBay Items I'm Watching page, and you can keep your eyes on the action.

All Items	Auctions	Buy It Now		⑦ Need help?

Home > All Categories · View Category: All

Basic Search

sterling (ice,iced) tea

☐ in titles & descriptions

[Search] Refine Search

Matching Categories

Antiques (46)
· Silver (46)
Home (4)
· Kitchen, Dining & Bar (4)

Display

· Gifts view 🎁
· Completed items
· Gallery view
· Items near me
· PayPal items
· Show all prices in $
· View ending times (Ends PST)

All Categories .... Add to My Favorite Searches

50 items found for **sterling (ice,iced) tea spoon**
Sort by items: **ending first** | newly listed | lowest priced | highest priced

Picture hide	Item Title	Price	Bids	Time Left
📷	Royal Crest Sterling Iced Tea Spoon	$9.99	-	10h 35m
📷	GORHAM STERLING CHANTILLY ICE TEA SPOON	$7.99	-	22h 05m
	6 International Sterling Silver Ice Tea Spoon	$51.00	2	22h 25m
	Gorham Sterling KING EDWARD ICE TEA SPOON	$9.99	1	23h 15m
	Gorham Sterling KING EDWARD ICE TEA SPOON	$9.99	1	23h 30m
	Gorham Sterling KING EDWARD ICE TEA SPOON	$9.99	2	23h 35m

Figure 5-2:
The results
of a quest
for a sterling
iced-tea
spoon, using
search
tricks.

✔ On the left side of the results page is a list of categories that your search term is listed under, which is a great reference. Next to each category is a number in parentheses that tells you how many times your search item appears in that category. Figure 5-3 shows a sample of the category spread. To view the items appearing only in a particular category, click that category (or subcategory) title.

eBay's Advanced Search

The Advanced Search tab of the search area throws quite a few more options into the package. Don't be intimidated by this area; you need to understand just a few important bells and whistles.

A completed items search

A Completed Items search returns results of auctions that have already ended. This is my favorite search option at eBay because you can use it as a strategic bidding tool. How? If you're bidding on an item and want to know if the prices are likely to go too high for your pocketbook, you can use this search option to compare the current price of the item to the selling price of similar items from auctions that have already ended.

You can also use this tool if you want to sell an item and are trying to determine what it's worth, how high the demand is, and whether this is the right time to list the item. (Chapter 10 offers the nuts, bolts, and monkey wrenches you need to set up your auction.)

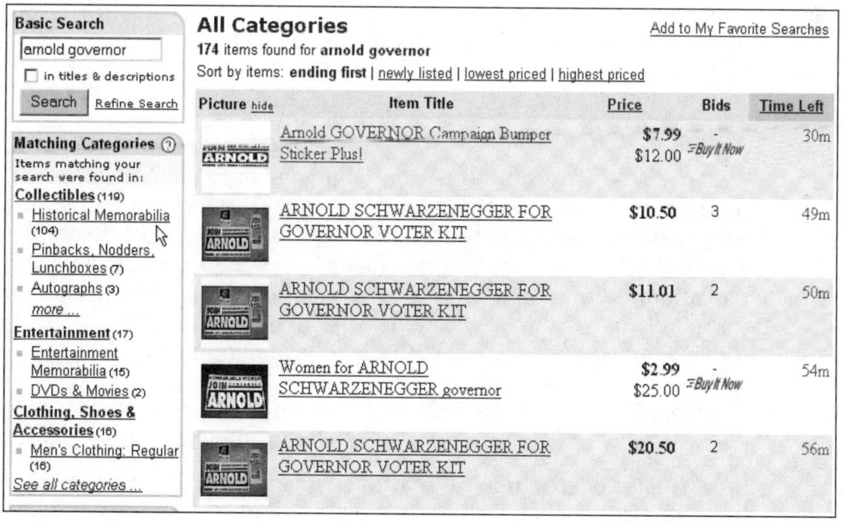

Figure 5-3: Search results category listings.

Type in your keyword criteria and scroll down the page to the Completed Items Only box. Step by step, here's how to do a Completed Items Only search:

1. **In the title search field, type in the title name or the keywords of the item you want to find.**

2. **Select the Completed Items Only check box to see completed listings as far back as the eBay search engine will permit.**

   Currently, you can go back about two weeks.

3. **Tell eBay how you want the results arranged.**

   In the Sort By area, choose one of the following four options:

   - **Items Ending First:** Include completed auctions starting with the oldest available (about two weeks).

   - **Newly Listed:** List the most recently completed auctions first.

   - **Lowest Prices First:** List auctions from the lowest price attained to the highest price paid for an item.

   - **Highest Prices First:** List completed items from highest to lowest. (This is very useful when you're searching for a 1967 Camaro and you want to buy a car and not a Hot Wheels toy).

4. **Click Search.**

   The search results appear in just a few seconds.

An alternate way to find completed items is to run a current auction search from any of the little search boxes on almost any eBay page. When the results of your auction show up, scroll down to the Display box in the left column and click the Completed Items link, as shown in Figure 5-4. That way, you can scout out the active auction competition quickly before moving on to the completed sales.

An international search

You can select any country (from Afghanistan to Zimbabwe, no kidding!) or narrow your search to the United States or Canada. Don't forget that you have to pay for shipping, so if you don't want to pay to ship a heavy Victorian-style fainting sofa from Hungary to Hoboken, New Jersey, stick close to home. The Location/International Search option is pretty much an international version of Search, and it's done the same way. You also have the choice of narrowing down your country search with the following options:

- ✔ **Items Available To:** The search engine looks for items within your own country or from international sellers willing to ship to you.

- ✔ **Items Located In:** The search engine looks for items from the specific country you entered in the box.

Basic Search		All Categories			Add to My Favorite Searches

Basic Search

chocolate truffle

☐ in titles & descriptions

Search | Refine Search

Matching Categories ⑦

Items matching your search were found in:

Home (34)
- Home Decor (24)
- Food & Wine (8)
- Crafting, Sewing, Art Supplies (2)

Everything Else (4)
- Health & Beauty (3)
- Gifts & Occasions (1)

Dolls & Bears (2)
- Bears (2)

Collectibles (1)

Display
- Gifts view
- Completed items
- Gallery view
- Items near me
- PayPal items
- Show all prices in $
- View ending times (Ends PDT)

All Categories

41 items found for **chocolate truffle**

Sort by items: **ending first** | newly listed | lowest priced | highest priced

Picture hide	Item Title	Price	Bids	Time Left
📷	Yankee Candle CHOCOLATE TRUFFLE TEALIGHTS	$7.99	-	2h 42m
	500+Chocolate Candy Fudge Truffle Recipes YUM	$2.49 ₌Buy It Now		3h 50m
	Yankee Candle CHOCOLATE TRUFFLE 22 oz RARE!	$15.95	-	4h 34m
📷	YANKEE CANDLE ~ 22 OZ CHOCOLATE TRUFFLE CHOC	$23.50 $25.00 ₌Buy It Now	-	5h 50m
📷	CANDLEWORKS 16oz Chocolate Raspberry Truffle	$8.95	-	6h 59m
📷	YANKEE CANDLES CANDLE-22 OZ CHOCOLATE TRUFFLE	$16.27	5	9h 12m
	CHOCOLATE TRUFFLE BOXED FAVORS	$60.00	-	9h 53m
📷	CHOCOLATE BLUEBERRY TRUFFLE FLAVORED COFFEE	$4.99	-	16h 35m
	24PK CARBOLITE CHOCOLATE	$21.51	4	1d 03h 13m

Figure 5-4: The convenient Show Only Completed Items link in the Display box of the search results page.

A seller search

The By Seller tab of the search area, shown in Figure 5-5, gives you a list of all the auctions a seller is running, and it's a great way for you to keep a list of people you have successfully done business with in the past. The By Seller page is also a strategy that eBay users use to assess the reputation of a seller. You can find out more about selling strategies in Chapter 9.

View all items by a single seller

To use the By Seller search option to search for all of a single seller's items, follow these steps:

1. **In the Single Seller search field, type the eBay User ID of the person you want to learn more about.**

2. **On the Include Bidder Emails line, tell eBay whether you want to see the e-mail addresses of other people who are bidding on auctions posted by the person you're searching for.**

   If you are the seller and want to view these addresses from this page, click the Yes option button. Note that to protect each member's privacy, e-mail addresses are available to you only if you are involved in a transaction with the other person.

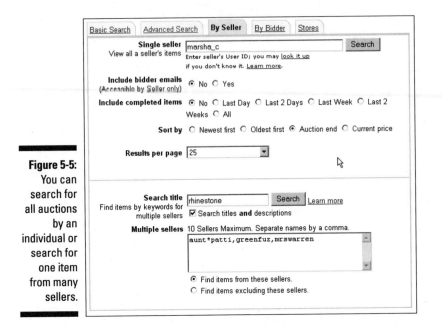

Figure 5-5:
You can
search for
all auctions
by an
individual or
search for
one item
from many
sellers.

3. **If you don't want to see auctions that this specific seller has conducted in the past, select No on the Include Completed Items line.**

   You can choose to see all current and previous auctions, as well as auctions that have ended in the last day, last two days, last week, or last two weeks.

   eBay keeps past auction results active for only 30 days; if you're looking for something auctioned 31 days (or longer) ago, sorry — no dice.

4. **On the Sort By line, select an option to control how you want the results of your search to appear on-screen.**

   If you want to see the auctions that are closing right away, select Auction End.

5. **Choose the number of results you want to see per page.**

   If the person you're looking up has 100 auctions running, you can limit the number of results to a manageable 25 listings on four separate pages. Doing so allows you to narrow down what you want to see.

6. **Click the Search button next to the Single Seller text box.**

   Figure 5-6 shows the results page of a By Seller search.

Items for Sale by marsha_c (2419 ★) ❖ Power Seller me ⓒstores

Find more great stuff at my eBay ⓒstore

19 items found.

View text-only format

| All items | Auctions | Buy It Now |

Picture *hide*	Item Title	Price	Bids	Time (Ends PDT)
	CLOUD DOME w 7 inch Ext Digital Macro Photos	$162.99 $168.99	- ⟶Buy It Now	Oct-14-03 14:05:40 PDT
	eBay Live 2003 TIPS for Dummies AUTHOR SIGNED	$3.99	1	Oct-14-03 14:05:40 PDT
	Starting an eBay Business for Dummies SIGNED	$21.99 $22.99	- ⟶Buy It Now	Oct-14-03 14:09:57 PDT
	Author SIGNED eBay for Dummies NEW 3rd Edit	$19.99 $20.99	- ⟶Buy It Now	Oct-14-03 14:09:57 PDT
	SIGNED Arnold Schwarzenegger Governor Ticket	$15.50	5	Oct-14-03 22:55:49 PDT
	Spanx Footless Body Shaping Pantyhose A NUDE	$13.99	⟶Buy It Now	Oct-16-03 09:07:29 PDT

Figure 5-6: The results of a By Seller search.

Finding items by keywords for multiple sellers

If you're looking for a specific item from a group of sellers, you can fill the search information in the bottom half of the By Seller search page, as shown earlier in Figure 5-5. You may need to perform this type of search after you settle into shopping on eBay and have several sellers that you like doing business with (or alternatively, you can exclude sellers you prefer not to do business with). With this method, you can limit the search for a particular item to just the sellers you want, rather than tens of thousands of sellers.

When you find a seller that you want to continue doing business with, you can add his or her link to your My eBay Favorite Sellers area. Just go to your My eBay page, and in the Favorites area, click the Add New Seller/Store link. You can add up to 30 sellers in this area, and can search their sales with a click of your mouse!

A bidder search

The By Bidder search option is unique because sellers and buyers alike use it when an auction is going on — to figure out their best strategies. After all, money is the name of the game. For information on conducting a By Bidder search, take a look at Chapter 7.

Narrowing down your eBay search

After you become familiar with each of eBay's search options, you need a crash course in what words to actually type into those nice little boxes. Too little information and you may not find your item. Too much and you're overwhelmed with information. If you're really into bean-bag toys, for example, you may be looking for Ty's Tabasco the Bull. But if you just search for *Tabasco*, you'll get swamped with results ranging from hot sauce to advertisements.

Some simple tricks can help narrow your eBay search results when you're searching from pages other than the main Search page (where you don't find all the searching bells and whistles). Table 5-2 has the details.

Table 5-2	Symbols and Keywords for Conducting Searches with the eBay Search Engine	
Symbol	*Impact on Search*	*Example*
No symbol, multiple words	Returns auctions with all included words in the title	**reagan letter** might return an auction for a mailed message from the former U.S. president, or it might return an auction for a mailed message from Boris Yeltsin to Ronald Reagan.
Quotes ""	Limits the search to items with the exact phrase inside the quotes	**"Wonder Woman"** returns items about the comic book/TV heroine. Quotes don't make the search term case sensitive. Using either upper- or lowercase in *any* eBay search gets you the same results.
Asterisk *	Serves as a wild card	**budd*** returns items that start with budd, such as Beanie Buddy, Beanie Buddies, or Buddy Holly.
Separating comma without spaces (a,b)	Finds items related to either the item before or after the comma	**(gi joe,g.i. joe)** returns all G.I. JOE items no matter which way the seller listed them.

Symbol	Impact on Search	Example
Minus sign –	Excludes results with the word after the –	Type in **box –lunch**, and you'd better not be hungry because you may find the box, but lunch won't be included.
Minus symbol and parentheses	Searches for auctions with words before the parentheses but excludes words inside the parentheses	**midge –(skipper,barbie)** means that auctions with the Midge doll won't have attention.
Parentheses	Searches for both versions of the word in parentheses	**political (pin,pins)** searches for political pin or political pins.

Here are additional tips to help you narrow down any eBay search:

- **Don't worry about capitalization:** You can capitalize proper names or leave them lowercase — the search engine doesn't care.

- **Don't use *and, a, an, or,* or *the*:** Called *noise words* in search lingo, these words are interpreted as part of your search. So if you want to find something from *The Sound of Music* and you type in **the sound of music**, you may not get any results. Most sellers drop noise words from the beginning of an item title when they list it, just as libraries drop noise words when they alphabetize books. So make your search for **sound music**. An even more precise search would be **"sound of music"** (in quotes).

- **Search within specific categories:** This type of search narrows down your results because you search only one niche of eBay — just the specific area you want. For example, if you want to find Tabasco the Bull, start at the home page and, under the Categories heading, click Toys and Bean Bag. The only problem with searching in a specific category is that sometimes an item can be in more than one place. For example, if you're searching for a Mickey Mouse infant snuggly in the Disney category, you may miss it because the item might be listed in infant wear.

Use the asterisk symbol often to locate misspellings. I've often found some great deals by finding items incorrectly posted by the sellers. Here are a few examples:

- **Rodri*.** In this search I look for items by the famous Cajun artist *George Rodrigue*. His Blue Dog paintings are world renowned and very valuable. By using this search, I managed to purchase a signed Blue Dog lithograph for under $200. (I resold it on eBay later that year for $900!)

- ✔ **Alumi* tree**. Remember the old aluminum Christmas trees from the '60s? They've had quite a resurgence in popularity these days. You can buy these "antiques" in stores for hundreds of dollars . . . or you can buy one on eBay for half the price. You can find them even cheaper if the seller can't spell *aluminum*. . . .

- ✔ **Cemet* plot**. If you're looking for that final place to retire, eBay has some great deals. Unfortunately, sellers haven't narrowed down whether they want to spell it *cemetery* or *cematary*. This search will find both.

After studying these examples, I'm sure you can think of many more instances in which your use of the asterisk can help you find the deals. Be sure to e-mail me and let me know when you find something special in this way!

Free hanging chads . . .

eBay gives you the opportunity to have the same fine museum-quality items as the Smithsonian Institution. In November of 2001, the Palm Beach County Board of County Commissioners found themselves in a bit of a pickle. Due to the infamous Presidential election of November 7, 2000 — fraught with hanging, pregnant, and dimpled chads — the announcement of the election winner was delayed for an unprecedented 37 days. As a result of this election, the Florida legislature outlawed the future use of punch-card voting systems — all Florida counties had to move to more stable, state-approved voting machines.

Palm Beach County chose to move to a touch-screen type of voting device, which cost its residents over $14 million. What to do with the old historic punch-card voting machines? Yep, donate one to the Smithsonian — and auction the rest off on eBay. Palm Beach County donated machine #1 to the Auction for America; it netted $4,550.01 for the Twin Towers fund.

The rest? Well, the Palm Beach County folks should have read this book. They ran a Dutch auction for 3,055 of the basic voting packages, with a starting bid of $300. Included with the voting machine was the iniquitous "butterfly ballot" with official stylus; a brass plaque certifying that it was used in the November 7 election; a Certificate of Authenticity signed by Theresa LePore, Palm Beach County Supervisor of Elections; 25 demonstrator punch cards for playing polling place at home; a signed photograph of the folks in charge of recounting the ballots: Palm Beach County Supervisor of Elections Theresa LePore, Palm Beach County Commissioner Carol Roberts, and Judge Charles Burton; and "any chads which are in the machine from previous elections." What a package! There also were 569 Premier packages, which included an Official Ballot box, starting at $600.

In the ten-day auctions (run at the same time!), Palm Beach County sold 78 of the Premier packages and 389 of the Basic voting-machine packages. I called the County Commissioner's office to find out why my voting machine hadn't arrived and asked when the rest would be auctioned. I was assured they would be put back up at eBay auction, but at a higher starting bid.

Palm Beach County should have followed the strategies in this book, like some smart eBay sellers did. Soon after, one of the basic packages sold after a seven-day auction for $670. Other entrepreneurial sellers have been selling voting machines from counties other than Palm Beach on eBay. Unfortunately for those who purchase them, only the Palm Beach County machines had the infamous butterfly ballot.

Finding eBay Members: The Gang's All Here

With millions of eBay users on the loose, you may think tracking folks down is hard. Nope. eBay's powerful search engine kicks into high gear to help you find other eBay members in seconds.

Here's how to find people or get info on them from eBay:

1. **From the main navigation bar at the top of most eBay pages, click the Search link.**

   This action takes you to the main Search page where three links pop up on the subnavigation bar: Find Items, Find Members, and Favorite Searches.

2. **Click the Find Members link on the subnavigation bar.**

   This link takes you to the main Find Members page, where you can search for specific About Me pages. (See Chapter 14 to find out how to create your own personal eBay Web page.) Here, you can also get a look at the feedback profile of a user (see Chapter 4 for details about feedback), find User ID histories of fellow eBay members (which comes in handy when you're bidding on items, as Chapter 7 avows), or get contact information when you're involved in a transaction.

3. **Fill in the appropriate boxes with what you're looking for and click the Search (or, in some cases, the Submit) button to get the info you want.**

   If you're looking for User ID histories or contact information and you haven't signed in, you have to do so at this point.

Clicking the Favorite Searches link on the subnavigation bar takes you to your My eBay Favorites page. You can tell eBay about the items you're looking for, and it does automatic searches for you. You can also have eBay e-mail you when auctions that match your descriptions crop up. (Chapter 18 gives you more info on how this works.)

Chapter 6

Shopping eBay: The Basics

*B*rowsing different categories of eBay, looking for nothing in particular, you spot that must-have item lurking among other Elvis paraphernalia in the Collectibles category. Sure, you *can* live without that faux gold Elvis pocket watch, but life would be so much sweeter *with* it. And even if it doesn't keep good time, at least it'll be right twice a day.

When you bid for items on eBay, you can get that same thrill that you would get at Sotheby's or Christie's for a lot less money, and the items you win are likely to be *slightly* more practical than an old Dutch masterpiece you're afraid to leave at the framer's. (Hey, you have to have a watch, and Elvis is the King.)

In this chapter, I give you the lowdown about the types of auctions available on eBay and a rundown of the nuts and bolts of bidding strategies. I also share some tried-and-true tips that'll give you a leg up on the competition.

The Auction Item Page

Because at any given point, you have more than a million pages of items that you can look at on eBay, auction item pages are the heart (better yet, the skeleton) of eBay auctions. All item pages on eBay — whether auctions, fixed-price items, or Buy It Now items — look about the same. For example, Figure 6-1 shows a conventional auction item page, and Figure 6-2 shows a fixed-price sale. Both item pages show the listing title at the top, bidding or buying info in the middle, and seller info on the right. Below this area you find a complete description of the item, along with shipping information.

Figure 6-1:
Here's
a typical
auction,
featuring
Buy It Now
and PayPal
payments.

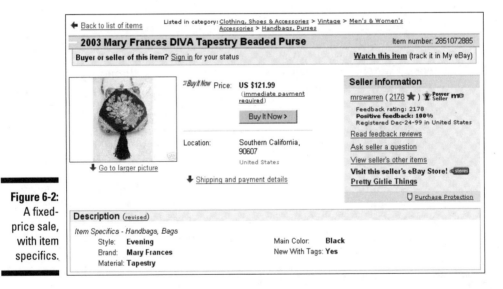

Figure 6-2:
A fixed-
price sale,
with item
specifics.

Of course, the two auction types have some subtle differences. (With a venue as big as eBay, you gotta have some flexibility.) Some auctions feature a picture at the top of the page, and some don't, depending on how the seller sets up his or her sale page. Some auctions have set item specifics in the description (as shown in Figure 6-2). This area is set up by eBay and filled in by the seller to give you a snapshot description of the item for sale. If the item you come to after your search is a fixed-price sale, you'll just see the words Buy It Now (also shown in Figure 6-2). But overall, the look and feel of these pages is the same.

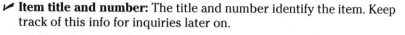

Here's a list of stuff you see as scroll down on a typical auction item page:

- **Item title and number:** The title and number identify the item. Keep track of this info for inquiries later on.

  If you're interested in a particular type of item, take note of the key words used in the title (you're likely to see them again in future titles). Doing so helps you in narrowing down your searches.

- **Item category:** Located just above the item title and number bar, you can click the category listing and do some comparison shopping. (Chapter 5 gives more searching strategies.)

- **Current Bid:** This field indicates the dollar amount the bidding has reached, which changes throughout the auction as people place bids. If no bids have been placed on the item, this field is called Starting Bid.

  Sometimes, next to the current dollar amount, you see *(Reserve not met)* or *(Reserve met)*. This means the seller has set a *reserve price* for the item — a secret price that must be reached before the seller will sell the item. If you don't see this note on an auction item page, don't be alarmed. Not all auctions have reserve prices. The majority don't.

- **Buy It Now price:** If you want the item immediately and the price quoted in this area is okay with you, click the Buy It Now link, which takes you to a page where you can complete your purchase.

- **Quantity:** This field appears only in a multiple item fixed-price sale or Dutch auction. It tells you how many items are available. If you see a number other than 1 in this field, you're looking at a Multiple Item (Dutch) auction, which is explained later in this chapter. It may also be a multiple unit, fixed-price sale (which means that you can buy just one — you don't have to buy the entire lot). You can tell if it's a fixed-price sale because you have no opportunity to bid — you can just use Buy It Now for whatever quantity of the item you desire. You'll be prompted for a quantity when you buy. But if a seller is selling two Elvis watches for the price of one, the item quantity still shows up as 1 (as in 1 set of 2 watches).

- **Time Left:** Although the clock never stops ticking at eBay, you must continue to refresh your browser to see the time remaining on the official clock. When the item gets down to the last hour of the auction, you'll see the time expressed in minutes and seconds. This field tells you the time remaining in this particular auction.

  Timing is the key in an eBay bidding strategy (covered in Chapter 7), so don't forget that, because eBay's world headquarters is in California, eBay uses Pacific Standard Time or Pacific Daylight Time as the standard, depending on the season.

- **History:** This field tells you how many bids have been placed. To use the number of bids to your advantage, you have to read between the lines. You can determine just how "hot" an item is by comparing the number of bids the item has received over time. Based on the amount of interest in an item, you can create a time strategy (which I talk about later in this chapter). The starting bid is listed in light gray next to the number of bids. If you click the number of bids, you can find out who is bidding and what date and time bids were placed on this item. The dollar amount of each bid is kept secret until the end of the auction.

- **High Bidder:** This field shows you the User ID and feedback rating of the current high bidder. *It could be you if you've placed a bid!*

Bidding is more an art than a science. Sometimes an item gets no bids because everyone's waiting until the last minute. You see a flurry of activity as bidders all try to outbid each other (called *sniping,* which Chapter 7 explains). But that's all part of the fun of eBay.

- **Location:** This field tells you at the very least the country where the seller is located, and you may also see more specific info, such as the city and geographic area where the seller is. (What you see depends on how detailed the seller wants to be.)

Factor in the geographic location of a seller when you consider bidding on an item. Knowing exactly where the item is can help you quickly calculate what the shipping charges will be — and how long it will take for the item to get to you. (Chapter 10 tackles that subject.) Also, if you buy from someone in your own state, you may also have to pay sales tax on your purchase. If the item is in Australia, for example, and you're in Vermont, you may decide that you don't really need that wrought-iron doorstop. (Remember, *you* pay the shipping charges.)

The region (located above the country in the Location field) lets you know if the item is included in eBay's regional auction areas. This is usually the city where the seller is located. It also makes it easy if the item is the sort you'd like to pick up directly from the seller. E-mail the seller first to see if he or she is up to meeting you at the local Starbucks to complete the transaction.

- **Watch This Item:** Click this link, and the item is magically added to the Bidding/Watching tab of your My eBay page so you can keep an eye on the progress of the auction — without actually bidding. If you haven't signed in, you have to type in your User ID and password before you can save the auction to your My eBay page.

- **Seller Information box:** This area gives you information about the seller. *Know thy seller* ranks right after *caveat emptor* as a phrase that pays at eBay. As I tell you nearly a million times in this book, *read the feedback rating!* (Okay, maybe not a million — it would drive the editors bonkers.) Human beings come in all shapes, sizes, and levels of honesty, and like any community, eBay has its share of good folks and bad folks. Your best defense is to read the seller's feedback. You'll see several things in the Seller Information box (as shown in Figure 6-3):

- **Feedback Rating:** This is the same number that's to the right of the seller's name in parentheses. Click the number next to the seller's ID to view his or her eBay ID card and entire feedback history just below it. Read, read, and reread all the feedback (hey, we're one closer to a million!) to make sure you feel comfortable doing business with this person.

- **Positive Feedback percentage:** The eBay computers cipher this figure. It's derived from all the positive and negative feedback that a user receives.

- **Registered:** This line lists the date the seller registered on eBay and the country in which he or she registered.

- **Read Feedback Reviews link:** This link does the same thing as clicking the Feedback Rating number.

- **Ask Seller a Question link:** Clicking this link hooks you up with eBay's e-mail system. You can ask the seller a question regarding the item here.

- **View Seller's Other Items link:** This link takes you to a page that lists all the seller's current auctions and fixed-price sales.

    If the seller has an eBay store, a link to it appears here as well. I give you a step-by-step guide on how these links work later in this chapter.

    If the seller accepts PayPal, that option is indicated in a shaded area. Also, if the seller qualifies for Buyer Protection, this is also indicated here, as shown in Figure 6-3.

- ✔ **Description bar:** Below this light blue shaded bar is the item description. Read all this information carefully before bidding. Read on to find out how to use this information.

Figure 6-3:
Lots of
data on the
seller here.

Seller information

marsha_c (2424 ⭐) 🏆 Power Seller me

Feedback rating: 2424
Positive feedback: 100%
Registered Jan-05-97 in United States

Read feedback reviews

Ask seller a question

View seller's other items

Visit this seller's eBay Store! stores
Marsha Collier's Fabulous Finds

PayPal ☑ Buyer Protection Offered
See coverage and eligibility

Below the seller's description area, you'll find some other important data on the typical auction item page, as shown in Figure 6-4:

✔ **Shipping and Payment Details:** Check here to see the details on shipping. You see

- Who pays (remember that on eBay, it's usually the buyer).

- Whether insurance is offered.

- Which states have to pay sales tax (if any).

- Whether the seller is willing to ship to your area. (Sometimes sellers won't ship internationally, and they'll let you know here.)

Also, always check the item description for other shipping information and terms.

If the item weighs more than a pound, the seller may have conveniently included eBay's shipping calculator in this area. Just type in your zip code, and you're presented with the shipping cost to your location.

✔ **Payment Methods Accepted:** This field tells you the payment methods that the seller accepts: checks, money orders, credit cards, or PayPal. Often, it tells you to read the item description for more details. I explain how to read item descriptions later in this chapter.

✔ **E-mail This Item to a Friend:** You can tip off a friend on a good find, get some advice from an antiques or collecting expert, or run the auction by a friend who's been around the eBay block a few times and ask for strategy advice. (You find this link below the shipping and payment areas.)

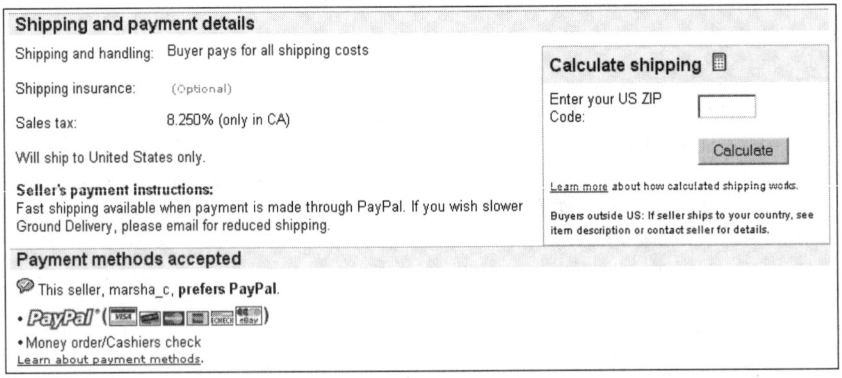

Figure 6-4:
Check the shipping and payment boxes below the item description to find out about additional costs, shipping, and tax that are applied when you buy.

Shipping and payment details

Shipping and handling: Buyer pays for all shipping costs

Shipping insurance: (Optional)

Sales tax: 8.250% (only in CA)

Will ship to United States only.

Seller's payment instructions:
Fast shipping available when payment is made through PayPal. If you wish slower Ground Delivery, please email for reduced shipping.

Calculate shipping

Enter your US ZIP Code:

Calculate

Learn more about how calculated shipping works.

Buyers outside US: If seller ships to your country, see item description or contact seller for details.

Payment methods accepted

This seller, marsha_c, prefers PayPal.

- PayPal (VISA)
- Money order/Cashiers check

Learn about payment methods.

Be sure to use the Watch This Item feature. Organization is the name of the game at eBay, especially if you plan to bid on multiple auctions while you're running auctions of your own. I figure you're in the bidding game to win, so start keeping track of items now.

Beating the Devil in the Details

As with any sale — whether you find it at Joe's Hardware, Bloomingdale's, or Target — carefully check out what you're buying. The item page gives you links to help you know what you're bidding on — and who you're potentially buying from. If you take advantage of these features, you won't have many problems. But, if you ignore these essential tips, you may end up unhappy with what you buy, who you buy it from, and how much you spend.

Read the item description carefully

The *item description* is the most critical item on the auction item page. This is where the seller lists the details about the item being sold. Read this page carefully and pay very close attention to what is, and *isn't,* written.

Don't judge a book by its cover — but do judge a seller by his or her item description. If the sentences are succinct, detailed, and well structured, you're most likely dealing with an individual who planned and executed the auction with care. It takes time and effort to post a good auction. If you see huge lapses in grammar, convoluted sentences, and misspellings, *you may be gonna get burnt!* Make sure that you feel comfortable dealing with this person; decide for yourself whether he or she is out to sell junk for a quick buck or is part of eBay for the long term.

If a picture is available, take a good look. The majority of eBay sellers jazz up their auctions with photos of their items. The seller should answer a few general questions in the item description. If these questions aren't answered, that doesn't necessarily mean that the seller's disreputable — only that if you're really interested, you should e-mail the seller and get those answers before you bid. In particular, ask questions like these:

- ✔ Is the item new or used?
- ✔ Is the item a first edition or a reprint? An original or a reissue? (See Chapter 5 for tips on how to assess what you're buying.)
- ✔ Is the item in its original packaging? Does it still have the original tags?
- ✔ Is the item under warranty?

Most sellers spell out in their item descriptions exactly how the item should be paid for and shipped. Check the Shipping and Payment Details box under the description to see whether an actual shipping charge applies — and if so, how much it'll cost you. Some sellers use eBay's incredibly convenient shipping calculator. Here are a few other things to consider regarding your item:

- ✔ If you're in a hurry to get the item, are delays likely? If so, what sort and how long?
- ✔ Can the seller guarantee you a refund if the item is broken or doesn't work upon delivery?
- ✔ What condition is the item in? Is it broken, scratched, flawed, or mint?

    Most experienced eBay buyers know that, depending on the item, a tiny scratch here or there may be worth the risk of making a bid. But a scratch or two may affect your bidding price. (Look at Chapter 5 for more expert advice for buying collectibles.)

- ✔ Is this item the genuine article or a reproduction, and if it's the real deal, does the seller have papers or labels certifying its authenticity?
- ✔ What size is the item? (That life-size fiberglass whale may not *fit* in your garage.)

If you win the item and find out the seller lied in the description, you have the right to request to return the item. But, if you win the item and discover that *you* overlooked a detail in the description, the seller isn't obligated to take the item back.

The seller is obligated to describe the item honestly and in detail, so if your questions aren't answered in the item description, then for goodness' sake, e-mail the seller for the facts. If a picture is available, is it clear enough that you can see any flaws? You can always ask the seller to e-mail you a picture taken from another angle.

Get the scoop on the seller

I can't tell you enough that the single most important way you can make an auction go well is to *know who you're dealing with.* Apparently, the eBay folks agree; they enable you to get info on the seller right from the auction item page. I recommend that you take advantage of the links offered there. (Chapter 5 demonstrates how to conduct a thorough By Seller search.) To get the full scoop on a seller, here's what you need to do:

- ✔ Click the number beside the seller's User ID to get his or her feedback history. Click the Me link (if there is one) next to the seller to view the seller's *About Me* page. It frequently gives you a good deal more information about the seller. (To set up your own free About Me page on eBay, check out Chapter 14.)

✔ Make note if you see the PowerSeller icon next to the seller's name. It means he or she is an eBay seller who has met certain stringent certifications. (For more on PowerSellers, see Chapter 20.)

✔ Click the View Seller's Other Auctions link to take a look at what else that person is selling. (If you win more than one auction from a seller, he or she will often combine the shipping costs.) Check the seller's feedback (message sound familiar?).

Check the seller's eBay ID card and feedback history. All together now — *check the feedback.* (Is there an echo in here?) What you will find are (for the most part) the honest thoughts and comments of buyers from previous transactions. No eBay user has control over the comments that others make, and feedback sticks to you like your permanent record from high school.

Read the feedback — the good, the bad, and the neutral — and unless you're prepared to kiss your money good-bye, I've found it safer not to buy from a seller who has a large percentage of negative comments.

eBay, like life, is full of shades of gray. Some sellers are unfairly hit with negative comments for something that wasn't their fault. If you suspect that a seller's received a bum rap (after you've read all his or her positive feedback), be sure to read the seller's response. (Look at Chapter 4 for more on reading and leaving feedback.)

Although scoping out an eBay member's ID card is *just that fast, just that simple,* you still need to take the time to read the feedback. (There's that echo again. Good thing it's a wise echo.) Someone with 500 positive feedback messages may look like a good seller, but if you take a closer look, you may find that his or her 10 most-recent feedback messages are negative.

View the seller's other auctions

To find out what other auctions the seller has going at eBay, all you have to do is click the corresponding link on the item page; you're whisked away to a list of the other auction pies the seller has a finger in. If the seller has no other auctions going and has no current feedback, you may want to do a more thorough investigation and conduct a By Seller search that will show you all that person's completed auctions in the last 30 days. (See Chapter 5 for details.)

Ask the seller a question

If anything about the auction is unclear to you, remember this one word: *ask.* Find out all the details about that item before you bid. If you wait until you've won the item before you ask questions, you may get stuck with something you don't want. Double-checking may save you woe and hassle later.

You can find out more about payment options, shipping charges, insurance, and other fun stuff in Chapters 8 and 12.

> ## How Swede it is!
>
> A savvy eBay user I know benefited from a major seller error. The seller titled his auction "Swede Star Trek Cast Jacket." My friend checked out the item description and found that it was written with bad spelling and incoherent grammar, so she e-mailed the seller for more information. The seller explained that the jacket was a suede cast jacket given as a wrap gift to the cast and crew of the movie *Star Trek: Generations.* He had won it in a local radio contest, and it was brand new. Because of the seller's mistake, only one bidder bid on this lovely green suede (silk-lined!) jacket, which my friend picked up for $150. Because of its *Star Trek* connection, the jacket is worth upwards of $400 to collectors. So study the item page carefully. You may get lucky and find that errors can work to your benefit. (And a word to the wise: Check your own spelling and grammar carefully when you put an item up for sale.)

If you're bidding on a reserve-price auction, don't be afraid to e-mail the seller and ask what the reserve is. Yeah, reserves are mostly kept secret, but there's no harm in asking — and many sellers gladly tell you.

To ask a seller a question, follow these steps:

1. **Click the Ask Seller a Question link on the item page.**

   If you *haven't* already signed in, you're automatically taken to the User ID request page. (This is beginning to sound as repetitive as checking feedback!) After you fill in your User ID and password and press Enter, you're presented with the Ask the Seller a Question form.

   You can always change your User ID, but your past life (in the form of feedback messages) stays with you at eBay. Along with your feedback from your previous User ID, all your previous User IDs are listed as well in a User ID history search from the eBay Search page.

   If you *have* already signed in, a preaddressed e-mail window opens for you.

2. **Fill in the message area and politely fire off your questions; then click Send Message.**

   Expect to hear back from the seller within a day. If it takes the seller more than a day or two to respond, and you get no explanation for the delay, think twice before putting in a bid.

Extend your scam antennae if a seller's reply to your question comes from an e-mail address that's different from the one you sent your question to. The seller should include an explanation for a difference in addresses. If you don't receive an explanation, ask for one. Fraudulent sellers often use several e-mail addresses to hide their true identity. There may be nothing wrong with having several e-mail addresses, but if you're getting a gut feeling that the seller is playing hide-and-seek with addresses all over the place, *thank* your gut very much and rethink doing business with that person.

Factoring in the Extras

Before you think about placing a bid on an item, you should factor in the financial obligation you have to make. In every case, the maximum bid you place won't be all you spend on an item. I recommend that you look closely at the payment methods that the seller is willing to accept and also factor in shipping, insurance, and escrow costs (if any). If you have only $50 to spend, you shouldn't place a $50 bid on a fragile item that will be shipped a long distance because often the buyer (that would be you) pays for shipping and insurance. In addition, if you live in the same state as the seller, you may have to pay sales tax if the seller is running an official business.

Payment methods

Several payment options are available, but the seller has the right to refuse some forms of payment. Usually, the accepted forms of payment are laid out in the item's description or in the Shipping and Payment Details below the description area. If you don't see this info, ask the seller a question (as described in the previous section) and get a clear idea of your additional costs *before* you place a bid.

These are the forms of payment available to you:

- ✔ **Credit card:** Paying with a credit card is a favorite payment option, one that's mainly offered by businesses and dealers. I like paying with credit cards because they're fast and efficient. In addition, using a credit card offers you another ally, your credit card company, if you're not completely satisfied with the transaction.

  Sometimes sellers use a friend's company to run credit card payments for eBay auctions. So don't be surprised if you buy a vintage Tonka bulldozer and your credit card is billed from Holly's Hair-o-Rama.

- ✔ **PayPal:** I pay for almost all my eBay purchases through PayPal. Owned by eBay, PayPal is the largest Internet-wide payment network. Sellers who accept PayPal are identified with a special icon in the Seller Information box (as well as a large PayPal logo in the Payment Methods area below the description) and accept American Express, Visa, MasterCard, and Discover as well as electronic checks and debits. The service is integrated directly into eBay auctions, so paying is a mouse click away.

After you register with PayPal to pay for an item, PayPal debits your credit card or your bank checking account (or your account — if you have earned some money from sales) and sends the payment to the seller's account. PayPal does not charge buyers to use the service. Buyers can use PayPal to pay any seller within the United States (and around the world in over 35 countries). Some international bidders can pay for their eBay auctions from sellers in the United States. To see a current list of PayPal's international services go to www.paypal.com/cgi-bin/webscr?cmd=p/gen/approved_countries-outside.

PayPal deposits the money directly into the seller's checking or savings account. The service charges the seller a small transaction fee, so the seller absorbs the cost.

Your credit card information is known only to the PayPal service. The seller never sees your credit card info. Another major advantage is that you have protection behind you when you use PayPal. And you have the right to dispute charges if the item arrives damaged or doesn't show up at all. When you use PayPal to pay for a qualified eBay item from a Verified PayPal member, you may be covered by PayPal's Buyer Protection program for purchases up to $500. To find out whether your item is protected in this program, look for the information at the bottom of the Seller Information box (refer to Figure 6-3).

For more details, check out the PayPal Web site (www.paypal.com).

✔ **Money order:** My second-favorite method of payment — and the most popular at eBay — is the money order. Sellers love money orders because they don't have to wait for a check to clear.

Money orders are the same as cash. As soon as the seller gets your money order, he or she has no reason to wait to send the item. You can buy money orders at banks, supermarkets, convenience stores, and your local post office. The average cost is about a dollar. If you're purchasing an item that's being shipped internationally, you can pay with an international money order from the U.S. Postal Service, which costs about $3.00.

International buyers may purchase a Western Union money order; www.westernunion.com provides locations in different cities around the world. The United Kingdom alone has hundreds of Western Union agents ready to receive your payment. Western Union money orders are also available online through BidPay.com for $1.95 for money orders under $10.00. The amount is charged to your credit card, and BidPay mails the money order to the seller for you.

✔ **Personal or cashier's check:** Paying by check is convenient but has its drawbacks. Most sellers won't ship you the goods until after your check clears, which means a lag time of a couple of weeks or more. If a seller takes personal checks, the item's description usually states how long the seller will wait for the check to clear before shipping the item. Unfortunately, that means that while the seller is waiting for your check to clear, your merchandise is collecting dust in a box somewhere. This is no fun for you or for the seller. Cashier's checks are available at your bank but often cost much more than a money order. It's not worth the extra money — have fun and buy more eBay items instead.

Before you send a personal check, make sure that you have enough money to cover your purchase. A bounced check can earn you negative feedback — too many negative transactions will bounce you off eBay.

The good news about checks is that you can track whether or not they've been cashed. Personal checks leave a paper trail that you can follow if a problem occurs later on.

The bad news about checks is that you're revealing personal information, such as your bank account number, to a stranger.

✔ **C.O.D.:** No, I'm not talking about codfish. I'm talking about *Cash on Delivery.* As a buyer, you may like the idea that you have to pay for an item only if it shows up. But paying C.O.D. has two problems:

- You have to have the money on hand — the exact amount. When was the last time any of us had exact change for anything?

- Even if you have exact change, if you're not around when the item's delivered, you're out of luck.

If you miss Mr. C.O.D., the shipment heads back to Bolivia or Oblivion or wherever it came from, never to be seen again. And what do you get? A lot of angry e-mails and maybe some negative feedback. No wonder sellers rarely use this option.

Most business at eBay is conducted in U.S. dollars. If you happen to buy an item from an international seller, you may need to convert American dollars into another currency. eBay has a currency converter. Type the following URL in your browser: `pages.ebay.com/services/buyandsell/currencyconverter.html`. Just select your choice of currency, type in the amount, and click Perform Currency Conversion.

Never use a form of payment that doesn't let you keep a paper trail. (Read into this: **Don't Wire Money!**) If a seller asks for cash, quote Nancy Reagan — just say no. Occasionally, I hear of international buyers sending U.S. greenbacks in the mail. But, if a seller asks for cash, chances are that you may never see the item or your money again. And, if a seller asks you to send your payment to a post office box, get a phone number. Many legitimate sellers use post office boxes, but so do the bad guys.

Using an escrow service

Even though most sales at eBay are for items that cost $100 or less, using an escrow service comes in handy on occasion — like when you buy a big-ticket item or something extremely rare. *Escrow* is a service that allows a buyer and seller to protect a transaction by placing the money in the hands of a neutral third party until a specified set of conditions are met. Sellers note in their item descriptions if they're willing to accept escrow. If you're nervous about sending a lot of money to someone you don't really know (like a user named Clumsy who has only two feedback comments and is shipping you bone china from Broken Hill, Australia), consider using an escrow company.

Using an escrow company is worthwhile only if the item you're bidding on is expensive, rare, or fragile, or traveling a long distance. If you're spending less than $200 for the item, I recommend that you purchase insurance from your shipper instead — just in case. Remember, with purchases under $200, you're also protected against fraud through eBay. (You may be protected up to $500 if you pay through PayPal — see the section "Payment methods" section, earlier in this chapter.)

eBay has a partnership with Escrow.com that handles eBay auction escrow sales in Canada and the U.S. After an auction closes, the buyer sends the payment to the escrow company. After the escrow company receives the money, it e-mails the seller to ship the merchandise. After the buyer receives the item, he or she has an agreed-on period of time (normally two business days) to look it over and let the escrow service know that all's well. If everything's okay, the escrow service sends the payment to the seller. If the buyer is unhappy with the item, he or she must ship it back to the seller. When the escrow service receives word from the seller that the item has been returned, the service returns the payment to the buyer (minus the escrow company's handling fee).

Before you start an escrow transaction, make sure that you and the seller agree on these terms (use e-mail to sort it out). Here are three questions about escrow that you should know the answers to before you bid:

- ✔ Who pays the escrow fee? (Normally, the buyer does, though sometimes the buyer and seller split the cost.)
- ✔ How long is the inspection period? (Routinely, it's two business days after receipt of the merchandise.)
- ✔ Who pays for return shipping if the item is rejected? (The buyer, usually.)

If you use a credit card or bank wire, you can pay return shipping costs right from your computer. If you're not comfortable giving your credit card number online, you can print out the escrow company's credit card form and fax it to the company.

Shipping and insurance costs

Don't let the sale go down with the shipping. Most auction descriptions end with "buyer to pay shipping charges." If the item is not an odd shape, excessively large, or fragile, experienced sellers calculate the shipping based on Priority Mail at the U.S. Postal Service, which is the unofficial eBay standard. Expect to pay $3.85 for the first pound and another $0.45 for tracking the item.

It has also become somewhat routine for the seller to add about a dollar for packing materials like paper, bubble wrap, tape, and such. A dollar or so is a reasonable handling charge because the cost of these items can add up over time.

You may come across sellers trying to nickel-and-dime their way to a fortune by jacking up the prices on shipping to ridiculous proportions. If you have a question about shipping costs, ask before you bid on the item.

Before bidding on big stuff, like a barber's chair or a sofa, check for something in the item description that says "Buyer Pays Actual Shipping Charges." When you see that, always e-mail the seller prior to your bid to find out what those shipping charges would be to your home. On larger items, you may need to factor in packing and crating charges. The seller may also suggest a specific shipping company.

As the bumper sticker says, (ahem) *stuff* happens — sometimes to the stuff you buy. But before you give up and just stuff it, consider insuring it. eBay transactions sometimes involve two types of insurance that may have an impact on your pocketbook:

✔ **Shipping insurance:** This insurance covers your item as it travels through the U.S. Postal Service, UPS, FedEx, or any of the other carriers.

Some savvy sellers have signed up with a company called Package In-Transit Coverage, which insures all their packages through an annual policy. This way the seller doesn't have to stand in line at the post office to get the insurance stamp from the clerk. The seller logs the packages and reports on them on a monthly basis. Sellers will let you know that they use this service when they ship your item.

Although many sellers offer shipping insurance as an option, others don't bother because if the price of the item is low, they'd rather refund your money and keep you happy than go through all that insurance paperwork. Don't forget that if you want shipping insurance, you pay for it. (See Chapter 12 for details on shipping insurance.)

✔ **Fraud insurance:** eBay provides some nominal insurance against fraud, eBay's Fraud Protection Program. eBay's Fraud Protection insurance pays up to $175 (a maximum of $200 minus a $25 deductible). So if you file a $50 claim, you get $25. If you file a $5,000 claim, you still only get $175. (All the details of this type of insurance are covered in Chapter 16.) Remember if you pay via PayPal, you may be covered for purchases up to $500.

Placing Your Bid

Okay, you've found the perfect item to track (say a really classy Elvis Presley wristwatch), and it's in your price range. You're more than interested — you're ready to bid. If this were a live auction, some stodgy-looking guy in a gray suit would see you nod your head and start the bidding at, say, $2. Then some woman with a severe hairdo would yank on her ear, and the Elvis watch would jump to $3.

eBay reality is more like this: You're sitting at home in your fuzzy slippers, sipping coffee in front of the computer; all the other bidders are cruising cyberspace in their pajamas, too. You just can't see 'em. (Be real thankful for little favors.)

When you're ready to jump into the eBay fray, you can find the bidding form (shown in Figure 6-5) at the bottom of the auction item page (or click the Place Bid button at the top of the auction page). When you get to the bottom of the page, if the item includes a Buy It Now option, you see that next to the bid form.

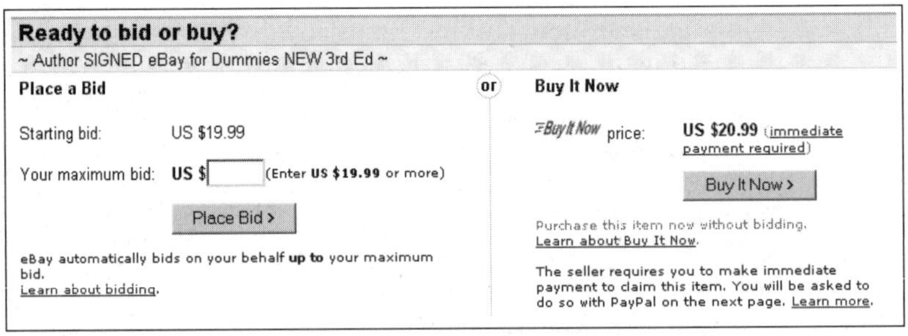

Figure 6-5:
You can find the bidding form at the bottom of every auction page.

Ready to bid or buy?
~ Author SIGNED eBay for Dummies NEW 3rd Ed ~

Place a Bid   (or)   **Buy It Now**

Starting bid: US $19.99

Your maximum bid: **US $** [____] (Enter US $19.99 or more)

[Place Bid >]

eBay automatically bids on your behalf **up to** your maximum bid.
Learn about bidding.

≡*Buy It Now* price: **US $20.99** (immediate payment required)

[Buy It Now >]

Purchase this item now without bidding.
Learn about Buy It Now.

The seller requires you to make immediate payment to claim this item. You will be asked to do so with PayPal on the next page. Learn more.

To fill out the bidding form and place a bid, first make sure that you're registered (see Chapter 2 for details) and then follow these steps. After you make your first bid on an item, you can instantly get to auctions you're bidding on from your My eBay page. (If you need some tips on how to set up My eBay, see Chapter 4.)

1. **Enter your maximum bid in the appropriate box.**

   The bid needs to be higher than the current minimum bid.

2. **If this is a Multiple Item auction, enter the quantity of items that you're bidding on.**

   (If it's not a Multiple Item auction, the quantity is always 1.) Figure 6-6 shows a Multiple Item auction bidding form.

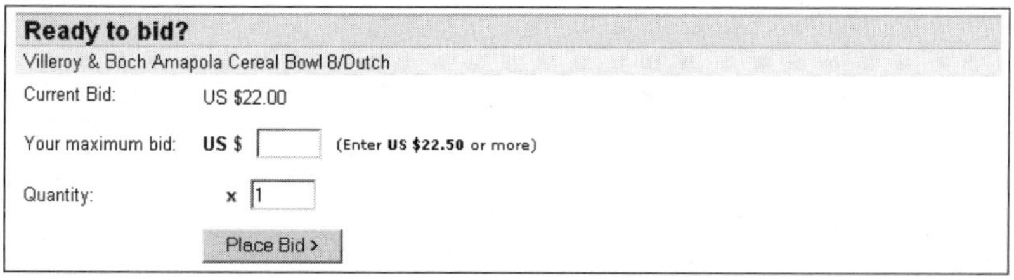

Figure 6-6:
The Multiple
Item auction
bidding form
requires you
to enter the
quantity of
the items.

Ready to bid?

Villeroy & Boch Amapola Cereal Bowl 8/Dutch

Current Bid:	US $22.00
Your maximum bid:	US $ [　　　] (Enter **US $22.50** or more)
Quantity:	x [1]

Place Bid >

You don't need to put in the dollar sign but do use a decimal point — unless you really *want* to pay $1,049.00 instead of $10.49. If you make a mistake with an incorrect decimal point, you can retract your bid (see "Retracting your bid" later in this chapter).

3. **Click Place Bid.**

   The Review Bid page appears on your screen, filling it with a wealth of legalese. This is your last chance to change your mind: Do you really want the item, and can you really buy it? The bottom line is this: If you bid on it and you win, you buy it. eBay really means it.

4. **At this point, you have to sign in if you haven't already. If you're signed in, skip to Step 5.**

5. **If you agree to the terms, click Submit.**

   After you agree, the Bid Confirmation screen appears.

When you first start out on eBay, I suggest that you start with a *token bid* — a small bid that won't win you the auction but that can help you keep tabs on the auction's progress.

After you bid on an item, the item number and title appear on your My eBay page, listed under (big surprise) Items I'm Bidding On, as shown in Figure 6-7. (See Chapter 4 for more information on My eBay.) The Items I'm Bidding On list makes tracking your auction (or auctions, if you're bidding on multiple items) easy.

eBay sends you an e-mail confirming your bid. However, eBay's mail server can be as slow as a tree-sloth marathon (yours would be too if you had a few million auctions to keep track of), so don't rely on eBay to keep track of your auctions. After all, this is your money at stake.

Items I'm Bidding On (4 Items)   ▶See totals | All item details 🔼 ➖

Items that you are currently winning are green and bold, those that you are **not** currently winning are red.

Item #	Start Price	Current Price	My Max Bid	Qty	# of Bids	Start Date	(PST) End Date	Time Left
McQUEEN KINGDOM GIFT SET! NEW! NO RESERVE								
2958802796	$3.00	$3.00	$3.00	1	1	Oct-18	Oct-21 20:15:33	2d 2h 16m
coiner "Rouge Baiser" signed Gruau (reserve price not yet met)								
3632455011	$1.00	$1.00	$2.51	1	1	Oct-17	Oct-24 11:30:25	4d 17h 31m
Gay Parisienne Barbie 1959 Repro Doll								
2958713804	$19.99	$21.55	$21.05	1	2	Oct-18	Oct-25 11:55:20	5d 17h 56m
DARLING ENESCO COLLECTIBLE/PIGGY BANK/BANK								
3248225137	$0.99	$0.99	$2.01	1	1	Oct-17	Oct-27 17:30:00	8d 0h 30m

Totals	Start Price	Current Price	My Max Bid	Total Qty	# of Bids			
All items	$24.98	$26.54	$28.57	4	5			
Items that I'm winning	$3.99	$3.99	$5.01	2	2			

Figure 6-7: Keep track of items you're bidding on right from your My eBay page.

REMEMBER

eBay considers a bid on an item to be a binding contract. You can save yourself a lot of heartache if you make a promise to yourself — *never bid on an item you don't intend to buy* — and keep to it. Don't make practice bids, assuming that because you're new to eBay, you can't win; if you do that, you'll probably win simply because you've left yourself open to Murphy's Law. Therefore, before you go to the bidding form, be sure that you're in this auction for the long haul and make yourself another promise — *figure out the maximum you're willing to spend* — and stick to it. (Read the section "The Agony (?) of Buyer's Remorse," later in this chapter, for doleful accounts of what can happen if you bid idly or get buyer's remorse.)

Bidding to the Max: Proxy Bidding

When you make a maximum bid on the bidding form, you actually make several small bids — again and again — until the bidding reaches where you told it to stop. For example, if the current bid is up to $19.99 and you put in a maximum of $45.02, your bid automatically increases incrementally so that you're ahead of the competition — at least until someone else's maximum bid exceeds yours. Basically, you bid by *proxy,* which means that your bid rises incrementally in response to other bidders' bids.

No one else knows for sure whether you're bidding by proxy, and no one knows how high your maximum bid is. And the best part is that you can be out having a life of your own while the proxy bid happens automatically. Buyers and sellers have no control over the increments (appropriately called *bid increments)* that eBay sets. The bid increment is the amount of money by which a bid is raised, and eBay's system can work in mysterious ways. The current maximum bid can jump up a nickel or a quarter or even an Andrew Jackson, but there is a method to the madness, even though you may not think so. eBay uses a *bid-increment formula,* which uses the current high bid to determine how much to increase the bid increment. For example:

- ✔ A 5-quart bottle of cold cream has a current high bid of $14.95. The bid increment is $0.50 — meaning that if you bid by proxy, your proxy will bid $15.45.

- ✔ But a 5-ounce can of top-notch caviar has a high bid of $200. The bid increment is $2.50. If you choose to bid by proxy, your proxy will bid $202.50.

Table 6-1 shows you what kind of magic happens when you put the proxy system and a bid-increment formula together in the same cyber-room.

Table 6-1			**Proxy Bidding and Bid Increments**	
Current Bid	*Bid Increment*	*Minimum Bid*	*eBay Auctioneer*	*Bidders*
$2.50	$0.25	$2.75	"Do I hear $2.75?"	Joe Bidder tells his proxy that his maximum bid is $8. He's the current high bidder at $2.75.
$2.75	$0.25	$3	"Do I hear $3?"	You tell your proxy your maximum bid is $25 and take a nice, relaxing bath while your proxy calls out your $3 bid, making you the current high bidder.
$3	$0.25	$3.25	"I hear $3 from proxy. Do I proxy hear $3.25?"	Joe Bidder's proxy bids $3.25, and while Joe Bidder is out walking his dog, he becomes the high bidder.
A heated bidding war ensues between Joe Bidder's proxy and your proxy while the two of you go on with your lives. The bid increment inches from $0.25 to $0.50 as the current high bid increases.				
$7.50	$0.50	$8	"Do I hear $8?"	Joe Bidder's proxy calls out $8, his final offer.
$8	$0.50	$8.50	"The bid is at $8. Do I hear $8.50?"	Your proxy calls out $8.50 on your behalf, and having outbid your opponent, you win the auction.

Specialized Auction Categories

After you get the hang of bidding at eBay, you may venture to the specialized auction areas. You can purchase fine art from eBay's Live Auctions, a car or car parts and accessories from eBay Motors, or your own piece of land or a new home in the Real Estate category. eBay is always adding new specialty areas, so be sure to check the announcements as well as the home page.

Should you reach the big-time bidding, be aware that if you bid over $15,000 in an auction, you *must* register a credit card with eBay. All items in the special categories are searchable in eBay's search engine, so don't worry about missing your dream Corvette when you use the Search page.

eBay Motors

Visiting the automotive area of eBay is an auto enthusiast's dream. You can also find some great deals in used cars, and eBay offers these creative ways to make buying vehicles of all shapes and sizes (as well as the largest array of parts you'll find anywhere on the planet) easy for you. Visit eBay Motors, by clicking the eBay Motors link on the home page or by going to `www.ebaymotors.com`.

- ✔ **Search engine:** If you want to search for cars without coming up with hundreds of die-cast vehicles, eBay motors has its own search available from the eBay Motors home page.

- ✔ **Vehicle shipping:** If you don't want to drive across the country to pick up your new vehicle, you can have it shipped through Dependable Auto shippers. Check online for a free quote.

- ✔ **Inspections:** Many used-car sellers take advantage of the inspection service available through Pep Boys. Pep Boys offer a comprehensive inspection covering the mechanical condition and cosmetic appearance and a detailed inspection report. Car auctions from sellers who have their cars inspected have their auctions listed with an Inspection icon.

- ✔ **Lemon Check:** With the vehicle's VIN (Vehicle Identification Number), you can run a lemon check right from eBay Motors through CARFAX.

- ✔ **Escrow:** Escrow.com is one of the safest ways to purchase a vehicle online. Escrow.com verifies and secures the buyer's payment and releases payment to the seller only after the buyer inspects and is completely satisfied with the vehicle.

Buyer's remorse can pay off

Sometimes buyer's remorse does pay off. I know one eBay buyer who got a serious case of remorse after winning an auction. She decided to do the right thing and pay for the item even though she didn't want it. After receiving the item, she turned around and *sold* it on eBay for triple what she paid. If you really don't want the item, think like a seller — see whether you can turn a horrible mistake into a profitable venture. For more information on the benefits of selling, take a look at Chapter 9.

eBay Live Auctions

If I don't check out eBay Live Auctions at least once a month, I feel like I'm missing something. eBay Live Auctions is the very cool hub for auction houses and dealers from around the world. Here you find items that are so rare, you'll never find 'em anywhere else. I just wasted (er, *enriched*) about half an hour of my life looking over some wonderful things up for auction. I saw autographs from Abraham Lincoln, illuminated manuscripts from the 1700s, and signed letters from Albert Schweitzer — how cool. I can't afford any of these items, but perusing eBay Live Auctions is like spending time in the fine galleries of the world — it's my version of virtual window-shopping!

Live Auctions allows you to participate in real-time auctions as they happen at the finest auction houses around the world. You can get to eBay Live Auctions through the eBay home page (it's listed at the bottom of the categories list). Remember to read the terms carefully, because often you must pay a bidder's premium (an additional amount added to your bid of up to 20 percent) on Live Auction items.

You may find yourself (or fantasize about) bidding against other famous people for these amazing items — that, in itself, is a lot of fun! If you don't have the money at the moment to buy one of these fine items, you can just click View Live, and your computer gives you a real time view of the auction. Take a look at Figure 6-8; it's an item I'd love to have, but just can't afford!

If you think that there's the slightest chance that you may want to bid on something, be sure to register for the auction first. You must register in advance to participate in eBay Live Auctions. There's nothing worse than not being registered and seeing an item that you thought you couldn't afford go on the block, observing very few bids, and watching it sell for a price within your range.

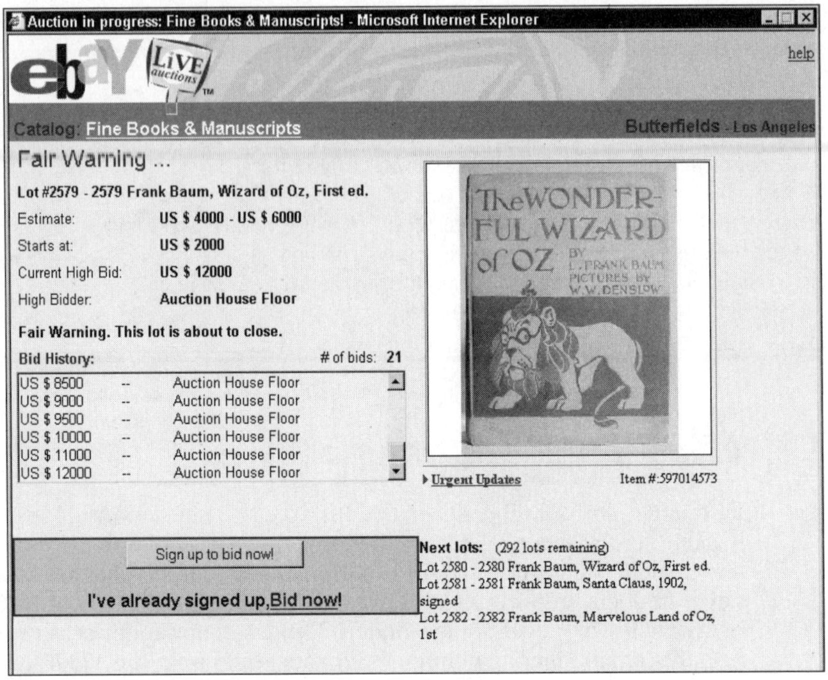

Figure 6-8:
A screen
from one of
Butterfield's
Live Auction
items,
tempting
me to bid.

Making purchases on the spot!

There's more to eBay than auctions. Aside from the Buy It Now offer available on some auctions, eBay holds venues for various items that you can buy *right now!*

eBay Stores

The newly instituted eBay Stores are a quick, easy, and convenient way to find items for sale that you can buy now. A large number of eBay sellers have opened eBay stores as an inexpensive way to display more items for sale. They're offered a much lower listing fee for their items, only five cents, and the items stay in their stores for as long as they want. The lower listing fees are quite a savings over the fees for listing an item for auction, and sellers often pass the savings onto you.

When you're perusing the auctions at eBay, look for the little red Stores tag next to a seller's name. If you click the tag, you're magically transported to the seller's virtual storefront at eBay. Figure 6-9 shows you the eBay Stores hub. You get there by clicking the eBay Stores link on the upper-left side of the home page.

Figure 6-9:
The eBay
Stores
hub — from
here, you
can browse
categories,
visit stores,
or search
all items
in all eBay
Stores.

eBay Stores have a separate search engine from eBay auctions. If you don't find the item you're looking for at eBay auctions, look at the column on the left side of the page. Under the Related Stores heading is a list of eBay stores that may contain the item you're looking for and a Search Stores link. Click the link, and eBay performs the same search for you in all eBay Stores.

The Agony (?) of Buyer's Remorse

Maybe you're used to going into a shopping mall and purchasing something that you're not sure you like. What's the worst that could happen? You end up back at the mall, receipt in hand, returning the item. Not so on eBay. Even if you realize you already have a purple feather boa in your closet that's just like the one you won yesterday on eBay, deciding that you don't want to go through with a transaction *is* a big deal. Not only can it earn you some nasty feedback, but it can also give you the reputation of a deadbeat.

It would be a shame to float around eBay with the equivalent of a scarlet *D* (for *deadbeat*) above your User ID. Okay, eBay uses a kinder term — *non-paying bidder* — but for many members, it boils down to the same thing. If you won an auction and have to back out of your obligation as the winner — even through no fault of your own — you need some info that can keep you in good (well, okay, *better*) standing. Look no further; you've found it.

After the auction: Side deals or personal offers?

If a bidder is outbid on an item that he or she really wants or if the auction's reserve price isn't met, the bidder may send an e-mail to the seller and see if the seller is willing to make another deal. Maybe the seller has another similar item or is willing to sell the item directly rather than run a whole new auction. You need to know that this could happen — but eBay doesn't sanction this outside activity.

If the original auction winner doesn't go through with the deal, the seller can make a Second Chance offer. This is a legal eBay-sanctioned second chance for underbidders (unsuccessful bidders) who participated in the auction.

Any side deals other than Second Chance offers are unprotected. My friend Jack collects autographed final scripts from hit television sitcoms. So when the curtain fell on *Seinfeld,* he had to have a script. Not surprisingly, he found one on eBay with a final price tag that was way out of his league. But he knew that by placing a bid,

someone else with a signed script to sell might see his name and try to make a deal. And he was right.

After the auction closed, he received an e-mail from a guy who worked on the final show and had a script signed by all the actors. He offered it to Jack for $1,000 less than the final auction price at eBay. Tempted as he was to take the offer, Jack understood that eBay's rules and regulations wouldn't help him out if the deal turned sour. He was also aware that he wouldn't receive the benefit of feedback (which is the pillar of the eBay community) or any eBay Fraud Protection insurance for the transaction.

If you even *think about* making a side deal, remember that not only does eBay *strictly* prohibit this activity, but eBay can also suspend you if you are reported for making a side deal. And if you're the victim of a side-deal scam, eBay's rules and regulations don't offer you any protection. My advice? Watch out!

Retracting your bid

Remember, many states consider your bid a binding contract, just like any other contract. You can't retract your bid unless one of these three outstandingly unusual circumstances applies:

- ✔ If your bid is clearly a typographical error (you submitted a bid for $4,567 when you really meant $45.67), you may retract your bid. If this occurs, you should reenter the correct bid amount immediately.

  You won't get any sympathy if you try to retract an $18.25 bid by saying you meant to bid $15.25, so review your bid before you send it.

- ✔ You have tried to contact the seller to answer questions on the item, and he or she doesn't reply.

- ✔ If the seller substantially changes the description of an item after you place a bid (the description of the item changes from "can of tennis balls" to "a tennis ball," for example), you may retract your bid.

If you simply must retract a bid, try to do so long before the auction ends — and have a good reason for your retraction. eBay users are understanding, up to a point. If you have a good explanation, you should come out of the situation all right. So admit you've made a mistake.

If you've made an error, you must retract your bid prior to the last 12 hours of the auction. At this point, a retraction removes all bids you have placed in the auction. Mistakes or not, when you retract a bid that was placed within the last 12 hours of the listing, only the most recent bid you made is retracted — your bids placed prior to the last 12 hours are still active.

Here's how to retract a bid while the auction's still going on:

1. **Click the Services link on the main navigation bar.**

2. **Go to the Buying and Selling Tools area.**

   Click the Go Directly to Buying and Selling Tools link.

3. **Scroll down to Buyer Tools and click Retract My Bid.**

   You may have to sign in again; when you do, the Bid Retraction page appears.

4. **Read the legalese and scroll down the page. Enter the item number of the auction you're retracting your bid from. Then open the drop-down menu and select one of the three legitimate reasons for retracting your bid.**

5. **Click the Retract Bid button.**

   You receive a confirmation of your bid retraction via e-mail. Keep a copy of it until the auction is completed.

The seller may send you an e-mail to ask for a more lengthy explanation of your retraction, especially if the item was a hot seller that received a lot of bids. You may also get e-mails from other bidders. Keep your replies courteous. After you retract one bid on an item, all your lower bids on that item are also retracted (unless the retraction is done within the last 12 hours), and your retraction goes into the bidding history — another good reason to have a really good reason for the retraction. The number of bids you've retracted also goes on your feedback rating scorecard.

Avoiding deadbeat (non-paying bidder) status

Some bidders are more like kidders — they bid even though they have no intention of buying a thing. But those folks don't last long on eBay because of all the negative feedback they get. In fact, when honest eBay members spot these ne'er-do-wells, they often post the deadbeats' User IDs on eBay's message boards. Some eBay members have created entire Web sites to warn others about dealing with the deadbeats . . . ahem . . . *non-paying bidders.* (Civilized but chilly, isn't it?)

Exceptions to the deadbeat (er, sorry, *non-paying bidder*) rule may include the following human mishaps:

✔ A death in the family

✔ Computer failure

✔ A huge misunderstanding

If you have a good reason to call off your purchase, make sure that the seller knows about it. The seller is the only one who can excuse you from the sale.

If you receive a non-paying bidder warning but you've paid for the item, eBay requires proof of payment. That would include a copy of the check (front and back) or money order, a copy of the payment confirmation from PayPal (or other online payment service), or an e-mail from the seller acknowledging receipt of payment. If the seller excused you from the auction, you need to forward the e-mail with all headers.

✔ Fax hard copies to eBay at 888-379-6251.

✔ Mail copies of the documents to

> eBay, Inc.
> Bidder Appeal Dept.
> P.O. Box 1469
> Draper, UT 84020

✔ Send the e-mail via an online form. Go to `pages.ebay.com/help/policies/appeal-npb.html`, click the link to the online form, and plead your case.

Here's how to plead your case if you've received a non-paying bidder warning:

1. **Click the Help link on the main navigation bar.**

   You're taken to the Help Overview page.

2. **Click the Rules and Safety link in the subnavigation bar.**

   You're taken to the Rules & Safety Overview page.

3. **Scroll down to the Policies heading and click the Non-Paying Bidder Policy link.**

   You're taken to the Non-Paying Bidder Program page, where you can read eBay's policy and instructions on how to make an appeal.

4. Scroll down the page and click the Non-Paying Bidder Appeal Form link.

You're taken to the Non-Paying Bidder Appeal form.

5. Sign In again.

For your security, this is an additional sign-in area.

6. In the Message box, write the reasons for your appeal and also include the following information:

- The transaction number for the item

- Any supporting information you have to plead your case

7. Review the information you've given. If you have to change anything you've written, click the Clear All Data button and start over.

8. Click the Send Inquiry button.

All done. Now sit back and cross your fingers.

There's no guarantee that your non-paying bidder appeal will be accepted. eBay will contact you after an investigation and let you know whether your appeal was successful.

eBay has a message for non-paying bidders: The policy is *three strikes and you're out.* After the first complaint about a non-paying (deadbeat) bidder, eBay gives the bad guy or gal a warning. After the third offense, the non-paying bidder is suspended from eBay for good and becomes *NARU* (Not A Registered User). Nobody's tarred and feathered, but you probably won't see hide nor hair of that user again on eBay.

Chapter 7

Power-Bidding Strategies

*W*hen I travel the country teaching classes about eBay, I speak to so many people who find an item at eBay, bid on it, and at the last minute — the last hour or the last day — are outbid. Sad and dejected, they feel like real losers.

You're not a loser if you lost at eBay. You just don't know the fine art of sneaky bidding. Sneaky bidding is my way of saying *educated* bidding.

Sports teams study their rivals, and political candidates scout out what the opposition is doing. Bidding in competition against other bidders is just as serious an enterprise. Follow the tips in this chapter and see if you can come up with a strong bidding strategy of your own. Feel free to e-mail me with any scathingly brilliant plans; I'm always open to new theories.

Get to Know the High Bidder

The User ID of the person the item would belong to if the auction ended right now is listed on the auction item page (assuming someone has bid on the item). Take a look at this name because you may see it again in auctions for similar items. If the high bidder has lots of feedback, he or she may know the ropes — and be back to fight if you up the ante.

You can use the By Bidder search option, shown in Figure 7-1 on the eBay Search page, to find out the bidder's recent auction experience. If you're bidding on an item, conducting a bidder search can be a valuable asset: You can size up your competition.

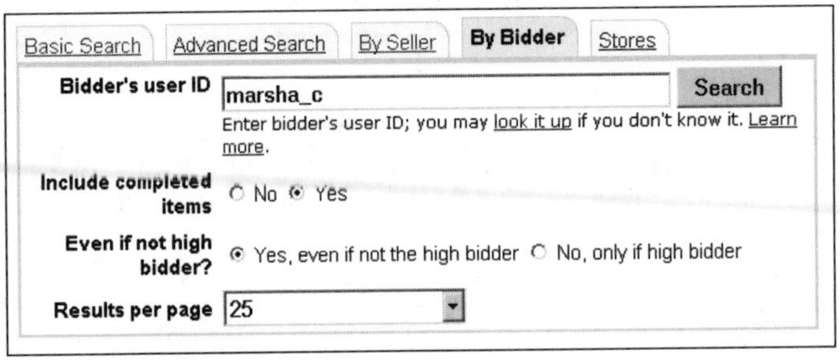

Figure 7-1:
Use a By
Bidder
search to
get an idea
of the com-
petition's
bidding
patterns.

| Basic Search | Advanced Search | By Seller | **By Bidder** | Stores |

Bidder's user ID | marsha_c | **Search**

Enter bidder's user ID; you may <u>look it up</u> if you don't know it. <u>Learn more</u>.

Include completed items ○ No ⦿ Yes

Even if not high bidder? ⦿ Yes, even if not the high bidder ○ No, only if high bidder

Results per page | 25

To get the skinny on a bidder, here's the move:

1. **Type in the User ID of the bidder you want to search for.**

2. **If you want to see auctions that this user has bid on in the past, select the Yes option button on the Include Completed Items line.**

   You should check completed auctions. They give you a sense of how often and at what time of day the user participates in auctions.

   Remember that eBay has a 30-day limit on the auction information it returns, so don't expect to see results from a year ago. By clicking the item number in your search results, you can see at what times your main competition tends to bid and then bid when you know those folks won't be looking.

3. **Tell eBay whether you also want to see the person's bid even if he or she is not the high bidder.**

   Selecting Yes means that you want to see the bidder's activity in every auction, even if the person is not the *current* high bidder. Selecting No limits the search to auctions where the bidder is the current top dog. I think you should check all of the bidder's auctions to see how aggressively he or she bids on items. You can also see how badly a bidder wants specific items.

   If the bidder was bidding on the same item in the past that you're both interested in now, you can also get a fairly good idea of how high that person is willing to go for the item.

4. **Choose the number of items you want to see per page.**

5. **Click Search.**

You may be tempted to try to contact a bidder you're competing with so you can get information about the person more easily. This is not only bad form but could also get you suspended. Don't do it.

AUCTION ANECDOTE

The tale of the 3-plus-negative seller

A friend of mine took a risk and bid on an old Winchester rifle (now a banned item — see Chapter 9 for a rundown of what you're allowed and not allowed to sell at eBay) without reading the seller's feedback. The seller had a (+3) next to his User ID, which is an okay rating. Good thing my friend lost the auction. It turned out that the seller had a whopping 20 negative feedback messages. He had 23 positives, mostly posted by suspicious-looking names. Repeat after me: *Always read the feedback comments!*

Find Out an Item's Bidding History

The bidding *history,* shown on the auction item page, lists everybody who is bidding on an item. You can see how often and at what time bids are placed, but you can't see *how much* each bidder bids until the auction ends. Look at Figure 7-2 to see a typical bidding history list. You can see bid amounts because this auction has ended.

eBay.com Bid History for
Bob Hope SIGNED 1st Ed Book ~DON'T SHOOT~ OOP (Item # 3339693778)

Currently	$132.50	First bid	$0.99
Quantity	1	# of bids	17
Time left	Auction has ended.		
Started	Jul-28-03 15:49:29 PDT		
Ends	Aug-04-03 15:49:29 PDT		
Seller (Rating)	marsha_c (2376 ★) me stores		

View page with email addresses (Accessible by Seller only) Learn more.

Bidding History (Highest bids first)

User ID	Bid Amount	Date of Bid
(15 ☆)	$132.50	Aug-04-03 15:48:22 PDT
(6)	$130.00	Aug-03-03 23:04:26 PDT
(15 ☆)	$125.00	Aug-03-03 20:37:44 PDT
(6)	$125.00	Aug-03-03 23:04:06 PDT
(6)	$110.00	Aug-03-03 23:03:33 PDT
(6)	$100.00	Jul-29-03 09:28:04 PDT
(15 ☆)	$100.00	Aug-03-03 20:36:18 PDT
(56 ★) stores	$65.00	Jul-30-03 18:48:48 PDT

Figure 7-2: The bidding history tells you the date and time of day at which the bidders placed their bids.

Pay attention to the times at which bidders are placing their bids, and you may find that, like many eBay users, the people bidding in this auction seem to be creatures of habit — making their bids about once a day and at a particular time of day. They may be logging on before work, during lunch, or after work. Whatever their schedules, you have great info at your disposal in the event that a bidding war breaks out: Just bid after your competition traditionally logs out, and you increase your odds of winning the auction.

Early in an auction, there may not be much of a bidding history for an item, but that doesn't mean you can't still check out the dates and times a bidder places bids. You can also tell if a bidder practices *sniping* (discussed later in this chapter) if his or her bid is in the last few minutes of the auction. You may have a fight on your hands if the bidder does do sniping.

Strategies to Help You Outsmart the Competition

Your two cents does matter — at least at eBay. Here's why: Many eBay members tend to round off their bids to the nearest dollar figure. Some choose nice, familiar coin increments like 25, 50, or 75 cents. But the most successful eBay bidders have found that adding two or three cents to a routine bid can mean the difference between winning and losing. So I recommend that you make your bids in oddish figures, like $15.02 or $45.57, as an inexpensive way to edge out your competition. For the first time ever, your two cents may actually pay off!

That's just one of the many strategies to get you ahead of the rest of the bidding pack without paying more than you should. *Note:* The strategies in this section are for bidders who are tracking an item over the course of a week or so, so be sure you have time to track the item and plan your next moves. Also, get a few auctions under your belt before you throw yourself into the middle of a bidding war.

Multiple Item (Dutch) auction strategy

Multiple Item (Dutch) auctions (explained in Chapter 1) are funky. Yes, that's a technical term that means that a Multiple Item auction strategy is a little different. After all, each winner pays the same amount for the item, and Multiple Item auctions don't have a super-secret reserve price.

But *winning* a Multiple Item auction isn't all that different from winning other auctions. Therefore, wait until the closing minutes of the auction to bid and then follow my sage advice for optimum success.

Here are the key things to remember about a Multiple Item auction:

- ✔ **The seller must sell all the items at the *lowest winning price* at the end of the auction, no matter what.**

- ✔ **Winners are based on the *highest* bids received.** If you up the ante, you could win the auction and pay only the *lowest winning price,* which may be lower than your bid.

  Confused yet? Say the minimum bid for each of ten Elvis watches is $10, and 20 people bid at $10, each person bidding for one watch. The first ten bidders win the watch. But suppose you come along at the end of the auction and bid $15 as the 21st bidder. You get a watch (as do the first nine people who bid $10), *and* you get the watch for the lowest successful bid — which is $10! Get it?

- ✔ **Know where you stand in the pecking order.** You can see a list of high bidders (and their bids) on the auction page, so you always know where you stand in the pecking order.

- ✔ **Avoid being the lowest or the highest high bidder.** The highest bidder is sure to win, so the usual bidding strategy is to knock out the lowest high bidder. The lowest high bidder is said to be *on the bubble* and on the verge of losing the auction by a couple of pennies. To avoid being the bidder on the bubble, keep your bid just above the second-lowest winning bid.

- ✔ **If you want to buy more than one of an item up for auction, make sure you have that number of successful high bids as the auction draws to a close.** Huh? Remember, winners are based on the *highest* bids. If you're in a Multiple Item auction for ten items and place five $15 bids, nothing guarantees that you'll win five of the item. Nine other people who want the item could bid $20 apiece. Then they each win one of the items at $15, and you end up with only one of the item. (At least you still pay only $15 for it.)

Pirates of the Caribbean . . . or Carribean?

Just before the movie *Pirates of the Caribbean* premiered; Disneyland gave out exclusive movie posters to their visitors. My daughter, savvy eBayer that she is, snagged several copies to sell on the site. She listed them (one at a time) when the movie opened and couldn't get more than the starting bid of $9.99 for each of them.

When we searched eBay for *pirates poster*, we found that the very same posters listed with a misspelled title, Pirates of the Carribean, were selling for as high as $30 each. After selling out her initial stock, she found another seller that had 10 for sale — in one auction — with the proper spelling. She bought those as well (for $5.00 each) and sold them with misspelled titles on the site for between $15 and $27!

Bidding strategies eBay doesn't talk about

Here's a list of Do's and Don'ts that can help you win your item. Of course, some of these tips *are* eBay-endorsed, but I had to get you to notice what I had to say somehow.

✔ **Don't bid early and high.** Bidding early *and high* shows that you have a clear interest in the item. It also shows that you're a rookie, apt to make mistakes. If you bid early and high, you may give away just how much you want the item.

  Of course, a higher bid does mean more bucks for the seller and a healthy cut for the middleman. So it's no big mystery that many sellers recommend it. In fact, when you sell an item, you may want to encourage it too.

  If you must bid early and can't follow the auction action (you mean you have a life?), use software or an online sniping service. Then feel free to place your highest possible bid! You can find out more about that in Chapter 20.

✔ **Do wait and watch your auction.** If you're interested in an item and you have the time to watch it from beginning to end, I say that the best strategy is to wait. Mark the auction to Watch This Item on your My eBay page and remember to check it daily. But if you don't have the time, then go ahead — put in your maximum bid early and cross your fingers.

✔ **Don't freak out if you find yourself in a bidding war.** Don't keel over if, at the split second you're convinced that you're the high bidder with your $45.02, someone beats you out at $45.50.

  You can increase your maximum bid to $46.02, but if your bidding foe also has a maximum of $46.02, the tie goes to the person who put in the highest bid first. Bid as high as you're willing to go, but bid at the very end of the auction.

✔ **Do check the item's bidding history.** If you find yourself in a bidding war and want an item badly enough, check the bidding history and identify your fiercest competitor; then refer to the earlier section "Get to Know the High Bidder" for a pre-auction briefing.

  To get a pretty exact picture of your opponent's bidding habits, make special note of the times of day when he or she has bid on other auctions. You can adjust your bidding times accordingly.

✔ **Do remember that most deals go through without a problem.** The overwhelming majority of deals at eBay are closed with no trouble, which means that if the auction you're bidding in is typical and you come in second place, you've lost.

However, if the winning bidder backs out of the auction or the seller has more than one of the item, the seller *could* (but isn't obligated to) come to another bidder and offer to sell the item at the second bidder's price through eBay's Second Chance option. (See Chapter 13 for more details on this feature.)

Time Is Money: Strategy by the Clock

You can use different bidding strategies depending on how much time is left in an auction. By paying attention to the clock, you can learn about your competition, beat them out, and end up paying less for your item.

Most auctions at eBay run for a week; the auction item page always lists how much time is left. However, sellers can run auctions for as short as one day or as long as ten days. So synchronize your computer clock with eBay's master time and become the most precise eBay bidder around. Figure 7-3 shows eBay's Official Time page.

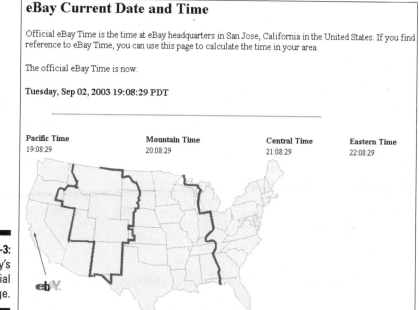

Figure 7-3:
eBay's
Official
Time page.

eBay Current Date and Time

Official eBay Time is the time at eBay headquarters in San Jose, California in the United States. If you find reference to eBay Time, you can use this page to calculate the time in your area.

The official eBay Time is now:

Tuesday, Sep 02, 2003 19:08:29 PDT

Pacific Time	Mountain Time	Central Time	Eastern Time
19:08:29	20:08:29	21:08:29	22:08:29

To synchronize your clock, make sure that you're logged on to the Internet and can easily access the eBay Web site. Then follow these steps:

1. **Go into your computer's Control Panel and double-click the icon that represents your system's date and time functions.**

2. **On the eBay Web site, go to the Site Map by clicking its link above the navigation bar on the top of every eBay page.**

3. **Click the eBay Official Time link.**

    This link is located at the bottom of the Browse column on the left side of the page.

4. **Check your computer's time against eBay's current time.**

5. **Click the minutes in your computer's clock and then click the Reload button (sometimes it's called Refresh) on your browser.**

    Clicking Reload ensures that you see the latest, correct time from eBay.

6. **Type in the minutes displayed on the eBay Official Time page as soon as the newly reloaded page appears.**

7. **Repeat Steps 5 and 6 to synchronize your computer's seconds display with eBay's.**

This process takes a little practice, but it can mean the difference between winning and losing an auction.

You don't need to worry about the hour display unless you don't mind your system clock displaying Pacific Time.

Most bidding at eBay goes on during East Coast work time and early evening hours, which gives you a leg up if you live out West. Night-owl bidders will find that after 10 p.m. Pacific Time (about 1 a.m. Eastern Time), lots of bargains are to be had. And believe it or not, lots of auctions end in the wee hours of the morning. Holidays are also great for bargains — especially Thanksgiving and the day after. While everyone is in the living room digesting and arguing about what to watch on TV, fire up eBay and be thankful for the great bargains you can win.

Using the lounging-around strategy

Sometimes the best strategy at the beginning of an auction is to do nothing at all. That's right; relax, take off your shoes, and loaf. Go ahead. You may want to make a *token bid* (the very lowest you are allowed) or mark the page to watch in your My eBay area. I generally take this attitude through the first six days of a week-long auction I want to bid on, and it works pretty well. Of course, I check in every day just to keep tabs on the items I'm watching in my My eBay page, and revise my strategy as time goes by.

The seller has the right to up his minimum bid — if his auction has received no bids — up to 12 hours before the auction ends. If the seller has set a ridiculously low minimum bid and then sees that the auction is getting no action, the seller may choose to up the minimum bid to protect his sale. By placing the minimum token bid when you first see the auction, you can foil a Buy It Now from another bidder (because Buy It Now is disabled after a bid has been placed) or prevent the seller from upping the minimum. If it's important enough, you can see whether the seller has done this in the past, by searching the Seller's completed auctions (see "Get to Know the High Bidder" earlier in this chapter to find out how to do this search). All preclosing changes are available for public view; just click Revised next to the word *Description* on the item page. See Figure 7-4 for a sample.

If you see an item that you absolutely must have, mark it to watch on your My eBay page (or make that token bid) and plan and revise your maximum bid as the auction goes on. I can't stress enough how important this is.

As you check back each day, take a look at the other bids and the high bidder. Is someone starting a bidding war? Look at the time that the competition is bidding and note patterns. Maybe at noon Eastern Time? During lunch? If you know what time your major competition is bidding, then when the time is right, you can safely bid after he or she does (preferably when your foe is stuck in rush-hour traffic).

If you play the wait-and-see method, you can decide if you really want to increase your bid or wait around for the item to show up again sometime. You may decide you really don't want the item after all. Or you may feel no rush because many sellers who offer multiple items put them up one at a time.

Figure 7-4:
This page shows the revisions made by the seller during this auction.

eb**a**Y®   home | sign out | services | site map | help ⓘ

| Browse | Search | Sell | My eBay | Community | Powered By IBM |

Item Revisions summary for item #2949092959

The seller has revised the following item information:

Date	Time	Revised Information
Sep-02-03	19:16:13 PDT	Description
Sep-02-03	19:17:32 PDT	Buy It Now Price Minimum Bid Price
Sep-02-03	19:19:12 PDT	Description

AUCTION ANECDOTE

The story of the Snipe sisters

Cory and Bonnie are sisters and avid eBay buyers. Bonnie collects vases. She had her eye on a Fenton Dragon Flies Ruby Verdena vase, but the auction closed while she was at work and didn't have access to a computer. Knowing that, sister Cory decided to snipe for it. With 37 seconds to go, she inserted the high bid on behalf of her sister. Bang, she was high bidder at $63. But, with 17 seconds left, another bidder sniped back and raised the price to $73. It was, of course, Bonnie, who had found a way to get access to a computer from where she was. Bonnie got the vase, and they both had a good laugh.

Using the beat-the-clock strategy

You should rev up your bidding strategy during the final 24 hours of an auction and decide, once and for all, whether you really *have* to have the item you've been eyeing. Maybe you put in a maximum bid of $45.02 earlier in the week. Now's the time to decide whether you're willing to go as high as $50.02. Maybe $56.03?

No one wants to spend the day in front of the computer (ask almost anyone who does). You can camp out by the refrigerator or at your desk or wherever you want to be. Just place a sticky note where you're likely to see it, reminding you of the exact time the auction ends. If you're not going to be near a computer when the auction closes, you can also use an automatic bidding software program to bid for you; see Chapter 20 for details.

In the last half hour

With a half hour left before the auction becomes ancient history, head for the computer and dig in for the last battle of the bidding war. I recommend that you log on to eBay about 10 to 15 minutes before the auction ends. The last thing you want to have happen is to get caught in Internet gridlock and not get access to the Web site. Go to the items you're watching and click the auction title.

With 10 minutes to go, if there's a lot of action on your auction, click Reload or Refresh every 30 seconds to get the most current info on how many people are bidding.

Sniping to the finish: The final minutes

The rapid-fire, final flurry of bidding is called *sniping*. Sniping is the fine art of waiting until the very last seconds of an eBay auction and then outbidding the current high bidder just in time. Of course, you've got to expect that the current high bidder is probably sniping back.

With a hot item, open a second window on your browser (by pressing the Ctrl key and the N key together), keep one open for bidding and the other open or constant reloading during the final few minutes. With the countdown at 60 seconds or less, make your final bid at the absolute highest amount you will pay for the item. The longer you can hold off — I'm talking down to around 20 seconds — the better. It all depends on the speed of your Internet connection, so practice on some small auctions so you know how much time to allow when you're bidding on your prize item. Keep reloading or refreshing your browser as fast as you can and watch the time tick to the end of the auction.

If you want to be truly fancy, you can open a third window (see Figure 7-5) and have a back-up high bid in case you catch another sniper swooping in on your item immediately after your first snipe. (I recently received an e-mail from one of my readers who used my somewhat paranoid method that she learned from a previous edition of this book — and by using the second snipe, she won her item!) You can avoid the third window routine if you've bid your highest bid with the first snipe. Then if you're outbid, you know that the item went for more than you were willing to pay. I know; it's some consolation, but not much.

Some eBay members consider the practice of sniping highly unseemly and uncivilized — like when dozens of parents used to mob the department store clerks to get to the handful of Cabbage Patch dolls that were just delivered. (Come to think of it, whatever happened to *those* collectibles?) Of course, sometimes a little uncivilized behavior can be a hoot.

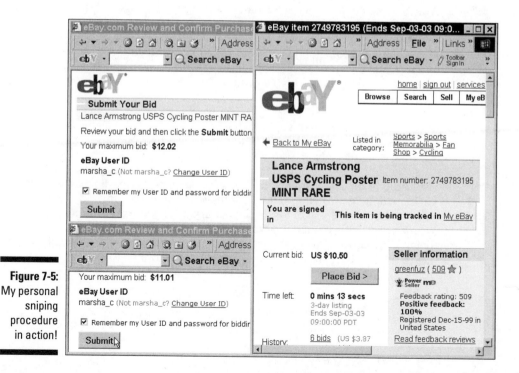

Figure 7-5: My personal sniping procedure in action!

I say that sniping is an addictive, fun part of life at eBay. And it's a blast. So my recommendation is that you try sniping. You're likely to benefit from the results and enjoy your eBay experience even more — especially if you're an adrenaline junkie.

Here's a list of things to keep in mind when you get ready to place your last bid:

- ✔ Know how high you're willing to go.

  If you know you're facing a lot of competition, figure out your highest bid to the penny. You should have already researched the item and know its value at this point. Raise your bid only to the level where you're sure you're getting a good return on your investment and don't go overboard. Certainly, if the item has some emotional value to you and you just have to have it, bid as high as you want. But remember, you'll have to pay the piper later. You win it, you own it!

- ✔ Know how fast (or slow) your Internet connection is.

- ✔ Remember, this is a game, and sometimes it's a game of chance, so don't lose heart if you lose the auction.

Although sellers love sniping because it drives up prices and bidders love it because it's fun, a sniper can ruin a week's careful work on an auction strategy. The most skillful snipers sneak in a bid so close to the end of the auction that you have no chance to counter-bid, which means you lose. Losing too often, especially to the same sniper, can be a drag.

If your Internet connection is slower than most, and you want to do some sniping, make your final bid two minutes before the auction ends and adjust the amount of the bid as high as you feel comfortable so you can beat out the competition.

If you can make the highest bid with just 20 seconds left, you most likely will win. With so many bids coming in the final seconds, your bid might be the last one eBay records.

This stuff is supposed to be fun, so don't lose perspective. If you can't afford an item, don't get caught up in a bidding war. Otherwise, the only person who wins is the seller. If you're losing sleep, barking at your cat, or biting your nails over any item, it's time to rethink what you're doing. Shopping at eBay is like being in a long line in a busy department store. If it's taking too much of your life or an item costs too much, be willing to walk away — or log off — and live to bid (or shop) another day.

Chapter 8

After You Win the Auction

*T*he thrill of the chase is over, and you've won your first eBay item. Congratulations — now what do you do? You have to follow up on your victory and keep a sharp eye on what you're doing. The post-auction process can be loaded with pitfalls and potential headaches if you don't watch out. Remember, sometimes money, like a full moon, does strange things to people.

In this chapter, you can get a handle on what's in store for you after you win the auction. I clue you in on what the seller's supposed to do to make the transaction go smoothly and show you how to grab hold of your responsibilities as a buyer. I give you info here about following proper post-auction etiquette, including the best way to get organized, communicate with the seller professionally, and send your payment without hazards. I also brief you on how to handle an imperfect transaction.

eBay Calling: You're a Winner

The Bidding/Watching section of your My eBay page highlights the titles of auctions you've won and indicates the amount of your winning bid. If you think you may have won the auction and don't want to wait around for eBay to contact you, check out the Bidding/Watching section for yourself and find out — are you a winner?

Throughout the bidding process, dollar amounts of items that you're winning appear in green on your My eBay page. If you've been outbid, they appear in red. After the auction ends, there's no marching band, no visit from Ed McMahon and his camera crew, no armful of roses, and no oversized check to duck behind. In fact, you're more likely to find out that you've won the auction from either the seller or the Items I'm Bidding On section of your My eBay page than you are to hear it right away from eBay. eBay tries to get its End of Auction e-mails (EOAs) out pronto, but sometimes there's a bit of lag time. For a look at all the contact information in the End of Auction e-mail, see Figure 8-1.

If you can receive text messages on your cell phone, eBay will send EOA notices to your mobile. Find out your wireless e-mail address from your cell phone provider — it's usually available from the provider's home page, for example www.nextel.com, www.tmobile.com, or the like. Then go to your My eBay Preferences page and click the Change My Wireless Email Address link. After you've entered your contact information there, click the Change My Notification Preferences link (also on the Preferences page) and select which notifications you want sent to your mobile phone. That way, no matter where y ou are, you'll know when you've won your item (and need to get payment out ASAP)!

Figure 8-1: Everything you need to know about contacting your buyer or seller is included in eBay's End of Auction e-mail.

Getting Your Paperwork Together

Yeah, I know that PCs were supposed to create a paperless society, but cars were supposed to fly by the year 2000, too. Maybe it's just as well that some predictions don't come true (think of the way some people drive). Paper still has its uses; printing out hard copies of your auction records can help you keep your transactions straight.

Your auction page shows the amount of your winning bid, the item's description, and other relevant information. The second you find out you've won the auction, print out *two* copies of the auction page if you're mailing the payment to the seller. Keep a copy for your files. Send the second copy to the seller along with your payment; doing so is not only efficient but also polite.

eBay displays auctions for only 30 days in the Bidder search, so don't put off printing out that final auction page for your records. If you save your End of Auction e-mails that you get from eBay, you can access the auction for up to 90 days if you use the link in the e-mail.

Many sellers have multiple auctions going at the same time, so the more organized you are, the more likely you will receive the correct item (and positive feedback) from the seller. Here's a list of the items you should keep in your auction purchases file:

- A copy of your EOA e-mail from eBay. *Don't* delete the EOA e-mail — at least not until you print a copy and keep it for your records. You may need to refer to the EOA e-mail later, and there's no way to get another copy.

- Printed copies of any e-mail correspondence between you and the seller that details specific information about the item or special payment and shipping arrangements.

- A printed copy of the final auction page.

Sellers can edit and update their auctions even while they're in progress, so keep your eyes peeled for changes in the auction as you monitor it. If the seller makes major changes in the auction, you are within your rights to withdraw your bid. (Check out Chapter 6 for more on the bidding process.)

An order of fries with a menu on the side

One seller, in 1999, auctioned off an old menu from Howard Johnson's, estimating its era as the 1950s based on the cars pictured on the cover — and the prices (fried clams were $1.25). Also included was a separate menu card that listed fresh seafood and had a liquor menu (with Pieman logo) on the back — plus a list of locations in the New York City area. Except for a couple of staple holes at the top of the front cover (maybe evidence of daily specials past), the menu was in very good condition. The starting bid was $5; the item sold for $64. These menus are even harder to come by now, but are still selling in the $65 range.

(I wonder how much they want for fried clams in New York these days. . . .)

Getting Contact Information

The eBay rules and regulations say that buyers and sellers must contact each other by e-mail within three business days of the auction's end. So, if an item closes on a Saturday, you need to make contact by Wednesday.

Most sellers contact auction winners promptly because they want to complete the transaction and get paid. Few buyers or sellers wait for the official eBay EOA e-mail to contact each other.

If you've won an item and intend to pay through PayPal, it's de rigueur for you to go to the item as soon as possible after you've won and to use the Pay Now link on the item page.

If you need to contact the seller before sending payment, you have several ways to find contact information:

- ✔ Click the Ask Seller a Question link on the auction page, which takes you to the Ask Seller a Question form.
- ✔ Click the Site Map link, located in the top-right corner of every eBay page, and then click the Search for Members link.
- ✔ Click the Search link on the main navigation bar and then click the Find Members link on the submenu.

Within the first three business days after an auction or a Buy it Now transaction, limit yourself to using the Ask Seller a Question form. The seller (if signed in) sees the buyer's e-mail address on the item page after the sale is closed.

So, What's Your Number?

If you don't hear from the seller after three business days and you've already tried sending an e-mail, you need to get more contact information. Remember back when you registered and eBay asked for a phone number? eBay keeps this information for times like this.

To get an eBay member's phone number, go back to the Find Members page and fill out the Contact Info form by entering the seller's User ID, your User ID, and the number of the item that you're trading with the other member; then click the Submit button.

If all the information is correct, you automatically see a request-confirmation page, and eBay automatically generates an e-mail to both you and the other user, as shown in Figure 8-2.

eBay's e-mail includes the seller's User ID, name, company, city, state, and country of residence, as well as the seller's phone number and date of initial registration. eBay sends this same information about you to the user you want to get in touch with.

Often, sellers jump to attention when they receive this e-mail from eBay and get the ball rolling to complete the transaction.

eBay doesn't tolerate any abuses of its contact system. Make sure that you use this resource only to communicate with another user about a specific transaction in which you are participating. To use contact information to complete a deal outside of eBay is an infringement of the rules. If you abuse the contact system, eBay can investigate you and kick you off the site.

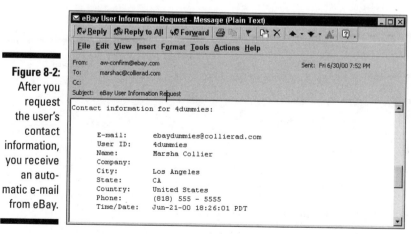

Figure 8-2: After you request the user's contact information, you receive an automatic e-mail from eBay.

```
eBay User Information Request - Message (Plain Text)

Reply  Reply to All  Forward

File  Edit  View  Insert  Format  Tools  Actions  Help

From:    aw-confirm@ebay.com                        Sent: Fri 6/30/00 7:52 PM
To:      marshac@collierad.com
Cc:
Subject: eBay User Information Request

Contact information for 4dummies:

        E-mail:      ebaydummies@collierad.com
        User ID:     4dummies
        Name:        Marsha Collier
        Company:
        City:        Los Angeles
        State:       CA
        Country:     United States
        Phone:       (818) 555 - 5555
        Time/Date:   Jun-21-00 18:26:01 PDT
```

If the seller doesn't contact you within three business days, you may have to do some nudging to complete the transaction. (See "Keeping in Touch: Dealing with an AWOL Seller," later in this chapter, and take a look at Chapter 13.)

Checking Out

When you buy something in a store, you need to check out to pay. eBay isn't much different. eBay's Checkout is a very convenient way to pay for your completed auctions or Buy it Now sales with a credit card or eCheck through PayPal. You may also use Checkout to exchange your information with the seller and pay for your item at a place other than PayPal (such as by money order, check, or another payment service that the seller accepts).

Checkout is integrated directly onto the item page so that you can win and pay for an item in less than a minute. Some sellers indicate, in their description, that they will send you a link to their private checkout page. When the sale is over, the item page will have checkout information, as shown in Figure 8-3.

When you click the Pay Now button, you are taken step-by-step through the checkout process. You pay for the item, and the seller is notified. You also get an e-mail confirming your payment, along with the seller's e-mail address.

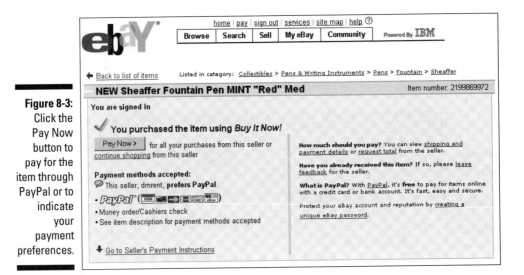

Figure 8-3: Click the Pay Now button to pay for the item through PayPal or to indicate your payment preferences.

You can make an immediate payment only if the seller chooses to accept PayPal. If the seller chooses to accept other forms of payment, such as personal checks or money orders, you can still go through the process to send the seller your shipping information (but not your actual payment). If the shipping cost is based on your zip code, the seller can also use this information to send you an invoice or to update the checkout information on the item page. When that's done, you can go ahead and send payment.

Communicating with the Seller

Top-notch sellers know that communication is the absolute key to a successful transaction, and they do everything they can to set a positive tone for the entire process with speedy and courteous e-mails.

A good e-mail from a professional eBay seller should include the following information:

- Confirmation of the winning price
- The address for sending payment or a phone number for credit card processing
- A review of the shipping options and price (the fee you pay)
- Confirmation of escrow (if offered in the auction)
- The date the item will be shipped

When you read the seller's e-mail, be sure to compare the terms the seller's laid out in his or her e-mail with the terms laid out on the auction page. And make sure that the form of payment and where it should be sent are clear to you.

When you e-mail the seller a reply, you should

- Let the seller know what form of payment you're using. For info on payment options, see Chapter 6.
- Include your address, name, and User ID.
- Include the item's title and number so that the seller knows exactly what you're referring to and can get your item ready to ship as soon as the payment arrives.

✔ Include your phone number if you plan to pay with a credit card. If there's a problem with the credit card number you've given, the seller can contact you promptly to let you know.

✔ Request that the seller e-mail you any shipping information, such as tracking numbers and an approximate arrival date.

The e-mail you receive from the seller after the auction is over should be a confirmation of the options laid out on the auction item page. If you see significant differences between what the seller's saying now and what is on your printout of the auction item page, address them immediately with the seller before you proceed with the transaction. For more on clarifying payment options during the bidding process, see Chapter 6.

Sending Out the Payment Promptly and Securely

So how many times have you heard the saying "The check is in the mail"? Yeah, I've heard it about a thousand times, too. If you're on the selling end of a transaction, hearing this line from the buyer but not getting the money is frustrating. If you're on the buying end, it's very bad form and may also lead to bad feedback for you.

Being the good buyer that you are (you're here finding out how to do the right thing, right?), naturally you'll get your payment out pronto. If you've purchased an item and intend to pay via PayPal, do it immediately — why wait? (The sooner you pay, the sooner you get that charming Flying Monkey decanter you won!)

Most sellers expect to get paid within seven business days after the close of the auction. Although this timeline isn't mandatory, it makes good sense to let the seller know payment is on the way.

Send your payment promptly. If you have to delay payment for any reason (you have to go out of town, you ran out of checks, you broke your leg), let the seller know as soon as possible. Most sellers understand if you send them a kind and honest e-mail. Let the seller know what's up, give him or her a date by which the money can be expected, and then meet that deadline. If the wait is unreasonably long, the seller may cancel the transaction. In that case, you can expect to get some bad feedback.

Here are some tips on how to make sure that your payment reaches the seller promptly and safely:

✔ Have your name and address printed on your checks. A check without a printed name or address sends up a big red flag to sellers that the check may not clear. For privacy and safety reasons, though, *never* put your driver's license number or Social Security number on your check.

✔ Always write the item title and your User ID on a check or money order and enclose a printout of the final auction page in the envelope. The Number 1 pet peeve of most eBay sellers is that they get a payment but don't know what it's for — that buyers send checks without any auction information.

✔ If you're paying with a credit card without using a payment service and you want to give the seller the number over the telephone, be sure to request the seller's phone number in your reply to the seller's initial e-mail and explain why you want it.

✔ You can safely e-mail your credit card information over the course of several e-mails, each containing four numbers from your credit card. Stagger your e-mails so that they're about 20 minutes apart and don't forget to let the seller know what kind of credit card you're using. Also, give the card's expiration date.

Buyers routinely send out payments without their name, their address, or a clue as to what they've purchased. No matter how you pay, be sure to include a copy of the eBay confirmation letter, a printout of the auction page, or a copy of the e-mail the seller sent you. If you pay with a credit card via e-mail or over the phone, you should still send this info through the mail just to be on the safe side.

Using PayPal, a person-to-person payment service

Chapter 6 covers the pros and cons of using PayPal to pay for your auctions. Here's where I show you why PayPal is the safest way to pay on eBay. eBay sees to it that PayPal is incredibly easy to use because PayPal is the official payment service at eBay. After the auction is over, a link to pay appears. If you'd prefer, wait until you hear from the seller. (I always like to have the seller's full name and address for my records before I send payment — especially if the amount of the transaction exceeds eBay's Fraud Protection Program limit.)

You can make your payment in three different ways.

- ✔ **Credit Card:** You can use your American Express, Discover, Visa, or MasterCard to make your payment through PayPal. The cost of the item is charged to your card, and your statement will reflect a PayPal payment with the seller's ID.

- ✔ **eCheck:** Sending money with an eCheck is easy. It debits your checking account just like a paper check. It does not clear immediately, and the seller probably won't ship until PayPal tells them it has cleared your bank.

- ✔ **Instant Transfer:** An Instant Transfer is just like an eCheck, except that it clears immediately, and the money is directly posted to the seller's account. To send an Instant Transfer, you must have a credit card on file with PayPal as a backup (should the payment from your bank be denied).

PayPal is my favorite payment service for another reason. PayPal has a buyer protection program, which will cover your purchases, over and above the $200 supplied by eBay's Fraud Protection plan. Read more about that in Chapter 16.

When the auction is over, you can click the Pay Now button to check out and enter the PayPal site. If you don't pay immediately from the item page, click the Pay link in the eBay navigation bar or just type **www.paypal.com** in your browser. If you go direct to the PayPal site, follow these steps:

1. **If this is your first visit to the PayPal site, register.**

   If you're already a registered user, go ahead and log in by following the steps on screen.

2. **Click the Auction Tools tab and then scroll down and click Pay for an Auction.**

PayPal takes you step-by-step through the process of filling out a payment form to identify the auction you're paying for as well as your shipping information. You're all done. Your credit card information is held safely with PayPal, and the payment is deposited into the seller's PayPal account. The seller receives notice of your payment and notifies you about how quickly he or she will ship your item.

By paying with PayPal, you can instantly pay for an auction without hassle. Your credit card information is kept private, and your payment is deposited into the seller's PayPal account.

You can always view your checkout status by going to your My eBay Items I've Won area, shown in Figure 8-4. Click the link in the Next Steps/Status column for the item in question.

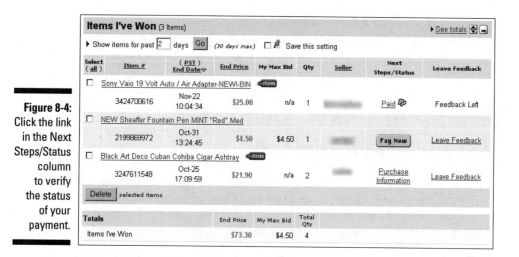

Select (all)	Item #	(PST) End Date	End Price	My Max Bid	Qty	Seller	Next Steps/Status	Leave Feedback
☐ Sony Vaio 19 Volt Auto / Air Adapter-NEW!-BIN [stores]								
	3424700616	Nov-22 10:04:34	$25.00	n/a	1		Paid 📦	Feedback Left
☐ NEW Sheaffer Fountain Pen MINT "Red" Med								
	2199869972	Oct-31 13:24:45	$4.50	$4.50	1		[Pay Now]	Leave Feedback
☐ Black Art Deco Cuban Cohiba Cigar Ashtray [stores]								
	3247611548	Oct-25 17:09:59	$21.90	n/a	2		Purchase Information	Leave Feedback

Delete | selected items

Totals			End Price	My Max Bid	Total Qty			
Items I've Won			$73.30	$4.50	4			

Figure 8-4: Click the link in the Next Steps/Status column to verify the status of your payment.

Using escrow

If you and the seller have agreed to use escrow to complete your transaction, you must first register your auction for an escrow transaction.

To sign up for escrow from any eBay page, step right up:

1. **Click the Services link on the main navigation bar.**

   You're taken to the Services Overview page.

2. **Scroll down to the SafeHarbor area and click Escrow Services.**

   You're taken to the Escrow help page.

3. **Click the How Escrow Works link.**

4. **On the Escrow.com eBay page, scroll down the page and get the current scoop on escrow.**

5. **Click the Start New Transaction button.**

   You're taken to the beginning of the escrow process. Input the item number of the transaction in question.

6. **Click the Continue button.**

   You're presented with a summary of the item. Be sure that everything is correct and read the terms and conditions; this is your last chance to cancel the process. eBay sends the information to the escrow company, an Internet escrow company, for processing.

   7. Click the I Agree button.

   Your escrow is in the works, and the escrow company either calls or
   e-mails you with information regarding the details of this transaction.

Keeping in Touch: Dealing with an AWOL Seller

The eBay community, like local towns and cities, is not without its problems.
With the millions of transactions that go on every week, transactional difficulties do pop up now and then.

The most common problem is the AWOL seller — the kind of person who
pesters you for payment and then disappears. Just as you're expected to
hustle and get your payment off to the seller within a week, the seller has
an obligation to notify you within a week of receiving your payment with an
e-mail that says the item has been shipped. If you sent the money but you
haven't heard a peep in a while, don't jump the gun and assume the person is
trying to cheat you.

Follow this week-by-week approach if you've already paid for the item but
haven't heard from the seller:

   ✔ **Week one, the gentle-nudge approach:** Remind the seller with an e-mail
      about the auction item, its number, and the closing date. "Perhaps this
      slipped your mind and got lost in the shuffle of your other auctions" is
      a good way to broach the subject. Chances are good that you'll get an
      apologetic e-mail about some family emergency or last-minute business
      trip. You'll find that the old saying "You can attract a lot more bees with
      honey than with vinegar" works great at eBay.

   ✔ **Week two, the civil-but-firm approach:** Send an e-mail again. Be civil but
      firm. Set a date for when you expect to be contacted. Meanwhile, tap into
      some of eBay's resources. See the section "Getting Contact Information,"
      earlier in this chapter, to find out how to get an eBay user's phone
      number. After you have this information, you can send a follow-up letter
      or make direct contact and set a deadline for some sort of action.

   ✔ **Week three, the take-action time:** If you still haven't heard from the seller,
      e-mail the seller once more and let him or her know that you're filing a
      complaint. Then go to SafeHarbor and file a grievance for Seller Non-
      Performance. Explain in detail what has transpired. eBay will launch its
      own internal investigation. Turn to Chapter 16 to find out more about
      filing complaints and using other tools to resolve problems.

You Get the Item (Uh-Oh What's This?)

The vast majority of eBay transactions go without a hitch. You win, you send your payment, you get the item, you check it out, you're happy. If that's the case — a happy result for your auction — then skip this section and go leave some positive feedback for the seller!

On the other hand, if you're not happy with the item you receive, the seller may have some 'splaining to do. E-mail or call the seller immediately and politely ask for an explanation if the item isn't as described. Some indications of a foul-up are pretty obvious:

- ✔ The item's color, shape, or size doesn't match the description.
- ✔ The item's scratched, broken, or dented.
- ✔ You won an auction for a set of candlesticks and received a vase instead.

A snag in the transaction is annoying, but don't get steamed right away. Contact the seller and see if you can work things out. Keep the conversation civilized. The majority of sellers want a clean track record and good feedback, so they'll respond to your concerns and make things right. Assume the best about the seller's honesty, unless you have a real reason to suspect foul play. Remember, you take some risks whenever you buy something that you can't touch. If the item has a slight problem that you can live with, leave it alone and don't go to the trouble of leaving negative feedback about an otherwise pleasant, honest eBay seller.

Of course, while I can give you advice on what you *deserve* from a seller, you're the one who has to live with the item. If you and the seller can't reach a compromise and you really think you deserve a refund, ask for one.

If you paid the U.S. Postal Service to insure the item, and it arrives at your home pretty well pulverized, call the seller to alert him or her about the problem. Find out the details of the insurance purchased by the seller. After you have all the details, follow the seller's instructions on how to make a claim. If the item was shipped through the post office, take the whole mangled shebang back to the post office and talk to the good folks there about filing a claim. Check out Chapter 12 for more tips on how to deal with a shipping catastrophe. And jump over to Chapter 16 to find out how to file your eBay and/or PayPal insurance claim.

Don't Forget to Leave Feedback

Good sellers should be rewarded, and potential buyers should be informed. That's why no eBay transaction is complete until the buyer fills out the feedback form. Before leaving any feedback, though, always remember that sometimes no one's really at fault when transactions get fouled up; communication meltdowns can happen to anyone. (For more info on leaving feedback, see Chapter 4.) Here are some handy hints on what kind of feedback to leave for a seller:

- Give the seller the benefit of the doubt. If the transaction could have been a nightmare, but the seller really tried to make it right and meet you halfway, that's an easy call — leave positive feedback.

- Whenever possible, reward someone who seems honest or tried to fix a bad situation. For example, if the seller worked at a snail's pace but you eventually got your item and you're thrilled with it, you may want to leave positive feedback with a caveat. Something like "Item as described, good seller, but very slow to deliver" sends the right feedback message.

- If the seller worked at a snail's pace and did adequate packaging and the item was kinda-sorta what you thought, you may want to leave neutral feedback; it wasn't bad enough for negative but didn't deserve praise. Here's an example: "Really slow to deliver, didn't say item condition was good not excellent, but did deliver." Wishy-washy is okay as a response to so-so; at least the next buyer will know to ask very specific questions.

- If the seller doesn't ship your item, or if the item doesn't match the description and the seller won't make things right, you need to leave negative feedback. But never write negative feedback in the heat of the moment and never make it personal. Do expect a response but don't get into a negative feedback war. Life's interesting enough without taking on extra hassles.

The Accidental Deadbeat might be an intriguing title for a movie someday, but being a deadbeat isn't much fun in real life. See Chapter 6 for details on buyer's remorse and retracting a bid *before* the end of an auction.

Part III
Are You Selling What They're Buying?

The 5th Wave   By Rich Tennant

@RICHTENNANT

"Oh, we're doing just great. Philip and I are selling decorative jelly jars at eBay. I manage the listings and Philip sort of controls the inventory."

In this part . . .

A lot of different factors are at work when a seller makes a nice profit on an item he or she has put up for auction.

If you're new to selling, you can find out all the benefits of selling and get pointed in the right direction to find items that could make you a tidy profit. In fact, you may be sitting on major profits hiding in your own home! eBay has its rules, though, so when you assess an item's value to prepare for your auction, you need to make sure the item isn't prohibited from being sold at the eBay site.

In this part, I walk you through the paperwork you need to fill out to list an item for auction, and I show you how to close the deal and ship the item without any hassles. But even though I'm good, I can't stop problems from occurring, which is why I try to walk you through every conceivable mishap. There's also a chapter for those eBay newbies out there who already know that a picture's worth a thousand words. That's right — if you really want to make money at eBay, you can't miss the advanced strategies.

Chapter 9

Selling in Your Fuzzy Slippers
for Fun and Profit

· ·

In This Chapter

▶ Discovering the benefits of selling

▶ Looking for inventory in your own backyard

▶ Knowing what to sell, when to sell, and how much to ask

▶ Staying out of trouble — what you can't sell at eBay

▶ Paying the piper with eBay fees

▶ Keeping the taxman happy (or at least friendly)

· ·

*F*inding items to sell can be as easy as opening up your closet and as challenging as acquiring antiques overseas. Either way, establishing yourself as an eBay seller isn't that difficult when you know the ropes. In this chapter, you find out how to look for items under your own roof, figure out what they're worth, and turn them into instant cash. But before you pick your house clean (I know eBay can be habit-forming, but, please, keep a *few* things for yourself!), read up on the eBay rules of the road — like how to sell, when to sell, and what *not* to sell. If you're interested in finding out how to set up your auction page, get acquainted with Chapter 10; if you want to read up on advanced selling strategies, Appendix A is where to find them.

Why Should You Sell Stuff on eBay?

Whether you need to clear out 35 years of odd and wacky knickknacks cluttering your basement or you seriously want to earn extra money, the benefits of selling at eBay are as diverse as the people doing the selling. The biggest plus to selling at eBay is wheeling and dealing from your home in pajamas and fuzzy slippers (every day is Casual Friday in my office). But no matter where you conduct your business or how you dress, many more important big-time rewards exist for selling at eBay.

Life lessons learned at eBay

If you have kids, get them involved with your eBay selling. They'll learn real-life lessons they can't learn in school. Give them a feel for meeting deadlines and fulfilling promises. Get them writing e-mails (if they aren't already) and helping to pack the items. eBay is a great place to learn basic economics and how to handle money. When I first started on eBay, I taught my pre-teen daughter about geography by using eBay. Every time I completed a transaction, she looked up the city in which the buyer (or seller) lived on a search engine and then marked the city by placing a pin on a huge map of the United States. She's graduating college now and coincidentally majored in Business and Marketing. (Thank you eBay!)

Get creative and make eBay a profitable learning experience, too. Remember, however, that eBay doesn't let anyone under the age of 18 register, buy, or sell, so make sure you're in charge of handling all transactions. Your kids can help out, but they need to be under your supervision at all times.

Most people starting a business have to worry about rounding up investment capital (start-up money they may lose), building inventory (buying stuff to sell), and finding a selling location like a booth at a swap meet or even a small store. Today, even a little Mom and Pop start-up operation requires a major investment. eBay has helped to level the playing field a bit; everybody can get an equal chance to start a small business with just a little money. Anyone who wants to take a stab at doing business can get started with just enough money to cover the Insertion Fee.

Get a few transactions under your belt. See how you like the responsibilities of marketing, collecting money, shipping, and customer service. Grow a bit more, and you'll find yourself spotting trends, acquiring inventory, and marketing your items for maximum profit. In no time, you'll be making items disappear faster than David Copperfield (though you may have a little trouble with the Statue of Liberty — how'd he *do* that, anyway?). If you think you're ready to make eBay a full- or part-time business, take a look at Appendix B. If you still want to go long on eBay, please take a look at my book, *Starting an eBay Business For Dummies* (Wiley Publishing, Inc). It gives you just what you need to ramp up from hobbyist to big-time eBay tycoon!

A fun way to get your feet wet on eBay is to buy some small items. When I say small, I mean it. Some of the least expensive items you can buy on eBay are recipes. Type **recipe** in the search box and sort the results by Lowest Prices First. You'll find recipes for a dollar and under. You don't have to pay a shipping charge, either. The sellers usually e-mail the recipe direct to you after the auction. You can also begin selling your very own secret recipes. This is a great way to become familiar with how eBay works, and you'll be gaining experience with feedback — as well as building yours!

Mi Casa, Mi Cash-a: Finding Stuff to Sell

Finding merchandise to sell at eBay is as easy as opening up a closet and as tough as climbing up to the attic. Just about anything you bought and stashed away (because you didn't want it, forgot about it, or it didn't fit) is fair game. Think about all those really awful birthday and holiday presents (hey, it was the thought that counted — and the giver may have forgotten about them, too). Now you have a place you can try to unload them. They could even make somebody happy.

In your closet, find what's just hanging around:

- Clothing that no longer fits or is out of fashion. (Do you really want to keep it if you wouldn't be caught dead in it or you know it will never fit?) Don't forget that pair of shoes you wore once and put away.

- Kids' clothes. (Kids outgrow things fast. Use profits from the old items to buy new clothes they can grow into. Now that's recycling.)

Have the articles of clothing in the best condition possible before you put them up for sale. For example, shoes can be cleaned and buffed up to like new. According to eBay's policies, clothing *must* be cleaned prior to shipping.

And consider what's parked in your basement, garage, or attic:

- **Old radios, stereo and video equipment, and 8-track systems.** Watch these items fly out of your house — especially the 8-track players (believe it or not, people love 'em).

- **Books you finished reading long ago and don't want to read again.** Some books with early copyright dates or first editions by famous authors earn big money at eBay.

- **Leftovers from an abandoned hobby.** (Who knew that building miniature dollhouses was so much work?)

- **Unwanted gifts.** Have a decade's worth of birthday, graduation, or holiday gifts collecting dust? Put them up at eBay and hope Grandma or Grandpa doesn't bid on them because they think you need another mustache spoon!

Saleable stuff may even be lounging around in your living room or bedroom:

- **Home décor you want to change.** Lamps, chairs, and rugs (especially if they're antiques) sell quickly. If you think an item is valuable but you're not sure, get it appraised first.

- **Exercise equipment.** If you're like most people, you bought this stuff with every intention of getting in shape, but now all that's building up is dust. Get some exercise carrying all that equipment to the post office after you've sold it at eBay.

✔ **Records, videotapes, and laser discs.** Sell them after you've upgraded to new audio and video formats such as DVD (Digital Versatile Disc) or DAT (Digital Audio Tape). (Think Betamax is dead? You may be surprised.)

✔ **Autographs.** All types of autographs — from sports figures, celebrities, and world leaders — are very popular at eBay. A word of caution, though. A lot of fakes are on the market, so make sure that what you're selling (or buying) is the real thing. If you're planning on selling autographs on eBay, be sure to review the special rules that apply to these items:

```
pages.ebay.com/help/policies/autographs.html
```

Know When to Sell

Warning . . . warning . . . I'm about to hit you with some clichés: *Timing is everything. Sell what you know and know when to sell. Buy low and sell high.*

Okay, granted, clichés may be painful to hear over and over again, but they do contain nuggets of good information. (Perhaps they're well known for a reason?)

Snapping up profits

Way back in 1980, when Pac-Man ruled, my friend Ric decided to try his hand at photography. Hoping to be the next Ansel Adams or to at least snap something in focus, he bought a 1/4 Kowa 66, one of those cameras you hold in front of your belt buckle while you look down into the viewfinder. Soon after he bought the camera, Ric's focus shifted. The camera sat in its box, instructions and all, for over 15 years until he threw a garage sale.

Ric and his wife didn't know much about his Kowa, but they knew that it was worth something. When he got an offer of $80 for it at the garage sale, his wife whispered "eBay!" in his ear, and he turned down the offer.

Ric and his wife posted the camera at eBay with the little information they had about its size and color, and the couple was flooded with questions and information about the camera from knowledgeable bidders. One bidder said that the silver-toned lens made it more valuable. Another gave them the camera's history.

Ric and his wife added each new bit of information to their description and watched as the bids increased with their every addition — until that unused camera went for more than $400 in a flurry of last-minute sniping in 1999. These days, when Ric posts an auction, he always asks for additional information and adds it to the auction page.

What difference does a year make? You'll learn that the values of all items on eBay trend up and down. In 2000, this camera sold at eBay for over $600; in late 2001, it sold for $455. In the winter of 2003, the interest was waning; it sold in the $375 to $400 range.

Experienced eBay sellers know that when planning an auction, timing is almost everything. You don't want to be caught with 200 Cabbage Patch Kids during a run on Furbies, and Superman action figures are good sellers unless a new Batman movie is coming out.

Some items, such as good antiques, rugs, baseball cards, and sports cars, are timeless. But timing still counts. Don't put your rare, antique paper cutter up for auction if someone else is selling one at the same time. I guarantee that will cut into your profits.

Timing is hardly an exact science. Rather, timing is a little bit of common sense, a dash of marketing, and a fair amount of information gathering. Do a little research among your friends. What are they interested in? Would they buy your item? Use eBay itself as a research tool. Search to see whether anyone's making money on the same type of item. If people are crazed for some fad item (say, Beanie Babies or Furbies) and you have a bunch, *yesterday* was the time to sell. (In other words, if you want your money out of 'em, get crackin' and get packin'.)

If the eBay market is already flooded with dozens of an item and no one is making money on them, you can afford to wait before you plan your auction.

Know Thy Stuff

At least that's what Socrates would have said if he'd been an eBay seller. Haven't had to do a homework assignment in a while? Time to dust off those old skills. Before selling your merchandise, do some digging to find out as much as you can about it.

Getting the goods on your goods

Here are some ideas to help you flesh out your knowledge of what you have to sell:

- ✔ **Hit the books.** Check your local library for books about the item. Study price guides and collector magazines.

  Even though collectors still use published price guides when they put a value on an item, so much fast-moving e-commerce is on the Internet that price guides often lag behind the markets they cover. Take their prices with a grain of salt.

✔ **Go surfin'.** Conduct a Web search and look for info on the item on other auction sites. If you find a print magazine that strikes your fancy, check to see whether the magazine is available on the Web by typing the title of the magazine into your browser's search window. (For detailed information on using search engines to conduct a more thorough online search, check out Chapter 5.)

✔ **When the going gets tough, go shopping.** Browse local stores that specialize in your item. Price it at several locations.

When you understand what the demand for your product is (whether it's a collectible or a commodity) and how much you can realistically ask for it, you're on the right track to a successful auction.

✔ **Call in the pros.** Need a quick way to find the value of an item you want to sell? Call a dealer or a collector and say you want to *buy* one. A merchant who smells a sale will give you a current selling price.

✔ **eBay to the rescue.** eBay offers some guidance for your research on its category pages. eBay offers special features for each main category. Click Browse on the navigation bar and select your favorite category. As you scroll the page, eBay places links to stories and features specifically for this category. Also, eBay has category-specific chat rooms, where you can read what other collectors are writing about items in a particular category. See Chapter 17 for more on eBay's Chat area.

For information on how items are graded and valued by professional collectors, jump to Chapter 5, where I discuss grading your items.

Be certain you know what you have — not only what it is and what it's for, but also *whether it's genuine.* Make sure it's the real McCoy. You are responsible for your item's authenticity; counterfeits and knock-offs are not welcome at eBay. In addition, manufacturers are keeping an eye on eBay for counterfeit and stolen goods and may tip off law enforcement.

Here's the lowdown on collectors' price guides from Lee Bernstein, my favorite antiques and collectible maven: The prices quoted in most collectors' books are intended to be flexible reference points to help guide shoppers. The guidelines at the beginning of every good collecting book lay out how the author has determined the prices you see listed. For more advice on collectibles, visit Lee's Web site at www.elee.com.

Spy versus spy: Comparison selling

Back in the old days, successful retailers like Gimbel and Macy spied on each other to figure out ways to get a leg up on the competition. Today, in the bustling world of e-commerce, the spying continues, and dipping into the intrigue of surveilling the competition is as easy as clicking your mouse.

Say that you're the biggest *Dukes of Hazzard* fan ever and you collect *Dukes of Hazzard* stuff, such as VHS tapes from the show, General Lee models, and lunchboxes. Well, good news: That piece of tin that holds your lunchtime PB&J may very well fetch a nice sum of money. To find out for sure, you can do some research at eBay. To find out the current market price for a *Dukes of Hazzard* lunchbox, you can conduct a Completed Items search on the Search page (as described in Chapter 5) and find out exactly how many *Dukes of Hazzard* lunchboxes have been on the auction block in the past couple of weeks. You can also find out their high selling prices and how many bids the lunchboxes received by the time the auctions were over. And repeating a completed auction search in a week or two is not a bad idea so that you can get at least a month's worth of data to price your item. Figure 9-1 shows the results of a Completed Items search sorted by highest prices first.

TIP

eBay makes saving a search easy. Just click the link in the top-right corner (you can also see it in Figure 9-1) to add this to your favorite searches. Then it's on your My eBay Favorites page, and you can repeat the search with a click of your mouse.

WARNING!

Sometimes sellers make errors when they write item titles. In the case of a *Dukes of Hazzard* lunchbox, when you conduct a search for such an item, I suggest that you use one of my favorite search tricks featured in Chapter 5. Type your search this way: **Dukes Hazzard (lunchbox,"lunch box")**. (Be sure that you drop the noise word *of.*) This way, you find all instances of *Dukes Hazzard lunch box* and *Dukes Hazzard lunchbox.*

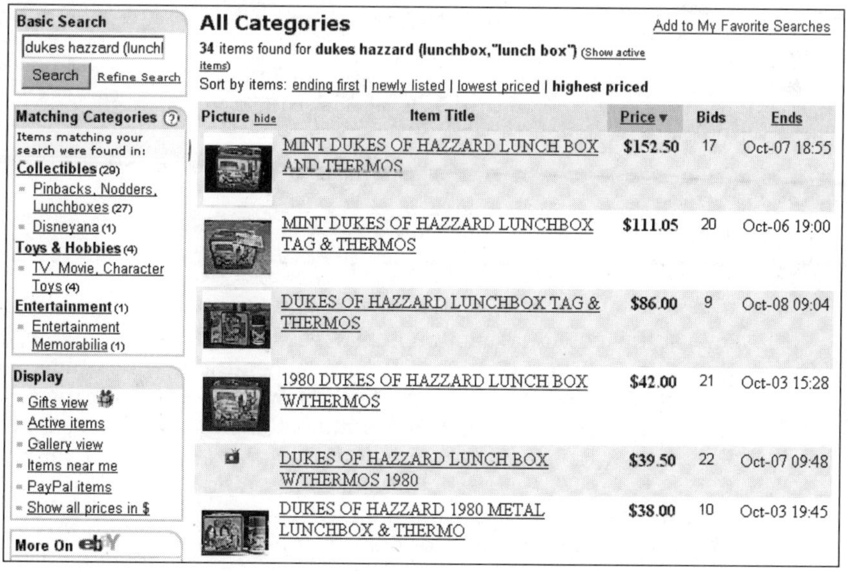

Figure 9-1:
Use the
Completed
Items
search to
find out
what an
item is
selling for,
how many
bids it has
received,
and how
many have
been up for
sale for the
past few
weeks.

Basic Search	All Categories			Add to My Favorite Searches
dukes hazzard (lunchl	**34** items found for **dukes hazzard (lunchbox,"lunch box")** (Show active items)			
Search Refine Search	Sort by items: ending first	newly listed	lowest priced	**highest priced**			

Picture hide	Item Title	Price ▼	Bids	Ends
	MINT DUKES OF HAZZARD LUNCH BOX AND THERMOS	$152.50	17	Oct-07 18:55
	MINT DUKES OF HAZZARD LUNCHBOX TAG & THERMOS	$111.05	20	Oct-06 19:00
	DUKES OF HAZZARD LUNCHBOX TAG & THERMOS	$86.00	9	Oct-08 09:04
	1980 DUKES OF HAZZARD LUNCH BOX W/THERMOS	$42.00	21	Oct-03 15:28
	DUKES OF HAZZARD LUNCH BOX W/THERMOS 1980	$39.50	22	Oct-07 09:48
	DUKES OF HAZZARD 1980 METAL LUNCHBOX & THERMO	$38.00	10	Oct-03 19:45

Matching Categories (?)
Items matching your search were found in:
Collectibles (29)
 • Pinbacks, Nodders, Lunchboxes (27)
 • Disneyana (1)
Toys & Hobbies (4)
 • TV, Movie, Character Toys (4)
Entertainment (1)
 • Entertainment Memorabilia (1)

Display
 • Gifts view
 • Active items
 • Gallery view
 • Items near me
 • PayPal items
 • Show all prices in $

More On eb Y

Sure enough, when I tried this tactic, I found a considerable number of additional listings for a *Dukes of Hazzard Lunch Box (lunchbox, "lunch box")*. Coincidentally, when I changed my search (remember, sellers *do* make mistakes) to **dukes (hazzard,hazard) (lunchbox, "lunch box")**, my search results went from 34 lunchboxes to 49! The best deals for buyers (and for sellers to resell) are always when the seller misspells a name or brand in the title.

Always search for the same item with different word variations or spellings. This is about the only time "creative" spelling can actually help you.

Lunchboxes have always been a hot item at eBay. Check out Figure 9-2 to see some top sellers.

Basic Search	All Categories			Add to My Favorite Searches

Figure 9-2:
A completed items search for *lunchbox* and *lunch box.*

Basic Search
(lunchbox,"lunch box"
[Search] [Refine Search]

Matching Categories ⑦
Items matching your search were found in:
Collectibles (9388)
 ▪ Pinbacks, Nodders, Lunchboxes (5897)
 ▪ Animation Art, Characters (976)
 ▪ Disneyana (791)
  more ...
Toys & Hobbies (2111)
 ▪ TV, Movie, Character Toys (1268)
 ▪ Action Figures (555)
 ▪ Pretend Play, Preschool (51)
  more ...
Sports (1057)
 ▪ Fan Shop (942)
 ▪ Sporting Goods (53)
 ▪ Cards (37)
  more ...
See all categories ...
Display
 ▪ Gifts view 🎁

All Categories   Add to My Favorite Searches
14836 items found for **(lunchbox,"lunch box")** (Show active items)
Sort by items: ending first | newly listed | lowest priced | **highest priced**

Picture hide	Featured – Item Title	Price ▼	Bids	Ends
	NM RARE 1974 MOSKOWITZ JAPAN DOME LUNCH-BOX 🎁	$725.00	-	Sep-28 00:21

To find out how to be listed in this section and seen by thousands, please visit this link Featured Auctions

Picture	Item Title	Price ▼	Bids	Ends
	1963 Jetsons Dome Top Lunchbox Aladdin	$750.00	30	Sep-28 18:45
	NM RARE 1974 MOSKOWITZ JAPAN DOME LUNCH-BOX 🎁	$725.00	-	Sep-28 00:21
📷	1935 Mickey Mouse Lunch Box - True Vintage	$670.00	28	Sep-27 13:24
📷	1966 ATOM ANT LUNCHBOX & THERMOS	$607.55	32	Oct-09 18:35
📷	1984 MICKEY MOUSE SCHOOL DAYS LUNCHBOX & THER	$595.00	9	Oct-09 18:41
📷	1965 MUNSTERS LUNCHBOX **UNUSED NEAR MINT**	$595.00	11	Oct-09 18:34
	Vtg 1963 Jetsons Dome Metal Lunchbox	$502.78	16	Oct-09 18:05

Look at the individual auction item pages for each item that your Completed Items search turns up. That way, you can confirm that the items (lunchboxes, for example) are identical to the one you want to sell. And when you do your research, factor in your item's condition. Read the individual item descriptions. If your item is in better condition, expect (and ask for) more money for it; if your item is in worse condition, expect (and ask for) less. Also, note the categories the items are listed under; they may give you a clue about where eBay members are looking for items just like yours.

If you want to be extremely thorough in your comparison selling, go to a search engine to see whether the results of your eBay search mesh with what's going on elsewhere. If you find that no items like yours are for sale anywhere else online, and are pretty sure people are looking for what you have, you may just find yourself in Fat City.

Don't forget to factor in the history of an item when you assess its value. Getting an idea of what people are watching, listening to, and collecting can help you assess trends and figure out what's hot. For more about using trend-spotting skills to sniff out potential profits, take a look at Appendix A.

Know What You Can (And Can't) Sell

The majority of auctions found at eBay are aboveboard. But sometimes eBay finds out about auctions that are either illegal (in the eyes of the state or federal government) or prohibited by eBay's rules and regulations. In either case, eBay steps in, calls a foul, and makes the auction invalid.

eBay doesn't have rules and regulations just for the heck of it. eBay wants to keep you educated so you won't unwittingly bid on — or sell — an item that has been misrepresented. eBay also wants you to know what's okay and what's prohibited so that if you run across an auction that looks fishy, you'll help out your fellow eBay members by reporting it. And eBay wants you to know that getting your auction shut down is the least of your worries: You can be suspended if you knowingly list items that are prohibited. And I won't even talk about criminal prosecution.

You need to know about these three categories at eBay:

- ✔ **Prohibited** lists the items that may *not* be sold at eBay under any circumstances.

- ✔ **Questionable** lists the items that may be sold under certain conditions.

- ✔ **Potentially Infringing** lists the types of items that may be in violation of copyrights, trademarks, or other rights.

You may not even offer to give away for free a prohibited or infringing item, nor can you give away a questionable item that eBay disallows; giving it away doesn't relieve you of potential liability.

The items that you absolutely *cannot* sell at eBay can fit into *all three* categories. Those items can be legally ambiguous at best, not to mention potentially risky and all kinds of sticky. To find a detailed description of which items are prohibited on the eBay Web site, follow these steps:

1. **Click the Policies link on the bottom of all eBay pages.**

   You arrive at the friendly eBay Policies page.

2. **Scroll to the Prohibited and Restricted items link and click.**

   Ta-da! Finally you are presented with the lists and links that will help you decipher whether or not your item is legal.

   You can also click the Site Map, go to the Help heading, and click the Is My Item Allowed on eBay link. Or, if you don't mind typing, you can go directly to `pages.ebay.com/help/sell/item_allowed.html`.

Sometimes an item is okay to own but not to sell. Other times the item is prohibited from being *sold and possessed.* To complicate matters even more, some items may be legal in one part of the United States but not in others. Or an item may be illegal in the United States but legal in other countries.

Because eBay's base of operations is in California, United States law is enforced — even if both the buyer and seller are from other countries. Cuban cigars, for example, are legal to buy and sell in Canada, but even if the buyer *and* the seller are from Canada, eBay says *"No permiso"* and shuts down auctions of Havanas fast. Figure 9-3 shows an auction that was shut down soon after I found it.

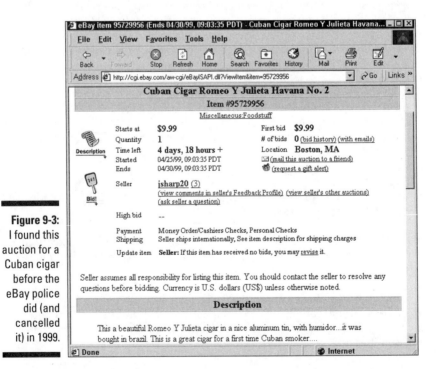

Figure 9-3:
I found this auction for a Cuban cigar before the eBay police did (and cancelled it) in 1999.

Prohibited items

Even though possessing (and selling) many of the items in the following list is legal in the United States and elsewhere, you are absolutely, positively *prohibited* from buying and selling the following at eBay:

- ✔ **Firearms of all types.** This also means firearm accessories, including antique, collectible, sport, or hunting guns; air guns; BB guns; silencers; converters; kits for creating guns; gunpowder; high-capacity ammunition magazines (receptacles designed to feed ten rounds or more into a gun, not the publications about ammo); and armor-piercing bullets. You can't even sell a gun that doesn't work.

  You *can* buy and sell single bullets, shells, and even antique bombs and musket balls as long as they have nothing explosive in them.

- ✔ **Firearms and military weapons.** No way can you sell any type of firearm that is designed to propel a metal (or similar) projectile, regardless of whether it works. Military weapons? Items included are bazookas, grenades, and mortars.

- ✔ **Police and other law-enforcement badges and IDs.** Stop in the name of the law if you're thinking about buying or selling any of these items, including actual United States federal badges or imitation badges. In fact, selling just about any U.S. government badge can get you in hot water.

  You also can't own or sell those agencies' identification cards or credential cases or those really cool jackets they use in raids. Selling a copy or reproduction of any of these items is prohibited, too, because these items are copyrighted (see the section on infringing items in this chapter).

  If you find a badge that's legal to sell and own, you need to provide a letter of authorization from the agency. The same letter of authorization is required for fake badges, such as reproductions or movie props.

- ✔ **Replicas of official government identification documents or licenses.** Birth certificates, drivers' licenses, and passports fall into this category.

- ✔ **Current vehicle license plates or plates that claim to resemble current ones.** Note that expired license plates (at least 5 years old) are considered collectible as long as they are no longer valid for use on a vehicle.

- ✔ **Locksmithing devices.** These items can be sold only to authorized recipients. Federal law prohibits the mailing of such devices.

- ✔ **Human parts and remains.** Hey, we all have two kidneys, but if you get the urge to sell one to pay off your bills, eBay is not the place to sell it. You can't sell your sperm, eggs, blood, or anything else you manage to extricate from your body. What's more, you can't even give away any of these items as a free bonus with one of your auctions.

- ✔ **Drugs or drug paraphernalia.** Narcotics, steroids, or other controlled substances may not be listed, as well as gamma hydroxybutyrate (GHB). Drug paraphernalia includes all items that are primarily intended or designed for use in manufacturing, concealing, or using a controlled substance, including 1960s vintage cigarette papers, bongs, and water pipes.

- ✔ **Anything that requires a prescription from a doctor, dentist, or optometrist to dispense.** Listen, just because it's legal to use doesn't mean it doesn't require special permission to get. For example, even though penicillin is legal to buy in the U.S., only a doctor can prescribe it, which is why when you get sick you have to stand in that *loooong* line at the pharmacy sneezing on all the other sick people. And if you're looking for Viagra auctions at eBay, don't even *go* there.

- ✔ **Stocks, bonds, or negotiable securities.** Nope, you can't sell stock in your new pie baking company or an investment in property you may own. And if you're thinking of offering credit to someone, you can't do that either. Note that antique and collectible items are permitted.

- ✔ **Bulk e-mail lists.** No bulk e-mail or mailing lists that contain personal identifying information. You may not even sell tools or software designed to send unsolicited commercial e-mail.

- ✔ **Pets and wildlife, including animal parts from endangered species.** If you've had it with Buster, your pet ferret, don't look to eBay for help in finding him a new home. And you can't sell your stuffed spotted owls or rhino-horn love potions, either. If you're in the animal business — *any* animal business — eBay is not the place for you.

- ✔ **Child pornography.** Note that this material is strictly prohibited at eBay, but you can sell other forms of erotica. (See the section later in this chapter about questionable items.)

- ✔ **Forged items.** Autographs from celebrities and sports figures are big business — and a big opportunity for forgers. Selling a forgery is a criminal act. The state of New York is taking the lead on this issue, investigating at least two dozen suspected forgery cases linked with online auctions.

If you're in the market for an autograph, don't even consider bidding on one unless it comes with a *Certificate of Authenticity* (COA). Many sellers take authenticity so seriously that they give buyers the right to a full refund if any doubt about authenticity crops ups. Figure 9-4 shows an item that comes with a COA from an auction at eBay. Find out more about authentication services in Chapter 15.

- ✔ **Items that infringe on someone else's copyright or trademark.** Take a look at the very next section for details on infringing items.

✔ **Satellite and cable TV descramblers.** Although the Internet is loaded with hardware and instructions on how to get around cable TV scrambling, eBay prohibits the sales of anything in this arena. After all, it is illegal to get around these technologies.

✔ **Stolen items.** Need I say more? (Seems obvious, but you'd be surprised.) If what you're selling came to you by way of a five-finger discount, fell off a truck, or is hot, don't sell it at eBay.

Ignorance is no excuse. If you list an item that's in any way prohibited on eBay, eBay will end your auction. If you have any questions, always check eBay's Rules & Safety department at pages.ebay.com/help/sell/item_allowed.html.

Figure 9-4: When bidding on an item with a COA, be sure that the seller is reputable (hint, hint, check the feedback).

The item you are bidding on is a 3x5 Card, Autographed by the late James Stewart ....

The card is white and in mint condition... Signed bold and clear, in black felt tip pen ...

This Autograph is 100% Genuine, and I will provide my COA that Guarantees it for life...

Infringing items

In school, if you copied someone's work, you were busted for plagiarism. Even if you've been out of school for a while, you can get busted for copying someone else's work. Profiting from a copy of someone else's legally owned *intellectual property* is an *infringement* violation. Infringement, also known as *piracy*, is the encroachment on another person's legal ownership rights on an item, a trademark, or a copyright. eBay prohibits the selling of infringing items at its site.

Hot property busted

In 1961, a young jockey named John Sellers won his first Kentucky Derby on a horse named Carry Back. He was so emotional about the victory that he was crying as he crossed the finish line. Seventeen years later, someone broke into his California home and stole his priceless trophy. But today, more than two decades after it was stolen, it's back in his possession — thanks to an observant eBay member. The prized trophy was put up for auction in 1999 by a seller who had bought it legitimately. An eBay member who knows the history of the trophy saw that it was for sale and alerted the seller. The seller stopped the auction immediately, contacted the former jockey, and personally returned the trophy to him. Now that's a great finish!

All the legal mumbo-jumbo, translated to English, comes down to this: Profiting from someone else's idea, original work, or patented invention is very, very bad and can get you in hot water.

Here's a checklist of no-no items commonly found at the center of infringement violations:

✔ Music that's been recorded from an original compact disc, cassette tape, or record.

✔ Movies that have been recorded from an original DVD, laser disc, or commercial VHS tape.

✔ Television shows that have been recorded off the air, off cable, or from a satellite service.

Selling a used original CD, tape, commercial VHS movie cassette, DVD, or CD-ROM is perfectly legal. Some television shows have sold episodes on tape; you can sell those originals as well. But if you're tempted to sell a personal copy that you made of an original, you are committing an infringing violation.

✔ Software and computer games that have been copied from CD-ROMs or disks (and that includes hard disks — anybody's).

✔ Counterfeit items (also called *knock-offs*), such as clothes and jewelry, that have been produced, copied, or imitated without the permission of the manufacturer. (Bart Simpson knock-off T-shirts abounded in the early '90s.)

If you pick up a brand-name item dirt cheap from a discount store, you can check to see whether it's counterfeit by taking a look at the label. If something isn't quite right, the item is probably a knock-off.

Trademark and copyright protection doesn't just cover software, music, and movies. Clothing, toys, sunglasses, and books are among the items covered by law.

Intellectual property owners actively defend their rights and, along with help from average eBay users, continually tip off eBay to fraudulent and infringing auctions. Rights owners can use eBay's Verified Rights Owner (VeRO) program, as well as law-enforcement agencies. (See "VeRO to the Rescue," later in this chapter, for info about the VeRO program.)

Questionable items: Know the laws

Because some items are prohibited in one place and not another, eBay lists a few items that you can trade but that are restricted and regulated. As a member of eBay, you're responsible for knowing the restrictions in your area as well as on the eBay Web site.

Certain items are illegal in one geographic area and not another. This list mentions a few of the major questionables:

- ✔ **Event tickets:** Laws regarding the sale of event tickets vary from state to state, even city to city. Some laws prohibit reselling the ticket for a price higher than the amount printed on the face of the ticket. Some states limit the amount that you can add to the ticket's face value.

  If you're planning to sell event tickets, visit `pages.ebay.com/help/community/png-tickets.html` or `pages.ebay.com/help/policies/event-tickets.html` for details. These pages have details featuring the various states' legal requirements. Be sure to double-check this page to be certain you're following the appropriate laws for your area.

- ✔ **Wine and alcohol:** Selling wine and alcohol at eBay — and anywhere else, for that matter — is tricky business. For starters, you have no business in this business unless you're at least 21 years old. eBay does not permit sales of any alcohol products unless they are sold for their "collectible" containers. You may sell alcoholic beverages for consumption if you have a liquor license and are preapproved by eBay. In the case of collectible bottles, some strict rules apply:

  - The value must be in the collectible container, not in its contents. You can't auction off your uncle's Chateaux Margaux because the value is in the wine — not the bottle.

  - The bottle must be unopened, and your auction must state that the contents are not meant for consumption.

  - The container's value must substantially exceed the price of the alcohol in the container, and it must not be available at a retail outlet.

- You must be sure that the buyer is at least 21 years old.

- You must be sure that the sale complies with all laws and shipping rules. Every state has its own laws about shipping alcohol and wine. Some states require licenses to transport it; some limit the amount you can ship. You're responsible for knowing what your state laws are (and are expected to conduct your auctions accordingly).

For a state-by-state legal summary, plus contact names, numbers, and all the clickable links you need to keep your wine-shipping business on the good side of the law, visit www.wineinstitute.org/shipwine/ analysis/intro_analysis.htm or check with the Alcoholic Beverage Control (ABC) agency of your state. To find the phone number and address for your state's ABC, visit www.wineinstitute.org/shipwine/ state_abcz/abcz.htm.

- **Erotica:** Some forms of erotica are allowed at eBay. To see what eBay allows and what it prohibits, type pages.ebay.com/help/policies/ mature-audiences.html in your browser.

One thing that's definitely illegal, wrong, and criminal is child pornography. If someone reports that you're selling child pornography, eBay forwards your registration information to law enforcement for criminal prosecution.

Forbidden auctions

The folks at eBay didn't just fall off the turnip truck. eBay staffers have seen just about every scam to get around paying fees or following policy guidelines. Chances are good that if you try one of these scams, you'll get caught. eBay cancels the auction and credits you for the listing fee. Do it once, and shame on you. Do it a lot, and you're out of eBay.

The following items are definitely forbidden:

- **Raffles and prizes:** You need to sell something in your auction; you can't offer tickets or chances for a giveaway.

- **Want ads:** If you want something, you have to search for it. Don't try to run your needs as an ad thinly disguised as an auction. I explain in Chapter 14.

- **Advertisements:** An eBay auction is not the place to make a sales pitch (other than attractive copy describing your item, that is). Some eBay bad guys list an auction name and then use the auction to send bidders to some other auction or Web site. The Real Estate category is one exception. You can run an ad there for your property.

✔ **Bait-and-switch tactics:** These are a variation on the ugly old sales technique of pretending to sell what you're not really selling. Some eBay users who are selling an unfamiliar brand of item try to snag bidders by putting a more familiar brand in the title. For instance, writing *Designer Chanel purse — not really, but a lot like it!* is a fake-out. eBay calls it *keyword spamming.* I call it lousy.

✔ **Choice auctions:** These are like Multiple Item (Dutch) auctions gone crazy. Normally, sellers can offer only one item per auction in a regular auction and multiples of the same item in a Multiple Item auction. Choice auctions offer a mishmash of multiple items from which bidders choose. For example, if you're selling T-shirts, an auction can be for only one particular size per sale. If you want to list small, medium, and large sizes, I suggest that you run an auction for one size and open an eBay store (see Chapter 11) where you can list single sales for each size.

✔ **Mixing apples with oranges:** This gambit tries to attract more bidders to view an item by putting it in a high-traffic category where it doesn't belong. Forget it. eBay will move it for you if necessary, but keeping that rutabaga recipe book *away* from the list of automotive repair manuals is more considerate.

✔ **Catalogs:** "Buy my catalog so you can buy more stuff from me!" Uh-huh. I don't know why anyone would put a *bid* on a catalog (unless it's a Sears-Roebuck antique). If it's only a booklet that shows off all the cool junk you're selling, you can't offer it as an auction item.

Reporting a Problem Auction

You probably don't think that eBay can monitor millions of auctions on a daily basis. You're right; it can't. eBay relies on eBay members like you to let it know when a shady auction is afoot. If you ever smell something fishy, for goodness' sake, report it to eBay. Sometimes eBay takes a few days to cancel an auction, but rest assured that eBay invests a lot of time protecting its users from fraudulent auctions.

If you see an auction that just doesn't look right, you should report the auction via an online form at one of the following addresses:

```
pages.ebay.com/help/contact_inline/index.html
pages.ebay.com/securitycenter/
```

REMEMBER

eBay doesn't personally prosecute its users and wouldn't want such a huge responsibility. However, eBay does have a stake in protecting its honest users and acts as an intermediary between honest eBay users and law-enforcement agencies.

VeRO to the Rescue

If you own intellectual property that you think is being infringed upon on the eBay site, eBay has a program called the Verified Rights Owner (VeRO) program. Owners of trademarked or copyrighted items and logos, as well as other forms of intellectual property, can become members of this program for free.

You can find out more about the VeRO program by clicking the Help link above the main navigation bar. To get eBay's current VeRO policy, go to `pages.ebay.com/help/confidence/vero-rights-owner.html`. Read the information, and if you qualify, click to download the form, fill it out, and fax it to eBay. Then you're on your way to protecting your intellectual property from being auctioned to the highest bidder. Remember, only *you* can stop the infringement madness. If eBay agrees with you that your intellectual property is being infringed upon, it invalidates the auction and informs the seller by e-mail that the auction "is not authorized." The high bidders in the auction are also notified and warned that they may be breaking the law if they continue the transaction.

If you qualify and become a VeRO member, you'll be pleased to know that eBay has teamed up with Ranger Online to find and report the infringements. Visit `www.rangerinc.com/channel/vero` for details.

eBay understands that sometimes people don't know that they're selling infringing items, but it draws a hard line on repeat offenders. eBay not only shuts down the offenders' auctions, but also suspends repeat offenders of this ilk. Also, eBay cooperates with the proper authorities on behalf of its VeRO program members.

If eBay deems your auction invalid because the item doesn't meet eBay's policies and guidelines, you can find out why by checking the page at `pages.ebay.com/help/confidence/vero-removed-listing.html`. If you still feel you're in the right, scroll down the page to the Contact Us link. Click there to plead your case.

eBay Fees? What eBay Fees? Oops . . .

The Cliché Police are going to raid me sooner or later, but here's one I'm poking a few holes in this time around: *You gotta spend it to make it.* This old-time business chestnut means that you need to invest a fair amount of money before you can turn a profit. Although the principle still holds true in the real world (at least most of the time), at eBay you don't have to spend much to run your business. This is one reason why eBay has become one of the most successful e-commerce companies on the Internet and a darling of Wall Street. eBay keeps fees low and volume high.

eBay charges the following types of fees for conducting auctions:

✔ Regular auction Insertion Fees ($0.30 to $3.30).

✔ Real estate listing fees. These can vary because you have the choice of listing your property as an ad rather than an auction. Because eBay real estate auctions are *non-binding* (due to legalities), you may be better off running an ad. eBay charges different prices for different types of real estate:

• **Timeshares and Land**

Auctions: 3-, 5-, 7-, or 10-day listing ($35); 30-day listing ($50)

Ad format: 30-day listing ($150); 90-day listing ($300)

• **Residential, Commercial, and Other Real Estate**

Auctions: 3-, 5-, 7-, or 10-day listing ($100); 30-day listing ($150)

Ad format: 30-day listing ($150), 90-day listing ($300)

✔ Automotive fees ($40); motorcycles are only $25.

✔ Additional reserve auction fees, which are refundable if your item meets the reserve and sells ($0.50 to $1; auctions with reserves over $100, 1 percent of the reserve with a maximum of $100).

✔ Final value fees (a percentage of the sales price).

✔ Optional fees (vary).

Insertion Fees

Every auction is charged an Insertion Fee. There's no way around it. The Insertion Fee is calculated on a sliding scale that's based on the *minimum bid* (your starting price) or on the *reserve price* (the secret lowest price that you're willing to sell your item for) of your item. (Later in this chapter, I explain how the reserve price affects what you eventually have to pay.) Take a look at Table 9-1 for eBay's Insertion Fee structure.

Table 9-1	Insertion Fee Charges
If Your Minimum Bid Is	*The Insertion Fee Is*
$0.01 to $9.99	$0.30
$10.00 to $24.99	$0.55
$25.00 to $49.99	$1.10
$50.00 to $199.99	$2.20
$200 to gazillions	$3.30

If you're running a reserve-price auction (explained in detail in Chapter 10), eBay bases its Insertion Fee on the reserve price, not the minimum bid. eBay also charges a fee to run a reserve-price auction.

Here's a snapshot of how a reserve price affects your Insertion Fee. If you set a minimum bid of $1 for a gold Rolex watch (say what?) but your reserve price is $5,000 (that's more like it), you're charged a $3.30 Insertion Fee based on the $5,000 reserve price plus a $50 *(refundable if the item sells)* reserve fee. (See Table 9-4, later in this chapter, for the reserve auction fees.)

In a Multiple Item (Dutch) auction (explained in Chapter 10), the Insertion Fee is based on the minimum bid — as in a regular auction — but then eBay multiplies it by the number of items you list. So if you set a minimum bid of $1 for 300 glow-in-the-dark refrigerator magnets, you pay a $3.30 Insertion Fee for the listing.

So what does the Insertion Fee buy you at eBay?

- ✔ A really snazzy-looking auction page of your item that millions of eBay members can see, admire, and breathlessly respond to. (Well, I can hope.)

- ✔ The use of eBay services, such as the SafeHarbor program, that somewhat ease your auction experience. (Chapter 15 tells you how to use SafeHarbor during and after your auctions.)

Final Value Fees

If you follow the movie business, you hear about some big A-list stars who take a relatively small fee for making a film but negotiate a big percentage of the gross profits. This is known as a *back-end deal* — in effect, a commission based on how much the movie brings in. eBay does the same thing, taking a small Insertion Fee when you list your item and then a commission on the back end when you sell your item. This commission is called the *Final Value Fee* and is based on the final selling price of your item.

eBay doesn't charge a Final Value Fee on an auction in the Real Estate/ Timeshares category as in other categories. You pay a flat Final Value Fee of $35 for Timeshares and Land, and no fees for Commercial or Residential. But in the Automotive category, you pay a flat Transaction Services Fee of $40 for vehicles and $25 for motorcycles if your auction ends with a winning bidder (and the reserve has been met).

In real life, when you pay sales commissions on a big purchase like a house, you usually pay a fixed percentage. eBay's Final Value Fee structure is different: It's set up as a three-tiered system. Table 9-2 covers the calculation of Final Value Fees.

Table 9-2	Final Value Fees
Closing Bid	*To Find Your Final Value Fee*
$.01 to $25	Multiply the final sale price by **5 percent**. If the final sale price is $25, multiply 25 by 5 percent. You owe eBay $1.25.
$25.01 to $1,000	You pay $1.25 for the first $25 of the final sale price (which is 5 percent). Subtract $25 from your final closing bid and then multiply this amount by **2.5 percent**. Add this total to the $1.25 you owe for the first $25. The sum is what you owe eBay. If the final sale price is $1,000, multiply 975 by 0.025. (**Hint:** The answer is $24.38.) **Now**, add $24.38 and $1.25. You owe eBay $25.63.
$1,000.01 and over	You owe $1.25 for the first $25 of the final sale price (which is 5 percent). But you also have to pay $24.38 for the remainder of the price between $25.01 through $1,000 (which is 2.5 percent). This amount is $25.63. **Now**, subtract $1,000 from the final sale price (you've already calculated those fees) and multiply the final sale amount that is over $1,000 by 1.25 percent. Add this amount to $25.63. The sum is the amount you owe eBay. If the final sales price is $3,000, multiply $2,000 by **1.25 percent**. (**Hint:** The answer is $25.) Add $25.63 to $25. The sum, $50.63, is what you owe eBay. You won't be graded on this.

So how do all these percentages translate to actual dollar amounts? Take a look at Table 9-3. I calculated the Final Value Fees on some sample selling prices.

Table 9-3	Sample Prices and Commissions	
Closing Bid Price	*Percentage*	*What You Owe eBay*
$10	5.25 percent of $10	$0.53
$256	5.25 percent of $25 plus 2.75 percent of $231	$7.66
$1,284.53	5.25 percent of $25 plus 2.75 percent of $975 plus 1. 5 percent of $284.53	$32.39
$1,000,000	5.25 percent of $25 plus 2.75 percent of $975 plus 1.5 percent of $999,000	$15,013.12 (yikes!)

When selling a vehicle (car, truck, or RV) through eBay Motors, you're getting a great deal. Although you pay a $40 fee to list your item, when it sells, the Transaction Services Fee is only $40.

If you try to work out your own Final Value Fees, you may get an extreme headache — and come up with fractional cents. Know that eBay rounds up fees of $0.005 and more, and below $0.005, drops it. These roundings are done on a per transaction basis and generally even out over time.

If you're starting to get dizzy just reading these examples, perhaps doing your own calculations isn't for you. It's certainly not for me — this stuff makes my eyes glaze over! There's a very cool software program that can handle all these calculations for you. Visit www.hammertap.com/coolebaytools for a free trial and discount.

Because of the sliding percentages, the higher the final selling price, the lower the commission eBay charges. I guess math can be a beautiful thing, when applied in my benefit.

Optional fees

You don't have to pay a license fee and destination charge, but setting up your auction can be like buying a car. eBay has all sorts of options to jazz up your auction. (Sorry, eBay is fresh out of two-tone metallic paint — but how about a nice pair of fuzzy dice for your mirror?) I explain how all these bells, whistles, and white sidewalls dress up your auction in Chapter 10.

As a hint of things to come, Table 9-4 lists the eBay auction options and what they'll cost you.

Table 9-4	eBay Optional Feature Fees
Option	*Fee*
Boldface Title	$1.00, $4.00 for vehicles in Motors
Home Page Featured	$99.95, $199.95 for multiple items
Featured Plus! (formerly Featured in Category)	$19.95
List in two categories	Double listing and upgrade fees
10-Day auction	$0.10
Highlight	$5.00
Listing Designer	$0.10
Scheduled Listings	$0.10

Option	*Fee*	
Gift Services	$0.25	
Subtitle	$0.50	
Picture Services	First picture free, each additional $0.15	
The Gallery	$0.25 and $19.95 (Featured Auction in Gallery), free Gallery for vehicles in Motors	
Auction BIN (Buy It Now) fee	$0.05	
eBay Motors vehicle BIN fee	$1.00 for Vehicles, $0.50 Motorcycles	
Vehicle Reserve Fee	$0.01 – $24.99	$0.50
	$25.00 – $199.99	$1.00
	$200.00 and up	$2.00

Keep current on your cash flow

When you've done all the legwork needed to make some money, do some eye-work to keep track of your results. The best place to keep watch on your eBay accounting is on your My eBay page, a great place to stay organized while you're conducting all your eBay business. I describe all the functions of the page in Chapter 4.

Here's a checklist of what to watch out for after the auction closes:

✔ **Keep an eye on how much you're spending to place items up for auction at eBay.** You don't want any nasty surprises, and you don't want to find out that you spent more money to set up your auction than you received selling your item.

✔ **If you decide to turn your eBay selling into a business, keep track of your expenses for your taxes.** (I explain Uncle Sam's tax position at eBay later in this chapter — next, in fact. Stay tuned.)

✔ **Make sure that you get refunds and credits when they're due.**

✔ **Double-check your figures to make certain eBay hasn't made mistakes.** If you have any questions about the accounting, let eBay know.

Find an error or something that isn't quite right with your account? Use the form at pages.ebay.com/help/contact_inline/index.html to get your questions answered.

Uncle Sam Wants You — to Pay Your Taxes

What would a chapter about money be without taxes? As Ben Franklin knew (and we've all found out since his time), you can't escape death and taxes. (C'mon, it's not a cliché; it's traditional wisdom.) Whether in cyberspace or face-to-face life, never forget that Uncle Sam is always your business partner.

If you live outside the United States, check the tax laws in that country so you don't end up with a real headache down the road.

As with offline transactions, knowledge is power. The more you know about buying and selling at eBay before you actually start doing it, the more savvy the impression you make — and the more satisfying your experience.

For more details on taxes and bookkeeping, check out my book, *Starting an eBay Business For Dummies.*

Two wild rumors about federal taxes

I've heard some rumors about not having to pay taxes on eBay profits. If you hear any variation on this theme, smile politely and don't believe a word of it. I discuss two of the more popular (and seriously mistaken) tax notions running around the eBay community these days.

The U.S. government uses two laws on the books to go after eBay outlaws. One is the Federal Trade Commission (FTC) Act, which prohibits deceptive or misleading transactions in commerce. The other is the Mail or Telephone Order Merchandise Rule, which requires sellers to ship merchandise in a timely manner or offer to refund a consumer's money. The FTC is in charge of pursuing these violations. If you have a question about federal laws, you can find a lot of information online. For example, I found these three Web sites that keep fairly current lists of U.S. law and federal codes:

```
www4.law.cornell.edu/uscode
www.ftc.gov
www.fourmilab.ch/ustax/ustax.html
```

Rumor #1: E-commerce isn't taxed

One story claims that "there will be no taxes on e-commerce sales (sales conducted online) for three years." No one ever seems to know when those three years start or end.

Some people confuse state sales tax issues with income tax issues. You don't pay Internet sales taxes, but that's not the same as not reporting income from the Internet or selling within your home state.

Congress's Internet Tax Freedom Act stated that until October 2001, Congress and state legislatures couldn't institute *new* taxes on Internet transactions. President Bush signed a unanimously approved law that extended a ban on multiple and discriminatory Internet taxes and Internet access taxes through November 1, 2003. (The moratorium did not apply to sales taxes or federal taxes.) The legislation also lengthened the "Sense of the Congress" resolution that there should be no federal taxes on Internet access or electronic commerce, and that the United States should work aggressively through the EU (European Union) and WTO (World Trade Organization) to keep electronic commerce free from tariffs and discriminatory taxes.

Even though November 1, 2003, has passed, there's still discussion about the law. Some people want to exempt online merchants if they bring in less than $25,000 per year. Others say no taxes should be imposed unless the merchant has sales of $5 million a year. As of this writing, the rules are up in the air. Please continue to check my Web site, www.coolebaytools.com, for news on Internet sales tax when it applies.

Rumor #2: Profits from garage sales are tax-exempt

"eBay is like a garage sale, and you don't have to pay taxes on garage sales."

(Uh-huh. And the calories in ice cream don't count if you eat it out of the carton. Who comes up with this stuff anyway?)

This notion is just an urban (or shall I say *suburban*) legend — somebody's wishful thinking that's become folklore. If you make money on a garage sale, you have to declare it as income — just like anything else you make money on. Most people never make any money on garage sales because they usually sell things for far less than they bought them for. However, the exact opposite is often true of an eBay transaction.

Even if you lose money, you may have to prove it to the government, especially if you're running a small business. You most definitely should have a heart-to-heart talk with your accountant or tax professional as to how to file your taxes. Remember that if something might look bad in an audit if you *don't* declare it, consider that a big hint.

To get the reliable word, I checked with the IRS's e-commerce office. The good folks there told me that even if you make as little as a buck on any eBay sale after all your expenses (the cost of the item, eBay fees, shipping charges), you still have to declare it as income on your federal tax return.

For the latest, up-to-date information on taxes and how they apply to e-commerce, visit `ecommercetax.com`.

If you have questions about eBay sales and your taxes, check with your personal accountant, call the IRS Help Line at 800-829-1040, or visit the IRS Web site at `www.irs.ustreas.gov`. And be friendly. (Just in case.)

State sales tax

If your state has sales tax, a *sales tax number* is required before you *officially* sell something. If sales tax applies, you may have to collect the appropriate sales tax for every sale that falls within the state that your business is in. A 1992 U.S. Supreme Court decision said that states can only require sellers that have a physical presence in the same state as the consumer to collect so-called use taxes.

To find the regulations for your state, visit one of the following sites, which supply links to every state's tax board. The tax board should have the answers to your questions.

```
www.taxsites.com/agencies.html
www.aicpa.org/yellow/yptstax.htm
```

State income taxes

Yes, it's true. Not only is Uncle Sam in Washington, D.C., looking for his slice of your eBay profits, but your state government may be hankering to join the feast.

If you have a good accountant, give that esteemed individual a call. If you don't have one, find a tax professional in your area. Tax professionals actually do more than just process your income tax returns once a year; they can help you avoid major pitfalls even before April 15.

Here's how to find out what your responsibilities are in your home state:

✔ You may need to collect and pay state sales taxes, but only if you sell to someone in your state.

✔ You can get tax information online at this Web site:

```
www.taxadmin.org/fta/rate/tax_stru.html
```

The site has links to tax information for all 50 states.

✔ You can also call your state tax office and let the good folks there explain what the requirements are. The state tax office should be listed in the government section of your phone book.

Chapter 10

Time to Sell: Completing the Cyber Paperwork

$\mathbf{A}$re you ready to make some money? Yes? (Call it an inspired guess.) You're on the threshold of adding your items to the hundreds of thousands that go up for auction at eBay every day. Some auctions are so hot that the sellers quadruple their investments. Other items, unfortunately, are so stone cold that they may not even register a single bid.

In this chapter, I explain all the facets of the Sell Your Item page — the page you fill out to get your auction going at eBay. You get some advice that can increase your odds of making money, and you find out the best way to position your item so buyers can see it and bid on it. I also show you how to modify, relist, or end your auction whenever you need to.

Getting Ready to List Your Item

After you decide what you want to sell, find out as much as you can about it and conduct a little market research. Then you should have a good idea of the item's popularity and value. To get this info, check out Chapter 9.

Before you list your item, make sure that you've got these bases covered:

✔ **The specific category under which you want the item listed.** Ask your friends or family where they'd look for such an item and remember the categories you saw most frequently when you conducted your market research with the eBay search function.

To find out which category will pay off best for your item, run a search and then check Completed Auctions. See how many of the item are selling now (and if people are actually bidding on it). Then scroll down to the left of the page and click Completed Items. Sort your results by highest prices first and then look over the auctions to see which categories they're listed in. For more information on how to get ahead of the crowd through eBay's search, visit Chapter 5.

✔ **What you want to say in your auction item description.** Jot down your ideas. Take a good look at your item and make a list of keywords that describe your item. Keywords are single descriptive words that can include

- Brand names

- Size of the item (citing measurements if appropriate)

- Age or date of manufacture

- Condition

- Rarity

- Color

- Size

- Material

     . . . and more

I know all about writer's block. If you're daunted by the Sell Your Item page, struggle through it anyway. This way you've already done the hard work before you even begin.

✔ **Whether you want to attach a picture (or pictures) to your description via a Uniform Resource Locator (URL).** Pictures help sell items, but you don't have to use them. (This information won't be on the test, but if you want to know more about using pictures in your auctions, see Chapter 14.)

✔ **The price at which you think you can sell the item.** Be as realistic as you can. (That's where the market research comes in.)

Examining the Sell Your Item Page

The Sell Your Item form is where your auction is born. Filling out your auction paperwork requires a couple of minutes of clicking, typing, and answering all kinds of questions. The good news is that when you're done, your auction is up and running and (hopefully) starting to earn you money.

Before you begin, you have to be a registered eBay user. If you still need to register, go to Chapter 2 and fill out the preliminary online paperwork. If you've registered but haven't provided eBay with your financial information (credit card or checking account), you'll be asked for this information before you proceed. Fill in the data on the secure form. Then you're ready to set up your auction.

Just like the dizzying menu in a Chinese restaurant, you have four ways to sell an item on eBay, as shown in Figure 10-1. Four ways may not seem to be very dizzying, unless you're trying to psychically decide just which format is the best for you. Here's what you need to know about each type:

- **Online Auction:** This is the tried-and-true traditional sale format on eBay. This is what the newbies look for, and you can combine this with a Buy It Now for those who want the item immediately. Often, if you're selling a collectible item, letting it go to auction may net you a much higher profit — remember to do your research before listing.

- **Fixed Price:** Just like shopping at the corner store, a fixed-price sale is easy for the buyer to complete. The only problem is that many potential buyers may lean toward an auction because of the perception that they *may* get a better deal.

- **Sell in Your eBay Store:** Chapter 11 covers eBay Stores — a convenient place to sell related items to your auctions or fixed-price sales.

- **Advertise Real Estate:** If you don't want to put your property up for auction and you'd like to correspond with the prospective buyers, this is the option for you.

Say, for example, that you want to list a good, old-fashioned eBay auction. You want to sell your item for a fixed price but are willing to let it go to auction.

To find eBay's Sell Your Item page from the eBay Home page, you can use either of these methods:

- Click the Sell link on the navigation bar at the top of the page, and you're whisked there immediately. eBay allows you to select your category and download the Sell Your Item page in seconds.

- You can also start your auction from your My eBay page. Just click the Selling tab and scroll down the page to Related Links. Click the Sell Your Item link and the Sell Your Item page magically appears.

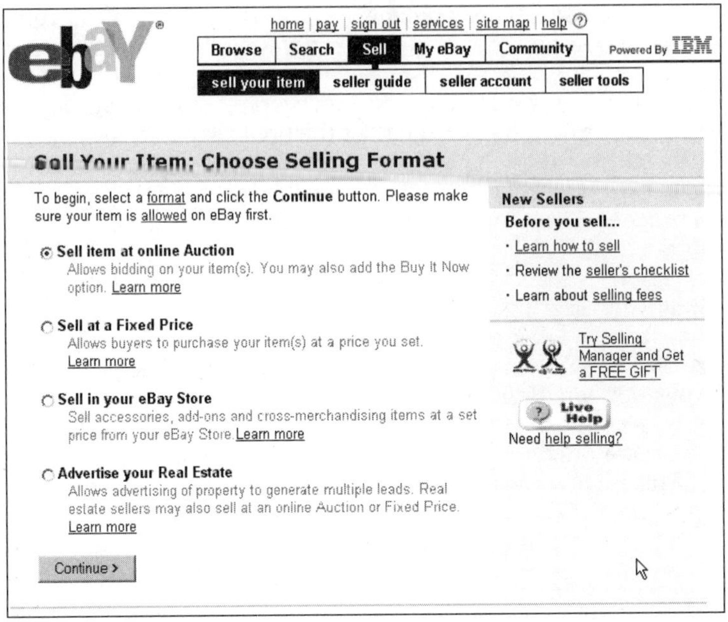

Figure 10-1:
Select your
selling for-
mat before
you list
your item.

When listing your item, here's the info you're asked to fill out (each of these items is discussed in detail later in this chapter):

- **User ID and Password:** If you're not signed in, you need to sign in before you list an item for sale.

- **Category:** The category where you've decided to list your item (required).

- **Title:** The name of your item (required).

- **Description:** What you want to tell eBay buyers about your item (required).

- **eBay Picture Services or Image URL:** The Web address of any pictures you want to add (optional). Note that you get a free Preview picture at the top of your auction. Chapter 14 has more information on using images in your auction.

- **The Gallery:** You can add your item's picture to eBay's photo gallery (optional). eBay charges $0.25 extra to add the item to the Gallery and $19.95 to make your item a featured auction in the Gallery. (You can find more on the Gallery later in this chapter.)

- **Gallery Image URL:** The Web address of the JPG image you want to place in the Gallery (optional). (If you're using eBay Picture Services, the first photo you upload is resized for the Gallery.) See Chapter 14.

- **Item Location:** The region, city, and country from which the item will be shipped (required).

✔ **Quantity:** The number of items you're offering in this auction is always one unless you plan to run a Dutch (Multiple Item) auction (required).

✔ **Minimum Bid:** The starting price you set (required).

✔ **Duration:** The number of days you want the auction to run (required).

✔ **Reserve Price:** The hidden target price you set. This is the price that must be met before this item can be sold (optional). eBay charges you a fee for this feature.

✔ **Private Auction:** You can keep the identity of all bidders secret with this option (optional). This type of auction is used only in rare circumstances.

✔ **Buy It Now:** You can sell your item directly to the first buyer who meets this price (optional).

✔ **List Item in Two Categories:** If you want to double your exposure, you can list your item in two different categories. Note that double exposure equals double listing fees (optional).

✔ **Home Page Featured:** You can place your auction in a premium viewing section and have the possibility that your listing will cycle through the direct links from the front page (optional). eBay charges $99.95 extra for this feature.

✔ **Featured Plus!:** You can have your auction appear at the top of the category in which you list it (optional). eBay charges $19.95 extra for this feature.

✔ **Highlight:** Your item title is highlighted in the auction listings and search listings with a lilac-colored band, which may draw eBay members' eyes right to your auction (optional). eBay charges $5 extra for this feature.

✔ **Boldface Title:** A selling option to make your item listing stand out. eBay charges $1 extra for this feature (optional).

✔ **Free Counter:** If you wish to avail yourself of Andale.com's counters, indicate so here (optional).

✔ **Ship-to-Locations:** Here's where you can indicate where you're willing to ship an item. If you don't want the hassle of shipping out of the United States, check that option only. You can individually select different countries as well (optional).

You may want to consider whether you *really* want to be in the international shipping business. Buyers usually pick up the tab, but you have to deal with customs forms and post office paperwork. If time is money, you may want to skip it entirely — or at least have all the forms filled out before you get in line at the post office. But remember that if you don't ship internationally, you're blocking out a bunch of possible high bidders. Depending on what you're selling, shipping internationally just may not be worth the investment in extra time.

✔ **Who Pays for Shipping:** Select the options that apply to who pays the shipping and handling charges in your auction.

 ✔ **Shipping and Handling Charges:** When prospective buyers know the shipping cost in advance (assuming it's a realistic price), they're more likely to bid right then and there. If they have to e-mail you with questions, they may find another auction for the same item — with reasonable shipping — and bid on that one. Also, if you list the shipping charges on the page, winning bidders can pay you instantly through PayPal. See information on eBay's handy shipping calculator, later in this chapter.

 ✔ **Payment Instructions:** Here's the place you put any after-sale information. If you don't want buyers to use Checkout, state that here. If you want them to pay with a different payment service, mention that as well. This information appears at the top of your sale when the sale is completed, at the bottom of the auction while it's active, and in the End of Auction e-mail (optional).

 ✔ **PayPal and Immediate Payment:** Fill out this area if you want to require the high bidder to pay through PayPal immediately when using Buy It Now. Add the Immediate Payment option if you know the shipping amount and would like the winner to pay with a click of the mouse (optional).

 ✔ **Escrow:** If using escrow is an option you'd like to offer the high bidder, (a good idea for high-dollar items), select the option as to who will pay the fees (optional).

Filling in the Required Blanks

Yes, the Sell Your Item form page looks daunting, but filling out its many sections doesn't take as long as you may think. Some of the questions you're asked aren't things you even have to think about; just click an answer and off you go — unless you forget your password. Other questions ask you to type in information. Don't sweat a thing; all the answers you need are right here. You can find info on all the required stuff, and later in this chapter, I talk about optional stuff. After you click your main category, you land on the official Sell Your Item page.

Selecting a category

Many eBay sellers will tell you that selecting the exact category isn't crucial to achieving the highest price for your item — and they're right. The bulk of buyers (who know what they're looking for) just input search keywords into eBay's search box and look for their items. Potential buyers, though, will select a category and, just like when you go to the mall, peruse the items and see if one strikes their fancy.

On the first page of the Sell Your Item form, you need to select the main category for your item.

Here's where your creativity can come into play. Who says that a box of Blue Dog (the famous doggie icon painted by Cajun artist George Rodrigue) note cards belongs in *Everything Else: Gifts & Occasions: Greeting Cards: Other Cards.* If you use the Find Suggested Categories tool (in a yellow shaded box) in the upper-right corner of the Select Category area, you may find some other creative places to list your item. Check to see if anyone else is selling the item (and in which category) or just let this tool help you pick a good category. Figure 10-2 shows you how easy it is to select a main category.

Select a Suggested Main Category

Top 10 categories found for **note cards**

You can select a suggested main category below and click **Save**, or use different keywords to refine your search.

Find Suggested Categories

Enter descriptive **item keywords** to see categories sellers have chosen for similar items.

[note cards] [Find] Tips

Category suggestions are based on the keywords you specified. **% Items Found** is an estimate of all items listed by sellers in select eBay categories containing your keywords.

Category	% Items Found
Everything Else : Gifts & Occasions : Greeting Cards : Other Cards	(9%)
Everything Else : Gifts & Occasions : Greeting Cards : Assortments	(7%)
Collectibles : Animals : Dog : Other Dogs	(6%)
Collectibles : Postcards & Paper : Greeting Cards : Other	(4%)
Home : Pet Supplies : Dogs : Other	(4%)
Specialty Services : Printing & Personalization : Stationery	(4%)
Collectibles : Animals : Bird : Parrot	(3%)
Art : Other Art	(2%)
Collectibles : Animals : Dog : Scottish Terrier	(2%)
Collectibles : Decorative Collectibles : Mary Engelbreit : Other Items	(2%)

Figure 10-2: Let eBay do some of the work in finding the proper category for your item.

After you select your main category, you need to select from the thousands of subcategories. eBay offers you this wealth of choices in a handy point-and-click way. If you're unfamiliar with the types of items you can actually *find* in those categories, you may want to pore over Chapter 3 before you choose a category to describe *your* item. Figure 10-3 shows you how to narrow down the subcategory listings on the Sell Your Item page.

To select a category, here's the drill:

1. **Click one of the main categories.**

   On the next page, you see a list of subcategories.

2. **Select the most appropriate subcategory.**

3. **Continue selecting subcategories until you have narrowed down your item listing as much as possible.**

   You know you've come to the last subcategory when you don't see any more right-pointing arrows in the category list.

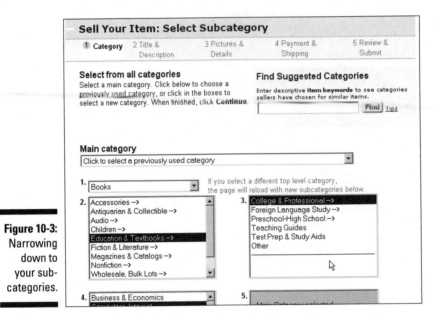

Figure 10-3: Narrowing down to your subcategories.

Most bidders scan for specific items in subcategories. For example, if you're selling a Bakelite fruit pin, don't just list it under Jewelry; keep narrowing down your choices. In this case, you can put it in a costume jewelry category that is especially for Bakelite. I guarantee that the real Bakelite jewelry collectors out there know where to look to find the jewelry they love. eBay makes it easy to narrow down the category of your item: Just keep clicking until you hit the end of the line.

If you've chosen to list an item, bid on an item, or even just browse in the Everything Else: Mature Audiences category, you need to follow separate, specific guidelines because that category contains graphic nudity or sexual content that may offend some community members. You must

✔ Be at least 18 years of age (but you already know that all eBay customers must be 18 or older).

✔ Have a valid credit card.

✔ Complete a waiver stating that you're voluntarily choosing to access adults-only materials. For more on how to do this (and a handy primer on privacy issues), see Chapter 15.

If you have Adult/Erotica items that you'd like to sell in a private auction, study the section later in this chapter that details the Private Auction option.

Creating the perfect item title

After you figure out what category you want to list in, eBay wants to get down to the nitty-gritty — what the heck to call that thing you're trying to sell.

Think of your item title as a great newspaper headline. The most valuable real estate on eBay is the 45-character title of your item. The majority of buyers do title searches, and that's where your item must come up to be sold! Give the most essential information right away to grab the eye of the reader who's just browsing. Be clear and informative enough to get noticed by eBay's search engine. Figure 10-4 shows examples of good titles.

Figure 10-4:
These item
titles are
effective
because
they're
clear, con-
cise, and
easy on
the eyes.

NEW womens ADIDAS Tennis Shirt Skirt sz M $80
1971 ROLLS ROYCE Corniche Sales BROCHURE
Pink 3 Plumerias Sterling Silver Pendant NEW
DICK TRACY RECALLED ADVANCE MOVIE POSTER + B
Alexander McQUEEN Kingdom 30ml Eau De Parfum
EASY French Normandy Original Classic Recipes
2 Photography Photo Light NIB Lighting Kit

Here are some ideas to help you write your item title:

- ✔ Use the most common name for the item.
- ✔ If the item is rare or hard to find, mention that.
- ✔ Mention the item's condition and whether it's new or old.
- ✔ Mention the item's special qualities, like its style, model, or edition.
- ✔ Avoid fancy punctuation or unusual characters, such as $, hyphens, and L@@K, because they just clutter up the title — buyers rarely search for them.

Don't put any HTML tags in your title. (*HTML* stands for HyperText Markup Language, which in plain English means that it's the special code you use to create Web pages.) As a matter of fact, despite what you may have been told, you don't need an extensive knowledge of HTML to have successful, good-looking auctions at eBay. In Table 10-2, I list a few HTML codes to use in your description (some photo-related code is in Chapter 14), and in Chapter 20, I give you some tips on where you can find some easy programs that produce the minor HTML coding that you may want to use to dress up your auctions.

Ordinarily, I don't throw out French phrases just for the fun of it. But where making a profit is an issue, I definitely have to agree with the French that picking or not picking *le mot juste* can mean the difference between having potential bidders merely see your auction and having an all-out bidding war on your hands. Read on for tips about picking *the best words* to let your auction item shine.

Look for a phrase that pays

Here's a crash course in eBay lingo that can help bring you up to speed on attracting buyers to your auction. The following words are used frequently in eBay auctions, and they can do wonders to jump-start your title:

- Mint
- One of a kind (or OOAK — see abbreviation list in Table 10-1)
- Vintage
- Collectible
- Rare
- Unique
- Primitive
- Well-loved

There's a whole science (called *grading*) to figuring out the value of a collectible. You're ahead of the game if you have a pretty good idea of what most eBay members mean. Do your homework before you assign a grade to your item. If you need more information on what these grades actually mean, Chapter 5 provides a translation.

eBay lingo at a glance

Common grading terms and the phrases in the preceding section aren't the only marketing standards you have at your eBay disposal. As eBay has grown, so has the lingo that members use as shortcuts to describe their merchandise.

Table 10-1 gives you a handy list of common abbreviations and phrases used to describe items. (**Hint:** Mint means "may as well be brand new," not "cool chocolate treat attached.")

Table 10-1	A Quick List of eBay Abbreviations	
eBay Code	*What It Abbreviates*	*What It Means*
MIB	Mint in Box	The item is in the original box, in great shape, and just the way you'd expect to find it in a store.
MIMB	Mint in Mint Box	The box has never been opened and looks like it just left the factory.
MOC	Mint on Card	The item is mounted on its original display card, attached with the original fastenings, in store-new condition.
NRFB	Never Removed from Box	Just what it says, as in "bought but never opened."
COA	Certificate of Authenticity	Documentation that vouches for the genuineness of an item, such as an autograph or painting.
MWBMT	Mint with Both Mint Tags	Refers to stuffed animals, which have a hang tag (usually paper or card) and a tush tag (that's what they call the sewn-on tag — really) in perfect condition with no bends or tears.
OEM	Original Equipment Manufacture	You're selling the item and all the equipment that originally came with it, but you don't have the original box, owner's manual, or instructions.
OOAK	One of a Kind	You are selling the only one in existence!
NR	No Reserve Price	A reserve price is the price you can set when you begin your auction. If bids don't meet the reserve, you don't have to sell. Many buyers don't like reserve prices because they don't think that they can get a bargain. (For tips on how to allay these fears and get those bids in reserve price auctions, see "Writing your description" later in this chapter.) If you're not listing a reserve for your item, let bidders know.

(continued)

Table 10-1 *(continued)*

eBay Code	What It Abbreviates	What It Means
NWT	New with Tags	An item, possibly apparel, is in new condition with the tags from the manufacturer still affixed.
HTF, OOP	Hard to Find, Out of Print	Out of print, only a few ever made, or people grabbed up all there were. (HTF doesn't mean you spent a week looking for it in the attic.)

Normally, you can rely on eBay slang to get your point across, but make sure that you mean it and that you're using it accurately. Don't label something MIB (Mint in Box) when it looks like it's been Mashed in Box by a meat grinder. You'll find more abbreviations on my Web site, www.coolebaytools.com.

Don't let your title ruin your auction

Imagine going to a supermarket and asking someone to show you where the stringy stuff that you boil is instead of asking where the spaghetti is. You might end up with mung bean sprouts — delicious to some but hardly what you had in mind. That's why you should check and recheck your spelling. Savvy buyers use the eBay search engine to find merchandise; if the name of your item is spelled wrong, the search engine can't find it. Poor spelling and incomprehensible grammar also reflect badly on you. If you're in competition with another seller, the buyer is likelier to trust the seller *hoo nose gud speling*.

If you've finished writing your item title and you have spaces left over, **please** fight the urge to dress it up with lots of exclamation points and asterisks. No matter how gung-ho you are about your item, the eBay search engine may overlook your item if the title is encrusted with meaningless **** and !!!! symbols. If bidders do see your title, they may become annoyed by the virtual shrillness and ignore it anyway!!!!!!!! (See what I mean?)

Another distracting habit is overdoing capital letters. To buyers, seeing everything in caps is LIKE SEEING A CRAZED SALESMAN SCREAMING AT THEM TO BUY NOW! All that is considered *shouting,* which is rude and tough on the eyes. Use capitalization SPARINGLY, and only to finesse a particular point.

Giving the title punch with a subtitle

A new feature at eBay is the availability of subtitles. eBay allows you to buy an additional 45 characters, which will appear under your item title in a search. The fee for this extra promotion is $0.50, and in a few circumstances, it is definitely worth your while. Any text that you input will really make your item stand out in the crowd — but (you knew there would be a *but* didn't you?) these additional 45 characters won't come up in a title search. So if you have all those words in your description, the words will be found either way with a title and description search. Keep in mind that a subtitle essentially *doubles* your listing fee.

Writing your description

After you hook potential bidders with your title, reel 'em in with a fabulous description. Don't think Hemingway here; think infomercial (the classier the better). Figure 10-5 shows a great description of some silver dollars. You can write a magnificent description, as well — all you have to do is click in the box and start typing.

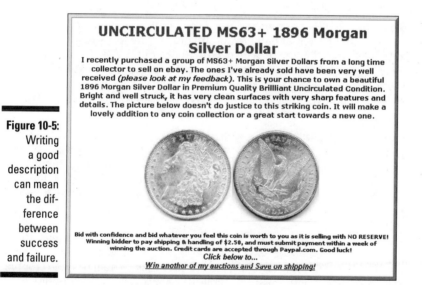

UNCIRCULATED MS63+ 1896 Morgan Silver Dollar

I recently purchased a group of MS63+ Morgan Silver Dollars from a long time collector to sell on ebay. The ones I've already sold have been very well received *(please look at my feedback)*. This is your chance to own a beautiful 1896 Morgan Silver Dollar in Premium Quality Brillliant Uncirculated Condition. Bright and well struck, it has very clean surfaces with very sharp features and details. The picture below doesn't do justice to this striking coin. It will make a lovely addition to any coin collection or a great start towards a new one.

Bid with confidence and bid whatever you feel this coin is worth to you as it is selling with NO RESERVE! Winning bidder to pay shipping & handling of $2.50, and must submit payment within a week of winning the auction. Credit cards are accepted through Paypal.com. Good luck!
Click below to...
Win another of my auctions and Save on shipping!

Figure 10-5: Writing a good description can mean the difference between success and failure.

Here's a list of suggestions for writing an item description:

- ✔ **Accentuate the positive.** Give the buyer a reason to buy your item and be enthusiastic when you list all the reasons everyone should bid on it. Unlike the title, you can use as much space as you want. Even if you use a photo, be precise in your description — how big it is, what color, what kind of fabric, what design, and so on. Refer to "Creating the perfect item title" earlier in this chapter, as well as Table 10-1, for ideas on what to emphasize and how to word your description.

- ✔ **Include the negative.** Don't hide the truth of your item's condition. Trying to conceal flaws costs you in the long run: You'll get tagged with bad feedback. If the item has a scratch, a nick, a dent, a crack, a ding, a tear, a rip, missing pieces, replacement parts, faded color, dirty smudges, or a bad smell (especially if cleaning might damage the item), mention it in the description. If your item has been overhauled, rebuilt, repainted, or hot-rodded (say, a "Pentium computer" that was a 386 till you put in the new motherboard), say so. You don't want the buyer to send back your merchandise because you weren't truthful about imperfections or modifications. This type of omission can lead to a fraud investigation.

- ✔ **Be precise about all the logistical details of the post-auction transaction.** Even though you're not required to list any special S&H (shipping and handling) or payment requirements in your item description, the majority of eBay users do. Try to figure out the cost of shipping the item in the United States and add that to your description. If you offer shipping insurance, add it to your item description.

- ✔ **While you're at it, promote yourself too.** As you accumulate positive feedback, tell potential bidders about your terrific track record. Add statements like "I'm great to deal with. Check out my feedback section." You can even take it a step further by inviting prospective bidders to your About Me page (where you may also include a link to your personal Web site — if you have one). (Chapter 14 gives you some tips on how to make your auction seen by a wider audience.)

- ✔ **Wish your potential bidders well.** Communication is the key to a good transaction, and you can set the tone for your auction and post-auction exchanges by including some simple phrases that show your friendly side. Always end your description by wishing bidders good luck, inviting potential bidders to e-mail you with questions, and offering the option of providing additional photos of the item if you have them.

When you input your description, you have the option of jazzing things up with a bit of HTML coding, or you can use eBay's new HTML text editor, shown in Figure 10-6. If you know how to use a word processor, you'll have no trouble touching up your text with this tool. Table 10-2 shows you a few additional codes to help you pretty things up.

You can go back and forth from the HTML text editor to the regular input and add additional codes here and there by clicking the View/Edit HTML check box (when you're in the HTML text editor). I prepare all my auctions ahead of time in a program called CuteHTML and save them in my computer as plain HTML files — that way they're always retrievable for use (I just copy and paste) — no matter what program or form I'm using to list my auctions. See Chapter 20 for more on software to help you with your auctions.

Figure 10-6:
The HTML
text editor
shows
you the
description
area with
HTML-
coded text.

Table 10-2	A Short List of HTML Codes	
HTML Code	**How to Use It**	**What It Does**
`<b></b>`	`<b>cool collectible</b>`	**cool collectible** (bold type)
`<I></I>`	`<I>cool collectible</I>`	*cool collectible* (italic type)
`<b><I></I></b>`	`<b><i>cool collectible </b></i>`	***cool collectible*** (bold and italic type)
`<font color =red></font>`	`<font color=red>cool collectible</font>`	Selected text appears in red. (This book is in black and white so you can't see it.)
`<font size= +1></font>`	`<font size=+3>cool</font> collectible`	cool collectible (font size normal +1 through 4, increases size *x* times)
` `	`cool collectible`	cool collectible (inserts line break)

(continued)

Table 10-2 *(continued)*

HTML Code	How to Use It	What It Does
`<p>`	`cool<p>collectible`	cool collectible (inserts paragraph space)
`<hr>`	`cool collectible<hr>cheap`	cool collectible _____ cheap (inserts horizontal rule)
`<h1><h1>`	`<h1>cool collectible</h1>`	**cool collectible** (converts text to headline size)

Occasionally, sellers offer an item as a *presell,* or an item that the seller doesn't yet have in stock but expects to. If you're offering this kind of item, make sure that you spell out all the details in the description. eBay policy states that you must ship a presell item within 30 days of the auction's end, so be sure you will have the item within that time span. Don't forget to include the actual shipping date. I have found that putting an item up for sale without actually having it in hand is a practice fraught with risk. The item you're expecting may not arrive in time or arrive damaged. I've heard of one too many sellers who have had to go out and purchase an item at retail for a buyer in order to preserve their feedback when caught in this situation.

Listing the number of items for sale

Unless you're planning on holding a Multiple Item (Dutch) auction, the number of items is always 1, which means you're holding a traditional auction. If you need to change the quantity number from 1, just type the number in the box.

A matching set of cuff links is considered one item, as is the complete 37-volume set of *The Smith Family Ancestry and Genealogical History since 1270.* If you have more than one of the same item, I suggest that you sell the items one at a time, because you will more than likely get higher final bids for your items when you sell them individually.

Whether you list your items individually in auctions or together in a Multiple Item auction, eBay won't allow you to list the same item in more than ten auctions at one time.

Setting a minimum bid — how low can you go?

What do a baseball autographed by JFK, a used walkie-talkie, and a Jaguar sports car all have in common? They all started with a $1 minimum bid. eBay requires you to set a *minimum bid,* the lowest bid allowed in an auction. You may be surprised to see stuff worth tens of thousands of dollars starting at just a buck. These sellers haven't lost their minds. Neither are they worried someone could be tooling down the highway in a $100,000 sports car they bought for the price of a burger.

Setting an incredibly low minimum (just type it in the box *without* the dollar sign but *with* the decimal point) is a subtle strategy that gives you more bang for your buck. You can use a low minimum bid to attract more bidders who will, in turn, drive up the price to the item's real value — especially if, after doing your research, you know that the item is particularly hot. If you're worried about the outcome of the final bid, you can protect your item by using a *reserve price* (the price the bidding needs to reach before the item can be sold). Then you won't have to sell your item for a bargain-basement price because your reserve price protects your investment. The best advice is to set a reserve price that is the lowest amount you'll take for your item and then set a minimum bid that is ridiculously low. Use a reserve only when absolutely necessary because some bidders pass up reserve auctions. (For more info about setting a reserve price, see the section "Your secret safety net — reserve price," later in this chapter.)

Starting with a low minimum is also good for your pocketbook. eBay charges the seller an Insertion, or Placement, Fee — based on your opening bid. If you keep your opening bid low and set no reserve, you get to keep more of your money. (See Chapter 9 for more about eBay fees.)

The more bids you get, the more people who will want to bid on your item because they perceive the item as hot. A hot item with lots of bids draws even more bidders the way a magnet attracts paper clips.

Before you set any minimum bid, do your homework and make some savvy marketing decisions. If your auction isn't going as you hoped, you *could* end up selling Grandma Ethel's Ming vase for a dollar. Think about your strategy. See "Mid-Course Corrections: Fixing Current Auctions" later in this chapter on how you can make changes in your listing if you've made some egregious error.

When putting in your minimum bid, type in only the numbers and a decimal point. Don't use dollar signs ($) or cents signs (¢).

Buy It Now

eBay's Buy It Now (*BIN* in eBay-speak) is available for single-item auctions. This feature allows buyers who want to purchase an item *now* to do so. Have you ever wanted an item really badly and didn't want to wait until the end of an auction? If the seller offers Buy It Now, you can purchase that item immediately. Just specify the amount the item can sell for in the Buy It Now price area — the amount can be whatever you wish. If you choose to take advantage of selling a hot item, for example, during the holiday rush, you can make the BIN price as high as you think it can go. If you just want the item to move, make your BIN price the average price you see the item go for at eBay.

When your item receives a bid, the BIN option disappears, and the item goes through the normal auction process. If you have a reserve price on your item, the BIN feature doesn't disappear until a bidder meets your reserve price through the normal bidding process. To list an item with Buy It Now, you must have a feedback of 10 or be ID Verified. (See Chapter 16 for more details on ID Verify.)

Setting your auction time

How long do you want to run your auction? eBay gives you a choice — 1, 3, 5, 7, or 10 days. Just click the number you want in the box. If you choose a 10-day auction, you add $0.10 to your listing fee.

My auction-length strategy depends on the time of year and the item I'm selling, and I generally have great success. If you have an item that you think will sell pretty well, run a 7-day auction (be sure to cover a full weekend) so bidders have time to check it out before they decide to bid. However, if you know that you've got a red-hot item that's going to fly off the shelves — like a rare toy or a hard-to-get video game — choose a three-day auction. Eager bidders tend to bid higher and more often to beat out their competition if the item is hot and going fast. Three days is long enough to give trendy items exposure and ring up bids.

No matter how many days you choose to run your auction, it ends at exactly the same time of day as it starts. A seven-day auction that starts on Thursday at 9:03:02 a.m. ends the following Thursday at 9:03:02 a.m.

Although I know the folks at eBay are pretty laid back, they do run on military time. That means they use a 24-hour clock that's set to Pacific Time. So 3:30 in the afternoon is 15:30, and one minute after midnight is 00:01. Questions about time conversions? Check out www.timezoneconverter.com or look at the table on my Web site, which has a printable conversion chart of eBay times (www.coolebaytools.com). (And so you don't have to keep flipping back to this page, I also include these handy-dandy links on the Cheat Sheet at the front of this book.)

Going Dutch

If you've got 5 Dennis Rodman Wedding Dolls, 37 Breathalyzers, or 2,000 commemorative pins, and you want to sell them all at once to as many bidders as quickly as possible, sell them as multiple quantities in a fixed-price sale. (You can also sell the whole shebang in one lot in the Wholesale Lot category.) If you're not sure how much you can get for the items, you can always try a Dutch (Multiple Item) auction. Dutch auctions are mainly used by dealers and businesses that want to move lots of items fast.

eBay has requirements for starting a Dutch auction. You have to be an eBay member at least 14 days with a feedback rating of 30 or higher or go through ID Verify. Click the Dutch auction link on the Sell Your Item page for more information on how to conduct this type of auction, and check out Chapter 1 for more info on how a Dutch auction works. If you're interested in bidding on a Dutch auction, take a look at Chapter 6.

Once a week, eBay conducts database maintenance, which means that some features (or sometimes the whole site) close up shop on Fridays from 1 a.m. to 3 a.m. Pacific Time (that's 4 a.m. to 6 a.m. Eastern Time). Never post an auction right after this outage. eBay regulars won't be around to bid on it. Also, search updates are often 12 to 15 hours behind on Friday and Saturday following scheduled maintenance.

With auctions running 24 hours a day, 7 days a week, you should know when the most bidders are around to take a gander at your wares. Here are some times to think about:

✔ **Saturday/Sunday:** Always run an auction over a weekend. People log on and off of eBay all day.

Don't start or end your auction on a Saturday or Sunday — *unless* your completed auction research indicates that you should. Certain types of bidders love sitting at their computers waiting for auctions to end on the weekends, but many bidders are busy having lives, and their schedules are unpredictable. Some eager bidders may log on and place a maximum bid on your auction, but you can bet they won't be sitting at a computer making a last-minute flurry of competitive bids if they have something better to do on a Saturday or Sunday.

✔ **Holiday weekends:** If a holiday weekend's coming up around the time you're setting up your auction, run your auction through the weekend and end it a day after the "holiday" Monday. This gives prospective bidders a chance to catch up with the items they perused over the weekend and plan their bidding strategies.

Don't end an auction on the last day of a three-day holiday. People in the mood to shop are generally at department stores collecting bargains. If eBay members aren't shopping, they're out enjoying an extra day off.

✔ **Time of day:** The best times of day to start and end your auction are during eBay's peak hours of operation, which are 5 p.m. to 9 p.m. Pacific Time, right after work on the West Coast. Perform your completed auction research, however, to be sure that this strategy applies to your item, because this timing depends on the item you're auctioning and whether 5–9 p.m. Pacific Time is the middle of the night where you live.

Unless you're an insomniac or a vampire and want to sell to werewolves, don't let your auctions close in the middle of the night, at 02:30? Not enough bidders are around to cause any last-minute bidding that would bump up the price.

Your secret safety net — reserve price

Here's a little secret: The reason sellers list big-ticket items like Ferraris, grand pianos, and high-tech computer equipment with a starting bid of $1 is because they're protected from losing money with a *reserve price.* The reserve price is the lowest price that must be met before the item can be sold. It's not required by eBay but can protect you. eBay charges an additional fee for this feature that varies depending on how high your reserve is.

For example, say you list a first edition book of John Steinbeck's *The Grapes of Wrath*. You set the starting price at $1, and you set a reserve price at $80. That means that people can start bidding at $1, and if at the end of the auction the book hasn't reached the $80 reserve, you don't have to sell the book.

As with everything in life, using a reserve price for your auctions has an upside and a downside. Many choosy bidders and bargain hunters blast past reserve-price auctions because they see a reserve price as a sign that proclaims "No bargains here!" Many bidders figure they can get a better deal on the same item with an auction that proudly declares *NR* (for *no reserve*) in its description. As an enticement to those bidders, you see lots of NR listings in auction titles.

If you need to set a reserve on your item, help the bidder out. Many bidders shy away from an auction that has a reserve, but if they're really interested, they will read the item description. To dispel their fears that the item is way too expensive or out of their price range, add a line in your description that states the amount of your reserve price. "I have put a reserve of $75 on this item to protect my investment; the highest bid over $75 will win the item." A phrase such as this takes away the vagueness of the reserve auction and allows you to place a reserve with a low opening bid. (You want to reel 'em in, remember?)

On lower-priced items, I suggest that you set a higher minimum bid and set no reserve. Otherwise, if you're not sure about the market, set a low minimum bid but set a high reserve to protect yourself.

If bids don't reach a set reserve price, some sellers e-mail the highest bidder and offer the item at what the seller thinks is a fair price. Two caveats:

- ✔ eBay can suspend the seller *and* the buyer if the side deal is reported to SafeHarbor. This activity is strictly prohibited.

- ✔ eBay won't protect buyers or sellers if a side deal goes bad.

You can't use a reserve price in a Multiple Item (Dutch) auction.

I want to be alone: The private auction

In a private auction, bidders' User IDs are kept under wraps. Sellers typically use this option to protect the identities of bidders during auctions for high-priced big-ticket items (say, that restored World War II fighter). Wealthy eBay users may not want the world to know that they have the resources to buy expensive items. Private auctions are also held for items from the Adult/Erotica category. (Gee, there's a shocker.)

The famous sign that was pictured in almost every piece of Disney promotion (for the first 40 or so years of Disneyland's existence) was put up for sale on eBay in 2000. Legend has it that the sign was purchased by actor John Stamos for a high bid of $30,700. Unfortunately for John, the Disney auctions did not use the private auction feature. After news of the winner's name hit the tabloids — the entire world knew John's eBay User ID! He had to change his ID in a hurry to end the throngs of lovey-dovey e-mail headed to his computer!

In private auctions, the seller's e-mail address is accessible to bidders in case questions arise. Bidders' e-mail addresses remain unseen.

Put me in the Gallery

The Gallery is a visually graphic auction area that lets you post pictures to a special photo gallery that's accessible from the listings. It also causes a postage-stamp-size version of your image to appear next to your listing in the category or search. Many buyers enjoy browsing the Gallery catalog-style, and it's open to all categories. If you choose to go this route, your item is listed in both the Gallery and in the regular text listings. (I explain how to post your pictures in Chapter 14.)

The best thing about using a Gallery picture in your listings is that it increases the space your listing takes up on a search or category page. If you don't use a Gallery picture and just have an image in your auction, all that will be next to your listing is a teeny, tiny camera icon.

Filling out the item location

eBay wants you to list the general area and the country in which you live. The idea behind telling the bidder where you live is to give him or her a heads-up on what kind of shipping charges to expect. Don't be esoteric (listing where you live as *The Here and Now* isn't a whole lot of help) but don't go crazy with cross-streets, landmarks, or degrees of latitude. Listing the city and state you live in is enough.

eBay also wants you to indicate in which of its local regions you reside. Doing so allows your auction to be listed under the Regional eBay pages. You also have the option not to be listed. I recommend that, if you live in one of the listed metropolitan areas, you use the benefits of local trading and select your area.

If you live in a big area — say, suburban Los Angeles (who, me?), which sprawls on for miles — you may want to think about narrowing down your region a little. You may find a bidder who lives close to you, which could swing your auction. If you do a face-to-face transaction, doing it in a public place is a good idea. (I like doing my trades at Starbucks.)

A picture is worth a thousand words

Clichés again? Perhaps. But an item on eBay without a picture is almost a waste of time. If you haven't set up photo hosting elsewhere, you can list one picture with eBay's Pictures Service for free. Additional ones cost you $0.15 each.

Alternatively, you can put all the pictures you want in your auction description for free. See Chapter 14 for the necessary coding and instructions.

Listing Designer

How many times have you seen an item on eBay laid out on the page all pretty-like with a fancy border around the description? If that sort of thing appeals to you, eBay's Listing Designer will supply you with pretty borders for almost any type of item for $0.10. Will the pretty borders increase the amount of bids your auction will get? It's doubtful. A clean item description with a couple of good clear pictures of your item is really all you need.

Listing the payment methods you'll accept

Yeah, sure, eBay is loads of fun, but the bottom line to selling is the phrase "Show me the money!" You make the call on what you're willing to take as money from the high bidder of your auction. eBay offers the following payment options — just select the ones that you like:

✔ **Money Order/Cashier's Check:** From a seller's point of view, this is the safest method of payment. It's the closest thing you can get to cash. As a seller, you want to get paid with as little risk as possible. The only drawback? You have to wait for the buyer to mail it.

✔ **Credit Cards:** If you accept credit cards, using PayPal is the cheapest and most convenient way to go. If you have a merchant account through a retail store, be sure to select the little check boxes next to the credit cards you accept.

Offering a credit card payment option often attracts higher bids to your auctions. These higher bids usually more than cover the small percentage that credit card payment services charge you to use their services. See Chapter 8 for a more complete description on how to use these services.

Some sellers who use credit card services try attaching an additional fee (to cover their credit card processing fees) to the final payment. However, that's against the law in California, home of eBay, and therefore against eBay's rules. So forget about it. eBay can end your auction if it catches you.

✔ **C.O.D. (Cash on Delivery):** I think that this option is the least attractive for both buyers and sellers. The buyer has to be home with the cash ready to go on the day that the package arrives. Odds are that on the day the item's delivered, your buyer is taking his or her sick pet goldfish to the vet for a gill-cleaning. Then the item ends up back at your door, and you have no sale. It also often takes up to 30 days for you to get the money back in your hands.

✔ **See Item Description:** I think you should always state in your item description how you want to be paid. Why? Because there's no good reason not to and it takes away the mystery of shopping with you.

✔ **Personal Check:** This is an extremely popular option, but it comes with a risk: The check could bounce higher than a lob at Wimbledon. If you accept personal checks, explain in your item description how long you plan to wait for the check to clear before sending the merchandise. The average hold is about ten business days. Some sellers wait as long as two weeks. Accepting eChecks through PayPal leaves all the bookkeeping and waiting to PayPal; you don't have to call the bank for confirmation.

Cut down on the risk of bad checks by reading the bidder's feedback when the auction's underway. Be wary of accepting checks from people with negative comments. (I explain all about feedback in Chapter 4.) Never ship an item until you're certain the check has cleared the buyer's bank.

eBay is trying to take some of the mystery and foreboding out of accepting checks with its ID Verify program, which allows VeriSign, a gigantic check-verification company, to run credit checks and present eBay members with a clean bill of health. (For more on ID Verify, see Chapter 16.)

✔ **Online Escrow:** An escrow service acts as a referee, a neutral third party. Unless you're selling an expensive item, however, offering escrow is overkill. Usually, the buyer pays for this service. Escrow companies typically charge 5 percent of the sale price. On big-ticket items, it may make the difference between a sale and a pass. Escrow gives bidders an added sense of security. If you do offer escrow, the winning bidder should inform you right after the auction if he or she intends to use it. You can find more on escrow in Chapter 6.

✔ **Other:** If you're offering payment options that aren't listed here, select this option. Some buyers (mostly international) like to pay in cash, but I think this is *way* too risky and recommend that you *never,* ever deal in cash. If a problem arises — for either buyer or seller — no one has evidence that payment was made or received. Avoid it.

Most sellers offer buyers several ways to pay. You can choose as many as you want. When the auction page appears, your choices are noted at the top of the listing. Listing several payment options makes you look like a flexible, easygoing professional.

Setting shipping terms

Ahoy, matey! Hoist the bid! Okay, not quite. Before you run it up the mast, select your shipping options. Here are your choices:

✔ **Ship to the United States Only:** This option is selected by default; it means you only ship domestically.

✔ **Will Ship Worldwide:** The world is your oyster. But make sure that you can afford it.

✔ **Will Ship to United States and the Following Regions:** If you're comfortable shipping to certain countries but not to others, make your selections here, and they show up on your auction page.

When you indicate that you will ship internationally, your auction shows up on the international eBay sites, which is a fantastic way to attract new buyers! eBay has lots of good international users, so you may want to consider selling your items around the world. If you do, be sure to clearly state in the description all extra shipping costs and customs charges. (See Chapter 12 for more information on how to ship to customers abroad.)

Traditionally, the buyer pays for shipping, and this is the point at which you must decide how much to charge. You also have to calculate how much this item will cost you to ship. If it's a small item (weighing under a pound or so), you may decide to charge a flat rate to all buyers. To charge a flat rate, click the Flat Shipping Rates tab and fill in the shipping amount. Before you fill in the amount, be sure to include your charges for packing (see Chapter 12 for more info on how much to add for this task) and how much the insurance charges will be. When your item weighs two pounds or more, you may want to use eBay's versatile shipping calculator. Because UPS and the U.S. Postal Service now charge variable rates for packages of the same weight, based on distance, using the calculator simplifies things for your customers (and you). Be sure you've weighed the item and know how much your handling charge will be. The calculator allows you to input a handling amount and adds it to the overall shipping total. But does not break out the amount separately for the customer. The calculator also conveniently calculates the proper insurance amount for the item. Figure 10-7 shows how simple the form is.

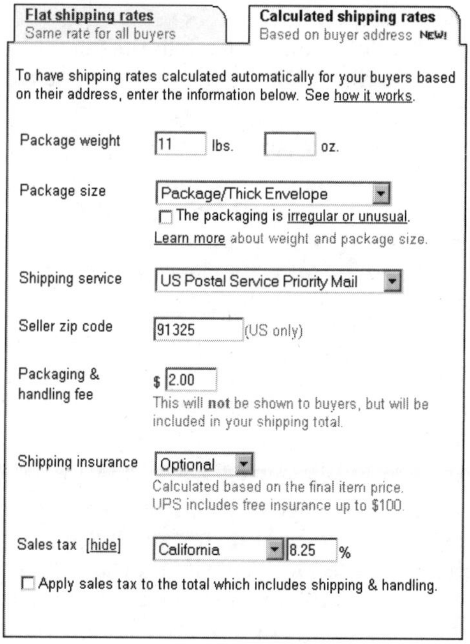

Figure 10-7:
Input your item shipping information in the calculator.

The calculator appears on the item page so that prospective buyers can type in their zip code and immediately know how much shipping will be to their location.

Check out Chapter 12 for more information on shipping options.

eBay Options: Ballyhoo on the Cheap

Although eBay's display options aren't quite as effective as a three-story neon sign in Times Square, they do bring greater attention to your auction. Here are your options:

✔ **Bold:** eBay fee: $1. Bold type does catch your attention but don't bother using it on items that'll bring in less than $25. Do use it if you're in hot competition with similar items and you want yours to stand out.

✔ **Highlight:** eBay fee: $5. Yellow highlighter is what I use to point out the high points in books I read. (You're using one now, aren't you?) The eBay highlight feature is lilac, but it can really make your item shine. Check out the category in which you choose to list before selecting this feature. Some categories are overwhelmed with sellers using the highlight option, and the pages look completely shaded in lilac. In these categories, *not* using highlight (and using perhaps a bold title instead) makes your auction stand out more.

✔ **Home Page Featured:** eBay fee: $99.95 ($199.95 for Multiple Item listings). As with expensive real estate, you pay a premium for location, location, location. The $99.95 gives you the highest level of visibility at eBay, and it occasionally appears smack dab in the middle of the eBay home page (although there's no guarantee that it will). Figure 10-8 shows the featured auctions on eBay's home page.

Bidders do browse the Featured Items to see what's there, just as you might head directly to the New Releases section of your video store. But, because the vast majority of auctions found at eBay are under $25, the average seller doesn't use the Featured Items option.

✔ **Featured Plus!** eBay fee: $19.95. You want top billing? You can buy it here. This option puts you on the first page of your item category and on search results pages. This is a good option for moving special merchandise. Often, bidders just scan the top items; if you want to be seen, you gotta be there. eBay's statistics say that items listed as Featured Plus! are 58 percent more likely to sell — but it really depends on what you're selling and when. Ask yourself this: Is it worth $20 to have more people see my item? If yes, then go for it. Figure 10-9 shows how items are listed in the Featured Plus! listings.

You need a feedback rating of at least 10 to make it to the Featured Items and Featured Plus! auctions.

Figure 10-8:
If you're lucky, your Home Page Featured auction will rotate through the home page at a premium time of day.

Featured Items   *all items...*

- New-In-Box WebTV Units & Keyboards $24 Web TV
- Not $60! Amazing Bust Enhancing Pills! $11.95
- 15% Police Pepper Spray & Holster $3.45 Hot!
- Original Bettie Betty Page Front Window
- $35 Rechargable Shaver & kit-ONLY $9.99!!WOW!
- HOCKEY Pens vs Boston 01-08 2nd Row !NR!
- *all featured items...*

Figure 10-9:
Featured items appear at the top of a search page or at the top of the category listings, as pictured here.

Home > All Categories > Coins > Coins: US > Quarters > Washington (1932-Now)   ⑦ **Questions**

Basic Search

☑ **only** in Washington (1932-Now)
☐ in titles & descriptions

[Search] Advanced Search

Related Items
- US Paper Money
- Political Memorabilia
- Coin Supplies
- Coin Operated Machines
- Coin Grading

Washington (1932-Now)   Sell your item in this category

281 items found

Show only: current | new today | **ending today** | going, going, gone | items near me

| All items | | Gallery items only | Updated:Jan-07 18:42:14 PST |

Picture hide

	Featured Items - Ending Today	Price	Bids	Ends PST
	GREAT SOFTWARE FOR YOUR *COIN* COLLECTIBLES! 📄 🔲	$12.95	5	Jan-08 16:25

To find out how to be listed in this section and seen by thousands, please visit this link Featured Auctions

Picture	All Items - Ending Today	Price	Bids	Ends PST
📷	1954 25c Washington ANACS MS 65 Coin	$18.00	-	Jan-07 19:14
📷	1953 25c Washington ANACS MS 65 Coin	$18.00	-	Jan-07 19:14
📷	1953-S 25c Washington ANACS MS 65 Coin	$21.00	-	Jan-07 19:15
📷	1956 25c Washington NGC MS 66 Coin	$21.00	-	Jan-07 19:15
📷	1964 25c/Washington NGC PF68 Coin ＝Buy It Now	$13.00	-	Jan-07 19:15
📷	1953-D 25c Washington ANACS MS 65 Coin	$19.00	-	Jan-07 19:16

Checking Your Work and Starting the Auction

After you've filled in all the blanks on the Sell Your Item page and you think you're ready to join the world of e-commerce, follow these steps:

1. **Click the Review button at the bottom of the Sell Your Item page.**

   You waft to the Verification page (shown in Figure 10-10), the place where you can catch mistakes before your item is listed. The Verification page shows you a condensed version of all your information and tallies up how much eBay is charging you in fees and options to run this auction. You also see a preview of how your auction description and pictures will look on the site.

   You also may find the Verification page helpful as a last-minute chance to get your bearings. If you've chosen a very general category, eBay asks you whether you're certain there isn't a more appropriate category. You can go back to any of the pages that need correcting by clicking the appropriate tab on the top of the Verification page. Make category changes or any other changes and additions, and then head for the Verification page again.

2. **Check for mistakes.**

   Nit-pick for common, careless errors; you won't be sorry. I've seen eBay members make goofs such as the wrong category listing, spelling and grammatical errors, and missing information about shipping, handling, insurance, and payment methods.

3. **When you're sure everything's accurate and you're happy with your item listing, click the Submit My Listing button.**

   An Auction Confirmation page pops up from eBay. At that precise moment, your auction begins, even though it may be a couple of hours before it appears in eBay's search and listings updates. If you want to see your auction right away and check for bids, your Auction Confirmation page provides a link for that purpose. Click the link, and you're there. You can also keep track of your auctions by using the My eBay page. (To find out how, see Chapter 4.)

All auction pages come with this friendly warning:

```
Seller assumes all responsibility for listing this item. You
should contact the seller to resolve any questions before
bidding.
```

Some eBay veterans just gloss over this warning after they've been wheeling and dealing for a while, but it's an important rule to remember. See Chapter 9 for details on the rules sellers must follow and Chapter 12 for tips on your role in closing the deal and receiving good feedback.

For the first 24 hours after your auction is underway, eBay stamps the Auction Item page with a funky sunrise icon next to the listing. This is just a little reminder for buyers to come take a look at the latest items up for sale.

Figure 10-10:
The Verification page is the last place you can double-check for errors before the listing begins.

Within the figure:

Revise Your Item: Review & Submit Listing

Item you are revising:
Starting an eBay Business for Dummies SIGNED (#2958092471)
Listed on: Oct-15-03 12:54:52 PM PDT
Item has NO BIDS/PURCHASES, more than 12 hours left

Click an 'Edit page' link to make changes. When you do, you'll be directed to a page where you can make your desired changes.

Starting an eBay Business for Dummies SIGNED — Edit Title

Description — Edit description

SQUARE TRADE
Oct. 15, 2003

eBay User ID:
marsha_c

SquareTrade Verified Seller
Click to Learn More

Best Seller Signed & Dedicated to the Winner by the Author

On the BusinessWeek Magazine BestSeller List!
eBay just gets better and better. If it's your intent to take the leap from casual seller to starting a full or part time business at eBay as a Power

Mid-Course Corrections: Fixing Current Auctions

Don't worry if you make a mistake filling out the Sell Your Item page but don't notice it until after the auction is up and running. Pencils have erasers, and eBay allows revisions. You can make changes at two stages of the game: before the first bid is placed and after the bidding war is underway. The following sections explain what you can (and can't) correct — and when you have to accept the little imperfections of your Auction Item page.

Making changes before bidding begins

Here's what you can change about your auction before bids have been placed (and when it does not end within 12 hours):

- The title or description of your auction
- The item category
- The item's Minimum Bid price

- ✔ The item's Buy It Now price

- ✔ The reserve price (you can add, change, or remove it)

- ✔ The duration of your listing

- ✔ The URL of the picture you're including with your auction

- ✔ A private auction designation (you can add or remove it)

- ✔ Accepted payment methods, checkout information, item location, and shipping terms

When you revise an auction, eBay puts a little notation on your auction page that reads: Description(revised). (Think of it as automatic common courtesy.)

To revise an auction before bids have been received, follow these steps:

1. **Go to the auction page and click the Revise Your Item link.**

   This link will only appear if you've Signed In to eBay. If the item hasn't received any bids, a message appears on your screen to indicate that you may update the item.

   You're taken to the Sign In page, which outlines the rules for revising your item. At the bottom, the item number will be filled in. Click Revise Item.

2. **You arrive at the Revise Item page which looks like the Sell Your Item form.**

   Click the link that corresponds to the area that you'd like to change.

3. **Make changes to the item information and then click the Save Changes button at the bottom of the page when you're finished.**

   A summary of your newly revised auction page appears on your screen.

4. **If you're happy with your revisions, click the Submit Revisions.**

   If not, click the Back button of your browser and redo the Update Your Information page.

   You're taken to your newly revised auction item page, where you see a disclaimer from eBay that says you've revised the auction before the first bid.

Making changes after bidding begins

If your auction is up and running and already receiving bids, you can still make some slight modifications to it. Newly added information is clearly separated from the original text and pictures. In addition, eBay puts a time stamp on the additional info in case questions from early bidders crop up later.

After your item receives bids, eBay allows you to add to your item's description. If you feel you were at a loss for words in writing your item's description or if a lot of potential bidders are asking the same questions, go ahead and make all the additions you want. But whatever you put there the first time around stays in the description as well.

You've discovered that the Apollo 11 cookie jar you thought was a reproduction is really an original? Better change that description before you sell it. When your item has received bids, you can add to your item's description.

Follow the same procedure for making changes before bidding begins. When you arrive at the Revise Your Item page, you'll *only* be given the option to add to your description, add features, or add additional payment information. Your initial listing will not be changed — only appended.

Alternatively, click Services in the navigation bar at the top of the page, scroll down to Manage Your Active Listings and click the Add to Item Description link. If you use this route, you'll have to have the item number written down, as it must be input prior to making any changes.

Don't let an oversight grow into a failure to communicate and don't ignore iffy communication until the auction is over. Correct any inaccuracies in your auction information now to avoid problems later on.

Always check your e-mail to see whether bidders have questions about your item. If a bidder wants to know about flaws, be truthful and courteous when returning e-mails. As you get more familiar with eBay (and with writing auction descriptions), the number of e-mail questions will decrease. If you enjoy good customer service in your day-to-day shopping, here's your chance to give some back.

Chapter 11

Forget the Car — Drive Your Mouse to an eBay Store

Sometimes you just don't wanna buy in an auction. Sometimes you want to buy your item *now*. No waiting for an auction to end — *now!* The easiest place to go for this type of transaction is the eBay Stores area, where you find fixed-price items that feature an eBay Buy It Now price.

All the fine — and funky — merchandise that you can find on eBay can also be found in the eBay Stores area. eBay Stores is located in a separate area from the regular auctions, and regular eBay sellers run these stores. eBay Stores is a place where sellers can list as many additional items for sale as they'd like for a reduced Insertion Fee. Buyers are lured to the store by the small red eBay Stores icon that appears next to the seller's User ID.

Whenever you're looking at an item, and you see that the seller has a store, be sure to click the store icon. The seller may have the very same merchandise in his or her eBay store for a lower buy price.

If a seller has an eBay store, he or she can list individual items for different sizes of an article of clothing, different variations of items that he or she sells in regular auctions, or anything that falls within eBay's listing policies. The store items have a listing time of at least 30 days, so sellers can also put up specialty items that may not sell well in a short auction term of only one to ten days.

The requirements to open an eBay store are pretty basic. I suggest that you transact business on the site for quite a while before you open a store. You need to have a solid understanding of how eBay works and know how to handle all types of transactions. These are eBay's requirements:

✔ You must be registered as an eBay seller, with a credit card on file.

✔ You must have a feedback rating or 20 or more (or be ID Verified).

✔ You must accept credit card payments, either through PayPal or through a merchant account.

TIP

The eBay search engine does not directly search the eBay Stores area. If you're looking for a particular item, search eBay, and then on the results page, look at the column of links on the left. Scroll down, and if a store has your item in stock, the store is listed with a clickable link in a box entitled More on eBay, Shop eBay Stores. This box appears under the Display option box.

To get to the eBay Stores main area, visit the eBay home page, look for the Specialty Sites link on the upper left (see Figure 11-1), and click the eBay Stores link. Alternatively, you can type **www.ebaystores.com** in the address box of your Web browser.

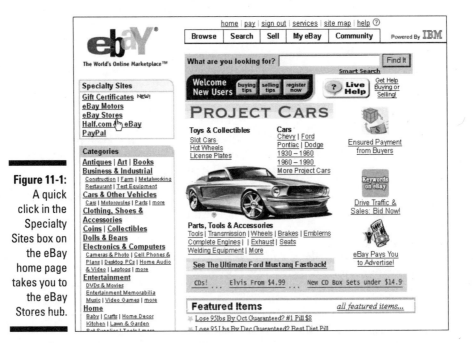

Figure 11-1:
A quick click in the Specialty Sites box on the eBay home page takes you to the eBay Stores hub.

Unlimited Shopping from the Stores Page

Okay, you've arrived! You've come to the hub of power shopping online, the eBay Stores home page (see Figure 11-2). Just like the eBay home page, this is your gateway to many incredible bargains. This section takes a look at what you find there, how to navigate the stores, and how to find the deals.

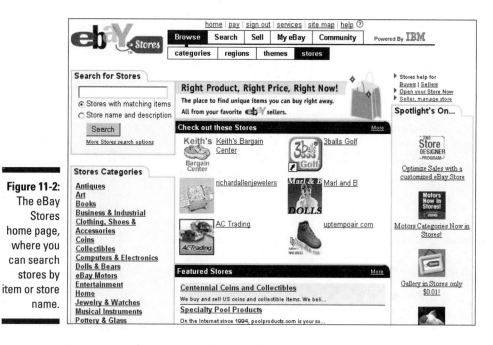

Figure 11-2:
The eBay
Stores
home page,
where you
can search
stores by
item or store
name.

eBay Stores search

On the top-left of the eBay Stores home page is the search engine for eBay
Stores. You can perform your search in eBay stores on different levels. You
can search for Buy It Now items — seems a tad bit too obvious for me, isn't
that why we're here? Anyway, if you type your keyword in the box and stay
with the default search, you'll find all the Buy it Now items in the stores that
match your keyword.

eBay Stores don't just list the Buy It Now items. If sellers have current auctions on eBay, those auctions are listed in their stores as well — only regular
auctions won't come up in an eBay Stores item search. So if you find an auction that interests you at eBay, click the item to read the description and
the condition of the item. If you want to buy the item, then click the Visit My
eBay Store link next to the store name on the top of the item page to go to the
seller's eBay store. You just may find some related items that you want. And
the seller probably combines shipping so that you save some money!

By the way, before you click Buy It Now, you should — all together now! —
double-check the seller's feedback.

When you get the results of an eBay Stores search, you can click the Find Related Auction Items in All eBay link at the bottom of the page to search for similar items on eBay auctions (see Figure 11-3). By clicking this link, you go to eBay (the auctions) to find auction items that match your search. I highly recommend clicking the link before you decide to buy — you may find your item on auction at a considerably lower price. Time is money, and if you have the time, you can save some money.

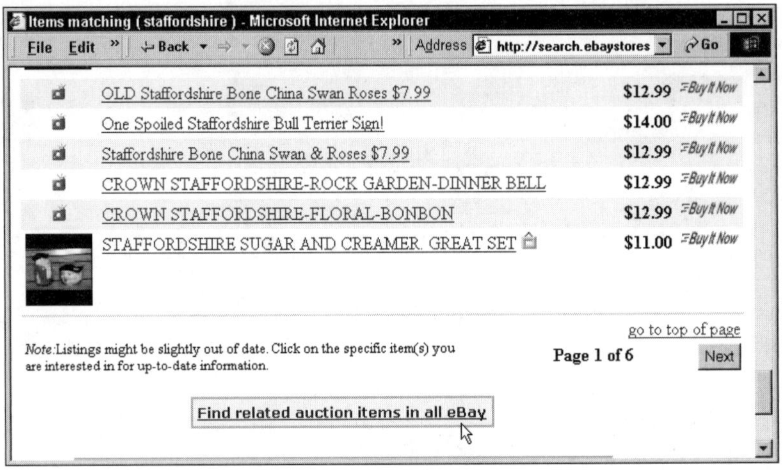

Figure 11-3: Here's a link to more items when performing an eBay Stores search.

OLD Staffordshire Bone China Swan Roses $7.99	$12.99	Buy It Now
One Spoiled Staffordshire Bull Terrier Sign!	$14.00	Buy It Now
Staffordshire Bone China Swan & Roses $7.99	$12.99	Buy It Now
CROWN STAFFORDSHIRE-ROCK GARDEN-DINNER BELL	$12.99	Buy It Now
CROWN STAFFORDSHIRE-FLORAL-BONBON	$12.99	Buy It Now
STAFFORDSHIRE SUGAR AND CREAMER. GREAT SET	$11.00	Buy It Now

Note: Listings might be slightly out of date. Click on the specific item(s) you are interested in for up-to-date information.

go to top of page
Page 1 of 6 Next

Find related auction items in all eBay

If you remember a particular seller's store name (or part of it), you can also search eBay Stores by store name. All you have to do is type the store name (or part of the store name), as shown in Figure 11-4 in the Search Stores box and select the Search Store Name and Description option button.

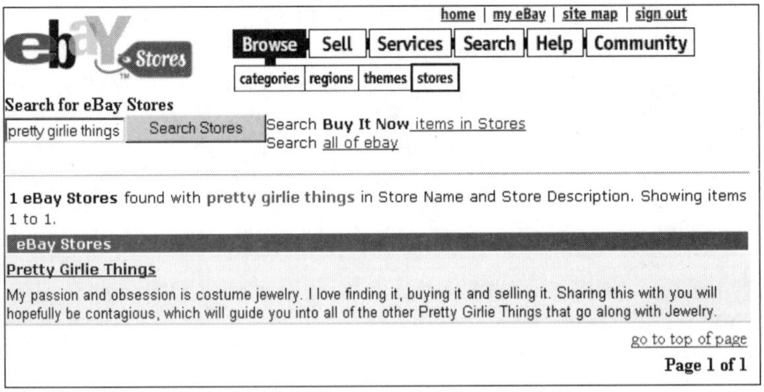

Figure 11-4: Finding a store by name.

home | my eBay | site map | sign out

eBay Stores

Browse | Sell | Services | Search | Help | Community
categories | regions | themes | stores

Search for eBay Stores
pretty girlie things Search Stores Search **Buy It Now** items in Stores
Search all of ebay

1 eBay Stores found with **pretty girlie things** in Store Name and Store Description. Showing items 1 to 1.

eBay Stores

Pretty Girlie Things
My passion and obsession is costume jewelry. I love finding it, buying it and selling it. Sharing this with you will hopefully be contagious, which will guide you into all of the other Pretty Girlie Things that go along with Jewelry.

go to top of page
Page 1 of 1

If you can't remember the store name, but you can remember what it sells, type the keywords in the search box while selecting the Search Store Name and Description option. For example, you can search for *terrier t-shirts*. If the seller has used those words in his or her store description or title, it shows up in the search results listing, as shown in Figure 11-5.

Figure 11-5: A search for keywords in the store description.

Browsing the store categories

Browsing store categories is a great idea when you're looking for a specialist — you know, someone who carries a particular type of item that appeals to you. Perhaps you have an affinity for jewelry, art, limited edition books, or needlepoint. Whatever your interest, you'll probably find a store here to suit your needs.

To browse eBay Stores, just click Browse in the navigation bar on any eBay page. In the subnavigation box that appears below it, click Stores, and you travel to the eBay Stores hub. Look for a list of categories on the left side of page; click a category that suits your fancy. When you do that, the left side of the page (surprise!) lists subcategories within that category. I clicked the category Coins and then the subcategory US Coins, and got the subcategory hub page shown in Figure 11-6.

Browsing eBay Stores categories is like strolling down a mall filled with your favorite items. Note that stores with the highest inventories in the category are listed towards the top.

Just like in the brick and mortar world, more "general" stores at eBay carry a wide breadth of merchandise. By browsing individual categories, you may be missing them. Try visiting the Everything Else category, and you'll find, well, everything else.

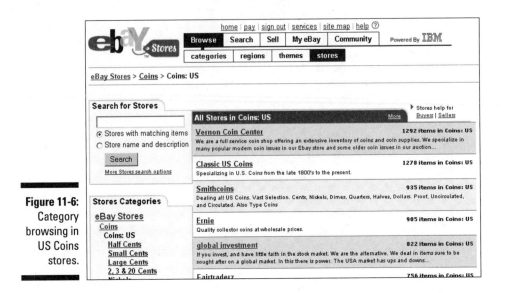

Figure 11-6:
Category
browsing in
US Coins
stores.

Selling from Your Own Virtual Storefront

After you've shopped the eBay Stores, you may be thinking that this is a good place to open your own store. There's great news on that end because eBay Stores have the most reasonable rent on the Internet. At an eBay Store, you are not constrained by the auction format of a one-to-ten day maximum. You can list your fixed-price items in your eBay store on a "good till cancelled" basis.

Paying the landlord

Monthly rent for an eBay store is as low as $9.95 per month. Featured stores have a rent of $49.95, and anchor stores (just like your local department store) pay $499.95 a month. Featured stores' listings are guaranteed to rotate through the special featured section on the eBay Stores home page. These listings also appear on the top level of their category directory page. Anchor stores get extra promotion, and their logos are showcased in the stores' directory pages.

The reasonable pricing behind eBay Stores is a remarkable bargain. For as little as $9.95 a month, you have the opportunity to sell your merchandise to over 73 million registered users! See Table 11-1 for eBay Store listing fees.

Table 11-1	eBay Store Listing Fees		
Listing Length (Days)	*Basic Fee*	*Surcharge*	*Total*
30 days	$0.05	$0.00	$0.05
60 days	0.05	0.05	0.10
90 days	0.05	0.10	0.15
120 days	0.05	0.15	0.20
Good Till Cancelled	0.05	0.05 for every additional 30 days	Depends on length of listing

Listing fees and monthly "rent" can be just the tip of the iceberg if you choose to get fancy by using all kinds of options. My recommendation? Don't spend too much on them until you're fully entrenched in an eBay business — by that time, you'll have the experience to know what to add and when. Stick with the basics. All the same Final Value Fees and listing option costs apply as in regular eBay auctions. (See Chapter 9 for the actual figures.)

The Gallery option fee is reduced for use in store listings only. For example, the very valuable option of a Gallery picture adds only $0.01 to your listing cost! That makes the total cost of your individual listing, with a Gallery picture, only $0.06!

Opening your eBay store

Because this book is your introduction to eBay, I'll just give you some ideas about opening an eBay store. In my advanced book, *Starting an eBay Business For Dummies* (Wiley Publishing, Inc.), I take you step-by-step through the basics of opening your store.

The easiest way for a beginner to open an eBay store is to get ahold of a large quantity of a single item, such as six dozen umbrellas, and then list these items separately. Keep in mind the costs of your items before pricing them. List an auction for one of the items and, within your description, mention that you have more in your eBay store. Also offer to combine shipping costs on multiple purchases.

Naming your store is your first challenge. Pick out a name that describes the type of items your store will carry or one that includes your User ID. Don't pick a name that is so esoteric or overly creative that it doesn't give possible shoppers a clue as to what you carry. A creative store name and graphic logo are pictured in Figure 11-7.

Figure 11-7:
The eBay
Stores page
for my store.

As you can see from my store page, each store can have its own categories. You get to make them up yourself so your customers can find items within your store in an organized manner. You can define up to 19 custom categories (a maximum of 29 characters for each name) in your store.

Your eBay store home page has links for your Store Information: Store Policies and About the Seller page. The About the Store Page is the same as your About Me page (discussed in Chapter 14).

Spend some serious time on eBay before you open the store. Study some of the very successful stores. You want to have enough know-how to make your store a success!

Chapter 12

Closing the Deal and Shipping It Out

. . . .

In This Chapter

▶ Staying organized

▶ Communicating with the buyer

▶ Packing and sending the item

▶ Purchasing stamps and services online

. . . .

*T*he auction's over, and you have a winning bidder, who (you hope) is eager to send you money. Sounds perfect, doesn't it? It is if you watch your step, keep on top of things, and communicate like a professional.

In this chapter, I help you figure out how to stay organized by showing you what documents you need to keep and for how long. I also include tips and etiquette on communicating with the buyer so that you're most likely to come out with positive feedback. In addition, you find out how to pack your item, assess costs, and make sure the item reaches the buyer when you say it will (oh, yeah . . . and in one piece).

Bookkeeping and Staying Organized

Although I don't recommend lining your nest with every scrap from every auction you run, you can safely keep some documents without mutating into a giant pack rat. Until you become an eBay expert and have other ways to electronically store your information, you should print and file these essentials:

 ✔ **The auction page as it appeared when the auction closed:** This page gives you a record of the item name and number, the bidding history, every bidder's User ID, and a lot of other useful information. The page also includes the auction item description (and any revisions you've made to it), which is handy if the buyer argues that an item's disintegrating before his eyes and you honestly believe it's just well loved.

You may think you don't need this information because you can always look it up, but here practicality rears its head: eBay makes completed auctions seem to disappear after 30 days. However, if you use the custom link that appears in your End of Auction e-mail (see the next bullet), you can access the auction online for up to 90 days. Print your auction page *before* you forget about it, file it where you know you can find it, and *then* forget about it.

✔ **The End of Auction (EOA) e-mail you receive from eBay that notifies you that the auction is over:** If you lose this e-mail, you can't get it back because eBay doesn't keep it.

I set up a separate folder in my Microsoft Outlook e-mail program for End of Auction e-mails. When one comes in, I read it and then drag it over to its special folder. That way, I can always check this folder for the information I need.

✔ **E-mail between you and the buyer:** In the virtual world, e-mail is as close to having a face-to-face conversation as most people get. Your e-mail correspondence is a living record of all the things you discuss with the buyer to complete the transaction. Even if you sell just a few items a month at eBay, keep track of who's paid up and who owes you money. And more importantly, if the buyer says, "I told you I'd be out of town," you can look through your e-mail and say, "Nope, it doesn't show up here," or "You're right! How was Timbuktu? Is the payment on the way?" Or something more polite. Be sure to keep that e-mail with the headers and date on it so that you can't be accused of (ahem) creative writing.

✔ **PayPal payment notices:** You get a notice from PayPal when the buyer pays for the item. The notice has the auction information and the buyer's shipping information. (When that e-mail arrives, the clock begins to tick on sending out the item.)

✔ **Any bank statements you receive that reflect a payment that doesn't clear:** Keep anything related to payments, especially payments that didn't go through. That way, if a buyer says he's sure he sent you a check, you can say, "Yes sir, Mr. X, you did send me a check, and it was made of the finest rubber." Or something kinder, especially if you want that payment.

✔ **Any insurance or escrow forms that you have:** Until the item has arrived and you're sure the customer is satisfied, be sure to keep those shipping and insurance receipts, as well as any documentation that goes along with an escrow sale.

✔ **Refund requests you make:** If you make a request to eBay for a refund from an auction that doesn't go through, hold on to it until the process is completed.

✔ **Receipts for items that you buy for the sole purpose of selling them on eBay:** This comes in handy as a reference so that you can see if you're making a profit. It can also be helpful at tax time.

Tales from the formerly Type A

Confession time. I used to keep all my paper-work — auctions, e-mails, the works. Now I keep the e-mails and receipts sent to me until I know a transaction is complete. Then they go wafting off to the Recycle Bin so that I can still find a file in my Outlook program.

These days, I stay on top of my eBay finances with auction-management software that helps me keep track of who has paid me and who hasn't. These programs also help me figure out my expenses, profits, and other financial calcu-lations, almost painlessly. (See Chapter 20 for more information on these programs.) They also help jazz up the look of my auctions. Ah, progress.

Someday, the Internal Revenue Service (or government agency in your area) may knock on your door. Scary, but true. Like hurricanes and asteroid strikes, audits happen. Any accountant worth his or her salt will tell you that the best way to handle the possibility of an audit is to be prepared for the worst — even if every eBay transaction you conduct runs smooth as silk and you've kept your nose sparkling clean. See Chapter 9 for more tax information.

If you accept online payments by PayPal (PayPal Premier or Business members only), you can download your transaction history for use in QuickBooks, Quicken, or Excel. Additionally, these programs are excellent sources for your documentation.

Once a month, conduct a By Seller search on yourself so that you can print out all the information on the bid histories of your most recent auctions. I do this independently of my auction software. Having the listings neatly printed out easily helps you see what sold for how much and when. Chapter 5 gives you the lowdown on how to perform this search.

When it comes to printouts of e-mails and documents about transactions, as soon as the item arrives at the destination and you get your positive feed-back, you can dump them. If you get negative feedback, hang on to your documentation a little longer (say, until you're sure the issues it raises are resolved and everyone's satisfied). If selling at eBay becomes a fairly regular source of income, save all receipts for items you've purchased to sell; for tax purposes, that's inventory.

If you sell specialized items, you can keep track of trends and who your fre-quent buyers are by saving your paperwork. This prudent habit becomes an excellent marketing strategy when you discover that a segment of eBay users faithfully bids on your auctions. An *audience*. Imagine that.

Talking to Buyers: The ABCs of Good Communication

You've heard it countless times — talk is cheap. Compared to what? Granted, empty promises are a dime a dozen, but honest-to-goodness talk and efficient e-mail are worth their weight in gold and good feedback — especially at eBay. Sometimes, *not* talking is costly.

A smooth exchange of money and merchandise really starts with you (the seller) and your attitude towards the transaction. Your auction description and then your first e-mail — soon after the auction is over — set the entire transaction in motion and set the tone for that transaction. If all goes well, *no more than* a week should elapse between getting paid and sending the item.

Take a proactive approach and start the ball rolling yourself. I suggest contacting the buyer even *before* you get eBay's EOA. Here's how to get the buyer's e-mail address:

1. **Start on the page of the item you sold.**

    Click the Contact the Buyer link next to the winner's name. If you signed in to eBay, you're taken to the User ID History page.

2. **Click the winner's e-mail address.**

    An e-mail window opens, showing the user's User ID history and e-mail information. This page tells you some needed information:

    - The person's e-mail address
    - The person's User ID (or multiple User IDs if the person did any name changes in the past)
    - The date the User ID became effective
    - The end date of the User ID (if this person had others in the past)

Signing in first puts a temporary cookie (a computer file that makes it easier to get around a Web site) in your computer so that you automatically get the e-mail addresses of eBay users (and other actions that you've specified on your My eBay Preferences page) without going through this process again. You have to set your preferences to do this on your My eBay page. If you selected the Keep Me Signed In on This Computer Unless I Sign Out check box when you signed into eBay, your password is saved even if you cut off your Internet connection. Your password is saved until you click the Sign Out link. For more tasty info on cookies, see Chapter 15.

Another way to access the buyer's information is to go to your My eBay page, scroll down to the Items I've Sold area, and click the buyer's name in the row of the auction in question.

Thank you — I mean it

What do all the successful big-name department stores have in common? Yes, great prices, good merchandise, and nice displays. But with all things being equal, customer service always wins hands-down. One department store in the United States, Nordstrom, has such a great reputation that the store happily took back a set of snow tires because a customer wasn't happy with them. No big deal, maybe — until you notice that Nordstrom doesn't even *sell* snow tires!

A friend of mine who owns restaurants calls this level of customer satisfaction the *Wow!* effect. If customers (no matter what they're buying) say, "Wow!" during or after the transaction — admiringly or happily — you've satisfied the customer. A good rule to go by: Give people the same level of service you expect when you're on the buying end.

The best way to start satisfying the buyer is with an introductory e-mail. Congratulate the person on winning the auction — making him or her feel good about the purchase — and thank the buyer for bidding on your item. Then provide these important details:

- ✔ Item name and auction number.
- ✔ Winning bid amount.
- ✔ Cost of shipping and packing, and any shipping or insurance restrictions. (I give pointers on determining shipping and packaging costs later in this chapter.)
- ✔ Payment options (check, money order, credit cards, or PayPal).
- ✔ How long you will hold the item waiting for a check to clear (usually 7 to 14 days).
- ✔ The shipping timetable.

You should also mind a few vital details in the first e-mail:

- ✔ Confirm the address (and daytime phone number if you think you need to call); ask whether this is where you should ship the item. If not, ask for the correct shipping address.
- ✔ Include your name and the address to which you want the payment sent.
- ✔ Remind buyers to write the item name, auction number, and shipping address on whatever form of payment they send. You'd be surprised how many buyers forget to give you the item number. Also ask buyers to print out and send a copy of your e-mail with the payment.
- ✔ If you're using an online payment service, such as PayPal, be sure to give buyers instructions on how they can pay for the auction online.

✔ Include your phone number if you think it will speed up the process.

✔ Suggest that if all goes well, you'll be happy to leave positive feedback for the buyer. (See Chapter 4 for more on feedback.)

You can also send an invoice from your My eBay page, Items I've Sold area. Just click the gray Send Invoice bar, verify all the information, and click Send Invoice. If you select the Copy Me check box on this invoice, you'll receive a copy. The buyer's copy has a link in the invoice, enabling the buyer to pay directly to PayPal (if you accept it for payment). Figure 12-1 shows what the invoice e-mail looks like.

Figure 12-1:
An eBay
invoice, as
sent to a
buyer.

Let's keep e-mailing

If you've got a good transaction going (and the majority of them are), the buyer will reply to your e-mail within three business days. Customarily, most replies come the next day. If your buyer has questions regarding anything you asked in your e-mail, you'll get those inquiries now. Most of the time, all you get back is, "Thanks. Payment on the way." Hey, that's good enough for me.

If any last-minute details need to be worked out, usually the buyer asks to set up a time to call or request further instructions about the transaction. Respond to this communication as soon as possible. If you can't deal with it at the moment, let the buyer know you're working on it and will shoot those answers back ASAP. *Never* let an e-mail go unanswered.

As soon as you get the hang of sending e-mail, you can add an eBay link that takes the buyer right to the Feedback Forum with just a click of the mouse. Buyers and sellers can also link to the Feedback Forum from the final auction page by clicking the Leave Feedback link.

For sample e-mail letters and deeper information, get your hands on a copy of my book on advanced eBay selling, *Starting an eBay Business For Dummies* (published by Wiley Publishing, Inc.).

Shipping without Going Postal

Shipping can be the most time-consuming (and most dreaded) task for eBay sellers. Even if the selling portion of your transaction goes flawlessly, the item has to get to the buyer in one piece. If it doesn't, the deal could be ruined — and so could your reputation.

This section briefs you on shipping etiquette, gives you details about the three most popular shipping options (the U.S. Postal Service, UPS, and FedEx Ground), and offers tips on how to make sure your package is ready to ride.

The best way to avoid shipping problems is to do your homework beforehand, determine which method is likely to work best, and spell out in your item description exactly how you intend to ship the item. I always say "Buyer pays actual shipping, handling, and insurance" in my item description, and that's what I charge, although I can make allowances if the buyer wants a specific method of shipment within reason. Here's how I handle the whole process:

1. **After the auction, get the package ready to ship.**

   You don't have to seal the package right away, but you should have it ready to seal because the two critical factors in shipping are weight and time. The more a package weighs and the faster it has to be delivered, the higher the charge. (I cover packing materials and tips later in this section.) The time to think about packing and shipping is *before* you put the item up for auction — that way, last-minute surprises are less likely to arise while your buyer waits impatiently for the item!

2. **Know your carrier options.**

   In the United States, the three main shipping options for most eBay transactions are the U.S. Postal Service, FedEx, and UPS. See the section "Shopping for a shipper" (try saying *that* five times fast) for how you can get rate options from each service, painlessly and online. Compare costs and services.

3. **Before quoting the shipping fees, make sure that you include all appropriate costs.**

   I recommend that you charge a nominal handling fee (up to $1.50 isn't out of line) to cover your packing materials, which can add up quickly as you start making multiple transactions. You should also include any insurance costs and any delivery-confirmation costs. See the sidebar "Insuring your peace of mind (and your shipment)" for more information.

   Some eBay scam artists inflate shipping and handling costs to make added profit. *Shame, shame, shame on them.* Purposely overcharging is tacky, ugly, and immature. And the buyer often figures it out after one look at the postage on the box.

   It's best to post the shipping amount (or use the eBay online shipping calculator — see Chapter 10 for more on how to use this tool) to give buyers an idea of how much shipping will be. This way, buyers can include this cost when they consider their bidding strategies. Figure out what the packed item will weigh and then give a good guess; the online calculators can help. If the item is particularly heavy, and you need to use a shipping service that charges by weight and distance, be sure to say in your auction description that you're just giving an estimate, and that the final cost will be determined after the auction is over. Optionally, you can tell the bidder how much the item weighs, where you're shipping from, and what your handling charges are (a few bidders don't mind doing the math).

   Occasionally, shipping calculations can be off-target, and you may not know that until after you take the buyer's money. If the mistake is in your favor and is a biggie, notify the buyer and offer a refund. But if shipping ends up costing you a bit more, take your lumps and pay it. You can always let the buyer know what happened and that you paid the extra cost. Who knows, it may show up on your feedback from the buyer! (Even if it doesn't, spreading goodwill never hurts.)

4. **E-mail the buyer and congratulate him or her on winning; reiterate what your shipping choice is and how long you expect it'll take.**

   Make sure you're both talking about the same timetable. If the buyer balks at either the price or the shipping time, try working out an option that will make the buyer happy.

5. **Send the package.**

   When should you ship the package? Common courtesy says it should go out as soon as the item and shipping charges are paid. If the buyer has followed through with his or her side of the bargain, you should do the same. Ship that package no more than a week after payment (or after the check clears). If you can't, immediately e-mail the buyer and explain the delay. You should e-mail the buyer as soon as you send the package and ask for an e-mail to confirm arrival after the item gets there. (Don't forget to put in a plug for positive feedback.)

Insuring your peace of mind (and your shipment)

Sure, "lost in the mail" is an excuse we've all heard hundreds of times, but despite everyone's best efforts, sometimes things do get damaged or misplaced during shipment. The universe is a dangerous place; that's what insurance is for. I usually offer to get insurance from the shipper if the buyer wants to pay for it, and always get it on expensive items, one-of-a-kind items, or very fragile items. I spell out in my item description that the buyer pays for the insurance.

The major shippers all offer insurance that's fairly reasonably priced, so check out their rates at their Web sites. But don't forget to read the details. For example, many items at eBay are sold MIMB (Mint in Mint Box). True, the condition of the original box often has a bearing on the final value of the item inside, but the U.S. Postal Service insures only what is *in* the box. So, if you sold a Malibu Barbie mint in a mint box, USPS insures only the doll and not the original box. Pack carefully so that your buyer gets what's been paid for. Be mindful that shippers won't make good on insurance claims if they suspect you of causing the damage by doing a lousy job of packing.

Alternatively, when you're selling on eBay in earnest, you can purchase your own parcel protection policy from a private insurer. (See Appendix B for more information.) When you use this type of insurance, combined with preprinted electronic postage, you no longer have to stand in line at the post office to have your insured packaged logged in by the clerk at the counter.

Some sellers also offer their own type of *self-insurance*. No, they're not pretending they're State Farm or Allstate (though their hands *are* pretty good). Here's what I offer my buyers at no cost to them:

✔ On lower-priced items, I am willing to refund the buyer's money if the item is lost or damaged.

✔ On some items I sell, I have a *risk reserve*. That means I have more than one of the item I sold. If the item is lost or destroyed, I can send the backup item as a replacement.

Send a prompt follow-up e-mail to let the buyer know the item's on the way. In this e-mail, be sure to include when the item was sent, how long it should take to arrive, any special tracking number (if you have one), and a request for a return e-mail confirming arrival after the item gets there. I also include a thank-you note (a receipt would be a business-like addition) in each package I send out. I appreciate when I get one in eBay packages, and it always brings a smile to the recipient's face. It never hurts to take every opportunity to promote goodwill (and future business and positive feedback).

More often than not, you do get an e-mail back from the buyer to let you know the item arrived safely. If you don't, it doesn't hurt to send another e-mail (in about a week) to ask whether the item arrived in good condition. It jogs the buyer's memory and demonstrates your professionalism as a seller. Use this opportunity to gently remind buyers that you'll be leaving positive feedback for them. Ask whether they're satisfied and don't be bashful about suggesting they do the same for you. Leave positive feedback right away so that you don't forget.

Shopping for a shipper

If only you could transport your item the way they do on *Star Trek* — "Beam up that Beanie, Scotty!" Alas, it's not so. Priority Mail via the U.S. Postal Service is pretty much the eBay standard if you're shipping within the United States and Canada. Many Americans also rely on it to ship internationally as well. FedEx and UPS are global alternatives that work well, too.

Whether you're at the post office, UPS, FedEx, or your doctor's office, be ready, willing, and able to wait in line. I definitely have a "rush hour" at my neighborhood office — everybody's in a rush, so everything moves at a glacial pace. I avoid both the noontime and post-work crunches (easier on the nerves). A good time to ship is around 10:30 a.m., when everyone is still in a good mood. If I have to go in the afternoon, I go about 3:00 p.m., when the clerks are back from their lunch breaks and friendly faces (mine, too — I always smile!) can take the edge off those brusque lunchtime encounters. And no matter what shipper you use, fill out the shipping forms before you get to the drop-off center. That saves time and frustration.

Be sure to visit my Web site, www.coolebaytools.com, for introductory offers for much of the software and services that I mention in this book.

U.S. Postal Service

The U.S. Postal Service (USPS) is the butt of many unfair jokes and cheap shots, but when it comes right down to it, I think USPS is still the most efficient and inexpensive way to ship items — eBay or otherwise. It also supplies free boxes, labels, and tape for Priority and Express Mail packages. Here are some ways eBay members get their items from here to there via USPS:

- ✔ **Priority Mail:** As mentioned earlier, this is the *de facto* standard method of shipping for eBay users. I love the free boxes, and I like the rates. The promised delivery time is two to three days, although I've experienced rare delays of up to a week during peak holiday periods.

  Cost? As of this writing (rates are always subject to change), Priority Mail costs $3.85 for a 1-pound package. Over a pound, the charge is calculated according to weight and distance.

  A $3.85 flat-rate Priority envelope is also available. You can ship as much stuff as you want — as long as you can fit it into the supplied 9½ x 12½ envelope. You can reinforce the envelope with Priority Mail packing tape.

- ✔ **Express Mail:** If the item needs to be delivered the next day, use Express Mail. The Postal Service promises delivery no later than noon the following afternoon (even on weekends or holidays). And you can get free boxes.

Cost? Express Mail runs $13.65 for packages 8 ounces and under, $17.85 for packages 8 ounces to 2 pounds, and about $3 additional for every pound over 2 (up to 10 pounds). Express Mail also has a flat-rate envelope, which is the same size as the Priority flat-rate envelope and ships for $13.85.

The Postal Service makes a special pickup for Priority Mail and Express Mail. It's a flat rate for no matter how many separate packages are included. If you have several packages, this is an excellent option to consider, and the extra cost can be covered in your handling charge.

Get to know your mail carrier, and have your parcels ready and stacked up for him or her for the regular stop at your home. The mail carrier will usually be happy to take your packages back to the post office at no charge. (A bottle of icy-cold water for your letter carrier on hot days will go a long way in your relationship!)

✔ **First-Class Mail:** If your item weighs 13 ounces or less, you can use First-Class Mail. First-Class Mail is slightly cheaper than Priority Mail — the first ounce is $0.37, and every additional ounce is $0.23.

✔ **Media Mail:** This is a popular option among those who sell books on eBay. It's the *new* name for two older products, Book Rate and Special Standard Mail. Media Mail rates start at $1.42 for the first pound and increase by $0.42 cents for each additional pound.

✔ **Other options:** The Postal Service offers all sorts of add-ons. I always get the Delivery Confirmation service that you can add to Priority Mail, as well as other mailing services. A mere $0.45 cents ($0.55 on First-Class Mail, Parcel Post, or Media Mail) buys you the knowledge of when and where your item was delivered. With the parcel's tracking number, you can check on whether the package was delivered (or whether an attempt was made to deliver it) by calling 800-222-1811 in the U.S. If you go online at www.usps.com/shipping/trackandconfirm.htm, you can get a more complete report.

Free delivery confirmations? Yes! If you send out more than 18 packages a month with delivery confirmations, you can save yourself some serious cash if you go to www.shippertools.com. Get unlimited delivery confirmations for just $6.95 a month! The site gives small shippers a gateway to the same USPS electronic Delivery Confirmation system that the big-time shippers use. You can print out prenumbered delivery confirmations on plain paper (no weird labels to buy!) right from your computer, plus use its system to track the package and send customer follow-up messages after shipping. This is a convenient and handy service for eBay sellers!

If you're an occasional shipper (you *buy* more than you sell on eBay), you can print out bar-coded shipping labels with free delivery confirmation (for Priority Mail only) at the USPS site. No online e-mail functions are available, so you have to do all the e-mailing and record keeping yourself. But hey, the service is free. Just go to www.usps.com/cgi-bin/api/shipping_label.htm.

Delivery confirmation also comes in handy if you try to collect insurance for an item that was never delivered or if the buyer says the item was never delivered. It gives you proof from the Postal Service that the item was sent. (I explain insuring shipments later in this chapter.) But understand that you cannot accurately track your package. Delivery confirmation is merely proof that the package was mailed and delivered. If your package gets lost in the mail for a few weeks, this number won't act as a tracking number and won't reveal the location of your package until it's delivered.

The USPS Web site (www.usps.com) gives you an overview of the U.S. Postal Service rates so that you can see all your options. It sure beats standing in that endless line! For a complete explanation of domestic rates, check out this page at www.usps.com/consumers/domestic.htm.

Even better, USPS has a page that can help you determine exactly what your item costs to mail (after you've packaged it and weighed it, of course). Start at the Domestic Rate Calculator page at postcalc.usps.gov and follow the instructions. To find rates for sending packages from the United States to foreign countries, go to the International Rate Calculator at ircalc.usps.gov.

UPS

The folks in the brown UPS trucks love eBay. The options they offer vary, with everything from overnight service to the UPS Ground service. I use UPS for items that are heavy (say, antique barbells) or extremely large (such as a 1920s steamer trunk), because UPS ships anything up to 150 pounds in a single box — 80 more pounds than the U.S. Postal Service takes. UPS also takes many of the odd-shaped large boxes, such as those for computer equipment that the U.S. Postal Service won't.

UPS makes pickups, but you have to know the exact weight of your package so that you can pay when the UPS driver shows up. But the pickup service is free (my favorite price).

The rates for the same UPS shipment can vary based on whether you have a business account with UPS, whether the package goes to or is picked up at a residence, and whether you use the right kind of form. If you're going to use UPS regularly, be sure to set up an account directly with UPS.

You can find the UPS home page at www.ups.com. For rates, click the Shipping tab and then click Estimate Cost on the left side of the page, which gives you prices based on zip codes and package weights. (Note the ominous "estimate" rates.)

The UPS.com Quick Cost Calculator prices are based on what UPS charges regular and high-volume users. When you get to the counter, the price may be higher than what you find on the Web.

Sí, oui, ja, yes! Shipping internationally

Money's good no matter what country it comes from. I don't know why, but lots of people seem to be afraid to ship internationally and list "I don't ship overseas" on the auction page. Of course, sending an item that far away may be a burden if you're selling a car or a street-sweeper (they don't fit in boxes too well), but I've found that sending a package across the Atlantic can be just as easy as shipping across state lines. The only downside: My shipper of choice, the U.S. Postal Service, does not insure packages going to certain countries (check with your post office to find out which ones; they seem to change with the headlines), so I mail only to insured nations.

Here are a couple of other timely notes about shipping internationally:

✔ You need to tell what's inside the package. Be truthful when declaring value on customs forms. Be sure to use descriptions that customs agents can figure out without knowing eBay shorthand terms. For example, instead of declaring the contents as "MIB Furby," call it a "small stuffed animal toy that talks." Some countries require buyers to pay special duties and taxes, depending on the item and the value. But that's the buyer's headache.

✔ Wherever you send your package (especially if it's going to a country where English is not the native language), be sure to write legibly. (Imagine getting a package from Russia and having to decipher a label written in the Cyrillic alphabet. _'Nuff said._)

My favorite link on the UPS site is the transit map that shows the United States and how long it takes to reach any place in the country (based on the originating zip code). If you're thinking of shipping that compact refrigerator to Maine, you can check out this fun and informative page at `www.ups.com/using/services/servicemaps/servicemaps.html`.

If you have a UPS account, it's useful to buy the delivery confirmation option for $1.00. As soon as the package gets to its destination and is signed for, UPS sends you back a confirmation so that you have evidence that it has been delivered. But what's really cool is the free UPS online tracking. Every package is bar-coded and that code is read everywhere your package stops along its shipping route. You can follow its progress by entering the package number at `www.ups.com/tracking/tracking.html`.

FedEx

I use FedEx Express air all the time for rush business, but Express seems rather expensive for my eBay shipping. However, if the buyer wants it fast and is willing to pay, I'll send it by FedEx overnight, you bet. The new FedEx Ground Home Delivery service has competitive prices and carries all the best features of FedEx. I like the online tracking option for all packages, and FedEx Express takes packages over 150 pounds. For account holders, FedEx will pick up your package for a $3 charge.

---

iShip, you ship, we all ship

iShip (www.iship.com) is owned by UPS. It's an online shipping-pricing Web site that allows you to compare the charges from the four major shipping companies: USPS, FedEx Express air service (not FedEx Ground), UPS, and Airborne Express. Unfortunately (for us — fortunately for UPS), iShip does not quote rates for the FedEx Ground service, which tends to be cheaper than even UPS. To see the FedEx Ground fees to compare with the iShip responses, go to www.fedex.com/ratefinder/home?cc=US&language=en. iShip's handy site is easy to use, though sometimes slightly imprecise:

1. **On the Price It page (click the link from the home page), enter your zip code (or the zip code of the city you'll be sending the package from), the zip code of the address you're sending it to, and the size and weight of the package.**

2. **Click the Continue button.**

    On the following page, you're presented with various shipping options. Leave the

area asking for your handling fee blank so you can get the clearest idea of what it costs to ship.

3. **Click the Continue button again.**

    You're taken to a page that displays rates and delivery times. This page shows you the costs of the four major services and how many days it will take to ship the package to its final destination. Each service is represented by a specific color: red for Airborne Express, purple for FedEx Air, brown for UPS, and blue for the U.S. Postal Service. Click any of the color-coded rates for more information on that service.

I double-checked iShip's listed rates against the USPS, FedEx, and UPS online calculators and found that iShip is sometimes slightly off. Even so, iShip is a handy resource for getting the big picture of what it costs to send packages throughout the United States.

I also like the FedEx boxes. Like one of my favorite actors, Joe Pesci, from *My Cousin Vinny* and the *Lethal Weapon* movies, these boxes are small but tough. But if you're thinking of reusing these boxes to ship with another service, forget it. The FedEx logo is plastered all over every inch of the freebies, and the company may get seriously peeved about it. You can't use those fancy boxes for the Home Delivery service.

The FedEx Ground Home Delivery service is a major competitor for UPS. The rates are competitive, and FedEx offers a money-back guarantee (if it misses the delivery window) for residential ground delivery. A 2-pound package going from Los Angeles to a residence in New York City takes 5 days and costs $6.09. FedEx includes online package tracking and insurance up to $100 in this price. You have to be a business to avail yourself of home delivery — but plenty of home businesses exist.

The same two-pound U.S. Postal Service Priority Mail package with $100 insurance and a delivery confirmation costs you $6.20. (But remember, you know how to get free Delivery Confirmation forms!) Granted, the package will arrive within two to three days, but FedEx Ground guarantees a five-day delivery, and I've had a few Priority Mail packages take up to two weeks. FedEx Ground won't supply boxes for you, so you're on your own there. When you drop off your box at UPS, you can get five-day service for $8.05.

You can find the FedEx home page at www.fedex.com/us. The link for rates is conveniently located at the top of the page.

Getting the right (packing) stuff

You can never think about packing materials too early. You may think you're jumping the gun, but by the law of averages, if you wait until the last minute, you won't find the right-size box, approved tape, or the labels you need. Start thinking about shipping even before you sell your first item.

Before you pack, give your item the once-over. Here's a checklist of what to consider about your item before you call it a wrap (love that Hollywood lingo):

✔ **Is your item as you described it?** If the item has been dented or torn somehow, e-mail the winning bidder immediately and come clean. And if you sell an item with its original box or container, don't just check the item, make sure the box is in the same good condition as the item inside. Collectors place a high value on original boxes, so make sure the box lives up to what you described in your auction. Pack to protect it as well.

✔ **Is the item dirty or dusty, or does it smell of smoke?** Some buyers may complain if the item they receive is dirty or smelly, especially from cigarette smoke. Make sure the item is fresh and clean, even if it's used or vintage. If something's dirty, check to make sure you know how to clean it properly (you want to take the dirt off, not the paint), and then give it a spritz with an appropriate cleaner or just soap and water. If you can't get rid of the smell or the dirt, say so in your item description. Let the buyer decide whether the item is desirable with aromas and all.

If the item has a faint smell of smoke or is a bit musty, a product called Febreze may help. Just get a plastic bag, give your item a spritz, and keep it in the bag for a short while. *Note:* This is not recommended for cardboard. And, as with any solvent or cleaning agent, read the label before you spray. Or, if you're in a rush to mail the package, cut a 1-inch by 1-inch piece of sheet fabric softener and place it in a plastic bag with the product.

When the item's ready to go, you're ready to pack it up. The following sections give you suggestions on what you should consider using and where to find the right stuff.

Storing those bags of plump packing peanuts

By now, you may have realized that I have commandeered a large chunk of my home for my eBay business, and you might think that I live in a giant swamp of packing materials. Not really. Aside from the "lost" shower (see Appendix B), I have to store loads of packing peanuts. They're not heavy, but they sure are bulky!

If you have a house with a garage, you're set! Bear with me now, my plan isn't as crazy as it seems. Go to your local store and purchase some large screw-in cup hooks. Then purchase the largest *drawstring* plastic bags you can find. (I'm partial to Glad 39-gallon Lawn & Leaf bags.)

Screw the cup hooks into strategic locations on the ceiling rafters of your garage. Now fill the drawstring bags to capacity with packing peanuts and hang. When you've finished your garage will look like some bizarre art installation, but it gets the packing peanuts off the floor and out of your hair. I even set up a packing-peanuts barricade so I don't hit the end of my garage when I park!

Packing material: What to use

This may sound obvious, but you'd be surprised: Any list of packing material should start with a box. But you don't want just any box — you want a heavy cardboard type that's larger than the item. If the item is extremely fragile, I suggest you use two boxes, with the outer box about 3 inches larger on each side than the inner box that holds the item, to allow for extra padding. And if you still have the original shipping container for such things as electronic equipment, consider using the original, especially if it still has the original foam inserts (they were designed for the purpose, and this way they stay out of the environment awhile longer).

As for padding, Table 12-1 compares the most popular types of box-filler material.

Table 12-1	Box-Filler Materials	
Type	*Pros and Cons*	*Suggestions*
Bubble wrap	**Pros:** Lightweight, clean, cushions well. **Cons:** Cost.	Don't go overboard taping the bubble wrap. If the buyer has to battle to get the tape off, the item may go flying and end up damaged. And for crying out loud, don't pop all the little bubbles, okay?

Type	Pros and Cons	Suggestions
Newspaper	**Pros:** Cheap, cushions. **Cons:** Messy.	Seal fairly well. Put your item in a plastic bag to protect it from the ink. I like shredding the newspaper first. It's more manageable and doesn't seem to stain as much as wadded-up paper. I spent about $30 at an office-supply store for a shredder. (Or find one at eBay for much less.)
Cut-up cardboard	**Pros:** Handy, cheap. **Cons:** Transmits some shocks to item, hard to cut up.	If you have some old boxes that aren't sturdy enough to pack in, this is a pretty good use for them.
Styrofoam peanuts	**Pros:** Lightweight, absorb shock well, clean. **Cons:** Environmentally unfriendly, annoying.	Your item may shift if you don't put enough peanuts in the box, so make sure to fill the box. Also, don't buy these — instead, recycle them from stuff that was shipped to you (plastic trash bags are great for storing them). And never use plastic peanuts when packing electronic equipment, because they can create static electricity. Even a little spark can trash a computer chip.
Air-popped popcorn	**Pros:** Lightweight, environmentally friendly, absorbs shock well, clean (as long as you don't use salt and butter, but you knew that), low in calories. **Cons:** Cost, time to pop.	You don't want to send it anywhere there may be varmints who like it. The U.S. Postal Service suggests popcorn. Hey, at least you can eat the leftovers!

Whatever materials you use, make sure that you pack the item well and that you secure the box. Many shippers will contest insurance claims if they feel you did a lousy job of packing. Do all the little things that you'd want done if you were the buyer — using double boxes for really fragile items, wrapping lids separately from containers, and filling hollow breakables with some kind of padding. Here are a few other items you need:

- **Plastic bags:** Plastic bags protect your item from moisture. I once sent a MIB doll to the Northeast, and the package got caught in a snowstorm. The buyer e-mailed me with words of thanks for the extra plastic bag, which saved the item from being soaked along with the outer box. (Speaking of boxes, if you send an item in an original box, bag it.)

For small items, such as stuffed animals, you should always protect them in a lunch baggie. For slightly larger items, go to the 1-quart or 1-gallon size. Be sure to wrap any paper or cloth products, such as clothing and linens, in plastic before you ship.

✔ **Bubble-padded mailers:** The shipping cost for a package that weighs less than 13 ounces (First-Class Mail) is usually considerably cheaper than Priority. Many small items, clothing, books, and so on will fit comfortably into the many available sizes of padded envelopes. You can find them made of kraft paper or extra sturdy vinyl. A big plus is that they weigh considerably less than boxes — even when using extra padding. See Table 12-2 for standard sizes.

✔ **Address labels:** You'll need extras because it's always a good idea to toss a duplicate address label inside the box, with the destination address and a return address, in case the outside label falls off or becomes illegible.

✔ **Two- or 3-inch shipping tape:** Make sure that you use a strong shipping tape for the outside of the box. Use nylon-reinforced tape or pressure-sensitive package tape. Remember not to plaster every inch of box with tape; leave space for those *Fragile* and *Insured* rubber stamps.

✔ **Hand-held shipping tape dispensers:** It's quite a bit easier to zzzzzip! tape from a tape dispenser than unwind it and bite it off with your teeth. Have one dispenser for your shipping tape and one for your clear tape.

✔ **Two-inch clear tape:** For taping the padding around the inside items. I also use a clear strip of tape over the address on the outside of the box so that it won't disappear in the rain.

✔ **Scissors:** A pair of large, sharp scissors. Having a hobby knife to trim boxes or shred newspaper is also a good idea.

✔ **Handy liquids:** Three that I like are GOO GONE (which is available in the household supply section of most retail stores and is a wonder at removing unwanted stickers and price tags); WD-40 (the unstick-everything standby that works great on getting stickers off plastic); and Un-Du (the best liquid I've found to take labels off cardboard). If you can't find Un-Du in stores, visit my Web site, www.coolebaytools.com, for locations that carry it. Lighter fluid also does the trick, but be careful handling it and be sure to clean up thoroughly to remove any residue.

✔ **Rubber stamps:** Using custom rubber stamps can save you a bunch of time when preparing your packages. I purchased some return address self-inking rubber stamps (at an unbelievably low price) on eBay from the Melrose Stamp Company (eBay User ID melrose_stamp). I use these stamps to stamp all kinds of things that require my identification.

✔ **Thermal label printer:** Once I thought this was a flagrant waste of money, but now I wouldn't be without one. When you begin shipping several packages a week, you'll find it far more convenient to use a separate label printer for addressing and delivery confirmations. Dymo offers one of the best deals on a quality printer. Its new 330 model is one of the fastest you can get and available on eBay for about $100. If you want to get industrial, try one of the Zebra (I use the LP2844) thermal printers. These printers can print labels for FedEx and UPS as well as USPS.

✔ **Black permanent marker:** These are handy for writing information ("Please leave on porch behind the planter") and the all-important "Fragile" all over the box or "Do Not Bend" on envelopes. I like the big, fat Sharpie markers.

Table 12-2	Standard Bubble-Padded Mailer Sizes	
Size	*Measurements*	*Suggested Items*
#000	4" x 8"	Collector trading cards, jewelry, computer diskettes, coins
#00	5" x 10"	Postcards, paper ephemera
#0	6" x 10"	CDs, DVDs, Xbox or PS2 games
#1	7¼" x 12"	Cardboard sleeve VHS tapes, jewel-cased CDs and DVDs
#2	8½" x 12"	Clamshell VHS tapes
#3	8½" x 14½"	Toys, clothing, stuffed animals
#4	9½" x 14½"	Small books, trade paperbacks
#5	10½" x 16"	Hardcover books
#6	12½" x 19"	Clothing, soft boxed items
#7	14¼" x 20"	Much larger packaged items, framed items and plaques

Not sure how to pack your item? No problem — just call a store in your area that deals in that kind of item and ask the folks there how they pack for shipment. They'll probably be glad to offer you a few pointers. Or post a question to seasoned eBay veterans in the chat room for your auction's category. (I introduce you to chat rooms in Chapter 17.)

If you plan to sell on eBay in earnest, consider adding a 10-pound weight scale (for weighing packages) to your shipping department. I'm using a super small 13-pound maximum scale manufactured by Escali, which I bought on eBay for only $29.95.

When it comes to fragile items, dishes, pottery, porcelain, china — anything that can chip, crack, or smash into a thousand pieces — *double box.* The boxes should be about 3 inches different on each side. Make sure that you use enough padding so that the interior box is snug. Just give it a big shake. If nothing rattles, ship away!

Packing material: Where to find it

The place to start looking for packing material is the same place you should start looking for things to sell at eBay: your house. Between us, I've done over a thousand eBay transactions and never once paid for a carton. Because I buy most of my stuff from catalogs and online companies (I love e-commerce), I save all the boxes, bubble wrap, padding, and packing peanuts I get in the mail. Just empty your boxes of packing peanuts into large plastic trash bags — that way, they don't take up much storage space. If you recently got a mail-order shipment box that was used only once — and it's a good, sturdy box with no dents or dings — there's nothing wrong with using it again. Just be sure to completely cover any old labels so the delivery company doesn't get confused.

Beyond the ol' homestead, here are a couple of other suggestions for places where you can rustle up some packing stuff:

- ✔ **Your local supermarket, department store, or drugstore:** You won't be the first person pleading with a store manager for boxes. (Ah, fond memories of moving days past. . . .) Stores actually like giving them away because it saves them the extra work of compacting the boxes and throwing them away.

  I found that drugstores and beauty supply stores have a better variety of smaller boxes. But make sure that you don't take dirty boxes reeking of food smells.

- ✔ **The inside of your local supermarket, department store, or drugstore:** Places like Kmart, Wal-Mart, Target, and office-supply stores often have good selections of packing supplies.

- ✔ **Shippers like UPS, FedEx, and the U.S. Postal Service:** These shippers offer all kinds of free supplies as long as you use these supplies to ship things with their service.

  The Postal Service also ships free boxes, packing tape, labels, and shipping forms for Express Mail, Priority Mail, and Global Priority Mail to your house. In the U.S., you can order by phone (800-222-1811) or online (supplies.usps.gov). Here are a couple of rules for USPS orders:

  - Specify the service (Priority Mail, Express Mail, or Global Priority Mail) you're using because the tape, the boxes, and the labels all come with the service name printed all over them, and you can only use them for that specific service.

  - Order in bulk. For example, address labels come in rolls of 500 and boxes in packs of 25.

  - The boxes come flat, so you have to assemble them. Hey, don't look a gift box in the mouth — they're free!

- ✔ **eBay Sellers:** Many terrific eBay sellers are out to offer you really good deals. (You can't beat eBay sellers for quality goods, low prices, and great service.) I recommend the following family-run eBay stores:

- **Grasup** (GraMur Supply Co), based in Texas, is where I buy my vinyl padded envelope mailers for my eBay sales. It also has a super selection of multisized Ziplock bags for small items.

- **Bubblefast** — an eBay seller from the Chicago area — sells tons of reasonably priced bubble wrap, mailers, and more on eBay.

- **Gatorpack Shipping Supplies** is based in Tampa, Florida, and has many long-term customers in the eBay seller ranks. It sells everything from tape to peanuts!

- **ShippingSupply.com** (its eBay User ID and Web site address), located in Indiana, serves the selling community with a wide array of packing supplies.

Notice that I mention where these vendors are located. When ordering a large shipment, the distance it has to travel from the vendor's place to yours can tack on quite a bit of cash (and time) to your shipping costs!

Buying Postage Online

Isn't technology great? You no longer have to schlep to the post office every time you need stamps. What's even better, with the new print-it-yourself postage, you can give all your packages directly to your mail carrier. When you install your Internet postage software, you apply for a USPS postal license that allows you to print your own *Information Based Indicia* (IBI) for your postage. IBI is a bar code printed either on labels or directly on an envelope and has both human- and machine-readable information about where it was printed and security-related elements. IBI provides you, and the post office, with a much more secure way of getting your valuable packages through the mail.

You can print postage for First-Class, Priority, Express, and Parcel Post, and additional postage for delivery confirmations and insurance. If your printer mangles a sheet of labels or an envelope, you can send the printed piece to your Internet postage provider for a refund. Several vendors of Internet-based postage exist, but Endicia Internet Postage and Stamps.com are the most popular.

Endicia Internet Postage

In the early 90s, a couple guys came up with new software to enable people to design direct-mail pieces from the desktop. WOW! What an innovation. With the inexpensive software, you could also produce your own bar coding for the Postal Service. I used that software then, like I use DAZzle now.

DAZzle — combined with the patented Dial-A-Zip — became the basis for the software that comes free with the Endicia Internet Postage service. There isn't a more robust mailing program on the market.

Endicia has all the basic features and more:

- **Prints postage for all classes of mail, including international:** From Anniston, Alabama, to Bulawayo, Zimbabwe, the DAZzle software not only prints postage, but also lists all your shipping options and applicable rates.

  For international mailing, Endicia advises you about any prohibitions (no prison-made goods can be mailed to Botswana), any restrictions, any necessary customs forms, and areas served within the country.

- **Provides free delivery confirmations on Priority Mail:** You can print electronic delivery confirmations for First-Class, Parcel Post, and Media Mail for only $0.13 each (a savings of $0.42 from Postal Service purchase).

- **Enables you to design mail pieces:** The software enables you to design envelopes, postcards, and labels with color graphics, logos, and text messages. You can print your labels with postage and delivery confirmation on anything from plain paper (tape it on with clear tape) to 4 x 6 labels in a label printer.

- **Integrates with U-PIC insurance:** If you're saving time and money using a private package insurer (see Appendix A), you can send your monthly insurance logs electronically to U-PIC at the end of the month.

Endicia offers two levels of service. All the preceding features come with the standard plan for $9.99 a month (if paid annually, $99.95). The premium plan adds additional special features, customizable e-mail, enhanced online transaction reports and statistics, business reply mail, return shipping labels (prepaid so your customer won't have to pay for the return), and stealth indicias for $15.95 a month, or $174.94 paid annually.

A "stealth" indicia (also known as the postage-paid indicia) is an awesome tool for the eBay seller. By using this feature, your customers can't see the exact amount of postage that you paid for the package. This allows you to add reasonable shipping and handling costs and not inflame buyers when they see the final label.

Stamps.com

Stamps.com is truly an online postage system; you must be online to use it and to print your postage. After you accept the bargain du jour sign-up package from the Web site at `www.stamps.com` (today it's $20 in free postage), you can instantly download the software or request to have a CD sent to you. It's simple and convenient, and you don't have to buy a starter kit.

Stamps.com handles everything you need to do online. Your addresses are confirmed online, and the complete zip code is picked up directly from the Stamps.com servers. Delivery confirmations are free, as are most of the services you expect from an online postage service. The Stamps.com software integrates with many of the popular software packages that I use each day. You also have the option to print on envelopes or on special postage labels directly from your own printer.

Stamps.com's services are similar to other services in that it charges monthly fees. It has two levels of service:

- ✔ **Simple plan:** Charges you a monthly service fee of 10 percent of postage printed, with a monthly minimum of $4.49. If you send out 20 Priority Mail packages, each with a delivery confirmation, your total postage would be $71, and your fee to Stamps.com would be $7.10. If you print no postage in a given month, you still pay $4.49 to maintain the service.

- ✔ **Power plan:** Carries a $15.99 flat service fee per month (plus your postage purchases), no matter how much postage you print. You also get a free 5-pound digital scale to weigh your packages. This plan is perfect if you spend over $200 in postage per month.

If you go on vacation or don't run any auctions, you're still charged the monthly minimum for your plan.

Troubleshooting Your Auction

here's no getting around it: The more transactions you conduct at eBay, the more chances you have of facing some potential pitfalls. In this chapter, I give you pointers on how to handle an obnoxious buyer as if he or she is your new best friend (for a little while anyway). In addition, I explain how to keep an honest misunderstanding from blowing up into a vitriolic e-mail war. You find out how to handle a sale that's (shall I say) on a road to nowhere, how to get some attention, and if it all goes sour, how to sell to the next highest bidder legally, relist the item, and get back the Final Value Fee you paid eBay. There's no way that all of what I mention here will happen to you, but the more you know, the better prepared you'll be.

Dealing with a Buyer Who Doesn't Respond

Most of the time, the post-auction transaction between buyers and sellers goes smoothly. However, if you have difficulty communicating with the winner of your auction or store sale, you should know the best way to handle the situation.

You've come to the right place if you want help dealing with potential non-paying buyers (more commonly known as *deadbeat bidders,* which is how I refer to them). Of course, you should start with good initial post-auction communication; see Chapter 12 for details. (For more information on how to deal with a fraudulent seller, see Chapter 16.)

Going into nudge mode

Despite my best efforts, sometimes things fall through the cracks. Buyers (who want to pay for their item through an online service) should pay for the item without delay through PayPal, or, in the case of mail payments, buyers and sellers should contact each other within three business days of the close of the sale. Sometimes winners contact sellers immediately, and some use Checkout and pay for the item immediately, which saves you any hassle. However, if you don't hear from the buyer within three business days of your initial contact, my advice is *don't panic.*

People are busy; they travel, they get sick, computers crash, or sometimes your auction simply slips the winner's mind. After four days of no communication, you can go to your My eBay page and send out a payment reminder. You find the Payment Reminder icon in the Items I've Sold area, as shown in Figure 13-1.

Figure 13-1:
The
Payment
Reminder
icon in the
Items I've
Sold area.

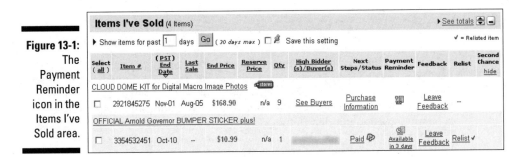

To send a payment reminder, follow these steps:

1. **Click My eBay on the navigation bar found at the top of every eBay page.**

2. **Scroll down to the Items I've Sold area and find the item in question.**

3. **Click the icon in the item's Payment Reminder column.**

   Note that if three days have not passed since the close of the item, you can't send a reminder.

   You're now at the decision-making page.

4. **Click the box next to each item that you want to appear in the e-mail.**

   Also, add the shipping amount in the area shown and decide whether you want your mailing address to appear in the e-mail.

5. **Click the Preview button to look over the e-mail eBay will send out in your behalf.**

   Figure 13-2 shows a preview of a payment reminder e-mail.

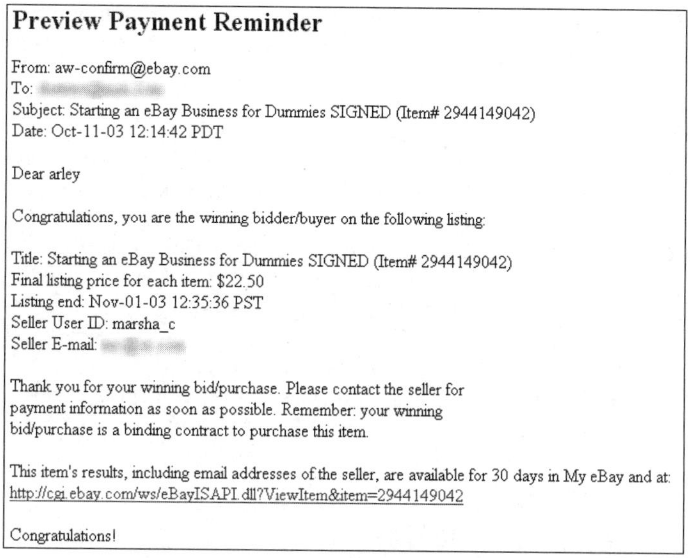

Preview Payment Reminder

From: aw-confirm@ebay.com
To: ░░░░░░░░░░░
Subject: Starting an eBay Business for Dummies SIGNED (Item# 2944149042)
Date: Oct-11-03 12:14:42 PDT

Dear arley

Congratulations, you are the winning bidder/buyer on the following listing:

Title: Starting an eBay Business for Dummies SIGNED (Item# 2944149042)
Final listing price for each item: $22.50
Listing end: Nov-01-03 12:35:36 PST
Seller User ID: marsha_c
Seller E-mail: ░░░░░░░░░░

Thank you for your winning bid/purchase. Please contact the seller for payment information as soon as possible. Remember: your winning bid/purchase is a binding contract to purchase this item.

This item's results, including email addresses of the seller, are available for 30 days in My eBay and at:
http://cgi.ebay.com/ws/eBayISAPI.dll?ViewItem&item=2944149042

Congratulations!

Figure 13-2:
A preview of the Payment Reminder e-mail.

6. **If you're happy with the way the information looks, click Go to send the e-mail now. If you want to edit the e-mail further, click the Edit E-Mail button and click Go to go back and make changes.**

If a week passes and you haven't heard from the winner, you need to get into big-time *nudge-nudge mode* — as in, "Mr. X, remember me and your obligation to buy the Tiffany lamp you won at eBay last week?"

Send a friendly-but-firm e-mail letting Mr. X know that when he bid and won your auction, he became obligated to pay and complete the transaction. If Mr. X doesn't intend to buy your item for any reason, he needs to let you know immediately.

Don't threaten your buyer. The last thing you want to do is add insult to injury in case the buyer is facing a real problem. Besides, if the high bidder goes to sleep with the fishes, you'll *never* see your money.

Here's what to include in your nudge-nudge e-mail:

✔ A gentle admonishment, such as, "Perhaps this slipped your mind," or "You may have missed my e-mail to you," or "I'm sure you didn't mean to ignore my first e-mail."

✔ A gentle reminder that eBay's policy is that every bid is a binding contract. You can even refer the buyer to eBay's rules and regulations if you want.

✔ A statement that firmly (but gently) explains that, so far, you've held up your side of the deal and you'd appreciate it if he did the same.

✔ A date by which you expect to see payment. Gently explain that if the deadline isn't met, you'll have no other choice but to consider the deal invalid.

Technically, you can nullify the transaction if you don't hear from a buyer within three business days. However, eBay members are a forgiving bunch under the right circumstances. I think you should give your buyer a one-week grace period after the auction ends to get in touch with you and set up a payment plan. If, at the end of the grace period, you don't see any real progress towards closing the deal, say goodnight, Gracie. Consider the deal kaput and go directly to the section "Auction Going Badly? Cut Your Losses" (later in this chapter) to find out what recourse you have.

Be sure that you're not the one who erred. Did you type the winner's e-mail address correctly? If you didn't, that person may not have received your message!

Be a secret agent, man

I'd like to say that history repeats itself, but that would be a cliché. (All right, you caught me, but clichés are memorable because they're so often true.) After you send your polite and gentle nudge-nudge e-mail, but before you decide that the auction is a lost cause, take a look at the bidder's feedback history. Figure 13-3 shows you the feedback profile of an eBay user with several negative feedback ratings in the last month. Beware.

To check a bidder's feedback (starting at your item page), do the following:

1. **Click the number in parentheses next to your winner's User ID.**

   This takes you to the member's feedback profile page.

2. **Scroll down the feedback profile page and read the comments.**

   Check to see if the bidder has gotten negative feedback from previous sellers. Make a note of it in case you need some support and background information (should you be chastised at a later date for canceling an unwanted bid).

3. **Conduct a Bidder search.**

   Click Search on the main navigation bar and do a Bidder search to see the buyer's conduct in previous auctions. How many items has the buyer won? Click the item number to see the history of the auction. For more info on Bidder searches, check out Chapter 5.

If you're running an auction for a high-dollar item, you may want to prequalify your bidders. At the very least, be sure to check them out as the auction progresses. eBay helps out here by allowing you to preapprove bidders in your auctions. If bidders are not preapproved by you, they can't bid; eBay tells them they have to contact you by e-mail before their bids will be accepted. You can add or delete bidders from your list until the listing ends. You'll find a link to block or preapprove bidders on your My eBay Selling page in the Selling-Related Links. Or you can go directly to the Bidder Management area at pages.ebay.com/services/buyandsell/biddermanagement.html.

When all else fails, you may want to double-check with some of the bidder's previous sellers. It's okay to use eBay's e-mail system to contact previous sellers who've dealt with the bidder. They're often happy to give you details on how well (or badly) the transaction went.

If the buyer's feedback profile provides any indication that the buyer has gone AWOL in the past, start thinking about getting out of the transaction before too much time passes. If the buyer looks to be on the level, continue to give him or her the benefit of the doubt.

Be sure to ask previous sellers that dealt with the bidder the following questions (politely):

- Did Mr. X pay on time?
- Did his check clear?
- Did he communicate well?

Figure 13-3: You can get a good idea of whether a buyer will complete a sale by looking at his or her feedback profile.

When e-mailing a third party about any negative feedback he or she has left, choose your words carefully. There's no guarantee that if you trash the bidder, the third party will keep your e-mail private. Make sure that you stick to the facts. Writing false or malicious statements can put you in danger of being sued.

Stepping up your nudge a notch

If you don't hear from the winner after a week, your next course of action is to contact the winner by phone. To get the contact information of an eBay member for transaction purposes only, do the following:

1. **Click the Search link on the navigation bar at the top of most eBay pages.**

   A subnavigation bar appears below the main navigation bar.

2. **Click the Find Members link.**

3. **In the Contact Info box, enter the User ID of the person you're trying to contact and the item number of the transaction in question.**

4. **Enter your User ID (or e-mail address) and your password if you're asked for it.**

5. **Click the Submit button.**

   eBay e-mails you the contact information of the person with whom you want to be in touch and *also sends your contact information* to that person.

Wait a day before calling the person. I like sending the last-chance e-mail after ten days that says you want to put the item back up at eBay if the buyer is no longer interested. Also, mention that you want to apply for any credits you can get from eBay due to an incomplete transaction. If enough money is involved in the transaction, and you feel it's worth the investment, make the call to the winner. eBay automatically sends your request and your information to the bidder, and that may be enough of a nudge to get some action.

If you do get the person on the phone, keep the conversation like your e-mail — friendly but businesslike. Explain who you are and when the auction closed, and ask if any circumstances have delayed the bidder's reply. Often, the bidder will be so shocked to hear from you that you'll receive payment immediately, or you'll know this person is a complete deadbeat.

Trying a last-ditch emergency effort

If e-mails and phoning the winner don't work, and you really want to give the buyer one last chance to complete the transaction, check out eBay's Emergency Contact Board. (It's located in the Chat area of the main Community page). The Emergency Contact Board is where members who are having trouble contacting buyers and sellers leave word. Don't worry that the buyer may miss your message. A conscientious group of eBay pros man this area and try to help by passing on e-mails to the missing parties. Jump over to Chapter 17 for more information on this board and its group of regulars. Figure 13-4 shows you what the Emergency Contact Board looks like.

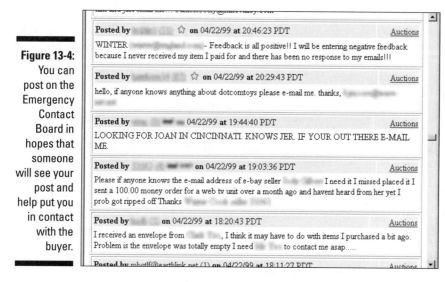

Figure 13-4:
You can post on the Emergency Contact Board in hopes that someone will see your post and help put you in contact with the buyer.

To post a message on the Emergency Contact Board, do the following:

1. Click the Community link on the main navigation bar at the top of most eBay pages.

You're taken to the Community hub page.

2. Click the Chat link in the Talk area of the page.

You're taken to the Talk Chat page, which lists all of eBay's chat boards.

3. In the General Chat Rooms category, click the Emergency Contact link.

You're taken to the Emergency Contact Board.

Before you post a message, scroll through the postings and look for messages from your AWOL buyer. Maybe he or she has been trying to get in touch with you, too.

4. If you haven't already signed in, type your User ID and password in the appropriate boxes. Then type your message where you want to post it.

Even though you may feel like the transaction is a lost cause when you get to the point of posting a message on the Emergency Contact Board, keep your message neutral and don't make accusations.

5. Check your message for errors and click the Save My Message button.

Your message is instantly posted.

Not sure what to post on the Emergency Contact Board? Start off by sticking to the facts of the transaction and say what you want your buyer to do. Have the item number and the buyer's User ID handy before you start your posting. Be sure not to post any personal information about the buyer, such as the buyer's real name and address. That is a violation of the eBay rules.

You can send messages to specific users or post a general cry for help. Here are two examples of short-but-sweet postings that get your message across:

- ✔ Dear Mr. X, I've been trying to reach you through e-mail and phone for two weeks about item number XXXXX and have had no response. Please contact me by *(leave date),* or I will invalidate the transaction and leave negative feedback.

- ✔ I've been trying to contact Mr. X for two weeks now regarding an auction. Does anybody know this person or have a new e-mail address for him? Did anybody get burned by this buyer in the past? Thanks.

For your postings to be useful, you need to check back often and read other eBay users' postings on the Emergency Contact Board. Check the board to see whether someone has responded to your message. Also, keep your eyes open as you scroll through the board. Don't trash anyone on this board — it's not good form — but many people do use the Emergency Contact Board to issue an all-points bulletin about bad eBay members.

Some Other Auction Problems

I'm not quite sure why, but where money is involved, sometimes people act kind of weird. Buyers may suddenly decide that they can't purchase an item after they've made a commitment, or there may be payment problems or shipping problems. Whatever the problem, look no further than this section to find out how to make things better.

The buyer backs out of the transaction

Every time eBay members place a bid or click Buy It Now, they make a commitment to purchase the item in question — in theory, anyway. In the real world, people have second thoughts, despite the rules. You have every right to be angry that you're losing money and wasting your time. Remind the buyer that making a bid is a binding contract. But, unfortunately, if the winner won't pay up, you can't do much except make the winner pay with negative feedback. Jump to Chapter 6 to find out more about buyer's remorse.

Keeping your cool

By all means, if the winner of your auction tells you that the transaction can't be completed, no matter what the reason, remain professional, despite your anger. For one thing, at least such a would-be buyer has the heart to break the news to you instead of ignoring your e-mail and phone calls.

When Plan A fails, try Plan B, or even C — Second Chance Offer

You have several options if the winner backs out:

- ✔ **You can make a Second Chance Offer: Offer the item to another bidder from the auction.** eBay offers a little-known feature called Second Chance Offer, which protects buyers just as if they were the winner of the auction. This is a great feature that turned the previously eBay-illegal practice of side deals into fair and approved auction deals. You can make a Second Chance Offer to any underbidder from your unpaid auction (at the amount of their high bid) for up to 60 days after the auction's end. The steps that follow this list detail how to make a Second Chance Offer.

- ✔ **You can request a full or partial Final Value Fee credit and then relist the item and hope it sells again.** (I give you more information on requesting a Final Value Fee credit and relisting your item, later in this chapter.) Who knows? This bidder may actually *earn* you money in the long run if you relist the item and get a higher winning bid.

To make a Second Chance Offer, follow these steps:

1. **Go to the completed auction page.**

2. **Scroll to the bottom of the blue shaded Seller Status area at the top of the page and click the Second Chance link.**

   You must be signed in to see the Seller Status area.

   You're taken to the Second Chance Offer page, which has the auction number already filled in.

3. **Click Continue.**

   The page shown in Figure 13-5 appears.

4. **Select an underbidder to offer the item to and then click the Review Second Chance Offer link.**

   When you make a Second Chance Offer, you can give the recipient one, three, five, or seven days to take you up on the offer. You are not charged a listing fee for the item, but you are responsible for Final Value Fees if the transaction is completed.

5. **Check over the offer and then click Submit to send it to the underbidder.**

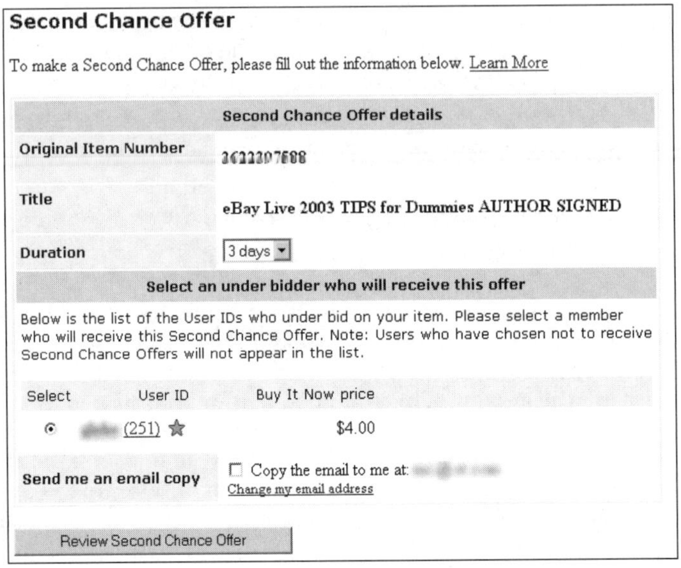

Second Chance Offer

To make a Second Chance Offer, please fill out the information below. Learn More

Second Chance Offer details	
Original Item Number	3622207588
Title	eBay Live 2003 TIPS for Dummies AUTHOR SIGNED
Duration	3 days ▾

Select an under bidder who will receive this offer		

Below is the list of the User IDs who under bid on your item. Please select a member who will receive this Second Chance Offer. Note: Users who have chosen not to receive Second Chance Offers will not appear in the list.

Select	User ID	Buy It Now price
⊙	___ (251) ☆	$4.00

Send me an email copy	☐ Copy the email to me at: ___
	Change my email address

Review Second Chance Offer

Figure 13-5: Here's where you may get out of a difficult situation by offering the item to one of the underbidders in the unsuccessful auction.

Houston, we have a payment problem

Lots of things can go wrong where money is concerned. Maybe you never receive the money or perhaps the check bounces. If the check bounces, contact the seller immediately. Honest winners will be completely embarrassed and make good whereas unscrupulous winners will offer lame excuses. Either way, insist on a more secure form of payment, like a money order or payment with a credit card through PayPal. I also require those who send bounced checks to include an extra $20 with their payment. This covers my bank's bounced-check charges and a little for my aggravation.

If the buyer pays by check, be sure to hang on to the item until you are positive that the check cleared and then ship the item. Call your bank to make sure that you have not received a return deposit item for the amount of the check.

The item you send is busted — and so are you

Uh-oh! Could it be true? Could you have sent the wrong item? Or is it possible that the crystal vase you thought you packed so well is a sad pile of shards at the bottom of a torn box? If so, read Chapter 12 as soon as you take care of this catastrophe so that you can get some hints on packing and insurance.

It's time to do some serious problem solving. If the buyer met his or her end of the deal, you need to do your best to fix the problem. Your communication skills are your number one asset in this situation, so get to work.

Picking up the pieces

No matter how carefully you pack an item, sometimes it arrives on the buyer's doorstep mangled, broken, or squashed. News of this unfortunate event travels back to you fast. The buyer will let you know in about 30 seconds how unhappy he or she is in an e-mail. Tell the buyer to locate the insurance stamp or paper tag that's attached to the package as proof of insurance and then take the whole mangled shebang back to his or her post office.

Here's what happens at the post office:

- ✔ If the item is insured for less than $50, the buyer immediately gets a Postal Service money order for the value of the item.

- ✔ If the item is insured for over $50, the buyer fills out a claim form, and you're contacted to fill out additional forms. You need to show your insurance receipt to the good people at the post office. You have to wait 60 to 90 days for the paperwork to be processed before you actually get paid.

- ✔ Of course, the post office won't refund the postage. Hey, they delivered the item, didn't they?

If a package is lost, you'll know it because the delivery confirmation never comes through, and the buyer tells you the package is a no-show. You need to go the post office from which you sent the item to file for insurance. Then the Postal Service checks around. If your item isn't located in 30 days, it's declared lost, and there's another round of paperwork and processing before you get your money. And no, you don't get a return on the postage either.

If you have private package insurance (discussed in Appendix B), the process is considerably simpler. You don't have to contact the shipper; you merely have to contact the insurance company and place a claim.

Boxed out of a claim

In my experience, neither UPS nor the United States Postal Service will pay on an insurance claim if they feel you did a lousy job of packing. So, don't be surprised if your claim is declined. Always use good packing products, wrap carefully, and get ready to plead your case.

Every shipping company has its own procedure for complaints. But here's the one thing they do have in common: No procedure is hassle-free. Call your shipper as soon as a problem arises.

Leaving feedback after an imperfect auction experience

If the buyer never materializes, backs out, bounces a check, or moves slower than a glacier to send your payment (but wants the item sent overnight from Boston to Khartoum at your expense), you need to think about how you want to word your feedback. You're well within your rights to leave negative feedback, but that doesn't mean you can go off the deep end. Remember to stick to the facts and don't get personal.

Here are a few feedback tips:

✔ If the transaction was shaky but everything turned out all right in the end, go ahead and leave neutral feedback.

✔ If a blizzard stopped planes out of Chicago for three days and that's why it took a long time to get your check, take a deep breath, blame the fates, and leave positive feedback.

✔ If the buyer was a living nightmare, take a long break before leaving negative feedback — and have someone you love and trust read it before you send something into the virtual world that you can't take back.

For more information on leaving feedback, check out Chapters 4 and 6.

You have regrets — seller's remorse

You've undoubtedly heard about buyer's remorse. Here's a new one for you — *seller's remorse.* If you're selling your velvet Elvis footstool because your spouse said, "It's me or that footstool!" and then decide that your spouse should have known how much you revered the King when you went to Graceland on your honeymoon, you can end the auction. Read "Try canceling bids first" and "If all else fails, end your auction early," later in this chapter.

Auction Going Badly? Cut Your Losses

So your auction is cruising along just fine for a couple of days when you notice that the same eBay user who didn't pay up on a previous auction is your current high bidder. You don't want to get burned again, do you? Of course not; *cancel* this deadbeat's bid before it's too late. Although canceling bids — or, for that matter, entire auctions — isn't easy (you have a load of explaining to do, pardner), eBay does allow it.

If you feel you have to wash your hands of an auction that's given you nothing but grief, it doesn't mean you have to lose money on the deal. Read on to find out the protocol for dumping untrustworthy bidders or (as a last resort) laying a bad auction to rest and beginning anew.

Many of these functions are also available from the Selling-Related Links area at the bottom of your My eBay Selling page.

Try canceling bids first

Face the facts: This auction is fast becoming a big-time loser. You did your very best, and things didn't work out. Before you kill an auction completely, see whether you can improve it by canceling bids first. Canceling a bid removes a bidder from your auction, but the auction continues running.

When you cancel a bid, you need to provide an explanation, which goes on record for all to see. You may have a million reasons for thinking your auction is a bust, but eBay says your explanation had better be good. Here are some eBay-approved reasons for canceling a bid (or even an entire auction):

- The high bidder informs you that he or she is retracting the bid.

- Despite your best efforts to determine who your high bidder is, you can't find out — and you get no response to your e-mails or phone calls.

- The bidder makes a dollar-amount mistake in the bid. (The bidder bids $100 instead of $10.)

- You decide mid-auction that you can't sell your item.

I can't drive this point home hard enough: *Explain why you're canceling a bid, and your explanation had better be good.* You can cancel any bid for any reason you want, but if you can't give a good explanation of why you did it, you will be sorry. Citing past transaction problems with the current high bidder is okay, but canceling a bidder who lives in Japan because you don't feel like shipping overseas after you said you'd ship internationally could give your feedback history the aroma of week-old sushi.

To cancel a bid (starting from most eBay pages), do the following:

1. **Click the Services link on the navigation bar.**

2. **In the Manage Your Active Listings area, click the Cancel Bids link.**

   You're taken to the Cancelling Bids Placed in Your Auction page, shown in Figure 13-6.

3. **Read all the fine print, and if you haven't signed in, type your User ID, password, item number, and an explanation of why you're canceling a bid, as well as the User ID of the person whose bid you're canceling.**

4. **Click the Cancel Bid button.**

   Be sure that you really want to cancel a bid before you click the Cancel Bid button. Canceled bids can never be reinstated.

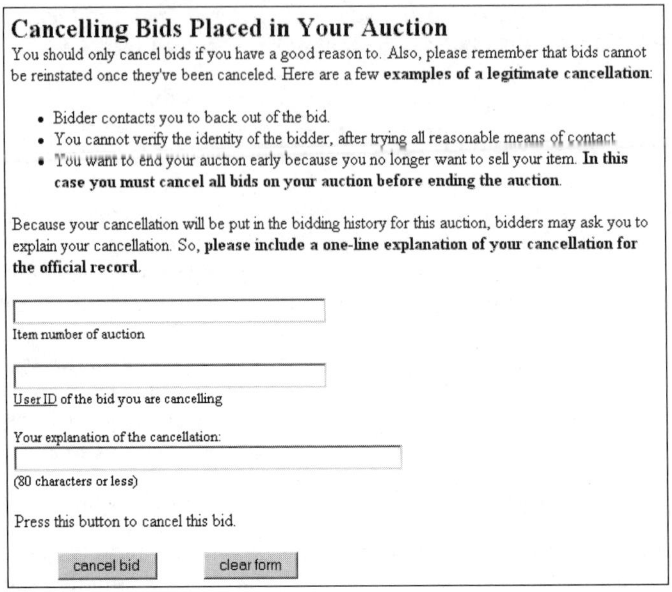

Cancelling Bids Placed in Your Auction

You should only cancel bids if you have a good reason to. Also, please remember that bids cannot be reinstated once they've been canceled. Here are a few **examples of a legitimate cancellation**:

- Bidder contacts you to back out of the bid.
- You cannot verify the identity of the bidder, after trying all reasonable means of contact
- You want to end your auction early because you no longer want to sell your item. **In this case you must cancel all bids on your auction before ending the auction.**

Because your cancellation will be put in the bidding history for this auction, bidders may ask you to explain your cancellation. So, **please include a one-line explanation of your cancellation for the official record**.

Item number of auction

User ID of the bid you are cancelling

Your explanation of the cancellation:

(80 characters or less)

Press this button to cancel this bid.

[cancel bid]   [clear form]

Figure 13-6:
Use this form to remove a bidder from one of your auctions.

Canceling bids means you removed an individual bidder (or several bidders) from your auction, but the auction itself continues running. If you want to end the auction completely, read on.

Blocking bidders

If you have a bidder who just doesn't get the message and continually bids on your auctions despite the fact you've e-mailed and told him or her not to, you can block the bidder from ever participating in your auctions. You can create a list of bidders to prevent them from bidding temporarily or permanently, and you can edit the list at any time.

You can find the page from the same Manage Your Active Listings area as described in the preceding section. Only this time, click Bidder Management and then create your list. Alternatively, you can go directly to this address:

```
pages.ebay.com/services/buyandsell/biddermanagement.html
```

eBay says that you can't receive feedback on a transaction that wasn't completed. So, if something in your gut says not to deal with a particular bidder, then don't.

If all else fails, end your auction early

If you put your auction up for a week and the next day your boss says you have to go to China for a month or your landlord says you have to move out immediately so that he can fumigate for a week, you can end your auction early. But ending an auction early isn't a decision to be taken lightly. You miss all the last-minute bidding action.

eBay makes it clear that ending your auction early does not relieve you of the obligation to sell this item to the highest bidder. To relieve your obligation, you must first cancel all the bids and then end the auction. Of course, if no one has bid, you have nothing to worry about.

When you cancel an auction, you have to write a short explanation (no more than 80 characters) that appears on the bidding history section of your auction page. Anyone who bid on the item may e-mail you for a written explanation. If bidders think your explanation doesn't hold water, don't be surprised if you get some nasty e-mail.

Bidding on your own item is against the rules. Once upon a time, you could cancel an auction by outbidding everyone on your own item and then ending the auction. But some eBay users abused this privilege by bidding on their own items merely to boost the sales price. Shame on them.

To end an auction early, go to the Manage Your Active Listings area (as described earlier in the "Try canceling bids first" section) and click the End Your Listing Early link. Then follow these steps:

1. **For your own security, you must Sign In again.**

   You're taken to the Ending Your Auction form.

2. **Enter the item number and then click Continue.**

3. **On the next page, shown in Figure 13-7, select a reason for ending your auction.**

4. **Click the End Your Listing button.**

   An Ended Auction page appears.

   eBay sends an End of Auction Confirmation e-mail to you and to the highest bidder.

If you know when you list the item that you'll be away when an auction ends, let potential bidders know when you plan to contact them in your item description. Bidders who are willing to wait will still be willing to bid. Alerting them to your absence can save you from losing money if you have to cut your auction short.

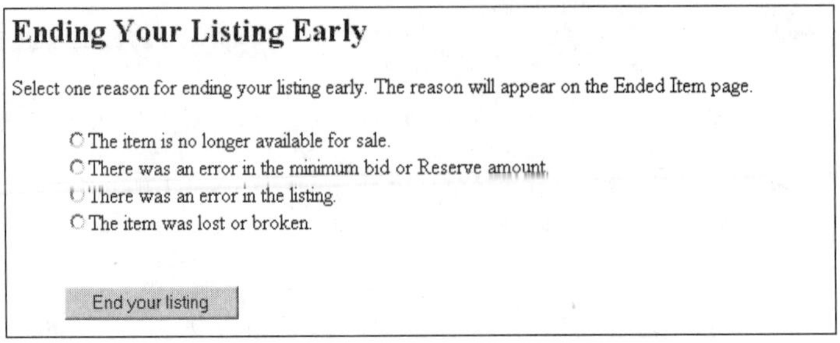

Ending Your Listing Early

Select one reason for ending your listing early. The reason will appear on the Ended Item page.

○ The item is no longer available for sale.
○ There was an error in the minimum bid or Reserve amount.
○ There was an error in the listing.
○ The item was lost or broken.

[End your listing]

Figure 13-7:
Select the
reason for
ending your
auction
early.

Extending your auction (not)

Is your auction red hot? Bids coming in fast and furious? Wish you could have more time? Well, the answer is you can't. eBay won't extend auctions under normal conditions.

However, eBay on occasion experiences *hard outages.* That's when the system goes offline and no one can place bids. (Of course, Murphy's Law would put the next hard outage right in the thick of a furious bidding war in the final minutes of *your* auction. Or so it seems.) Outages can last anywhere from five minutes to a few hours. Because so many bidders wait until the last minute to bid, this can be a disaster. To make nice, eBay extends auctions by 24 hours if any of these three things happen:

✔ The outage is unscheduled and lasts two hours or more.

✔ The auction was scheduled to end during the outage.

✔ The auction was scheduled to end one hour after the outage.

If your auction was set to end Thursday at 20:10:09 (remember, eBay uses military time, based on Pacific Time — which would make it 8:10 p.m.), the new ending time is Friday at 20:10:09. Same Bat-time, same Bat-channel, different day.

eBay also refunds all your auction fees for any hard outage that lasts more than two hours. That means the Insertion Fee, Final Value Fee, and any optional fees. You don't have to apply for anything; eBay automatically refunds the appropriate fees.

You can read about any hard outages at eBay's System Status Announcement Board. To get to an outage report, check the bottom of most eBay pages; you'll find an Announcements link that takes you to the General Announcements Board. From there, click the eBay System Announcements Board link.

If the Announcements link isn't there, start at the navigation bar (at the top of most eBay pages) and do the following:

1. **Click Community on the main navigation bar.**

   You're taken to the Community Overview page.

2. **In the News area, click the System Announcements link.**

   You go to the System Status Announcements Board.

Make it standard operating procedure to check the both the General and the System Announcements Boards when you're running auctions. Checking the Announcements Boards is sort of like checking the obituaries in the morning to make sure you're not listed. You can find more on the Announcements Boards in Chapter 17.

Filing for a Final Value Fee credit

Hard outages are not the only time you can collect a refund. If closing a successful auction is the thrill of victory, finding out that your buyer is a non-paying bidder or deadbeat is the agony of defeat. Adding insult to injury, eBay still charges you a Final Value Fee even if the high bidder never sends you a cent. But you can do something about it. You can file for a Final Value Fee credit.

To qualify for a Final Value Fee credit, you must prove to eBay that one of the following events occurred:

- ✔ The winning bidder never responded after numerous e-mail contacts.
- ✔ The winning bidder backed out of the sale.
- ✔ The winning bidder's payment did not clear or was never received.
- ✔ The winning bidder returned the item to you, and you refunded the payment.

So what happens if the sale goes through but for some reason you collect less than the final sale price listed? eBay has you covered there, too. But first you may ask, "Wait a second; how can that happen?" Let me count the ways. Here are a few of them:

- ✔ eBay miscalculates the final price. (This doesn't happen often, but always check.)
- ✔ You renegotiate a lower final sale price to appease an unhappy customer, and eBay still charges you on the basis of the posted high bid.
- ✔ Bidders in your Multiple Item (Dutch) auction back out.

If both you and the buyer decide that it's okay not to go through with the transaction, that's okay with eBay, too. eBay will allow you to get back your Final Value Fee by going through the refund process. You'll find an option in the Reason for Refund area that will absolve the buyer of any wrongdoing with eBay's Non-Paying Bidder police.

If at least seven days and no more than 45 days have elapsed since the end of the auction, you can apply for a full or partial credit. First, you must first file a Non-Paying Bidder Alert:

1. **Click the Services link on the navigation bar at the top of most eBay pages.**

2. **In the Manage Your Ended Listings area, click the Request a Final Value Fee Credit link.**

   You're taken to the Non-Paying-Bidder / Final Value Fee Credit Request Program page.

3. **Read the guidelines for applying for a Final Value Fee credit and click the Non-Paying Bidder Alert link.**

   You're taken to the Non-Paying Bidder Alert Form information page.

4. **Read all the current terms.**

5. **Type in the item number of the auction in question and then click the Send Request button.**

   The Non-Paying Bidder Alert Form appears, as shown in Figure 13-8.

6. **From the Reason for Non-Paying Bidder Alert drop-down menu, select the reason for your request. Then click the Submit button.**

   If your reason includes a Partial Credit request, or is that you and the buyer mutually agreed not to complete the transaction, when you click Submit, you're taken immediately to the Final Value Fee Credit request page. In these instances, you don't have to wait.

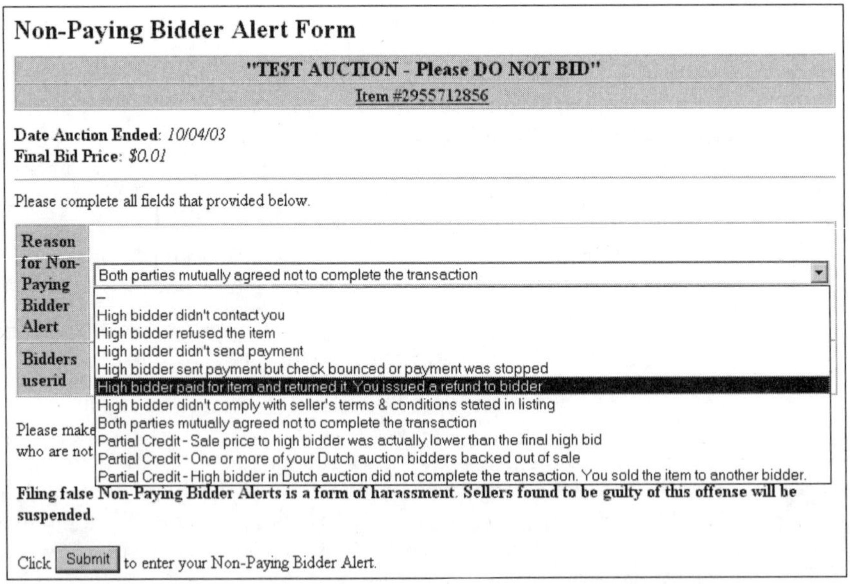

Figure 13-8: Selecting your reason for filing a Non-Paying Bidder Alert.

Non-Paying Bidder Alert Form

"TEST AUCTION - Please DO NOT BID"
Item #2955712856

Date Auction Ended: *10/04/03*
Final Bid Price: *$0.01*

Please complete all fields that provided below.

Reason for Non-Paying Bidder Alert:
Both parties mutually agreed not to complete the transaction

- High bidder didn't contact you
- High bidder refused the item
- High bidder didn't send payment
- High bidder sent payment but check bounced or payment was stopped
- High bidder paid for item and returned it. You issued a refund to bidder
- High bidder didn't comply with seller's terms & conditions stated in listing
- Both parties mutually agreed not to complete the transaction
- Partial Credit - Sale price to high bidder was actually lower than the final high bid
- Partial Credit - One or more of your Dutch auction bidders backed out of sale
- Partial Credit - High bidder in Dutch auction did not complete the transaction. You sold the item to another bidder.

Bidders userid

Please make who are not

Filing false Non-Paying Bidder Alerts is a form of harassment. Sellers found to be guilty of this offense will be suspended.

Click Submit to enter your Non-Paying Bidder Alert.

The instant you file for a Non-Paying Bidder Alert credit, eBay shoots off an e-mail to the winner of your auction (copying you on the e-mail) and warns the eBay user of the non-paying bidder status.

After three non-payment warnings, eBay can boot a deadbeat from the site.

You and your non-paying bidder now have ten days to work out your problems. If you make no progress after ten days, you may file for your Final Value Fee credit.

You need to wait *at least* seven days after the auction ends to file a Non-Paying Bidder Alert and then ten days before you can apply for a Final Value Fee credit. I think it's jumping the gun to label someone a non-paying bidder after only seven days — try to contact the bidder again unless the bidder sends you a message about backing out (or you have good cause to believe you've got a deadbeat on your hands). If you still want to file for your Final Value Fee credit after ten days, do the following:

1. **Follow Steps 1 and 2 in the preceding step list.**

   You're taken to the Non-Paying-Bidder / Final Value Fee Credit Request Program page.

2. **Under the Seller Accounts heading, click the Request Your Final Value Fee Credit link.**

   The Final Value Fee Credit Request Form page appears.

3. **Review the guidelines and input the item number in the text box. Then click Send Request.**

4. **Answer the following questions:**

   - **Did you receive any money from the bidder?** If you answer yes, type the amount in the box; use numerals and a decimal point. If you provided a full refund to the bidder, answer no to this question.

   - **Reason for refund.** Choose a reason for the refund from the drop-down menu.

5. **Click the Submit button on the bottom of the page.**

   You're taken to the Credit Request Process Completed page, which confirms that your refund is being processed by eBay, as shown in Figure 13-9.

When your auction ends, you have up to 60 days after the auction closes to request a full or partial credit. After 60 days, kiss your refund good-bye; eBay won't process it.

But is she a natural blonde?

Here's an example of an item that would have made the seller a bundle if she'd done a little more strategizing up front:

Platinum Mackie Barbie: Beautiful Platinum Bob Mackie Barbie. MIB (removed from box once only to scan). The doll comes with shoes, stand, booklet, and Mackie drawing. The original plastic protects her hair and earrings. Buyer adds $10 for shipping and insurance. Payment must be made within 10 days of auction by MO or cashier's check only.

The starting price was $9.99, and even though the bidding went to $256, the seller's reserve price was not met, and the item didn't sell.

When relisting this item, the seller should lower the reserve price and add much more to the description about the importance and rarity of the doll (unless, of course, $256 was far below what she wanted to make on the doll). Offering to accept credit cards through PayPal would have also helped her make the sale.

Figure 13-9:
eBay
processes
your Final
Value Fee
credit, and it
appears
on your
account
almost
immediately.

▸ Check out <u>Modern and Contemporary Art</u> on eBay Great Collections.

Search | tips
☐ Search titles **and** descriptions

Credit request process completed!

Your final value fee credit has been posted to your account for item #35123360

Your may review your account status at:
http://cgi3.ebay.com/aw-cgi/eBayISAPI.dll?ViewAccountStatus

Anyone caught applying for either a full or partial refund on a successful item transaction can be suspended or something worse — after all, this is a clear-cut case of fraud.

If you want to verify eBay's accounting, grab your calculator and use Table 9-2 in Chapter 9 to check the math. (Why couldn't I have had one of those in high-school algebra class?)

Always print out a copy of any refund and credit requests you make. This paper trail can help bail you out later if eBay asks for documentation.

Déjà vu — relisting your item

Despite all your best efforts, sometimes your auction ends with no bids or bids that are not even close to your reserve price. Or maybe a buyer won your auction, but the transaction didn't go through. eBay takes pity on you and offers you the chance to pick yourself up, dust yourself off, and start all over again.

The best way to improve your chances of selling a relisted item is by making changes to the auction. eBay says the majority of the items put up for auction sell. If you sell your item the second time around (in most cases), eBay rewards you with a refund of your Insertion Fee. You receive your refund after at least one billing cycle. Accept this refund as a reward for learning the ropes.

To be eligible for a refund of your Insertion Fee, here's the scoop:

- ✔ You must relist no more than 30 days after closing the original auction.

- ✔ You can get credit only if you got no bids in your original auction or if the bids you got did not equal the reserve in your reserve-price auction.

- ✔ You can change anything about your auction item description, price, duration, and minimum price, but you can't sell a different item.

- ✔ If you set a reserve price in your original auction, you must set the same reserve, lower it, or cancel the reserve altogether. If you set a higher reserve, you're not eligible for a relisting credit.

eBay's generosity has exceptions. It doesn't offer refunds for any listing options you paid for, such as **bold lettering** or use of Featured Plus!. Also, Multiple Item (Dutch) auctions aren't covered by this offer. And if you have a deadbeat on your hands, you can relist, but you don't get a return of your Insertion Fee. More bad news: If you don't sell the item the second time around, you're stuck paying *two* Insertion Fees. So work a little harder this time and give it your best shot!

To get your second shot at selling, do the following (from the Items I'm Selling section of your My eBay Selling page):

1. **Click the auction item listing that you want to relist.**

   You're taken to the main auction page of that item.

2. **Click the Relist Your Item link.**

   You're taken to the Relist Your Item form — basically, the Sell Your Item form with all the information filled in.

3. **Make your changes to the auction, launch it, and pray!**

Being as specific as possible with your item title improves your odds of being profitable. If you're selling an old Monopoly game, don't just title it **Old Monopoly board game**; call it **Rare 1959 Monopoly Game Complete in Box**. For more information about listing items, see Chapter 10.

Here's a list of ideas that you can use to improve your auction's odds for success:

- **Change the item category.** See if the item sold better in another category (see Chapter 3).

- **Add a picture.** If two identical items are up for auction at the same time, the item with a photo gets more and higher bids. Zoom in on Chapter 14.

- **Jazz up the title and description.** Make it enticing and grab those search engines. Breeze on over to Chapter 10.

- **Set a lower minimum bid.** The first bidders will think they're getting a bargain, and others will want a hot item. Mosey on over to Chapter 10.

- **Set a lower reserve price or cancel the reserve.** A reserve price often scares away bidders who fear it's too high. See (yup) Chapter 10 for ways to make your reserve more palatable to prospective bidders.

- **Offer more options for payment.** People may pop for an impulse item if they can put it on their credit card and pay for it later.

- **Change the duration of the auction.** Maybe you need some more time. Go to (you guessed it) Chapter 10.

Long-time eBay veterans say that reducing or canceling your reserve price makes your auction very attractive to buyers.

Chapter 14

Using Pictures and Strategies to Increase Your Profits

*Y*ou may be enjoying most of what eBay has to offer, and you're probably having some good buying adventures. If you're selling, you're experiencing the excitement of making money. But there's more. Welcome to eBay, the advanced class.

In this chapter, you go to the head of the class by discovering some insider tips on how to enhance your auctions with images and spiffy text. Successful eBay vendors know that pictures (also called images) really help sell items. This chapter gives you the basics on how to create great images. I also give you advice on linking pictures to your auctions so that buyers around the world can view them.

Using Images in Your Auctions

Will you buy an item you can't see? Most people won't, especially if they're interested in purchasing collectible items that they want to display — or clothes they intend to wear. Without a picture, you can't tell whether a seller's idea of good quality is anything like yours or if the item is exactly what you're looking for.

Welcome to the cyberworld of *imaging*, where pictures aren't called pictures, but *images*. With a digital camera or a scanner and software, you can manipulate your images — crop, color-correct, and add special effects — so that they grab viewers by the lapels. Even cooler: When you're happy with your creation, you can add it to your eBay auction for others to see.

Sellers, take heed and read these other reasons why you should use well-made digital images in your auction pages:

- ✔ If you don't have a picture, potential bidders may wonder whether you're deliberately hiding the item from view because you know something is wrong with it. Paranoid? Maybe. Practical? You bet.

- ✔ Fickle bidders don't even bother reading an item description if they can't see the item. Maybe they were traumatized in English class.

- ✔ Taking your own pictures shows that you have the item in your possession. Many scam artists take images from a manufacturer's Web site to illustrate their bogus sales on eBay. Why risk being suspect? Snap a quick picture!

- ✔ Everyone's doing it. I hate to pressure you, but digital images are the custom at eBay, so if you're not using them, you're not reaching the widest possible number of people who would bid on your item. From that point of view, you're not doing the most you can to serve your potential customers' needs. Hey, fads are *driven* by conformity. You may as well use them to your advantage.

So which is better for capturing images: digital cameras or digital scanners? As with all gadgets, here's the classic answer: It depends. For my money, it's hard to beat a digital camera. But before you go snag one, decide what kind of investment (and how big) you plan to make in your eBay auctions. If you're already comfortable with 35mm camera equipment, don't scrap it — scan (or find a digital SLR)! The scoop on both of these alternatives is coming right up.

Whether you buy new or used digital equipment at eBay, make sure it comes with a warranty. If you *don't* get a warranty, Murphy's Law practically ensures that your digital equipment will break the second time you use it.

Choosing a digital camera

If price isn't a factor, you should buy the highest-quality digital camera you can afford, especially if you plan to use images with a lot of your eBay auctions and the items you plan to sell vary in size and shape.

Sony, Olympus, and Nikon make good basic digital cameras, starting at around $300 (easily found on eBay for close to $100 less). Middle-of-the-road and quality used digital cameras sell for between $150 and $250. Compare prices at computer stores and in catalogs.

One of the most popular cameras used by eBay sellers is the Sony Mavica. It comes in two styles: the FD series uses an everyday 3½-inch floppy disk as the memory; the CD series burns the images directly onto a rewritable mini-CD.

Using the floppy Mavica is simple. Just take your pictures, and then pop out the floppy disk with the images and insert it into your computer. The images are now immediately accessible from your floppy drive. No fuss, no muss — no cards to input, no software to install. The CD models are similar, only you insert the CD in your CD drive. The files can be read off the disks from the camera as normal.

The models of the popular Sony cameras vary in image quality. It's interesting that a discontinued model, the FD-73, is the most popular among eBay sellers. The FD-73 is one of the few that has a 10x zoom, which helps with intricate close-ups. This camera has only VGA resolution, which makes it pretty unusable for large prints but perfect for your online images. Many newer digital cameras require color correcting and sharpening on your computer with programs like Photoshop. The FD-73 takes crisp, clean pictures without your having to make software adjustments. You just have to trim the images to size. You can find this camera either refurbished or used on eBay for under $200. I had an FD-73, and then bought a used FD-92 (a later model that adds a memory stick) — it's a deal.

A great place to buy digital cameras is (surprise!) eBay. Just do a search of some popular manufacturers, such as Olympus, Sony, and Nikon, and you will find pages of listings — both new and used digital cameras — that you can bid on and, if you win, buy.

When shopping for a digital camera, look at the following features:

- ✔ **Resolution:** Look for a camera that has a resolution of at least 640 x 480 pixels. This isn't hard to find because new cameras tout their strength in megapixels (millions of pixels). You don't need that high of a resolution for eBay because your pictures will ultimately be shown on a monitor, not printed on paper. A *pixel* is a tiny dot of information that, when grouped with other pixels, forms an image. The more pixels an image has, the clearer and sharper the image is; the more memory the image scarfs up, the slower it shows up on-screen. A 640-x-480-pixel resolution may seem paltry next to the 6-million-pixel punch of a high-end digital camera, but trust me: No one bidding on your auctions will ever know the difference.

- ✔ **Storage type:** Smart card? CompactFlash card? Memory Stick? Floppy disk? The instructions that come with your camera explain how to transfer images from your media type to your computer. (No instructions? Check the manufacturer's Web site.)

✔ **Extra features:** Make sure that the camera is capable of taking close-up images; you need to be close to an item you photograph for an auction — from 3 inches to 1 foot away. A flash also comes in handy.

If you plan to sell small or detailed items that require extreme close-ups (such as jewelry, stamps, currency, coins, or Tibetan beads), you might want a digital camera that lets you change lenses.

A more versatile way to get the best images of these items is to use a super new invention called a Cloud Dome. When photographing complex items, no matter how good your camera is, you may find it difficult to capture the item cleanly and exactly (especially the colors and brightness of gems and metals). Your camera attaches to the top of this Cloud Dome, and pictures are taken inside a translucent plastic dome. The dome diffuses the light over the entire surface of the object to reveal all the intricate details of the item. You can purchase Cloud Domes on eBay or from the manufacturer's Web site at `www.clouddome.com`. Even in black and white, you can see the difference that a cloud dome can make when taking pictures of jewelry, as shown Figure 14-1.

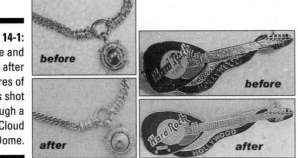

Figure 14-1: Before and after pictures of items shot through a Cloud Dome.

Choosing a scanner

If you plan to sell flat items such as autographs, stamps, books, or documents — or if you need a good piece of business equipment that can double as a photocopier — consider getting a digital scanner. You can pick up a brand new one for a under $100; you can also find scanners at eBay.

Here's what you need to look for when you buy a scanner:

✔ **Resolution:** As with printers and photocopiers, the resolution of digital scanning equipment is measured in *dots per inch* (dpi). The more dpi, the greater the resolution.

Some scanners can provide resolutions as high as 12,800 dpi, which looks awesome when you print the image, but to dress up your eBay auctions, all you need is (are you ready?) 72 dpi (dots or pixels per inch)! That's it. Your images will look great and won't take up much storage space on your computer's hard drive. Basic scanners can scan images up to 1,200 dpi, so even they are more powerful than you need for your eBay images.

✔ **Flatbed:** If you're planning to use your scanner to scan pictures of documents (or even items in boxes), a flatbed scanner is your best bet. Flatbeds work just like photocopiers. You simply lay your item or box on the glass and scan away.

Making Your Picture a Thing of Beauty

The idea behind using images in your auctions is to attract tons of potential buyers. With that goal in mind, you should try to create the best-looking images possible, no matter what kind of technology you're using to capture them.

Get it on camera

Point-and-shoot may be okay for a group shot at a historical monument, but illustrating your auction is a whole different idea. Whether you're using a traditional film camera (so that you can scan your developed photographs later) or a digital camera to capture your item, some basic photographic guidelines can give you better results.

Don't forget your camcorder!

The majority of eBay users use either a digital camera or scanner to dress up their auctions with images, but some just use what they already own — their handy-dandy camcorders! Yup, after videotaping your day at the beach, point your lens at that Victorian doll and shoot. With the help of a video-capturing device, you can create a digital image right from the camera.

Although several companies offer video-capturing devices, one that I'm most impressed with is Dazzle Digital Video Creator (from Pinnacle Systems). This device sells for under $100 and includes everything you need to transfer and save pictures from your camcorder (or VCR) to your computer. Visit the manufacturers' Web site (www.pinnaclesys.com) for details about how the product works and search eBay (of course) for the best prices.

For more on using 35mm cameras and scanners, zoom ahead to the next section, "Use traditional photos? Yes, I scan." Then c'mon back to these Do's and Don'ts to ensure that your digital image is a genuine enhancement to your auction:

- ✓ **Do** take the picture of your item outside, in daylight, whenever possible. That way, the camera can catch all possible details and color.

- ✓ **Do** forget about fancy backgrounds; they distract viewers from your item. Put small items on a neutral-colored, nonreflective towel or cloth; put larger items in front of a neutral-colored wall or curtain. You'll cut out almost all the background when you prepare the picture on your computer. (This chapter explains how to prepare your picture.)

- ✓ **Do** use extra lighting. You can do this with your camera's flash mode or with extra photo lighting on stands. Use extra lighting even when you're taking the picture outside. The extra lighting acts as *fill light* — it adds more light to the item, filling in some of the shadowed spots.

- ✓ **Don't** get so close to the item that the flash washes out (overexposes) the image. The easiest way to figure out the best distance is by trial and error. Start close and keep moving farther away until you get the results you want. This method can get pricey if you use film, but this is where digital cameras really shine: You can see the picture seconds after you shoot it, keep it and modify it, erase it, and start again.

- ✓ **Do** take two or three acceptable versions of your image; you can pick the best one later on your computer.

- ✓ If your item relies on detail (for example, an engraved signature or detailed gold trim), **do** take a wide shot of the entire item and then take a close-up or two of the detailed areas that you want buyers to see.

- ✓ **Do** make sure that you focus the camera; nothing is worse than a blurry picture. If your camera is a fixed-focus model (it can't be adjusted), get only as close as the manufacturer recommends. If you go beyond that distance, the item appears out of focus. (Automatic-focus cameras measure the distance and change the lens setting as needed.)

Taking pictures of your item from different angles gives the prospective buyer more information. When you have several images, use your photo-editing program to put them in one composite image, as shown in Figure 14-2.

Some eBay creeps, whether out of laziness or deceit, steal images from other eBay members. (They simply make a digital copy of the image and use it in their own auctions. This is so uncool because the copied image doesn't represent their actual item.) This pilfering has happened to me on several occasions. To prevent picture-snatching, you can add your User ID to all your photos. The next time somebody lifts one of your pictures, it has your name on it. If you're familiar with adding HTML code to your auctions, I offer a simple Java code on my Web site, `www.coolebaytools.com`, that you can insert into your auction descriptions to prevent scurrilous users from stealing your images.

Figure 14-2:
Making a composite image of pictures from several angles makes a most attractive auction.

Use traditional photos? Yes, I scan

If you use a scanner and 35mm camera to create images for your eBay auction, you've come to the right place. (Also check out the tips in the preceding section.) Here goes:

✔ Have the photo developer print your photos on glossy paper; it scans best.

✔ Avoid using incandescent or fluorescent lighting to illuminate the photos you plan to scan. Incandescent lighting tends to make items look yellowish, and fluorescent lights lend a bluish tone to your photos. One exception is *GE Reveal* incandescent bulbs; they throw a good natural light, and they're used by many eBay sellers.

✔ When you take traditional photos for scanning, get as close to your item as your camera allows. Enlarging photos in the scanner will only result in blurry (or, worse, jagged) images.

✔ Scan the box that the item came in, or if there's a photo of the item on the box, scan that portion of the box.

✔ If you're scanning a three-dimensional item (such as a doll, jewelry, or a box) and you can't close the scanner lid, put a black or white T-shirt over the item so that you will get a clean background and good light reflection from the scanner.

✔ If you want to scan an item that's too big to put on your scanner all at once, scan the item in sections and assemble the digital pieces with your image-editing software. The instructions that come with your software should explain how to do this.

Software that adds the artist's touch

After you take the picture (or scan it) and transfer it into your computer according to the manufacturer's instructions, the next step is to edit the picture. Much like a book or magazine editor, you get to cut, fix, resize, and reshape your picture until you think it's good enough to be seen by the public. If you're a non-techie type, don't get nervous. Many of the programs have one-button magical corrections that make your pictures look great.

The software program that comes with your digital camera or scanner puts at your disposal an arsenal of editing tools that help you turn a basic image of your item into something special. Although each program has its own collection of features, a few basic tools and techniques are common to all:

- ✔ **Image quality:** Enables you to enhance or correct colors, sharpen images, remove dust spots, and increase or reduce brightness or contrast.

- ✔ **Size:** Reduce or increase the size or shape of the image.

- ✔ **Orientation:** Rotate the image left or right; flip it horizontally or vertically.

- ✔ **Crop:** Trim your picture to show the item, rather than extraneous background.

- ✔ **Create an image format:** After the image is edited, you can save it in a specific format, such as .JPG, .GIF, or others. The best format for putting photos on the Web (and thus the preferred format at eBay and the one I strongly recommend) is .JPG (pronounced "JAY-peg").

Every image-editing software program has its own system requirements and capabilities. Study the software that comes with your camera or scanner. If you feel the program is too complicated (or doesn't give you the editing tools you need), investigate some of the other popular programs. You can get some excellent shareware (software that you can try out before you buy it) at www.tucows.com and www.shareware.com.

If you have Microsoft Office, check to see if you have Photo Editor in your Start menu under Microsoft Office Tools. (Sometimes it's even bundled with Windows.) You may even have to search your hard drive for the file, photoed.exe. If you don't see it on your computer, get out your Microsoft Office CD. Photo Editor is included on the CD but doesn't install automatically. Here's how to install it from Microsoft Office 2000:

1. **Insert the Office CD.**

2. **Click Add or Remove Features.**

   You see a screen of Office programs. Click the plus sign next to Office tools, and you see a screen similar to Figure 14-3.

3. **Scroll down the list of Office Tools until you see Microsoft Photo Editor.**

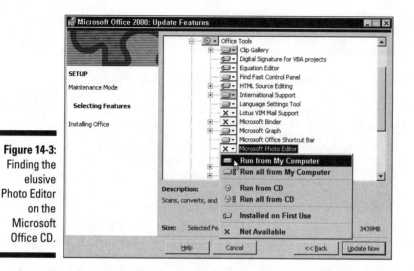

Figure 14-3:
Finding the
elusive
Photo Editor
on the
Microsoft
Office CD.

4. **Click the box next to Photo Editor (it will have an X in it), and from
   the drop-down menu that appears, select the Run from My Computer
   option.**

5. **Click Update Now in the lower-right corner.**

   Microsoft Photo Editor is then installed on your computer.

If your camera didn't come with software, you can purchase commercial
photo-editing software. The most widely used is the very complex Photoshop
and the pared down (but easier to use) Photoshop Elements; both are made
by Adobe. Another excellent choice is PhotoImpact by Ulead. This is high-
quality editing software, which you can easily purchase on eBay for under $50.

Copying someone else's auction text or images without permission can con-
stitute copyright infringement, which ends your auction and gets you suspended from eBay.

Making Your Images Web-Friendly

Because digital images are made up of pixels, and every pixel has a set of
instructions that has to be stored someplace, you have two difficulties facing
you right after you take the picture:

- Digital images contain computer instructions, so bigger pictures take up
  more memory.

- Very large digital images take longer to *build* (appear) on the buyer's
  screen, and time can be precious in an auction.

To get around both these problems, think small. Here's a checklist of tried-and-true techniques for preparing your elegantly slender, fast-loading images to display at eBay:

- ✔ **Set your image resolution at 72 pixels per inch.** You can do this with the settings for your scanner. Although 72 ppi may seem like a low resolution, it nibbles computer memory (instead of chomping), shows up fast on a buyer's screen, and looks great at eBay.

- ✔ **When using a digital camera, set the camera to no higher than the 640 x 480 format.** That's custom made for a VGA monitor. You can always crop the picture if it's too large. You can even save the image at 320 x 240, and it'll display well on eBay — but it will take up less space, and you can add more pictures!

- ✔ **Make the finished image no larger than 480 pixels wide.** When you size your picture in your image software, it's best to keep it no larger than 300 x 300 pixels or 4 inches square, even if it's a snapshot of a classic 4 x 4 monster truck. These dimensions are big enough for people to see without squinting, and the details of your item show up nicely.

- ✔ **Crop any unnecessary areas of the photo.** You need to show your item only; everything else is a waste.

- ✔ **Use your software to darken or change the photo's contrast.** When the image looks good on your computer screen, the image looks good on your eBay auction page.

- ✔ **Save your image as a .JPG file.** When you finish editing your picture, save it as a .JPG. (To do this, follow the instructions that come with your software.) .JPG is the best format for eBay; it compresses information into a small file that builds fast and reproduces nicely on the Internet.

- ✔ **Check the total size of your image.** After you save the image, check its total size. If the size hovers around 40K (kilobytes) or smaller, eBay users won't have a hard time seeing the image in a reasonable amount of time.

- ✔ **Reduce the size of your image if it's larger than 50K.** Small is fast, efficient, and beautiful. Big is slow, sluggish, and dangerous. Impatient eBay users will move on to the next listing if they have to wait to see your image.

The Image Is Perfect — Now What?

Now that your masterpiece is complete, you want to emblazon it on your auction for all the world to see. When most people first get the urge to dazzle prospective buyers with a picture, they poke around the eBay site looking for a place to put it. Trade secret: You're not actually putting pictures on eBay;

you're telling eBay's servers where to *find* your picture so that, like a good hunting dog, your auction *points* the buyers' browsers to the exact corner of the virtual universe where your picture is. That's why the picture has to load fast — it's coming in from a different location. (Yeah, it confused me in the beginning too, but now it makes perfect sense. Uh-huh. Sure.)

To help eBay find your image, all you have to do is type its address into the Picture URL box of the Sell Your Item form, so don't forget to write down the Web address (URL) of your image.

If you use eBay's Picture Services, your photo will be at eBay's servers and will upload once, directly from your computer. I talk more about that in just a minute.

You can highlight your image's URL with your cursor, right-click your mouse, and copy it to your computer's clipboard. Then go to the auction page you're filling out at eBay, put your cursor in the Picture URL window, and paste the address into the box.

A typical address (for someone using AOL) looks something like this: `members.aol.com/ebay4dummy/rolexwatch.jpg`.

Because your image needs an address, you have to find it a good home online. You have several options:

- ✔ **Your ISP (Internet service provider):** All the big ISPs — AOL, AT&T, Road Runner, and Earthlink — give you space to store your Internet stuff. You're already paying for an ISP, so you can park pictures there at no extra charge.

- ✔ **An image-hosting Web site:** Web sites that specialize in hosting pictures are popping up all over the Internet. Some charge a small fee; others are free. The upside here is that they're easy to use.

- ✔ **Your server:** If you have your own server (those of you who do know who you are), you can store those images right in your own home.

- ✔ **eBay Picture Services:** You can find out about using eBay's photo-hosting service later in this chapter.

Using an ISP to store your images

Every ISP has its own rules and procedures. Go to the help area of your ISP for directions on how to *access your personal area* and how to *upload your images*. (No, I'm not getting naughty, those are authentic computerese phrases!)

After you've uploaded your images to your ISP, get the Web address of your item's location and type it into the Picture URL box of eBay's Sell Your Item page. Now whenever someone views your auction page, the picture appears within the item description. Figure 14-4 shows you an auction description with a picture.

Figure 14-4:
Including pictures in your auctions takes practice, but the results are worth it.

Elegant Frosted & Clear
Floral Stopper Perfume Bottle

This charming and very Lalique style perfume bottle stands approx. 4" tall. The base features alternating swirls of frosted and clear cut glass and has no markings of any kind. The ground frosted stopper has two lovely flowers at the top. A great item for your vanity table, or a wonderful gift.
Bid with confidence and bid whatever you feel this bottle is worth to you as he is selling with **NO RESERVE!** *(Feel free to check my feedback!)* I pack all my items carefully. Winning bidder to pay shipping & handling of $4.55 and must submit payment within a week of winning the auction. I will accept credit cards through paypal.com (see below). Good luck on winning!

GOOD LUCK, HAPPY BIDDING!

Click below to...
View my other auctions - Win more than one and $AVE on shipping!

Using image-hosting Web sites to store images

Okay, realistically, many people are combing cyberspace looking for the next great thing. eBay's success has entrepreneurs all over the globe coming up with different kinds of auction-support businesses. As usual, a lot of junk pops up on the Internet in the wake of such trends — but one promising development caught my attention recently — *image-hosting* Web sites.

Image-hosting Web sites have changed from one-stop shops to mega-markets loaded with tons of services for your auctions. Some image-hosting sites let you post your pictures without requiring you to use their auction management software — not that I think auction management software is a bad thing; it's great! (Flip to Chapter 20 to find more info on auction management software.)

Here are a few convenient image-hosting sites that allow you to post a few of your images for free:

- FreePictureHosting.com (www.freepicturehosting.com)
- Picturetrail (www.picturetrail.com)
- PennyThings.com (www.pennythings.com)

MSN TV — the easiest way to upload pictures

You can upload images to MSN TV so quickly and easily that you may consider using it to upload images to the Web even if you own a computer. The restrictions? You must own (or borrow) a camcorder and, oh yeah, MSN TV.

Uploading images to MSN TV is simple. My low-tech suggestions should get you through the process:

1. **Place all your items on a kitchen counter or other flat, neutral surface and start filming.**

   Consider placing the items on a white sheet or towel to help create a background for the items.

2. **Pan your camcorder from one item to the next, zoom in and out of each item, and linger at the highlights of your collection.**

   Your camcorder's auto focus records quality images.

Don't turn your camcorder vertically, or your pictures will end up at eBay sideways. *I always wondered where sideways pictures came from.*

To load your images into your auction pages, you need to join an image-hosting site that's MSN TV friendly — all the image-hosting sites listed in this chapter are. After you log on and register, just connect your camera to the MSN TV box and follow the instructions provided by the image-hosting service.

Using eBay's Picture Services

eBay hosts one image per auction — for free. If you want more images, it costs only $0.15 to add additional pictures. (You can have a maximum of six images per auction item.)

If you use this service, your photos appear on your auction in a predesigned template. If you use more than one photo, the first photo shows up in a 400-x-300-pixel format. A miniature of the first image appears to the left of the larger image. The prospective bidder clicks the smaller picture, and it magically appears in the larger photo area.

When you prepare to list an item for auction, a page appears, and you're asked whether you'd like to use the photo service. If you don't want to use it, click the Your Own Web Hosting tab and input the URL of your picture. If you do want to use the service, follow the directions on-screen.

To post your photo, click the box, and an Open File dialog box appears. Find your image on your computer and click Open, and the image magically appears in the image box. Add more pictures if you want and click Submit Pictures and Continue. Figure 14-5 shows the upload page. eBay keeps an image online for the duration of your auction. After that, the image disappears (unless you relist the same auction). You can always post the image again if you need it later. (So be sure that you leave a copy of the image on your computer.) *Note:* This feature doesn't support the MSN TV platform.

Figure 14-5:
eBay's Full
Featured
Picture
Services.
Here's
where you
upload your
image from
the Sell Your
Item page. If
your upload
(on the Sell
Your Item
page)
doesn't look
like this,
click the link
on the right
to go to Full
Featured.

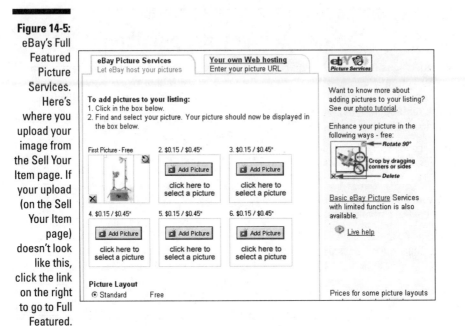

eBay's Gallery

Any discussion of images on eBay would be incomplete without a short
discussion of eBay's Gallery. The Gallery consists of the small pictures you
see next to items in category listings or in your searches. (If you perform a
search for just Gallery items, you'll see something like Figure 14-6.) It's obvious that using eBay's Gallery option draws more attention to your sales, but
have you ever noticed that not all Gallery images show up crisp and clear?
And that some are smaller than others? It's not by chance; eBay reduces the
same image you uploaded for the Gallery.

The technology that allows eBay's Picture Services to do its magic resizes the
seller's picture to fit the allotted space. In the case of the Gallery, a considerable amount of compression is applied to your image. The more compression
that's applied, the fuzzier and more distorted your image can get.

When you use your own photo hosting on eBay, you can use a different photo
for your Gallery image. Either use a different picture or reduce the main picture to a tiny 110 x 120 pixels. If you reduce the picture yourself, you'll notice
a big improvement in the way the Gallery picture looks.

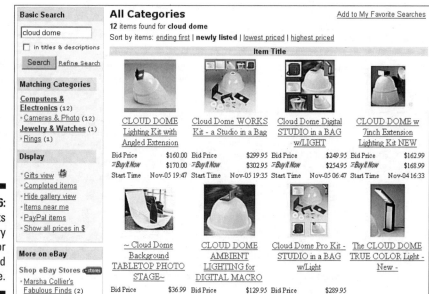

Figure 14-6:
The results
of a Gallery
Search for
Cloud
Dome.

Getting Your Item Noticed

Okay, you've got a great auction at eBay and great images to go with it. Now all you need to do is track the number of users peeking at your items and attract even more people to your auction. Read the following sections to find out how to make your auction even better.

Putting on the hits

Your auction is up and running at eBay, and you're dying to know how many people have stopped by to take a look. To easily monitor your auction's *hits* — the number of times visitors stop to look at the goods — you use a free public *counter* program from an online source. A counter is a useful marketing tool; for example, you can check the number of times people have looked at, but not bid on, your auctions. If you have lots more lookie-loos than bids, you may have a problem with your auction.

If your counter indicates you're not getting many hits, consider the following potential problems so that you can resurrect your auction:

✔ Does the picture take too long to load?

✔ Is the opening bid too high?

✔ Are those neon orange and lime green bell-bottoms just too funky to sell?

Multiple pictures in your descriptions

Here's the answer to *the most-asked* question when I teach a class on eBay. Many sellers have more than one picture within the auction description area. By putting extra images in the description, they do not have to pay extra for eBay's hosting services. This isn't magic; you can easily do it, too. Just add a tiny bit of HTML code in your auction description. Here is the HTML code to insert one picture in your auction:

```
<img src=http://www.yourserver.com/
        imagename.jpg>
```

Be sure to use the brackets to open and close your code (they're located above the comma and the period on your keyboard). This code reflects the URL of your picture and the coding img src= to tell eBay's server to insert a picture.

When you want to insert two pictures, just insert code for each picture, one after the other. If you want one picture to appear below the other, use the HTML code for line break, <BR>. Here's how to write that:

```
<img src=http://www.yourserver.com/
        imagenumber1.jpg> <BR>
<img src=http://www.yourserver.com/
        imagenumber2.jpg>
```

Counters are available at many auction-oriented Web sites. You can pick the free Andale.com counter at the eBay Sell Your Item page, or visit some of the other sites that supply counters. A couple of widely used ones are Vendio (www.vendio.com) for its "intelligent" counters and ManageAuctions.com (www.manageauctions.com) for its detailed hourly private counters.

Playing the links for fun and profit

By linking your eBay auctions to your personal or business Web page, you can get even more people to look at what you're selling. To link your auctions from your Web page (starting at the navigation bar found at the top of most eBay pages), do the following:

1. **Click the Services link.**

   You're taken to the Services Overview page.

2. **Scroll down the page to Manage Your Active Listings and click the Promote Your Listings Add Link Buttons link.**

   You can choose to link your item to the eBay home page, but why would you? Everyone visiting your auction already knows how to get there! Or you can choose to create a customized link that goes directly to a list of items you have for sale.

3. **Be bold — select the box that allows you to create a customized link.**

4. **Type in the URL of the Web site to which you want to link your auction.**

5. **Read eBay's link agreement and click the I Agree button. It's so much more civilized that way.**

6. **Read the Instructions for Installing Buttons on Your Site page.**

   eBay generates a piece of HTML code and displays it on your screen.

7. **Copy the handy HTML code that eBay generated for you; then use your computer's Clipboard to paste it into your Web site or text editor.**

   An eBay icon link appears on your personal or business Web page. Anyone who clicks this link is plucked from your Web page and automatically transported to your auctions.

The instant that you or another eBay user connects to a link that isn't owned or maintained by eBay, you're no longer protected by the eBay rules and regulations. eBay cancels any auctions that contain links to Web sites that offer to undersell an auction by touting the same item at a cheaper price — or offer to sell items forbidden at eBay.

It's against eBay policy to link to your Web site from your auction page, but you can link from your About Me page (see the next section). To add a link to your About Me page that takes eBay users to your Web site, type the following HTML code at the end of your item description:

```
Click below...<br>
<A HREF=http://www.YourOwnISP.com/~yourUserID/sale.htm>
Visit my Web site</A>
```

It's All About Me!

Want to know more about the people behind those User IDs? Thousands of eBay members have created their own personal Web pages at eBay, called About Me pages. About Me pages are easy to create and are as unique as each eBay member. eBay users with active About Me pages have a special ME icon next to their User IDs.

Take your time when you create your About Me page. A well-done About Me page improves your sales because people who come across your auctions and check out your About Me page can get a sense of who you are and how serious you are about your eBay activities. They instantly see that you're no fly-by-night seller.

Before you create your About Me page, I suggest that you look at what other users have done. eBay members often include pictures, links to other Web sites (including their personal or business home pages), and links to just about any Web location that reflects their personality, which is why they're so entertaining. If your purpose is to generate more business, I recommend that you keep your About Me page focused on your auction listings, with a link to your Web site.

Sellers with many auctions running at once often add a message to their About Me pages that indicates that they're willing to reduce shipping charges if bidders also bid on their other auctions. This direct tactic may lack nuance, but it increases the number of people who look at (and bid on) your auctions.

To create your About Me page (starting at the main navigation bar on most eBay pages), do the following:

1. **Click the Services link, and then on the Services Overview page, click the Create My About Me Page link.**

   You're taken to About Me: Create Your Own eBay Personal Page.

2. **If you haven't signed in, type your User ID and password in the appropriate boxes.**

3. **Click the Create and Edit Your Page button.**

   You're taken to the About Me layout page. You have three layout options, which eBay is kind enough to show you:

   • Two Column Layout

   • Newspaper Layout

   • Centered Layout

4. **Click the button that corresponds to the layout option you want.**

   You're taken to a second About Me creation page.

5. **Enter the following information:**

   • **Page Title:** Type the title of your About Me page (for example, **Larry's Lunchboxes**).

   • **Welcome Message:** Type a personal attention-grabbing headline, such as **Welcome to Larry Lunch's Lunchbox Place**.

   • **Text:** Type a short paragraph that greets your visitors (something like, **Hey, I like lunchboxes a lot** — only more exciting).

   • **Another Paragraph:** Type in another headline for the second paragraph of the page, such as **Vintage**, **Modern**, **Ancient**, or **I Collect All Kinds of Lunchboxes**.

   • **Text:** Type in another paragraph about yourself or your collection (such as, **I used to stare at lunchboxes in the school cafeteria . . .** only more, you know, *normal*).

   • **Picture:** If you're adding a picture, type in a sentence describing it, for example: **This is my wife Loretta with our lunchbox collection**.

- **URL:** Type in the Web site address (URL) where people can find your picture. See the section earlier in this chapter that shows you how to upload digital images.

- **Feedback:** Select how many of your feedback postings you want to appear on your About Me page. (You can opt not to show any feedback, but I think you should put in a few comments, especially if they're complimentary, as in, "Larry sent my lunchbox promptly, and it makes lunchtime a blast! Everybody stares at it. . . .")

- **Items for Sale:** Select how many of your current auctions you want to appear on your About Me page. If you don't have any auctions running at the moment, you can select the Show No Items option.

- **Caption:** Type a caption to introduce your auctions, for example: **Lunchboxes I'm Currently Selling**.

- **Favorite Links:** Type the names and URLs of any Web links you want visitors to see, for example, a Web site that appraises lunchboxes ("It's in excellent condition except for that petrified ham sandwich. . . .").

- **Favorite eBay Items:** Type the Item Numbers and select a comment from the options displayed to point out eBay auction items you think visitors should check out.

These text areas are shown in Figure 14-7.

6. **Click the Preview Your Page button, or, if you don't like your current layout, click the Choose New Layout button to go back to Step 1.**

   You're now looking at your final About Me page.

7. **Scroll down to the bottom of the page. You see a group of buttons:**

   - **Edit Some More:** Returns you to Step 2.

   - **Save My Page:** Saves your About Me page so that you're one step closer to publishing it at eBay.

   - **Edit Using HTML:** If you know HTML code, you can customize your About Me page. (You can insert pictures with the code I give you in the "Multiple pictures in your descriptions" sidebar, earlier in this chapter.)

   - **Start Over:** Takes you to a link page where you can delete what you created and begin again.

8. **When you're happy with your masterpiece, click the Save My Page button.**

   Yes, you did it; now anybody in the world with access to the Internet can now find your personal About Me page at eBay.

Figure 14-7:
Make *your* About Me page *your* home at eBay.

Don't forget to update your About Me page often. A good About Me page makes bidders eager to know more about your auctions. An out-of-date About Me page turns off potential bidders. If you choose to update, you need to edit it using HTML. If you don't use HTML, you have to create a whole new page.

You can link to your About Me page from your Web site or from your e-mail because all About Me pages have their own personal URLs. The address ends with your User ID. Here's the URL for my page:

```
members.eBay.com/aboutme/marsha_c
```

Part IV
Oy Vay, More eBay! Special Features

The 5th Wave   By Rich Tennant

"He saw your laptop and wants to know
if he can check his feedback rating."

In this part . . .

So you want to protect yourself from bad apples, not just at eBay but all over the Internet? You're not alone. I want to keep safe as well, and that's why I've tipped you off to the information in this part.

This is the place to come if you want to know just what eBay knows about you and is willing to share with other eBay members. I also introduce you to Rules & Safety (SafeHarbor), the next best thing to a superhero when it comes to protecting you from people who don't qualify for the eBay User of the Year Award.

eBay is a community, so you need to be let in on some of the ways you can commune with other collectors and get into the social scene. In this part, you find out about the special features that make eBay such a unique environment. Where else can you buy an item you really want and also help out a charity, all with the click of a mouse?

Chapter 15

Privacy: To Protect and Serve

. . . .

In This Chapter

▶ Digging up what eBay knows about you

▶ Determining how safe your information is at eBay

▶ Finding out what eBay does with your info

▶ Protecting your privacy

. . . .

*O*n the Internet, as in real life, you should never take your personal privacy for granted. Sure, you're ecstatic that you can shop and sell at eBay from the privacy of your home, but remember: Just because your front door is locked doesn't mean that your privacy is being protected. If you're new to the Internet, you may be surprised to find out what you reveal about yourself to the world, no matter how many precautions you take. (Yes, we all know about that neon blue exfoliating mask you wear when you're bidding . . . just kidding . . . honest.)

In this chapter, you find out how much eBay knows about you and who eBay shares your information with. I explain what you can do to protect your privacy and tell you some simple steps you can take to increase not only your Internet privacy but also your safety.

What (And How) eBay Knows about You

The irony of the Internet is that although you think you're sitting at home working anonymously, third parties such as advertisers and marketing companies are secretly getting to know you. (All together now: *Get-ting-to-know all a-bout youuu. . . .*)

While you're busy collecting World's Fair memorabilia and antique toasters, eBay is busy collecting nuggets of information about you. eBay gets some of this information from you and some of it from your computer. All the data eBay gets is stored in the mammoth eBay memory bank.

What you tell eBay

eBay gets much of what it knows about you *from* you. When you sign up, you voluntarily tell eBay important and personal information about yourself. Right off the bat, you give eBay these juicy tidbits:

- ✔ Name
- ✔ E-mail address
- ✔ Snail-mail address
- ✔ Phone number
- ✔ Password

"Okay, that's no big deal," you say, but if you're using your credit card to settle your eBay fees, you're also giving out the following personal financial information:

- ✔ Credit card number
- ✔ Expiration date
- ✔ Credit card billing address
- ✔ Credit card history

If you make a one-time payment with a personal check, register to pay by check through PayPal, or apply for ID Verify (see Chapter 16 for more on ID Verify), you give eBay even more information about yourself. eBay instantly knows your bank's name and your checking account number. The bottom line is that *every time* you pay by check, you give away personal info about yourself. eBay carefully locks up this information (in a high-tech Alcatraz, of sorts), but other companies or individuals may not be so protective. Before you put the check in the mail, make sure you're comfortable with where it's going.

If you fill in the optional questions when you sign up, eBay also knows the following information about you:

- ✔ Gender
- ✔ Date of birth
- ✔ Annual household income

What cookies gather

Web sites collect information about you by using *cookies*. No, they don't bribe you with chocolate-chip goodies. Cookies are nothing more than small files that companies (such as eBay) put on your hard drive to store data about your surfing habits.

Most Web site designers install cookies to help you navigate their sites. Sometimes the cookie becomes sort of an "admission ticket" so that you don't need to register every time you log on.

eBay has partnerships with companies that provide page-view and data-tracking technology, and advertisers who display advertising banners on eBay pages, whether you want to see the banners or not. If you click a banner, a cookie from that particular advertiser *may* go onto your computer, usually to prevent you from seeing it again.

Cookies can't steal information from other files on your computer. A cookie can access only the information that you provide to its Web site.

DoubleClick, a major player in the cookie-tracking field, says that it uses your information to limit the number of times that you see the same advertisement. DoubleClick also measures the kinds of ads that you respond to and tracks which member Web sites you visit and how often. The bottom line is that DoubleClick is just trying to sell you stuff with ads based on your personal interests. The upside is that you get to see stuff that you may like.

You can find out more about cookies at `www.cookiecentral.com/faq`. This site gives you simple instructions on how to handle cookies on your computer.

If you want to keep your information private, you can remove yourself from the DoubleClick cookie system by going to this Web site:

```
www.doubleclick.net/us/corporate/privacy/privacy/ad-cookie/
               default.asp?asp_object_1=&
```

Your eBay sign-in cookie

When you visit eBay and sign in, eBay gives you a special kind of cookie — not pecan shortbread — but an *end of session* or *permanent* cookie:

- ✔ **End of session:** This cookie type remains on your computer as long as you remain on the eBay site. It also disappears if you haven't been active on the site for over 40 minutes.

- ✔ **Permanent:** This flavor is perfect if you don't share your computer with anyone else; it permits your computer to always remain signed in to eBay.

eBay's sign-in cookie is a good thing. It prevents the previously repetitive task of typing your User ID and password at every turn. This cookie simplifies your participation in chats, bidding, watching items, viewing e-mail addresses, and so on. Because you don't have to sign in every time you do business at eBay, it's a real time saver.

Web beacons

Web beacons are clear, 1-pixel x 1-pixel images that are placed in the HTML (or Internet page code) for individual pages. Web beacons, like cookies, are used mainly for collecting marketing information. They track the traffic patterns of users from one page to another.

Web beacons are sneaky little things. They're invisible as cookies, but they're incorporated into Web pages without your knowing. Turning off cookies won't disable them. However, Web beacons are not as ominous as they may seem because the information collected is not personally identifiable.

What Web servers collect

Every time that you log on to the Internet, just like Hansel and Gretel you leave an electronic trail of information. eBay, like zillions of other Web sites, uses *servers,* which are immense programs that do nothing but collect and transfer bits (and bytes) of information day and night. Your Internet connection has a special address that identifies you to all servers when you surf the Net. This is called an IP (Internet Protocol) address and is often used to track those whose shenanigans wreak havoc on Web sites or other users.

Web servers all over the Internet track some or all of the following information:

- ✔ What Web site you came in from
- ✔ The ISP (Internet service provider) that you use
- ✔ Auctions that you're running
- ✔ The Web sites you linked your auctions to
- ✔ Your favorite Web sites (if you link them to your About Me page)

eBay collects the following information while you visit the eBay site. After you log off, the server discards the data:

- ✔ What you do while logged on to the site
- ✔ What times you log on and log off

Like incredible Internet archivists, eBay's servers keep a record of everything you bid on, win, and sell, which is great news if you have a problem with a transaction and need eBay to investigate. Also, eBay couldn't display feedback about you and other users if its servers didn't store all the feedback you write and receive. Have you ever sent an e-mail to eBay? eBay's servers record it and keep it in some murky recess of eBay's memory. Remember, we live in the age of electronic commerce, and the people at eBay run a serious business that depends on e-commerce. They have to keep everything in case they need it later.

Do seals bite back?

Because eBay pays to display the TRUSTe mark, some online critics say that the seal is nothing more than window dressing. These critics wonder whether it would be in the Web watch-dog's best financial interest to bite the hand that feeds it all those display fees. Critics complain that the seal offers a false sense of security — and suggest that you view the seal as nothing more than a disclaimer to be careful in your Internet dealings.

Technically, TRUSTe can pull its seal whenever a Web site becomes careless in its handling of privacy issues. However, the critics make a good point: *Always be careful in your Internet dealings,* no matter how much protection a site has.

To see a chart on what personal information is accessible by third parties, check out this address:

```
pages.ebay.com/help/policies/privacy-appendix.html
```

For an example of the type of information that can be gleaned from your computer as you surf the Internet, visit this Web site:

```
www.anonymizer.com/docs/resources/links.shtml
```

Cookie removal–ware

The other day, my daughter complained that her computer was getting slower and slower. I also noticed that it was opening extra windows and accessing the Internet spuriously. After checking to see whether she had a virus (no, she didn't), I went to the Internet to get her spyware removal software. Perhaps her problem was that too many people had inserted information-gathering cookies on her computer.

That was certainly the case. After installing and running the software, I found that she had over 350 cookies pulling information from her computer as she surfed. Once deleted, her computer ran much faster.

She certainly didn't give these people permission to spy on her comings and goings on the Internet. These cookies were placed on her computer without her knowledge. If you want to purge these uninvited spies from your computer, download any of the free spyware or malware software from the Internet. Two good free ones are Ad-aware from `www.lavasoftusa.com/software/adaware` and Spybot Search and Destroy, available from `www.security.kolla.de`.

If you're apprehensive about all the information that Web servers can collect about you while you innocently roam the Internet, I understand. But before you start looking out for Big Brother watching over your shoulder, consider this: On the Web, everybody's collecting information.

The odds are excellent that all the information that eBay knows about you is already in the hands of many other folks, too — your bank, your grocer, the staffs of any magazines you subscribe to, clubs you belong to, any airlines you've flown, and any insurance agencies you use. That's life these days. And if you're thinking, "Just because everybody knows all this stuff about me, that doesn't make it right," all I can say is, "You're right." But maybe you'll sleep better knowing that eBay is one place where folks take the privacy issue seriously. See the next section for details.

eBay's privacy policy

eBay had a privacy policy for all its users before privacy policies were even in vogue. Now eBay maintains the safety standards set forth by the pioneer in online safeguarding: TRUSTe.

TRUSTe (www.truste.org) sets a list of standards that its member Web sites have to follow to earn a "seal of approval." The hundreds of Web sites that subscribe to this watchdog group must adhere to its guidelines and set policies to protect privacy. eBay has been a member of TRUSTe since the privacy watchdog group was founded.

To review the policy that's earned eBay the TRUSTe seal of approval, click the Privacy Policy link that appears at the bottom of every eBay page.

In addition to setting and displaying a privacy policy, eBay follows these guidelines as well:

- ✔ eBay must make the TRUSTe links easily accessible to users. You can find the logo on eBay's home page. Click a TRUSTe link, and you're taken to the site for more information. Take advantage of this opportunity to find out how your privacy is being protected.

- ✔ eBay must disclose what personal information it collects and how it's using the info.

- ✔ Users must have an easy way to review the personal information that eBay has about them.

- ✔ Users must have an option — *opting out* — that lets them decline to share information.

- ✔ eBay must follow industry standards to make its Web site and database secure so that hackers and nonmembers have no access to the information. eBay uses Secure Sockets Layer (SSL), which is an encryption program that scrambles data until it gets to eBay. Unfortunately, no Web site, including the CIA's Web site, is completely secure, so you still have to be on your guard while you're online.

Grateful Dead cookie jar

In 1999, an auction description read: "This is one of the grooviest jars I have ever come across — a real find for the die-hard Grateful Dead fan or for the cookie jar collector who has it all. Made by Vandor, this Grateful Dead bus cookie jar looks like something the Dead *would* drive. Beautiful detailing on the peace signs; the roses are running lights. Painted windows. You have just got to see this piece. Only 10,000 made and I have only seen one other. Comes with box that has Grateful Dead logos on it. Buyer pays all shipping and insurance."

The cookie jar started at $1 and sold at eBay for $102.50. When I updated this book in 2002, it sold on eBay for $125. The Grateful Dead's bus cookie jar is even more valuable these days; an auction just closed with the final bid at $150.

Oh wow, dude — that's some far-out cookie jar. (Cue the band: *Keep truck-in'.* . . .)

If you ever have any questions about security at eBay, send an e-mail to privacy@ebay.com. You can also find some important eBay e-mail links at the following address:

pages.ebay.com/help/community/help-support-more.html

What Does eBay Do with Information about Me, Anyway?

Although eBay knows a good chunk of information about you, it puts the information to good use. The fact that it knows so much about you actually helps you in the long run.

Here's what eBay uses personal information for:

- **Upgrading eBay:** Like most e-commerce companies, eBay tracks members' use and habits to improve the Web site. For instance, if a particular item generates a lot of activity, eBay may add a category or a subcategory.

- **Clearing the way for transactions:** If eBay didn't collect personal information such as your e-mail address, your snail-mail address, and your phone number, after an auction was over, you couldn't complete the transaction you started. Bummer.

- **Billing:** You think it's important to keep track of your merchandise and money, don't you? So does eBay. It uses your personal information to keep an eye on your account and your paying habits — and on everybody else's. (Call it a gentle encouragement of honest trading habits.)

✓ **Policing the site:** Never forget that eBay tries to be tough on crime, and that if you break the rules or regulations, eBay will hunt you down and boot you out. Personal information is used to find eBay delinquents, and eBay makes it clear that it cooperates with law enforcement and with third parties whose merchandise you may be selling illegally. For more about this topic, read up on the VeRO program in Chapter 9.

Periodically, eBay runs surveys asking specific questions about your use of the site. It uses your answers to upgrade eBay. In addition, eBay asks whether it can forward your information to a marketing firm. eBay says that it does not forward any personally identifiable information, which means that any info you provide is given to third parties as raw data. However, if you're nervous about privacy, I suggest that you make it clear that you don't want your comments to leave eBay should you decide to participate in eBay surveys. If you don't participate in the surveys, you won't have any hand in creating new eBay features, though, so you can't complain if you don't like how the site looks. Sometimes, however, eBay advertises surveys that users can take part in on the eBay home page.

What Do Other eBay Members Know about Me?

eBay functions under the premise that eBay's members are buying, selling, working, and playing in an honest and open way. That means that anyone surfing can immediately find out some limited information about you:

✓ Your User ID and history

✓ Your feedback history

✓ All the auctions and eBay store sales you run

✓ Your current bids and any bids you've made within a given 30-day period

✓ Your e-mail address (only if the other party has completed a transaction with you)

eBay clearly states in its policies and guidelines that e-mail addresses should be used only for eBay business. If you abuse this policy, you can be suspended or even kicked off for good.

eBay provides limited eBay member registration information to its users. If another member involved in a transaction with you wants to know the following facts about you, they're available:

✓ Your name (and business name if you have provided that information)

✓ The city, state, and country that you provided to eBay

✓ The telephone number that you provided to eBay

Following the transaction, buyers and sellers exchange some real-world information. As I explain in Chapters 6 and 12, members initiate the exchange of merchandise and money by e-mail, providing personal addresses for both payments and shipments. Make sure that you're comfortable giving out your home address. If you're not, I explain alternatives in this chapter.

Spam — Not Just a Tasty Treat

Although you can find plenty of places to socialize and have fun at eBay, when it comes to business, eBay is . . . well, all business.

eBay's policy says that requests for registration information can be made only for people with whom you're transacting business on eBay. The contact information request form requires that you type in the item number of the transaction you're involved in as well as the User ID of the person whose contact info you want. If you're not involved in a transaction, as a bidder or a seller in the specified item number, you can't access the user information.

When it comes to e-mail addresses, your secret is safe until you win an auction or buy an item on eBay. The End of Auction notice contains your e-mail address so that the person on the other end of the transaction can contact you. After the other user has your e-mail address, eBay rules state that the user can use it only for eBay business.

Here's a list of "business" reasons for e-mail communication, generally accepted by all at eBay:

- ✔ Responding to feedback that you left
- ✔ Responding to feedback that you received
- ✔ Communicating with sellers or buyers during and after transactions
- ✔ Suggesting to other eBay members items that buyers may be interested in via the Mail This Auction to a Friend feature
- ✔ Leaving chat-room comments
- ✔ Discussing common interests with other members, such as shared hometowns, interesting collections, and past or current auctions

Sending spam versus eating it

Sending e-mail to other members is a great way to do business and make friends. But don't cross the line into spam. *Spam,* a Hormel canned meat product (I've given Spam its own sidebar), now has an alternate meaning. When you spell it with a small *s, spam* is unsolicited e-mail — most often, advertising — sent to multiple e-mail addresses gleaned from marketing lists. Eventually, it fills up your inbox the way "Spam, Spam, Spam, and Spam" filled up the menu in an old *Monty Python* restaurant skit.

Think of spam as the electronic version of the junk mail that you get via snail mail. Spam may be okay for eating (if you're into that kind of thing), but sending it can get you banned from eBay.

If you send an e-mail that advertises a product or service to people you don't know, you're guilty of spamming.

Trashing your junk mail

Sometimes spam can come in the form of mail from people you know and expect mail from. Your closest friend's computer may have been abducted by some weird Internet virus and replicated the virus to everyone in his or her e-mail address book. Obviously, this is not a good thing for those who receive and open the e-mail.

Don't open e-mail from anyone you don't know, especially if a file is attached to it. Sometimes, if a spammer is really slick, it's hard to tell that you've received spam. If you receive an e-mail with no subject line, however — or if the e-mail has an addressee name that isn't yours, or is coming from someone you never heard of — delete it. You never know; it could be just annoying spam — or worse, it could contain a computer virus as an attachment, just waiting for you to open and activate it.

Speaking of e-mail, if you're new to the technology, I recommend getting a good antivirus program that can scan e-mail attachments and rid your system of some annoying — and increasingly dangerous — computer bugs.

Spam I am

Spam, the unwanted electronic junk mail, is named after Spam, the canned meat product. (Spam collectibles at eBay are another matter entirely.) According to the Spam Web site (www.spam.com), more than 5 billion cans of Spam have been consumed worldwide. (By the way, Hawaiians eat more Spam than any other state in the union.) Spam is made from a secret recipe of pork shoulder, ham, and special spices. It was first produced in 1937 and got its name from the *SP* for *spice* and the *AM* from *ham*.

It's widely believed that spam (junk e-mail) got its name from the old *Monty Python* sketch because the refrain "Spam-Spam-Spam-Spam" drowned out all other conversation and one of the participants kept saying, "I don't want any Spam. I don't like Spam." Others say that it came from a bunch of computer geeks at USC who thought that junk e-mail was about as satisfying as a Spam sandwich. Perhaps they've never enjoyed a Spam luau in Hawaii under the moonlight — aloha!

For some interesting general anti-spam tips, drop in at spam.abuse.net. This Web site offers helpful advice for doing battle with spam artists. Also, I've been using a very handy software program called MailWasher, which allows me to preview my e-mail before it's downloaded to my computer. It even bounces spam back to the sender on command — as if your e-mail address didn't exist. Best of all, this program is free and available from www.mailwasher.net.

E-mail spoofing

E-mail spoofing has become the bane of the online community and can really wreak havoc. Spoofing is accomplished when crafty techno-geeks send out e-mail and make it appear to come from someone other than themselves — someone you know and expect e-mail from. Most often, this type of e-mail is programmed to invade your privacy or, even worse, bilk you out of confidential information.

A spate of e-mails have purportedly been sent from eBay, PayPal, and other major e-commerce sites, claiming that your membership has been suspended — or that your records need updating. The opportunistic e-mail then asks you to click a link to a page on the site, which then asks you to input your personal information. Don't do it!

Most sites will *never* ask you to provide sensitive information through e-mail, so don't do it. If you receive an e-mail saying your "account has been suspended," close the e-mail and go directly to the site in question — *without* using the supplied link in the e-mail. You'll know soon enough if there is a problem with your account.

If you get this sort of e-mail from eBay and want to confirm whether it is really from eBay, visit this eBay security page:

```
pages.ebay.com/help/confidence/isgw-account-theft-spoof.html
```

To help eBay in its investigation of these information thieves, send a copy of the e-mail (along with all identification headers) to spoof@ebay.com. When forwarding the e-mail, do not alter it in any way.

I Vant to Be Alone — and Vat You Can Do to Stay That Vay

The Internet has a long reach. Don't be surprised if you furnish your personal information freely on one Web site, and it turns up somewhere else. If you don't mind people knowing things about you (your name, your hobbies, where you live, and your phone number, for example), by all means share. But I think you should give only as much information as you need to do business.

Privacy is not secrecy. Don't feel obligated to reveal anything about yourself that isn't absolutely necessary. (Some personal facts are in the same league as body weight — private, even if hardly a secret.)

Although you can't prevent privacy leaks entirely, you can take some precautions to protect yourself. Here are some tips to keep your online information as safe and secure as possible:

- **User ID:** When eBay first started, members used their e-mail addresses to buy and sell; today, users appear on the site with a *nom de plume* (okay, User ID, but nom de plume sounds oh, so chic). Your first line of defense against everyone who surfs the eBay site is to choose a User ID that doesn't reveal too much about you. Chapter 2 gives you some pointers on how to choose your User ID.

- **Passwords:** Guard your password as if it were the key to your home. Don't give any buyers or sellers your password. If a window requesting your password pops up in an auction, skip it — it's somebody who is up to no good. Use your password *only* on official eBay screens. (See Chapter 2 for tips on choosing passwords.)

  If you're concerned that someone may have your password, change it immediately:

  1. **Go to your My eBay area and click the Preferences tab.**

  2. **In the Personal Information area, click the Change My Password link and follow the instructions.**

     Your password is immediately changed.

- **Credit card information:** Whenever you use your credit card at eBay, you can make sure that your private information is safe. Look for an SSL (SSL stands for *Security Sockets Layer*) link or check box. Sometimes you may see a link that says *You may also sign in securely.* This is an encryption program that scrambles the information so that hackers have almost no chance of getting your information. (I explain more about SSL in Chapter 2.)

  When buying from an auction that accepts credit cards, check the seller's feedback and carefully weigh the risks of giving your credit card number to someone you don't know versus the added time of paying by money order or personal check. An even safer way to pay is through PayPal, where your credit card number is not released.

  Never give anyone your Social Security number online. Guard yours as if it were your bank account number.

✔ **Registration information:** When you first register, eBay requests a phone number and address for billing and contact purposes. I have never had a problem with anyone requesting my registration information and then misusing it. However, many people want an added measure of anonymity. You can give eBay the information it wants in several ways without compromising your privacy:

- Instead of your home phone number, provide eBay with a cell phone number, a work phone number, or the phone number hooked up to your computer. Screen your calls with an answering machine. You can also use your beeper number.

- Use a post office box instead of your home address.

- Start a bank account solely for eBay transactions. Make it a TA account — as in *Trade As* — so that you can use an alternate name. Your bank can help you with this.

✔ **Chat rooms:** eBay has a multitude of chat rooms where members exchange information and sometimes heated arguments. (Chat rooms are thoroughly discussed in Chapter 17.) But heed this advice: Be careful what you reveal about yourself in a chat room. Don't expect that "just between us" means that at all. Chat rooms can be viewed by anyone who visits the eBay site, not just eBay members.

Never say anything online that you wouldn't feel comfortable saying to the next person who passed you on the street. Basically, that's who you're talking to. You can find stories of romances blossoming at eBay — and I'm delighted for the happy couples, I swear — but come on, that doesn't mean that you should lose your head. Don't give out any personal information to strangers; too often, that's asking for trouble. Have fun at eBay but hang on to your common sense.

Skim some of the category chat rooms, especially the Discuss eBay's Newest Features room, for warnings about security problems on the chat rooms and boards — and how to avoid 'em. Many A great bunch of users and eBay staffers frequent that board, and they're sure to give you good information.

✔ **Check feedback:** Yep, I sound like a broken record (in case you don't remember, *records* were the large, black, prone-to-breaking disks used by people to play music before cassette tapes and CDs were invented), but here it is again: *Check feedback.* eBay works because it's policed by its participants. The best way to learn about the folks whom you're dealing with is to see how others felt about them. If you take only one thing away from this book, it's to check feedback *before* you bid!

In the virtual world, as in the real world, cyberstalking is scary and illegal. If you think someone is using information from eBay to harass you, contact eBay immediately — as well as your local police. Chapter 16 gives you the ins and outs of contacting eBay's security team.

Fighting back

Robbin was minding her own business, selling software at eBay, when she ran into one of the world's nastiest eBay outlaws. He was a one-stop-shopping outlet of rule-breaking behaviors. First, he ruined her auctions by bidding ridiculously high amounts and then retracting bids at the last legal minute. He e-mailed her bidders, offering the same item but cheaper. He contacted Robbin's winning bidders to say he was accepting her payments. Then he started leaving messages on her answering machine. When she finally had enough, she contacted Rules & Safety (SafeHarbor), which suspended him.

But like a bad lunch, he came back up — with a new name. So Robbin fought back on her own. She got his registration information and sent him a letter. She also informed the support area at his ISP about what he was doing, and because he used his work e-mail address, she also contacted his boss.

Her efforts must have done the trick. He finally slipped out of eBay and slithered out of her life. The lesson: Don't rely completely on eBay to pick up the pieces. If you're being abused, stand up for your rights and fight back through the proper channels!

Chapter 16

eBay's Rules & Safety Program

Millions of people transact daily at eBay. If you're new to the Internet, however, you may need a reality check. With around ten million items selling every day, the law of averages dictates that you're bound to run into some rough seas. If you do, know that you can get the answers you need from eBay's SafeHarbor. In this chapter, I take you through the SafeHarbor resources — from reporting abuses to resolving insurance issues. This chapter explains how eBay enforces its rules and regulations, shows how you can use third-party escrow and mediation services, and even points out how to go outside eBay for help if you run into some really big-time problems.

Keeping eBay Safe with Rules & Safety

SafeHarbor is where eBay focuses on protecting the Web site from members who aren't playing by the rules. Through this department, eBay issues warnings and policy changes — and in some cases, it gives eBay bad guys the old heave-ho.

eBay's SafeHarbor can be found by clicking the Services link in the Navigation bar. The Services page is more than just a link to policies and information. It also connects you with a group of eBay staffers who handle complaints, field incoming tips about possible infractions, and dole out warnings and suspensions. The folks here investigate infractions and send out e-mails in response to tips. eBay staffers look at complaints on a case-by-case basis, in the order they receive them. Most complaints they receive are about these problems:

- ✔ Shill bidders (see the section on "Selling Abuses" in this chapter)
- ✔ Feedback issues and abuses (see the section on "Feedback abuses" in this chapter)

Keep in mind that eBay is a community of people, most of whom have never met each other. No matter what you buy or sell at eBay, don't expect eBay transactions to be any safer than buying or selling from a complete stranger. If you go in with this attitude, you can't be disappointed.

If you've been reading previous chapters in this book, you probably know about eBay's rules and regulations. For a closer online look at them, click the Policies link on the bottom of most eBay pages, and then check the User Agreement. (The agreement is revised regularly, so check it often.)

Another helpful link is the FAQ for the User Agreement, which explains the legalese in clearer English. To find it, go to

```
pages.ebay.com/help/policies/user-agreement-faqs.html
```

If you plan on being an active eBay member, it's probably worth your while to opt-in for eBay's User Agreement update e-mail. Go to your My eBay page and click the Preferences tab. Scroll down to the Personal Information area and click Change My Notification Preferences. At this point, you're asked to type in your password — this is to protect your security on eBay. Then you go to the magic page, where you can change *all* your eBay preferences, as well as the User Agreement update.

To go to the eBay Security Center (see Figure 16-1) for tips on current security issues on eBay, click the Safe Trading Tips link that you can find at the bottom of most eBay pages.

Abuses You Should Report to Rules & Safety

Before you even consider blowing the whistle on the guy who (gasp!) gave you negative feedback by reporting him to Rules & Safety, make sure that what you're encountering is actually a misuse of eBay. Some behavior isn't nice (no argument there), but it *also* isn't a violation of eBay rules — in which case, eBay can't do much about it. The following sections list the primary reasons you may start SafeHarbor investigations.

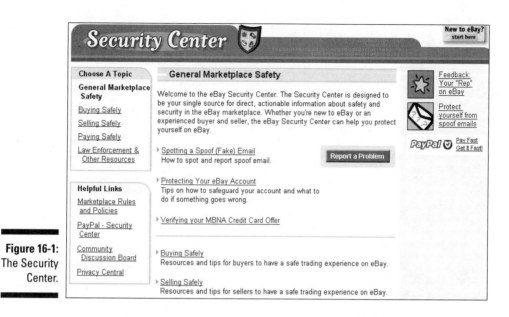

Figure 16-1:
The Security
Center.

Selling abuses

If you're on eBay long enough, you're bound to find an abuse of the service. It may happen on an auction you're bidding on, or it may be one of the sellers who compete with your auctions. Be a good community member and be on the lookout for the following:

- **Shill bidding:** A seller uses multiple User IDs to bid or has accomplices place bids to boost the price of his or her auction items. eBay investigators look for six telltale signs, including a single bidder putting in a really high bid, a bidder with really low feedback but a really high number of bids on items, a bidder with low feedback who has been an eBay member for a while but who's never won an auction, or excessive bids between two users.

- **Auction interception:** An unscrupulous user, pretending to be the actual seller, contacts the winner to set up terms of payment and shipping in an effort to get the buyer's payment. This violation can be easily avoided by paying with PayPal directly through the eBay site.

- **Fee avoidance:** A user reports a lower-than-actual final price and/or illegally submits a Final Value Fee credit. Final Value Fee credits are explained in Chapter 13.

- **Hot bid manipulation:** A user, with the help of accomplices, enters dozens of phony bids to make the auction appear to have a lot of bidding action. Let the experts at eBay decide on this one; but you may wonder if loads of bids come in rapid succession but the price moves very little.

Bidding abuses

If you want to know more about bidding in general, see Chapter 6. Here's a list of bidding abuses that eBay wants to know about:

- ✓ **Bid shielding:** Two users working in tandem: User A, with the help of accomplices, intentionally bids an unreasonably high amount and then retracts the bid in the closing moments of the auction — leaving a lower bid (which the offender or an accomplice places) as the winning bid.

- ✓ **Bid siphoning:** Users send e-mail to bidders of a current auction to offer the same merchandise for a lower price elsewhere.

- ✓ **Auction interference:** Users warn other bidders through e-mail to stay clear of a seller *during a current auction,* presumably to decrease the number of bids and keep the prices low.

- ✓ **Bid manipulation (or Invalid Bid Retraction):** A user bids a ridiculously high amount, raising the next highest bidder to maximum bid. The manipulator then retracts the bid and rebids *slightly* over the previous high bidder's maximum.

- ✓ **Non-paying bidder:** I call them deadbeats; the bottom line is that these people win auctions but never pay up.

- ✓ **Unwelcome bidder:** A user bids on a specific seller's auction despite the seller's warning that he or she won't accept that user's bids. (As in the case of not selling internationally and receiving international bids.) This practice is impolite and obnoxious. If you want to bar specific bidders from your auctions, you can exclude them. See Chapter 13 for the skinny on how to block bidders.

Feedback abuses

All you have at eBay is your reputation, and that reputation is made up of your Feedback history. eBay takes any violation of its Feedback system very seriously. Because eBay's feedback is now transaction-related, unscrupulous eBay members now have less opportunity to take advantage of this system. Here's a checklist of feedback abuses that you should report to Rules & Safety:

- ✓ **Feedback extortion:** A member threatens to post negative feedback if another eBay member doesn't follow through on some unwarranted demand.

- ✓ **Personal exposure:** A member leaves feedback for a user that exposes personal information that doesn't relate to transactions at eBay.

- ✓ **–4 Feedback:** Any user reaching a Net Feedback score of –4 is subject to suspension.

Identity abuses

Who you are at eBay is as important as what you sell (or buy). eBay monitors the identities of its members closely — and asks that you report any great pretenders in this area to Rules & Safety. Here's a checklist of identity abuses:

- ✔ **Identity misrepresentation:** A user claims to be an eBay staff member or another eBay user, or he or she registers under the name of another user.

- ✔ **False or missing contact information:** A user deliberately registers with false contact information or an invalid e-mail address.

- ✔ **Under age:** A user falsely claims to be 18 or older. (You must be at least 18 to enter into a legally binding contract.)

- ✔ **Dead/invalid e-mail addresses:** When e-mails bounce repeatedly from a user's registered e-mail address, chances are good that it's dead, Jim — and it's doing nobody any good. There's usually return e-mail indicating that the address is unknown.

- ✔ **Contact information:** One user publishes another user's contact information on the eBay site.

Operational abuses

If you see somebody trying to interfere with eBay's operation, eBay staffers want you to tell them about it. Here are two roguish operational abuses:

- ✔ **Hacking:** A user purposely interferes with eBay's computer operations (for example, by breaking into unauthorized files).
- ✔ **Spamming:** The user sends unsolicited e-mail to eBay users.

Miscellaneous abuses

The following are additional problems that you should alert eBay about:

- ✔ A user is threatening physical harm to another eBay member.
- ✔ A person uses racist, obscene, or harassing language in a public area of eBay.

For a complete list of offenses and how eBay runs each investigation, go to the following addresses: `pages.eBay.com/help/community/investigates.html` or `pages.ebay.com/help/confidence/programs-investigations.html`.

Reporting Abuses to Rules & Safety

If you suspect someone of abusing eBay's rules and regulations, go to the Security Center and click the green Report a Problem button. If you encounter any of the abuses in this chapter, go to the Security Center (a link is at the bottom of every eBay page), click Report a Problem, and then you'll be presented with this form, as shown in Figure 16-2. From this page, click the appropriate link for your issue.

The Security Center and Policies Page can give you a lot of good general information that can help you prevent something from going wrong in a future auction. Feel free to use these pages as a resource to help prevent problems.

If you've got a troubled auction and need to launch a report, follow these steps:

1. **Read all the information on the Investigations page before filing a new complaint.**

2. **Click any of the many Report links.**

   No matter which link you click, you're taken to an area that instructs you further and provides information about what offenses eBay can and cannot investigate.

3. **If you've found out that you have a legitimate case that should be investigated, click the Contact Rules & Safety link.**

   You go to that handy form I show in Figure 16-2.

   After clicking off the items that relate to your situation, click Continue. eBay may present you with a page full of links to teach you about their policies and some possible solutions to your issue. After reviewing them, scroll to the bottom of the page and click Contact Support.

4. **You're now at the Rules & Safety Support Send Message form. (Whew.)**

   Figure 16-3 shows you the form. Just type in the item number (or numbers if they are all part of a related problem) and give a thorough description of what transpired.

   Before you send your message to Support, be sure to review what you've written to confirm that your report is accurate.

5. **Send the report by clicking Submit.**

   Be sure you send only one report per case — and one case per report.

If you file a report, make your message clear and concise by including everything that happened, but don't editorialize. (Calling someone a "lowdown mud-sucking cretin" doesn't provide any useful info to anyone who can help you, and doesn't reflect well on you either.) Keep it businesslike — just the facts, ma'am. Do include all pertinent documentation, such as e-mails, receipts, canceled checks — and (of course) the auction number.

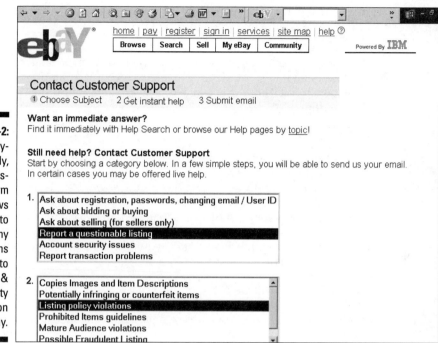

Figure 16-2:
The handy-dandy,
encompass-it-all form
allows
you to
report any
violations
directly to
the Rules &
Safety
division
of eBay.

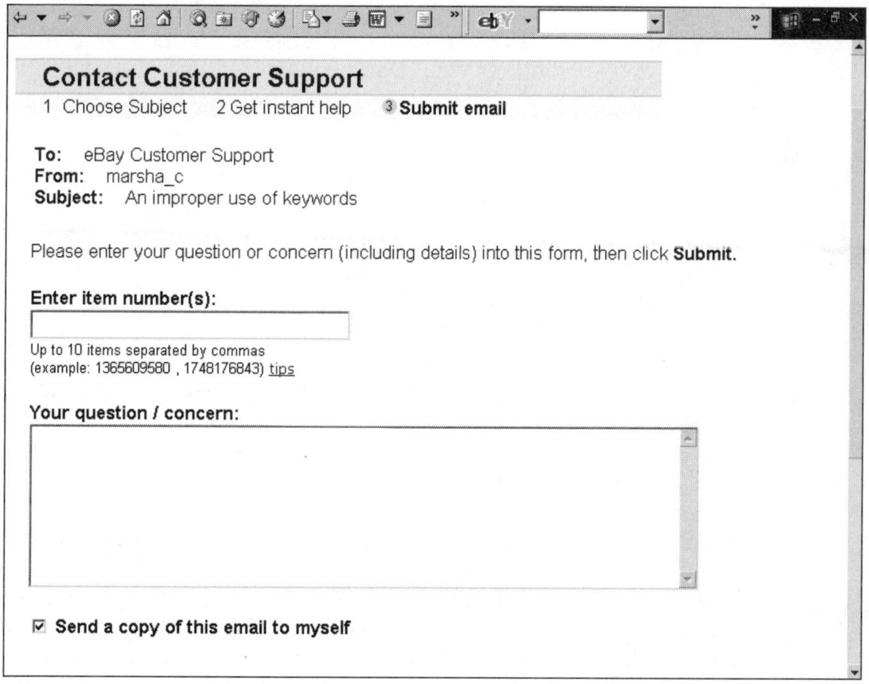

Figure 16-3:
Here's
where you
spill the
beans on
violators of
policy to
Rules &
Safety.

Here's a checklist of what you should include in your report to Rules & Safety:

- ✓ Write only the facts as you know them.
- ✓ Attach any pertinent e-mails with complete headers. (*Headers* are all the information found at the top of an e-mail message.) SafeHarbor uses the headers to verify how the e-mail was sent and to follow the trail back to the author.
- ✓ Be sure that the subject line of your report precisely names the violation.

If the clock is running out on your case (for example, you suspect bidding offenses in a current auction), I suggest that you avail yourself of the Live Help link that often appears on the eBay home page.

After eBay receives your report, you usually get an automatic response that your e-mail was received — although in practice, several days may go crawling by before eBay actually investigates your allegations. (They must look at a *lot* of transactions.)

Depending on the outcome of the probe, eBay may contact you with the results. If your problem becomes a legal matter, eBay may not let you know what's going on. The only indication you may get that some action was taken is that the eBay member you reported is suspended — or NARU *(Not A Registered User)*.

If your complaint doesn't warrant an investigation by the folks at Rules & Safety, they pass it along to someone at the overworked Customer Support staff, who then contacts you. (Don't bawl out the person if the attention you get is tardy.)

Unfortunately, NARU members can show up again on the eBay site. Typically nefarious sorts as these just use a different name. In fact, this practice is fairly common, so beware! If you suspect that someone who broke the rules once is back under another User ID, alert Rules & Safety. If you're a seller, you can refuse to accept bids from that person. If the person persists, alert Customer Support with e-mail.

As eBay has grown, so has the number of complaints about slow response from Customer Support. I don't doubt that eBay staffers are doing their best. Although slow response can get frustrating, avoid the temptation to initiate a reporting blitzkrieg by sending reports over and over until eBay can't ignore you. This practice is risky at best and inconsiderate at worst, and it just slows down the process for everyone — and won't endear the e-mail bombardier to the folks who could help. It's better to just grin and bear it.

If you're desperate for help, and can't find a Live Help link, you can post a message with your problem in one of the eBay chat rooms. eBay members participating in chat rooms often share the names of helpful staffers. Often you can find some eBay members who faced the same problem (sometimes with the same member) and can offer advice — or at the very least, compassion and a virtual ear. (Jump to Chapter 17 for more info on bulletin boards and chat rooms.)

If you're a PowerSeller, you can always contact PowerSeller support with your immediate problem.

Make sure that you don't violate any eBay rules by sharing any member's contact information as you share your story in a chat room. In addition, make sure that you don't threaten or libel (that is, say untrue things or spread rumors about) the person in your posting.

If you have a few hours to burn, eBay has a Customer Support e-mail response form that will get you an answer within 12 to 36 hours. You can find Customer Support creatively tucked away at

```
pages.ebay.com/help/contact_inline/index.html
```

Stuff eBay Won't Do Anything About

People are imperfect everywhere, even online. (Ya think?) You probably won't agree with some of the behavior that you run into at eBay (ranging from slightly annoying to just plain rotten). Although much of that conduct is detestable, it can (and does) go on as long as it doesn't break eBay rules.

In some cases, you may need to bite your tongue and chalk up someone's annoying behavior to ignorance of the unwritten rules of eBay etiquette. Just because people have computers and some things to sell or buy doesn't mean that they possess grown-up social skills. (But you knew that.)

Here's a gang of annoying issues that crop up pretty regularly but that *aren't* against eBay's rules and regulations:

✔ **You receive unwarranted or retaliatory feedback:** The biggest fear that haunts members who consider leaving negative feedback is that the recipient will retaliate with some more negative feedback. Remember that you can respond to negative feedback. Remember, however, that eBay will not remove a negative comment — no matter how unjustified you may think it is. eBay has agreed, however, that two parties can work through SquareTrade to remove feedback if they agree that the feedback was unwarranted. See "Negative feedback can be removed" later in this chapter.

Often, people who leave retaliatory feedback are also breaking some heftier eBay rules and (sooner or later) disappear from the site, never to rant again.

✔ **A seller sets astronomical shipping costs:** eBay policy says that shipping costs must be reasonable. Basically, eBay is wagging its finger and saying, "Don't gouge your buyers." Some sellers are trying to avoid fees or may be disappointed that a sale didn't make enough money, so they jack up shipping costs to increase their profit.

Under its rules, eBay can't really stop someone from charging too much for shipping. Bidders should always check shipping terms in the Auction Item description. Bidders must decide whether to agree to those terms before they bid. The best way to protect yourself from being swindled is to agree with a seller on shipping costs and terms in writing — *before* you bid.

✔ **A seller or buyer refuses to meet the terms that you mutually set:** eBay has the power only to warn or suspend members. It can't make anyone do anything — even someone who's violating a policy. If you want to make someone fulfill a transaction, you're more or less on your own.

I heard one story of a seller who refused to send a product after being paid. The seller said, "Come and get it." The buyer happened to be in town on business and did just that!

Often, reluctant eBay users just need a nudge from eBay in the form of a warning-to-comply. So go ahead and file a Final Value Fee Credit request (I explain how to do this in Chapter 13) and, if necessary, a fraud report (more on fraud reports later in this chapter).

✔ **E-mail spam:** An eBay member can send unwanted e-mail through eBay's Contact a Member Form, simply by clicking a member's User ID. eBay sees this as spam; you need to report any member who abuses this system. Although the items these spammers are selling may be perfectly good, eBay won't offer you any protection if you participate in these "off-the-site" deals. I suggest that you ignore these folks and avoid doing business with them in the future.

New eBay users are often the unwitting perpetrators of annoying behavior, but you're ahead of the pack now that you know what *not* to do. You can afford to cut the other newbies some slack and help them learn the ropes before you report them.

Using Mediation and Dispute Resolution Services

Even the best of friends sometimes have misunderstandings that can escalate to all-out war if they don't resolve their problems early enough. If the going gets tough, you need to call in the heavy artillery: a *mediator.* Just as pro boxing has its referees, auctions may need a level head to intervene in any squabble. eBay partners with SquareTrade, an online problem-solving service, and the service is available through the eBay Web site (or directly at www.squaretrade.com). Acting as a third party with no axe to grind, a mediator such as Square Trade can often hammer out an agreement or act as judge to resolve disputes.

To find SquareTrade at eBay, click the Dispute Resolution link in the SafeHarbor area of the Services page. After you click Services in the navigation bar, scroll to the bottom and click Dispute Resolution.

 SquareTrade offers online sellers the opportunity to get a SquareTrade Seal (like an online version of the Better Business Bureau) to post with your auctions. The SquareTrade Seal represents that the seller is committed to participating in online problem-solving, dedicated to superior customer service, is in compliance with SquareTrade standards and has been verified by SquareTrade. Find out more about obtaining the SquareTrade Seal by going to www.squaretrade.com.

Resolving a transaction dispute

If you file a complaint through the SquareTrade link, the service asks you to supply information regarding the offending transaction on an online form. SquareTrade then sends an e-mail to the offending party, outlining the situation. Both the complaint and the response from the other party appear on a secure Web page that only the offender, the mediator, and you can access.

SquareTrade uses a patent-pending technology to help smooth the mediation process. The mediator listens to both points of view and, if the parties can't reach an agreement, suggests a solution that he bases on the rules of fair play and good conduct. The use of a mediator doesn't, however, preclude the use of a lawyer if things truly hit an impasse.

Negative feedback can be removed!

You may find yourself in a situation where you've received unjustified feedback (as in the case of the nervous Nellie who left a negative because the item hadn't arrived but it was just hung up in the mail). If the problem gets resolved between the two of you, there is a way that you can get that feedback removed. eBay has agreed that if the two parties go through a SquareTrade mediation with a live mediator, and both parties agree that the feedback was unwarranted, the feedback will be expunged from your record.

You need to file an online Dispute Resolution with SquareTrade and request a mediator. There is a charge to involve a live mediator, $15 (eBay pays the balance of SquareTrade's fee). The process can take from two to six weeks, depending on how fast the other party responds to their SquareTrade e-mails. If the two of you agree ahead of time on the process, it can speed along quickly.

Walking the Plank: Suspensions

Playing by eBay's rules keeps you off the Rules & Safety radar screen. If you start violating eBay policy, the company's going to keep a close eye on you. Depending on the infraction, eBay may be all over you like jelly on peanut butter. Or you may safely lurk in the fringes until your feedback rating is lower than the temperature in Nome in November.

Here's a docket of eBay no-no's that can get members flogged and keel-hauled — or at least *suspended:*

- Feedback rating of –4
- Three instances of deadbeat bidding
- Repeated warning for the same infraction
- Feedback extortion
- Bid shielding
- Unwelcome bidding after a warning from the seller
- Shill bidding
- Auction interception
- Fee avoidance
- Fraudulent selling
- Identity misrepresentation
- Bidding when younger than age 18
- Hacking
- Physical threats

If you get a suspension but think you're innocent, respond directly to the person who suspended you to plead your case. Reversals do occur. Don't broadcast your suspicions on chat boards. If you're wrong, you may regret it. Even if you're right, it's oh-so-gauche.

Be careful about accusing members of cheating. Unless you're involved in a transaction, you don't know all the facts. Perry Mason moments are great on television, but they're fictional for a reason. In real life, drawing yourself into a possible confrontation is senseless. Start the complaint process, keep it businesslike, and let eBay's staff figure out what's going on.

Toss 'em a Life Saver: Insurance

One thing's for sure in this world: Nothing is for sure. That's why insurance companies exist. Several types of insurance are available for eBay users:

- ✔ Insurance that buyers purchase to cover shipping (see Chapter 12)
- ✔ eBay's Fraud Protection, which I discuss here
- ✔ eBay Motors Limited Warranty
- ✔ Warranties on Electronics
- ✔ PayPal's Buyer Protection

To cover loss from fraud, eBay has its own Fraud Protection Program. The insurance covers money that you pay for an item you never receive (as a result of fraud, not shipping problems) or receive but find to be materially different from the auction item's description. eBay insurance pays up to $175 (a maximum of $200 coverage minus a $25 deductible) for a single claim. So if you file a $50 claim, you get $25. If you file a $5,000 claim, you still get only $175. (Hey, it's better than nothing.)

Here's the checklist to qualify for an eBay insurance payment:

- ✔ The buyer and seller must be in good standing (no negative feedback ratings).
- ✔ The buyer must have proof that the item costs more than $25.
- ✔ The buyer must prove that the payment was sent.
- ✔ The buyer must prove that the seller didn't send the item.

    OR

- ✔ The buyer must prove that the item sent is substantially different from the auction description.

To be eligible for insurance, you must register a complaint with the Fraud Reporting System no sooner than 30 (and no later than 60) days after the auction closes. eBay then e-mails the seller that a complaint has been lodged. eBay hopes that by the time the 60 days are up, the differences are resolved and you can withdraw your complaint.

Extended warranties on electronics

eBay has teamed up with N.E.W. Customer Service Companies, a leading provider of extended service plans, to offer buyers of new, refurbished, or used electronics on eBay a 100-percent, one-year warranty. If you purchase this extended warranty and your product breaks during the warranty period, N.E.W. will repair it — parts and labor are 100 percent covered. If an item requires more than three repairs, the "no-lemon" guarantee will replace the item for free.

For more information on how this plan works, and how to purchase a policy, go to `pages.ebay.com/help/warranty/buyer_overview.html`.

eBay Motors Limited Warranty

Another beneficial eBay venture is its teaming up with 1Source Auto Warranty to offer a *free* limited warranty to anyone who purchases a car on eBay. To qualify (this is the easy part), the car you purchase must be under 10 years old, have fewer than 125,000 miles on it, and have no mechanical modifications. Qualified cars are identified in the listing description in the Item Specifics box, with the words *Free Limited Warranty.*

The warranty covers up to $10,000 in repairs with a $500 deductible per visit. You must redeem the warranty during the checkout process. You can find more information at eBay Motors:

```
pages.ebay.com/ebaymotors/services/warranty.html
```

PayPal Buyer Protection

Aside from safety, no PayPal offers an even better reason to pay through their service. If you've purchased your item through a PayPal-verified seller, you're covered for your purchase with an additional $300 of insurance. (Combined with the eBay insurance, that brings your total coverage to $500!)

This Protection covers you only for non-delivery of tangible items and tangible items that are received significantly not as described — not if you are disappointed with the item. This insurance kicks in after you have filed for the eBay Fraud Protection and your item exceeds the $200 cap.

If you've paid with a credit card through PayPal, be sure to make a claim with eBay first and *then* with PayPal. Do *not* make a claim with your credit card company. PayPal Protection is for PayPal purchases and you are not covered if you've made a claim with your credit card company.

For the latest information on this program, go to

```
pages.ebay.com/paypal/pbp.html or www.paypal.com/cgi-bin/
        webscr?cmd=p/gen/protections-buyer-outside
```

Launching a Fraud Report

The second that you complain about a seller who's taken money but hasn't delivered the goods, a SafeHarbor investigation automatically starts. To file an initial Fraud Alert for misrepresented or non-delivered items prior to eBay's 30-day waiting period, go to

`pages.ebay.com/help/confidence/programs-fraud.html`

and click the link to the Buyer Protection Program. Scroll down the page to the Report Suspicious Activity area and click the appropriate link to lodge your complaint.

To file an insurance claim with eBay, you must register a fraud report no sooner than 30 days, and no later than 60 days of the close of the auction. Be careful not to jump the gun and register a complaint too soon. I suggest waiting about two or three weeks before you register your complaint; double-check first to make sure that your e-mail is working and that you have the correct address of the person with whom you're having difficulties. After all, neither eBay nor your ISP is infallible.

Even if your insurance claim isn't worth a nickel after 30 days, you can still register a fraud report and help the investigation of a lousy, terrible, *allegedly* fraudulent eBay user. That's payment enough, ain't it?

After you register a complaint, eBay informs the other party that you're making a fraud claim. eBay says it will try to contact both parties and help reach a resolution. *Registering* the complaint is not the same thing as *filing* an insurance complaint. Registering starts the process; filing for insurance comes after a month-long grace period if the situation isn't resolved by then.

If you've clearly been ripped off, use eBay's Fraud Reporting program to file a complaint. Just follow these steps:

1. **On your My eBay page, scroll to the Buying-Related Links area and click the Filing a Fraud Complaint link.**

   If you can't find the link, go directly to the form at `crs.ebay.com/aw-cgi/ebayisapi.dll?crsstartpage`.

   You're now at the Fraud Protection Program page.

2. **Scroll down the page to the Online Fraud Complaint link and click it.**

   You go to the Online Fraud Reporting and Insurance Claim Form page.

3. **Read the step-by-step directions and click the Online Fraud Complaint Reporting Form link.**

   You're asked whether you want to file a complaint and insurance claim, and the page offers some ideas on how to resolve the problem.

4. **Click either the File a New Complaint button or the View a Complaint in Progress button.**

   You're forwarded to an ominous page that reads `Do you feel another eBay member has defrauded you?` If you've made it this far, I assume that you feel this way, so click Yes.

5. **On request, enter your User ID and password and click Sign In to move to the next page.**

   Even if you're permanently signed into eBay, you have to type in your password at this point — for your own protection.

6. **Verify your name, address, and contact info.**

   If it's wrong, click the appropriate button to correct the information.

7. **At this point, enter the item number and click the I Was Bidder button.**

8. **After you finish, print out the final page with the provided claim number.**

If the accusation you're registering refers to a clear violation, eBay gives you information on the kind of third-party assistance you can get to help resolve the problem. If eBay deems the problem a violation of the law, it reports the crime to the appropriate law-enforcement agency.

Docking with Escrow

Escrow is a relatively new concept for online trading. Escrow services act as the go-between between the seller and the buyer. The details of using escrow are spelled out in Chapter 6.

eBay has a direct link to an online escrow service. From the Services tab of the Navigation bar, scroll down and click the Escrow Services link. This action takes you to the Escrow Overview page. On this page, click the How Escrow Works link and follow the directions on the page that appears next.

Trimming in the Sales: Authentication and Appraising

Despite eBay's attempts to keep the buying and selling community honest, some people just refuse to play nice. After the New York City Department of Consumer Affairs launched an investigation into counterfeit sports memorabilia sold on the Web site, errant eBay outlaws experienced some anxious moments. I can always hope they mend their ways, while at the same time advising *Don't bet on it.* Fortunately, eBay is offering a proactive approach to preventing such occurrences from happening again.

Topmost among the countermeasures is easy member access to several services that can authenticate specific types of merchandise. The good news here is that you know what kind of item you're getting; the bad news is that, as does everything else in life, it costs you money.

Have a good working knowledge of what you're buying or selling. Before you bid, do some homework and get more information. And check the seller's or bidder's feedback. (Does this advice sound familiar?) See Chapters 5 and 9 for more information about conducting research.

Before you spend the money to have your item appraised and authenticated, ask yourself a few practical questions (regardless of whether you're buying or selling):

✔ **Is this item quality merchandise?** Am I selling/buying merchandise whose condition is subjective but important to its value — as in, *Is it really well-loved or just busted?* Is this item graded by some professionally accepted standard that I need to know?

✔ **Is this item the real thing?** Am I sure that I'm selling/buying a genuine item? Do I need an expert to tell me whether it's the real McCoy?

✔ **Do I know the value of the merchandise?** Do I have a good understanding of what this item's worth in the marketplace at this time, considering its condition?

✔ **Is the merchandise worth the price?** Is the risk of selling/buying a counterfeit, a fake, or an item I don't completely understand worth the cost of an appraisal?

If you answer "yes" to any of these questions, consider calling in a professional appraiser.

As for *selling* a counterfeit item — otherwise known as a knock-off, phony, or five-finger-discount item — that's a no-brainer: No way. Don't do it.

If you need items appraised, consider using an appraisal agency. Most agencies accessed from the Authentication Services link on the Rules & Safety overview page offer their services at discount to eBay members. eBay offers links to various appraising agencies:

✔ The **PCGS** (Professional Coin Grading Service) and **NGC** (Numismatic Guaranty Corporation) serves coin collectors:

`www.pcgs.com`

- **PSA/DNA** (a service of Professional Sports Authenticators) and **Online Authentics.com** authenticate your autographs. Both keep online databases of thousands of certified autographs for you to compare your purchases against. Their respective online addresses are

  www.psadna.com

  and

  www.onlineauthentics.com

- **PSE** (Professional Stamp Experts) authenticates your postal stamps:

  www.psestamp.com

- **CGC** (Comics Guaranty) grades and restores comic books:

  www.cgccomics.com/ebay_comic_book_grading.cfm

- **IGI** (International Gemological Institute) grades, authenticates, and identifies loose gemstones and jewelry:

  www.e-igi.com/ebay

- **PSA** (Professional Sports Authenticators) and **SGC** (Sportscard Guaranty) help guard against counterfeiting and fraud with sports memorabilia and trading cards. Their respective addresses are

  www.psacard.com

  and

  www.sgccard.com/ebay/ebay.html

  eBay has teamed up with these services to grade and authenticate trading cards.

Even if you use an appraiser or an authentication service, do some legwork yourself. Often, two experts can come up with wildly different opinions on the same item. The more you know, the better the questions you can ask.

If a seller isn't sure whether the item he or she is auctioning is authentic, you may find an appropriate comment (such as *Cannot verify authenticity*) in the auction item description. Knowledgeable eBay gurus always like to share what they know, and I have no doubt that someone on the appropriate chat board may be able to supply you with scads of helpful information. But be careful — some blarney artist (one of *those* is born every minute, too) may try to make a sucker out of you.

ID Verify

During the later years of the Cold War, Ronald Reagan said, "Trust but verify." The President's advice made sense for dealing with the old Soviet Union, and it makes good sense with your dealings at eBay, too! (Even if you're not dealing in nuclear warheads.)

To show other eBay members that you're an honest type — and to get special privileges when you're a newbie at eBay, you can buy a "trust but verify" option, known as *ID Verify,* from eBay for five bucks. The giant credit verification service, VeriSign, verifies your identity by asking for your wallet information, including the following:

- ✔ Name
- ✔ Address
- ✔ Phone number
- ✔ Social Security number
- ✔ Driver's license information
- ✔ Date of birth

VeriSign matches the info you give to what's in its database, and presents you with a list of questions from your credit file that only you should know the answer to. VeriSign may also ask you about any loans you have, (for example), or what kinds of credit cards you own (and how many).

Becoming ID-Verified can be a bonus for new users. It allows you to bypass some of eBay's more stringent requirements for participating in higher-level deals. By making sure that the community knows you're really who you say you are, you can get the green light for some higher-level activities:

- ✔ **Run Auctions with the Buy-It-Now option.** Ordinarily you need a feed-back rating of 10 to run a Buy-It-Now auction. This privilege may be worth the price of the verify, but honestly, how hard is it really to get you first ten feedbacks? Besides, the experience will be priceless.

- ✔ **Open an eBay store.** Although eBay requires a feedback rating of only 20 to open a store — I suggest you have much more. An eBay store (see Chapter 11 for more information) requires a bit more eBay savvy than the newbie seller can muster.

- ✔ **Run fixed-price auctions offering multiple items (and Dutch auctions).** Ordinarily an eBay seller must have more than a 30 feedback rating to perform this type of sale. I've spoken to several eBay veterans and they rarely participate in these types of sales.

- ✔ **Bid on items over $15,000.** Some form of verification is usually even required of eBay's old timers when bidding this high!

- ✔ **Sell items in the Mature Audiences Category.**

VeriSign sends only the results of its Identity Test to eBay (whether you pass the test) and *not* the answers to the private financial questions it asks you. VeriSign doesn't modify or add the information you provide to any of its databases.

VeriSign's questions are meant to protect you against anyone else who may come along and try to steal this information from you and assume your identity. The questions aren't a credit check, and your creditworthiness is never called into question. This info simply verifies that you are who you say you are.

If you pass the test and VeriSign can verify that you are who you say you are (and not your evil twin), you get a cool icon by your name for a year. If, after a year, you like the validation that comes from such verification, you can pay another fee and renew your seal.

Although you can feel secure knowing that a user who's verified is indeed who he or she claims to be, you still have no guarantee that he or she's not going to turn out to be a no-goodnik (or, for that matter, a well-meaning financial airhead) during auction transactions.

Even if an eBay member gets VeriSign verification, what makes this program so controversial is twofold:

- ✔ Many members object to giving out Social Security numbers. They see it as an unwarranted invasion of privacy.

- ✔ Some users also fear that this system creates a two-tiered eBay system, with verified users occupying a sort of upper class and anyone who's not verified stuck in the lower class. They're afraid that sellers may refuse to do business with *un*verified users.

You should consider all of eBay's current and future programs for protecting you from problematic transactions and people, but I think the "undisputed heavyweight champ" for finding out who someone *really is* (and keeping you out of trouble) is the first program eBay created. That's right, folks, *feedback* can show you other eBay members' track records and give you the best information on whether you want to do business with them or take a pass. Feedback is especially effective if you analyze it in conjunction with eBay's other protection programs. I suggest taking the time to read all about feedback in Chapter 4.

If It's Clearly Fraud

After filing either a fraud report or a Final Value Fee credit request, you can do more on your own. If the deal involves the post office in any way — if you mail a check or the seller sends you merchandise that's completely wrong and refuses to make good — file a mail-fraud complaint with the postal inspector.

In the United States, you can call your local post office or dial 800-275-8777 for a form to fill out. After you complete the form, the USPS sends the eBay bad guy a notice that you've filed a fraud complaint. Perhaps that *will* get his or her attention.

If you're interested in learning about mail-fraud law, go to the following Web site:

```
www.usps.com/websites/depart/inspect/usc18
```

In addition to the post office, you can turn to some other agencies for help:

- ✓ **The National Fraud Information Center.** NFIC has an online site devoted to combating fraud on the Internet. NFIC works closely with legal authorities. File a claim at `www.fraud.org/info/repoform.htm` or call toll free at 800-876-7060.

- ✓ **Law enforcement agencies.** Contact the local district attorney (or state Attorney General's office) and the local and state Consumer Affairs Department in the other person's state and city. (Look online for contact information or try your local agencies for contact numbers.)

- ✓ **Federal Trade Commission.** The FTC accepts complaints and investigates repeated cases of fraud. File a claim at

  ```
  https://rn.ftc.gov/dod/wsolcq$.startup?Z_ORG_CODE=PU01
  ```

- ✓ **Internet service provider.** Contact the member's ISP. You can get this bit of info from the person's e-mail address, just after the @ symbol. (See? This easy access to information does have its advantages.) Let the ISP know whom you have filed a complaint against, the nature of the problem, and the agencies that you've contacted.

Any time you contact another agency for help, keep Rules & Safety up to date on your progress by writing to them the old-fashioned way at eBay ATTN: Fraud Prevention, 2145 Hamilton Ave., San Jose, CA 95125.

A very thin line separates alerting other members to a particular person's poor behavior and breaking an eBay cardinal rule by interfering with an auction. Don't make unfounded and/or vitriolic accusations — especially if you were counting on them never to get back to the person they were about (or, for that matter, if you hoped they *would*). Trample the poison out of the gripes of wrath before you have your say. I recommend that you hunt for facts, but don't do any finger-pointing on public message boards or chat rooms. If it turns out that you're wrong, you can be sued for libel.

Communication and compromise are the keys to successful transactions. If you have a difference of opinion, write a polite e-mail outlining your expectations and offer to settle any dispute by phone. See Chapters 7, 12, and 13 for tips on communicating after the auction ends — and solving disputes *before* they turn wicked, aggressive, or unprintable.

Chapter 17

The eBay Community: Playing Nice with Other eBay Members

• •

• •

*e*Bay is more than just an Internet location for buying and selling great stuff. eBay wants the world to know that it has created (and works hard to maintain) a community. It's not a bad deal actually — prime real estate in *this* community costs only pennies! As in real-life communities, you participate as much as works for you. You can get involved in all sorts of neighborhood activities, or you can just sit back, mind your own business, and watch the world go by. eBay works exactly the same way.

As you've probably heard by now, one of the main ways to participate in the eBay community is through feedback (which I explain in detail in Chapter 6). In this chapter, I show you some other ways to become part of the community. You can socialize, learn from other members, leave messages, or just read what everybody's talking about through eBay's message boards, chat boards, and the corporate Announcements Board. I include tips on how to use all these places to your benefit, and then give you a change of scenery by surfing through some off-site message boards that can help you with your buying and selling.

On the navigation bar, there's a clickable link to Community. It's a handy link that connects you to the happenings on eBay; I use it regularly to check on proposed changes to the site in the General Announcements. But there's a whole lot more to the Community. Take a little time to explore it for yourself.

News and Chat, This and That

It's not quite like *The New York Times* ("All the News That's Fit to Print"), but you can find all the news, chat boards, and message boards links from the Community Overview page. Figure 17-1 shows you what the page looks like.

Here's a list of all the main headings of the main Community page. Each heading offers you links to the following specific eBay areas:

- ✔ **News:** This area contains links to the General Announcements page, which covers General News, Policy Changes, Technology Updates, System Announcements, and the eBay "Chatter" Newsletter.

- ✔ **Talk:** A click on these links whisks you to eBay's Discussion Boards, Chat Rooms, or the Answer Center.

- ✔ **Events:** Click here to find out what's going on at eBay.

- ✔ **People:** This is where you can get really social, join Groups, learn about Community Values, and get stories from eBay members about their bidding adventures.

Figure 17-1: The main community page features links to many informative places on eBay, including areas to chat and post messages.

Hear Ye, Hear Ye! eBay's Announcements Boards

If you were living in the 1700s, you'd see a strangely dressed guy in a funny hat ringing a bell and yelling, "Hear ye, hear ye!" every time you opened eBay's Announcements Boards. (Then again, if you were living in the 1700s, you'd have no electricity, computers, fast food, or anything else you probably consider fun.) In any case, eBay's Announcements Boards are the most important place to find out what's going on (directly from headquarters) on the Web site. And no one even needs to ring a bell.

You have your choice of two boards. First, the General Announcements Board, where eBay also lists any new features and policy changes. Visiting this page is like reading your morning eBay newspaper because eBay adds comments to this page almost every day. You find out about upcoming changes in categories, new promotions, and eBay goings-on. Reach this page at `www2.ebay.com/aw/marketing.shtml`. Figure 17-2 shows you eBay's General Announcements Board with information that could affect your auctions.

eBay also tips you off to the System Status (should you wonder whether the glitch is on your computer or on the eBay system). The System Announcements Board at `www2.ebay.com/aw/announce.shtml` is where eBay reports outages and critical changes in policies and procedures. eBay also uses this board to update users on glitches in the system and when those may be rectified.

Make a quick stop at the Announcements Boards a standard part of your eBay routine.

Figure 17-2:
Keep up-to-date on what's new at eBay by visiting the General Announcements Board.

Keep your eye out for the Outages listing in the Announcements Boards to see whether an outage may affect your auctions. Also on the boards, you can discover any new procedures and rules that could affect what you're selling.

Whenever eBay introduces new features, explanations, or links, they appear in General Announcements, which is in the News area of the Community Overview page.

eBay has close to 80 million members — a bigger population than some states — but it can still have that small-town feel through groups, chat boards, and discussion boards. Start on the main Talk page by clicking Community on the main navigation bar and then click Talk on the subnavigation bar. Now you can access more than over three-dozen category-specific chat and discussion boards, a bunch of general chat and discussion boards and help discussion boards.

When you arrive at the Community Overview page, and scroll down to find eBay's link for "Hot" items, don't get too excited. You have not found the secret trove of bonus information. Click it, and you find eBay reports for the top-selling categories within each category. Nope, that's not a typo; the categories are subdivided, apparently by bid ranking. eBay lists categories where "bidding growth has outpaced new listings growth and where bid-to item ratios are higher than other products in the same parent category." I'm sure that's some measure of sales, but as eBay sellers know, what sells today may be the overstock of tomorrow.

Help! I Need Somebody

If you ever have specific eBay questions to which you need answers, several eBay Discussion Help boards on the Community: Chat page can help you. You can also go directly to the chat rooms to pose your question to the eBay members currently in residence.

Boards work differently from chat rooms. Chat rooms are full of people who are hanging out talking to each other all at the same time, whereas users of Discussion Boards tend to go in, leave a message or ask a question, and pop out again. Also, in a message board, you need to start a thread by asking a question. Title your thread with your question, and you'll no doubt get an answer to your query posted swiftly. Take a look at the Technical Issues Board in Figure 17-3.

Most questions can be answered by going to eBay's Answer Center, which you can get to by clicking the Answer Center tab of the Talk area. You then see boards covering almost any topic you can think of regarding auctions at eBay. Just post your question and hopefully some kind eBay member will suggest an answer (but remember to take that advice with a grain of salt, just as you would any advice from someone with unknown credentials).

eBay > Community > Discussion Boards > Board Policies   Board log
>   in
Technical Issues

Welcome to the Technical Issues Discussion Board!
This board is for eBay members to learn more about the hardware and
software that is used to trade on eBay from other community members
with the support of eBay staff. If you are not an eBay registered user,
please register here first - it's fast and free! Otherwise, click below to start
a discussion or enter an existing thread. Prior to posting, please read and
familiarize yourself with the eBay Board Usage Policies.

List of Topics   ⊘ indicates new discussions.
                      ⊘ indicates updated discussions.
                      ebY indicates updated by eBay Staff.

Figure 17-3:
One of the
handy
Discussion
Boards on
eBay, the
Technical
Issues
Board.

(More) (To Last) (705 following items)

Updated	Replies	Topic (Started by)
Jan 6	511	ebY ⊘ If you are experiencing problems using sign-in, please read this
Jan 6	410	ebY ⊘ If you are experiencing problems listing, relisting or revising, please read this
Jan 6	3	⊘ HOW DO I GET A NEW BOARD USER ID????
Jan 6	1	⊘ I always get this message after I tried to set up my selling "Invalid Payment Option" What does it mean?
Jan 6	0	⊘ cannot load current auctions

eBay newbies often find that the boards are good places to add to their
knowledge of eBay. As you scroll on by, read the Q & A postings from the
past; your question may already be answered in an earlier posting. You can
even ask someone on this board to look at your auction listing and provide
an opinion on your descriptions or pictures.

Rating the member chat rooms and boards

You know you need help, but you don't know
which area is best for you. Here's my take on
which boards are most helpful.

✔ **Auction Listings:** This discussion board is a
catchall for many subjects. If you don't see a
board specific to your question (or if you
post to another board and get no reply), try
this one — it's always hopping with lots of
peeps.

✔ **Photos/HTML Board and Images/HTML
Chat:** Good help from other eBay members
for those with specific questions about using
HTML and posting pictures in your auctions.

✔ **Discuss eBay's Newest Features Chat:** This
board (also known as DNF) is where you
find many of the folks who are devoted to
protesting eBay's policies and new features. Brace yourself a bit — conversation
on this board can become nasty at times.
Keep in mind, however, that many of the
regulars on this board are extremely knowledgeable about eBay.

You can access a new board from any other
board by scrolling down the drop-down list
at the top of each Board page.

Community Chat Rooms

Because sending e-mail to eBay's Customer Service people can be frustratingly slow if you need an answer right away (they get bombarded with a gazillion questions a day), you may want to try for a faster answer by posting your question on one of the Community message boards.

You can always tell if an eBay staff member is replying on a board because the top border line of his or her post is in pink (not gray, as with regular users). They've earned the nickname "Pinks" on the boards.

Knowledgeable veteran eBay members or Customer Service "pinks" (if they're around) generally answer posted questions as best as they can. The answers are the opinions of members and are certainly not eBay gospel. But you get a fast and honest answer; often you get more than one response. Most questions are answered in about 15 minutes. If not, repost your question. Make sure that you post your question on the appropriate board, because each board has a specific topic of discussion.

Members who post on these boards often share helpful tips and Web sites and alert other members to scams. Newbies may find *lurking* (reading without posting) on some of these boards helpful to learn more about how eBay works. Occasionally, an eBay staffer shows up, which is kinda like inviting Bill Gates to a Windows XP new users' meeting. eBay staff members are usually hounded with questions.

If a new policy or some sort of big change occurs, the boards are most likely going to quickly fill with discussion about it. On slow days, however, you may need to wade through personal messages and "chat" with no connection to eBay. Many of the people who post on these boards are long-time members with histories (as well as feuds) that can rival any soap opera. On a rare occasion, the postings can get rather abusive. Getting involved in personality clashes or verbal warfare gains nothing.

No matter how peeved the users of a chat room or message board may get — and no matter how foul or raunchy the language may get — no one on eBay ever sees it. eBay uses a built-in "vulgarity checker" that deletes any (well, okay, *as many as possible*) words or phrases that eBay considers offensive or obscene.

One cardinal rule for eBay chat boards and message boards exists: no business. No advertising items for sale! Not now. Not ever. eBay bans any repeat offenders who break this rule from participating on these boards.

Remember that you're visiting eBay and that you're a member. It's not Speakers' Corner — that spot in a London park where protesters are free to stand on a soapbox and scream about the rats in government. If you feel the need to viciously complain about eBay, take it outside, as the bar bouncers say.

User-to-User Discussion Boards

eBay has some other boards that take a different tack on things. They're *discussion* boards as opposed to *chat* boards, which basically means that the topics are deliberately open-ended — just as the topics of discussions in coffee houses tend to vary depending on who happens to be in them at any given time. Check out these areas and read ongoing discussions about eBay's latest buzz. It's a lot of fun and good reading. Post your opinions to the category that suits you. Each discussion board carries as many topics as you can imagine. Here are few of my favorites:

- **The eBay Town Square** is a potpourri of various subjects and topics.
- **The Soapbox** is the place to voice your views and suggestions to help build a better eBay.
- **NightOwls Nest** is the fun locale for creatures of the night and their unique postings. (As I'm writing this, for example, there's a thread with spirited advice to a Community Member who needs help with his "gassy" cat.)
- **The Park** is an interesting place where Community Members join in for fun ideas and threads.

Other Chat Rooms (Message Boards)

About a dozen chat rooms at eBay specialize in everything from pure chat to charity work. The following sections describe a few of these boards.

Café society

The eBay Café (eBay's first message board from back when they were just selling Pez candy dispensers) and AOL Café message boards attract mostly regulars chatting about eBay gossip. Frequent postings include the sharing of personal milestones and whatever else is on people's minds. You can also find useful information about eBay and warnings about potential scams here.

Holiday Board

Although eBay suggests that this is the place to share your favorite holiday memories and thoughts, it's really a friendly place where people meet and chat about home and family. Stop by for cybermilk and cookies next time you've got a few minutes and want to visit with your fellow auction addicts.

Giving Board

eBay isn't only about making money. On the Giving Board, it's also about making a difference. Members in need post their stories and requests for assistance. Other members with items to donate post offers for everything from school supplies to clothing on this board.

If you feel like doing a good deed, conduct a member benefit auction, or donate directly to those in need. For information on how to participate, visit the Giving Board at www.givingboard.com.

Emergency Contact Board

It's no *Rescue 911,* but if your computer crashes and you lose all your info, this board is the place to put out an all-points bulletin for help. If your ISP goes on vacation, your phone line is on the fritz, or you're abducted by aliens and can't connect to your buyers or sellers, use a friend's computer to post a message on the Emergency Contact Board. There's a dedicated group of eBay users who frequent this board; they will try to help you by passing on your e-mails to the intended parties. Talk about a bunch of *givers!*

Recently, a bidder posted saying that her computer had crashed *and* that she was in the process of moving. She asked her sellers to be patient and she would get to them as soon as possible. The friendly regulars of the Emergency Contact Board looked up her bidding history and e-mailed the sellers whose auctions she'd won in the last week. Then they forwarded her the e-mails they'd sent on her behalf. The sellers understood the situation and did not leave negative feedback for the user for lack of communication.

If you're having trouble contacting another eBay member, posting for help from other members to track 'em down often gets the job done.

If you think you may be the victim of a rip-off, check the Emergency Contact Board. The buyer or seller may have left word about an e-mail problem. On the flip side, you may find out that you're not alone in trying to track down an eBay delinquent who seems to have skipped town. Posting information about a *potentially* bad eBay guy is (at the least) bad manners on most boards. If you wrap it in the guise of an emergency contact, however, you can clue in other members about a potential problem. Stick to the facts and make the post as honest and useful as you can.

To access the Emergency Contact Board, follow these steps:

1. **From the eBay navigation bar, click the Community link.**

    A subnavigation bar appears.

2. **Click the Chat link in the Talk area.**

   You are now on the main Chat page.

3. **Scroll down the Chat page and click Emergency Contact.**

   You see a message board full of messages from all the desperate sellers and buyers trying to locate each other.

eBay International Chat Boards

People from all around the world enjoy eBay. If you're considering buying or selling globally, visit the International Boards. They're a great place to post questions about shipping and payments for overseas transactions. Along with eBay chat, the International Boards turn up discussions about current events and international politics.

Got a seller or bidder in Italy? Spain? France? Translate your English messages into the appropriate language through the following Web site:

```
babelfish.altavista.digital.com
```

If you venture into unfamiliar foreign tongues, I suggest you keep things simple. Don't try to get fancy with your verbiage — stick to standard phrases that can translate literally with minimum hassle.

Category-Specific Chat Boards

Want to talk about Elvis, Louis XV, Sammy Sosa, or Howard the Duck? Currently over 20 category-specific chat boards enable you to tell eBay members what's on your mind about merchandise and auctions. You reach these boards by clicking Community on the main navigation bar and then clicking Chat in the Talk area.

Of course, you can buy and sell without ever going on a chat board, but you can certainly learn a lot from one. Discussions mainly focus on merchandise and the nuts and bolts of transactions. Category-specific chat boards are great for posting questions on items that you don't know much about.

At eBay, you get all kinds of responses from all kinds of people. Take some of the help you get with a grain of salt, because some of the folks who help you may be buyers or competitors.

These boards are also great for finding out where to go for more research and information on specific items. You can also find helpful sources for shipping information about items in that category (such as large furniture in the Antiques section or breakable items on the Glass chat board).

Don't be shy. As your second-grade teacher said, "No questions are dumb." Most eBay members love to share their knowledge of items.

eBay Groups

If you're the friendly type and would like an instant group of new friends, I suggest that you click the link in the Talk area to eBay Groups. Here you can find thousands of user groups, hosted on eBay — but run by eBay community members. They may be groups consisting of people from the same geographic area, those with similar hobbies, or those interested in buying or selling in particular categories.

eBay Groups may be public (open to all) or private (invited memberships only!) clubs with their own private boards. Only members of the groups can access these boards.

Joining a group is easy: Just click any of the links on the main Groups page, and you're presented with a dizzying array of groups to join. Your best bet though, is to participate in Chat or Discussions, and find other members that you'd like to join up with.

Chapter 18

Fun Stuff and Features

• •

In This Chapter

▶ Bidding for a good cause

▶ Using eBay's member specials

▶ Buying souvenirs at the eBay store

▶ Getting a personal cyber-shopper

• •

*N*o one can say that eBay isn't fun! The eBay staff is always trying to work with the community by filling needs and finding fun stuff to keep us happy. In this chapter, I show you how eBay members can get great inside deals from manufacturers, and I open the door of the eBay-o-rama store where you can get T-shirts and coffee cups with the official eBay logo on them. I also show you how you can help your favorite charity earn some well-deserved cash at eBay's charity auctions.

Over and over, eBay members show what big hearts they have. Yes, you actually can pocket some nice-sized profits from selling at the eBay Web site, but (just as in real life) people usually take the time to give a little back for worthy causes. But because we're talking about eBay, giving back means getting something fabulous in return.

Truly Righteous Stuff for Charity

Most of us have donated to charity in one form or another. But here at eBay, charities really rock. Do you need a *Jurassic Park* helmet signed by Steven Spielberg to round out your collection (and deflect the odd dino tooth)? Post a bid on one of the charity auctions. How about a signed original photograph of Jerry Seinfeld from *People* magazine? Yup, you can get that, too. All these and more have turned up in charity auctions. In short, having a big heart for charities has gotten a whole lot easier thanks to eBay.

Auction for America

In late December 2001, eBay took on one of its most ambitious attempts at fundraising: the Auction for America. In responses to requests by New York Governor George E. Pataki and Mayor Rudolph Giuliani, eBay called on the community to raise $100 million in 100 days. eBay and Billpoint (eBay's payment service at the time) waived all fees, and community members gave their all, donating and buying all kinds of items benefiting the New York State World Trade Center Relief Fund, the Twin Towers fund, the American Red Cross, and the September 11 Fund.

Community member Jay Leno sold his celebrity-autographed Harley Davidson for over $360,260; Tim Allen sold his 1956 Chevrolet Nomad for $46,000; and countless corporate sponsors joined in with the person-to-person community to raise funds. Over 100,000 sellers participated, and over 230,000 items were listed.

The auction ended on December 25, raising $10 million. This is an amazing tribute to the eBay members and their community spirit.

eBay Giving Works

November 2003 was a lucky time for this country's charities. That's the month that eBay launched the eBay Giving Works Charity auction area. Smartly, the folks at eBay teamed up with one of the finest charity sites on the Internet, MissionFish. MissionFish, a service of the Points of Light Foundation, has been around since early 2000 and has enabled charities to raise hundreds of thousands of dollars by turning in-kind donations into cash.

If you're involved with a charity, you can register your charity to get on the list of beneficiaries. You can also run your own fundraising events at eBay! Just go to www.ebay.com/givingworks or click the Charity link on the left-hand side of the eBay home page.

The best part about this new system is that *you* can run an auction to benefit your favorite charity. eBay sellers can list items for sale and designate those items to benefit a charity from the MissionFish directory of thousands of charities. The seller can also specify what percentage (from as little as 10 up to 100 percent) of the auction proceeds go to the charity. At the end of the sale, MissionFish e-mails a tax receipt to the seller. The page to select the charity of your choice and percentage to share is at

```
www.missionfish.org/Sell/SellerController?ACTION=
         BrowseAction&SUB_ACTION=GetSearchForNP
```

As you visit different areas of eBay, you can recognize the charity auctions by the small ribbon icon next to them in searches and category listings.

Creative charity auctions

New charities are popping up all the time at eBay. To see what auctions they're running, go to the Charity page. To get there, start at eBay's home page and click the Charity link. Here are some of the more creative charity auctions that have been held at eBay:

- ✔ Oprah Winfrey has jumped onto eBay with a bang! To fund her charity, the Angel Network, Oprah auctioned two chairs from her set. These were not just any chairs. Aside from being luxurious leather chairs designed by Ralph Lauren, they housed the behinds of famous names like John F. Kennedy, Jr., Halle Berry, Tom Hanks, Jim Carrey, and Michael Jordan, to name just a few. The seven day auction netted the charity an amazing $64,100.

- ✔ In honor of the introduction of Avon's newest fragrance, Little Black Dress, the company held an eBay auction of celebrity owned and donated little black dresses. All proceeds from the auction went to the Avon Breast Cancer Crusade to find a cure for breast cancer. Among the celebrities who donated dresses for auction were Elizabeth Taylor, Gillian Anderson, Christina Aguilera, and Sharon Stone.

- ✔ A *People* magazine auction offered signed and limited-edition celebrity photographs. The proceeds of this auction went to the Until There's A Cure Foundation. The foundation's goal is to help raise millions of dollars to fund HIV/AIDS youth education programs, scientific research, and care services for those who have the disease.

- ✔ To celebrate Chivas Regal's 200th year, the company chose eBay for CHIVAS 200, the largest online charity auction in the world. From September 6 to October 31, 2001, the Chivas folks auctioned more than 200 of the world's most-wanted items and experiences — all for the benefit of charity partners around the world. They auctioned items such as an opportunity to become a Russian space station astronaut.

- ✔ When I appeared on *The View* with Barbara Walters and Star Jones, all four stars of the show autographed a coffee cup that we auctioned off at eBay to benefit UNICEF. We raised over $1,000 on a single coffee cup!

If you go to the About Me page (by clicking the link from the Giving Works page) of any of the charities on the Charity Fundraising page, you can find out exactly where the money that eBay users bid goes. You can also get to the charity auctions by going to pages.ebay.com/givingworks.

And Now for Our Feature Presentation

As an eBay member, you're entitled to some features offered on the Web site. The perks aren't quite as high-end as you may receive with, say, a country club membership, but hey, your non-existent membership dues are a lot less! With about 73 million registered users, eBay can get outside companies and manufacturers to listen to what it has to say. You know the old saying about power in numbers? At eBay, you find "savings in numbers" on items or services that you can buy outside the Web site.

The following sections explain some of the savings and other services you can find at eBay.

Member specials

As eBay gains popularity, more and more outside companies are offering special deals exclusively for members. These deals aren't auctions but are conventional "pay the price and get the item or services" transactions.

To find the member specials, go to the very bottom of eBay's home page and click the affiliates' logos or links at the bottom of the page. eBay has a habit of moving features like this around the site, so you may also find these specials from the navigation bar under Services: Buying & Selling. eBay also has a page with most of the Power Trading features at `pages.ebay.com/services/buyandsell/member-specials.html`.

The special deals change all the time, but here's a small sampling of perks available to you as a member:

- ✔ **eBay Anything Points:** An eBay frequent flyer program — almost. You can get eBay points when you shop with the partner companies or sign up for their services. The points are applied to your PayPal account at a value of $0.01 each. Okay, this isn't a great exchange rate. But, if you want to deal with these companies, you might as well get the bonus from eBay. You can find more information at `pages.ebay.com/anything/points`.

- ✔ **eBay Gift Certificates:** WOW! It doesn't get much better than this. Now I never have to drag myself all over town looking for a gift. You can purchase these certificates in any amount from $5.00 to $200.00. You can print out the certificate and give it with a gift (I think my book, *eBay Bargain Shopping For Dummies*, would make an excellent companion for an eBay gift certificate), or you can have it e-mailed to the recipient. You can also find information at the secure site `https://certificates.ebay.com/`.

✔ **PayPal:** Online payments integrated directly into your eBay auctions.

✔ **Authentication services:** Get a special discount (usually 10 percent) if you authenticate coins through Professional Coin Grading Service (PCGS) or trading cards through Professional Sports Authenticator (PSA). See Chapter 16 for tips on authenticating your items.

As time passes, you can see additional benefits and programs that eBay creates for the community. The folks at eBay are aggressively searching out new and helpful affiliations to help you take care of your auction business. But don't leave the task of maintaining your auctions entirely to eBay — take it upon yourself to find new ways to make your auctions easier to manage.

A successful seller takes advantage of every program and service he or she can. The less time you spend tied to your computer, the more time you have to plan new auctions and find new items to sell. Investigate these programs and try them out for yourself.

Who's minding the eBay store?

eBay's minding the eBay store, of course (and freshening up its window-dressing from time to time). If you can't find the perfect item for your favorite eBay member with more than 11 million auctions (or so) running at any given time, go browse around eBay's General store, eBay Gear. You don't find any auctions here — just eBay logo items, such as shirts, bags, coffee mugs, and even an eBay gumball machine!

To get to eBay's online store, start at the home page. Scroll down to the very bottom and click the eBay-o-rama link. Just pick and choose what you like, add it to your shopping cart, and then check out when you're done. The store will ask you for specific billing information, so keep your credit card handy.

eBay's Favorite Searches e-mail service

If you're too busy to explore the nooks and crannies of eBay on a daily basis (or you're the type who wants to cut to the chase), sign up for eBay's personal shopper through your My eBay Favorites page.

This service is one of eBay's better ideas. It enables you to find what you're looking for and still have a life, because it sifts through the new listings for you 24 hours a day, looking for the items that meet your personalized description. eBay sniffs 'em out like a bloodhound. Then eBay sends you an e-mail containing a list of items that you may want to bid on, complete with links that take you right to those items. Hey, best of all, the service is free!

To register for the personal shopper e-mail service, begin on the navigation bar at the top of most eBay pages and follow these steps:

1. **Click Search on the navigation bar.**

   The subnavigation bar appears.

2. **Click the Favorite Searches link.**

   You go to the Favorites section of your My eBay page.

3. **Scroll down to the Favorite Searches box and click the Add New Search link.**

   This action takes you to the Search page.

4. **Complete the following information and then click the Search button:**

   • **Search:** Type the title of the item that interests you and select the Search Item Title and Description option. Searching item descriptions adds to the possibility of finding exactly what you're looking for.

   • **Price Range:** Enter the dollar amount (range) you're willing to spend. If you leave this blank, eBay searches all price ranges.

5. **After completing the search, just above the listings, you see the Add to My Favorite Searches link. Click this link to transfer that listing to your Favorite Searches page.**

   You see a list of your current searches. You have the option of simply adding the search, or deleting a search and adding this search in its place. Below the list of searches, you may select the period of time (from 7 days to 12 months) you'd like to receive the e-mails when items are listed. When you're happy with the results, click the link. The search appears in your Favorite Searches page.

   You may save up to 100 searches to be notified by e-mail. Yikes, don't do 100! All you'll get is e-mail from eBay!

Part V
The Part of Tens

The 5th Wave   By Rich Tennant

BUNGCO
BUNGEE CABLE
COMPANY

"Come on Walt — we need a shot of the product in
action to bring in more bids."

In this part . . .

1n keeping with a long tradition, this part gives you the short version, kinda like the CliffsNotes version. Check here for the golden rules every eBay user needs to know, whether you buy or sell (or, like most eBay members, do both).

I also give you information on some of the software programs available to help simplify your auction experience — from creating a catchy auction item page to helping you snipe the final bid while you're sleeping, walking Fido, washing your hair, or otherwise occupied. The best thing about some of these programs is that the price is right — you can get started for free.

Following the Part of Tens chapters, you get two appendixes. Appendix A gives you eBay fanatics exactly what you've been looking for — tips to help you acquire stock and take your auction habit to the next level by thinking strategically. And if you decide to really go into business and sell on eBay, Appendix B gives you some great ideas.

Chapter 19

Ten (Or So) Golden Rules for eBay Buyers and Sellers

. . . .

. . . .

*N*o matter how much experience an airplane pilot may have, he always keeps a checklist to go over. The same is true at eBay (although the only crashing that you need to worry about is on your computer). No matter how many times you buy, the advice in this chapter can help you survive and thrive at eBay.

Although conducting business at eBay is relatively smooth overall, any venture is bound to have a few bumps here and there. Here are ten (or so) easy, important golden rules for eBay. I note which tips are geared toward buyers or sellers. Happy hunting and gathering!

Keep these buyer and seller golden rules at the heart of all your dealings at eBay. After a while, posting auctions and bidding become rote. You can all too easily forget the basics, so look at this chapter every now and again and remember that, as an eBay member, you're part of a very special person-to-person community.

Buyer: Investigate Your Treasure before You Buy

In the excitement of finding just what you want, you may develop a tendency to leap before you look. Even if the item is closing soon, carefully read the item description. Does the item have any flaws? Can you live with it? Is something missing from the description that should be there? Did you read the terms of payment and shipping?

You can also communicate with the seller of the item that you're longing for. Don't be too shy or embarrassed. If you have any questions, send an e-mail! You're better off covering your bases before you place a bid than facing disappointment after making a purchase. Remember that when you click the bid or buy button, you are legally and morally obligated to go through with the transaction if you win. Make sure that parts are original and check for a warranty or return policy. Clarify everything upfront. If the seller doesn't answer back, consider that nonresponse an *early warning* that dealing with this person may be a mistake!

Buyer: Check the Seller's Feedback

Never bid without checking the seller's feedback. You need to be able to trust the person you're buying from. Don't just evaluate the Feedback percentage: Investigate the seller's feedback by clicking the number next to his or her name. Be sure to read the comments left by other users. Checking some of the seller's other auctions, past and present, to get an idea of the seller's history also can't hurt. As badly as you may want something, sending money to someone with a high feedback rating but who recently got a bunch of negatives could be risky business.

Buyer: Understand Post-Auction Charges and Payment Methods

Before you bid on an item, make sure that you and the seller agree on shipping and handling, insurance, and escrow fees (if applicable — see Chapter 6). Buying a $10 item and finding out that shipping and handling are going to cost more than your winning bid is a real bummer. Don't forget to ask about any "handling charges." Many sellers don't want the added hassle of an escrow service; make sure that they're agreeable if you want to use that option.

Also, make sure that you and the seller can agree on the form of payment before the deal closes. Is the seller willing to accept a personal check? Are you willing to wait to receive your purchase until a check clears? Is credit card payment available? Is the seller using a secure method of accepting credit cards like PayPal?

Buyer: Check the Item Price Tag and Bid Wisely

Before you bid, make sure that you have some knowledge of the item, even if you limit your search to completed auctions to get an idea of how much the item went for in the past. If a deal sounds too good to be true, it may well be.

I love eBay — but not for every single thing that I buy. Make sure that you can't get the item cheaper at the store or from an online seller.

Beware of getting caught up in the frenzy of last-minute bidding: It's an easy thing to do. Whether you choose proxy bidding or sniping (see Chapter 7 for my discussion on sniping), decide how much you're willing to pay before bidding. If you set a limit, you aren't overcome with the urge to spend more than an item is worth — or, worse, more than you have in your bank account.

Although eBay is lots of fun, it's also serious business. Bidding is a legal and binding contract. Don't get a bad reputation by retracting bids or becoming a deadbeat.

Buyer: Be a Good Buyer Bee

Always leave feedback after you put the finishing touches on a transaction. Leaving feedback, and thereby helping other members, is your responsibility.

Remember your manners, too, when sending off your payment. You like to be paid on time, right? And, speaking practically, the sooner you send in the dough, the sooner you get your stuff.

Buyer: Cover Your Assets

Remember that just because you're conducting transactions from the privacy of your home doesn't mean that you're doing everything you can to protect your privacy. Legitimate buyers and sellers *never* need to know your password or Social Security number. Do not respond to this sort of e-mail. See Chapter 15 about how to handle this sort of e-mail.

To fight back against computer viruses — which can spread through e-mail attachments and ruin your day, your auction, and maybe your computer — purchase a good antivirus software program and update it often. McAfee VirusScan (at www.mcafee.com) and Symantec's Norton AntiVirus (at www.nortonutilities.com) are both excellent antivirus programs.

Seller: Know Your Stuff

Do some homework. Know the value of your item. At the very least, get an idea of your item's value by searching completed auctions of similar items. Knowing your product also means that you can accurately describe what you have and never, ever pass off a fake as the real McCoy. Make sure that your item isn't prohibited, illegal, questionable, or infringing. It's your responsibility!

Before posting your auction, you should take the following actions:

- Establish what kinds of payment you're willing to accept.
- Set your check-holding policy (usually seven to ten days).
- Spell out your shipping and handling charges.

Add each of the preceding pieces of info to your item's description to avoid any unnecessary disputes later on.

Seller: Polish and Shine

Make sure that your title is descriptive enough to catch the eye of someone browsing a category and detailed enough for eBay's search engine to identify. Don't just write *1960s Board Game*. Instead, give some details: *Tiny Tim Vintage '60s Board Game MIB*. That gets 'em tiptoeing to your auction.

Play editor and scrutinize your text for grammar mistakes and misspellings. Typos in either your title or description can cost you money. For example, a search engine will keep skipping over your *Mikky Mouce Cokie Jare*. Spelling counts — and pays. Double-check your work!

Seller: Picture-Perfect Facts

Photos can be a boon or a bust at eBay. Double-check the photo of your item before you post it. Is the lighting okay? Does the photo paint a flattering image of the item? Crop out unnecessary backgrounds. Would *you* buy this item?

Make sure that your image actually appears on your auction page (and that it's not lost in cyberspace) and that it doesn't take too long to download. And just adding an image doesn't mean that you can skip writing a detailed item description.

Be factual and honest. At eBay, all you have is your reputation, so don't jeopardize it by lying about your item or terms. Tell potential buyers about any flaws. Give as complete a description as possible, with all the facts about the item that you can include.

Seller: Communication Is Key

Respond quickly and honestly to all questions sent via e-mail and use the contact to establish a good relationship. Don't let more than 24 hours pass without sending a response. If a bidder makes a reasonable request about payment or shipping, going along with that request is usually worth it to make a sale. *Remember:* The customer is always right! (Well, some of the time, anyway.)

Be upfront and fair when charging for sending merchandise to your buyer. You don't make a fortune overcharging for shipping and handling. After the item arrives, the buyer sees what it cost to ship. Unreasonable charges inevitably lead to bad feelings and negative feedback.

Seller: Be a Buyer's Dream

Just because you're transacting through the computer doesn't mean that you can forget your manners. Live by the golden rule: Do unto others as you would have others do unto you. Contact the buyer within three business days — within 24 hours is even better. And keep all your correspondence polite.

Ship the goods as soon as you can (in accordance with the shipping terms you outline in the item description, of course). An e-mail stating that the item is on its way is always a nice touch, too. That way, buyers can eagerly anticipate the arrival of their goods.

And, when shipping your items, use good packing materials and sturdy boxes to prevent disaster. Broken or damaged items can lead to reputation-damaging, negative feedback. Pack as if someone's out to destroy your package (or as if *you* had made this purchase). Your buyers are sure to appreciate the effort.

Seller: Listen to the Music

As I state in the golden rules for buyers, don't underestimate the power of positive feedback. Your reputation is at stake. Always generously dole out feedback when you complete a transaction. Your buyers will appreciate it and should return the favor.

What should you do if you get slammed unfairly with negative feedback? Don't freak out! Don't retaliate. Do, however, post a response to the feedback by using the Respond to Feedback link on your My eBay page. Those who read your feedback can often see past a single disgruntled message.

Buyers and Sellers: Keep Current, Keep Cool

You'd be surprised at the number of users who get suspended even though they have automatic credit card payment. Maybe they move. Or they change Internet service providers. Regardless, if you don't update your contact and credit card information, and eBay and other users can't contact you as a result, you can be suspended.

If you make any major moves (home address, billing address, ISP provider), let eBay know this new contact information. As soon as you know your new credit card number, your mailing address, e-mail address, or contact phone number, click Services on the main navigation bar. Scroll down to My eBay Preferences and update the appropriate information.

Chapter 20

Ten (Or So) Programs and Services to Ease Your Way on eBay

*R*eady to take your auctions to the next level? Are you looking for cool text or fancy layouts to make your auctions scream out, "Buy me!"? Need to slip in a bid in the middle of the night without losing sleep? If so, here's a list of ten (or so) software programs and services to make your bidding life easier and help put your auctions ahead of the pack.

As online auctions grow in popularity, software developers are constantly upgrading and developing new auction software to meet eBay's changes. Many of these programs even look for new versions of themselves — and update themselves as you start them. (Aladdin never had things so good.)

You don't have to use any of these programs or services to run an eBay auction successfully. When you're running more than several auctions a week, the addition of a "helper" makes things go ever so much smoother.

A massive amount of companies out there are offering online management service and offline programs. I can't cover them all, so the software that I mention in this chapter has been tried and tested by me. You may know of others, and I'd love to hear about them. I do know that these work and are good tools when you choose to expand your eBay sales.

Listed in this chapter are several auction-management Web sites. Each site has its own distinct personality. I also provide the names of some terrific offline software programs you can use to help manage your auctions, make your e-auctions elegant and eye-catching, find the best prices, and snatch up that bargain at the last minute.

Be sure to check my Web site www.coolebaytools.com for updates on software and services, as well as special discounts that are offered to my readers.

Online Services

You're comfortable transacting your auctions online, so why not manage them online as well? These sites offer incredibly useful services that save time in both posting your auctions and wrapping them up.

Auction Hawk

Auction Hawk is a fast-rising star of Web-based management services. The best part about its service is that you pay a flat monthly fee, based on the number of auctions you want to run per month. With its easy-to-use service, the little guy can get the same benefits as large-volume sellers but pay smaller fees. Auction Hawk has won many awards for its service including *Forbes* magazine's Best of the Web.

You can manage every aspect of your eBay sales, including image hosting, ad design, automated e-mail management, and report tracking. If you want to get fancy, you can design your item listing from any of Auction Hawk's over 300 templates. Here are some more features:

- ✔ Your customer can check out directly with you and pay through PayPal. Buyers can combine multiple purchases (with discounted shipping) for checkout and invoices. You can even schedule your listings in advance without incurring additional eBay fees.

- ✔ You get detailed, hourly counter statistics.

- ✔ The service integrates directly with Endicia.com for one of the speediest shipping solutions possible (see Chapter 12 for more information on Endicia).

- ✔ If you're not ready to dive right in for full management, Auction Hawk offers Web hosting for your eBay images for a low monthly fee.

Visit Auction Hawk's Web site (www.auctionhawk.com) for a free trial: You get 21 days of the full service (up to 50 listings) and image hosting.

Auctionworks

"The Leader in Marketplace Management" proclaims the Auctionworks home page, and indeed, that's just what the site delivers. Auctionworks was one of eBay's first preferred providers in 1999 and has been serving thousands of professional sellers since. It's used by many top PowerSellers who have to manage large inventories and launch lots of listings. It's a very professional and automated way to handle auctions.

Here are just a few of its many advanced features:

- **Advanced Inventory Management:** Auctionworks has an easy-to-use inventory-management system that enables you to post items in your own area on the site and list them at eBay whenever you want. You can organize them in individual folders that you create.
- **Robust Business Management:** Auctionworks tracks all functions relating to the selling process: notifications, payments, shipments, and feedback — all of which the system automates to save you time. It also integrates with PayPal to facilitate auction payments, and with UPS and the U.S. Postal Service for label printing.

By using its tools, sellers can manage inventory, images, customers, financial data, and post-auction tasks. Of course, Auctionworks also offers professionally designed description templates, image hosting, and a wide variety of counters. All sellers get a storefront, too — your very own e-commerce site.

Make sure that you check out what's new on the Auctionworks Web site (www.auctionworks.com), and you can sign up for a free two-week trial.

BidRobot

As you can tell by reading Chapter 7, I'm a big fan of sniping. It's my favorite way to win an auction. It makes the entire auction experience even more entertaining. Sadly, with the schedule I keep, I am rarely at my computer when the auctions close!

BidRobot to the rescue. When I find an auction that I'm serious about, I simply go to the BidRobot Web site, log in, and place my future snipe bids. All I have to do is type in the item number and my high bid, and that's it. I can shut off my computer knowing that BidRobot will do my bidding for me. Nobody on eBay will know what item I'm desperate to have, because the magical BidRobot doesn't place my bid until a few seconds before the auction closes. If I'm the high bidder, no one will have the chance to bid against me!

BidRobot's services are reasonably priced, based on the amount of time that you want to use the service. You pay a flat rate for all the snipes you can handle. You don't pay any extra charges for the service. BidRobot's Web site is www.bidrobot.com.

ManageAuctions

How you manage your auctions is a very personal choice. ManageAuctions provides complete, low-cost auction-management services, as well as easy-upload image hosting and hourly counters. You can determine not only how many people view your auctions, but also when they view them.

You don't need to post your auctions through the site, although it offers a patent-pending process for bulk launching at eBay. ManageAuctions can also retrieve your existing auctions from eBay and perform its services from any point in the auction's progress. The following list describes a few of the site's other services:

- ✔ E-mail management, and label and postage printing through its partner Stamps.com for after-the-auction shipping
- ✔ Photo hosting for your eBay images

Check out the site's services at www.manageauctions.com.

Software for Offline Use

Software for offline use can handily reside on your computer after a simple download from a Web site. As with online services, this software comes in a variety of flavors, so take a look and decide which program works best for you. Downloadable software may be available from Web sites that offer other services and can be used whether you are online or not. Offline software enables you to handle auctions in your spare time, without the limitations of ISPs or servers.

Auction Wizard 2000

Auction Wizard 2000 is a full-service professional auction-management software package developed by eBay sellers. The software is fairly simple and amazingly powerful. It expedites all the seller functions for running and completing auctions, including automating the following tasks:

- ✔ Inputting your inventory on the software's HTML templates and uploading auctions in bulk onto eBay.

✔ Automatically updating the software with the current status of your auctions, including who won, who is a runner-up, and the auction bidding history. The preformatted e-mail and feedback files automatically fill in the values from each auction and send them to the people you do business with directly through the software.

✔ Tracking income and expenses, as well as creating a full set of reports.

This software also really shines in its ability to track consignors' information. That's when you're selling items for someone else, on *consignment.* It even computes the fees that you're charging for your services.

Download a fully functional 60-day test drive with no inactive features and no restrictions from www.auctionwizard2000.com.

Cricket Software

Cricket Software has been around almost as long as eBay has been in the auction business, since 1997. The owner of Cricket Software was an eBay user who saw a need and invented the first sniping software. Over the years, he has expanded his interests and developed some very useful eBay utilities:

✔ **Cricket Jr. Power Sniper program:** Cricket Jr. automatically handles your bid sniping for you right from your home computer. (See Chapter 7 for more on bidding strategies.)

✔ **Safe2Bid:** Safe2Bid is an easy-to-use program that makes checking feedback a simple task. With this software, input a seller's (or a bidder's) User ID, and Safe2Bid does a thorough check of his or her eBay reputation. The program extracts all negative and neutral feedback for your examination. Safe2Bid also helps you detect shill bidding. (Beware shill bidders — see Chapter 16).

For more information, go to www.cricketsniper.com.

Finally for the Mac!

Rejoice! You Mac users out there now have a software utility that will help with your auctions at eBay. **eLister 2** is a full-powered offline listing program that allows you the freedom to write up auctions on your own time and includes a group of good-looking auction templates.

It includes an automatic HTML generator and an automatic listing fee calculator. Visit www.blackmagik.com/; the program is updated regularly to conform to any changes in eBay listing procedures.

SpoonFeeder

This software program made quite a splash at this year's "eBay Live." It comes in Basic, Standard, and Full versions. Because you're likely just starting out here, I'll tell you what you get with the Basic version. It's loaded with lots of options that you expect in auction software, including auction scheduling (as long as your computer is on). Here are some of its unique features:

- A photo editor is embedded in the listing creator. It really helps make your pictures clearer and ready for eBay.
- Free photo hosting for all SpoonFeeder users. (Yes, *free* hosting for *all* your eBay pictures.)
- A description builder that has a spell checker (sew very impurtent) and a thesaurus to help you find the right words for your description.
- Support for the specialized listings for eBay Motors.

The Basic version of SpoonFeeder is $19.95. A free trial download and information on the more advanced versions are available at www.spoonfeeder.com.

Virtual Auction Ad Pro

Virtual Auction Ad Pro is a snappy little HTML generator. It takes you through an easy-to-use process that helps spruce up your eBay auctions with an HTML touch. I like its simple approach, and it's easy for beginners to use. The software enables you to perform the following tasks:

- Design auction descriptions in four different fonts with seven different sizes in millions of colors. You can also use auction titles and subtitles in your descriptions in three different sizes.
- Create descriptions in a snap with six templates (layout designs) and add up to two photos with your description.

Download a trial version of Virtual Auction Ad Pro (bundled with two other auction utilities) at www.virtualnotions.com/vadpro.

eBay's Software and Services

When the users call, eBay answers! As eBay grew, the need for additional services and software also grew. eBay answered the need with Turbo Lister software and its PowerSeller program. Read on to see how these services tailored for the eBay user may benefit you.

eBay's Turbo Lister

Turbo Lister is free software that enables you to upload many auctions simultaneously. After you prepare your auctions offline, the software uploads your auctions to eBay with just the click of a button. You can edit, preview, and (whenever you're ready) launch all your auctions at once, or schedule them to launch at different times (which costs you $0.10 for each scheduled auction). Your items can include eBay's templates at no charge, and the items will remain archived on your computer for later use. The software is very convenient and simple to use even if you have only a few auctions at one time — although Turbo Lister will let you launch thousands of auctions at a time!

The program is free, and you can download it at `pages.ebay.com/ turbo_lister`. If your connection is slow and you don't want to wait for the 18MB download, you can get a CD from eBay at the eBay-o-rama store and just pay shipping costs.

Selling Manager and Selling Manager Pro

I have used Selling Manager for my eBay auctions, and I find it to be a very convenient way to track the progress of my sales, send e-mails, leave feedback, relist singly (or in bulk), and keep track of what has and hasn't sold. The program works very well when used in conjunction with Turbo Lister.

As you can see from Figure 20-1, Selling Manager replaces the Selling tab in your My eBay area. This thorough data is updated automatically from eBay's servers and PayPal, so you have up-to-the-minute data.

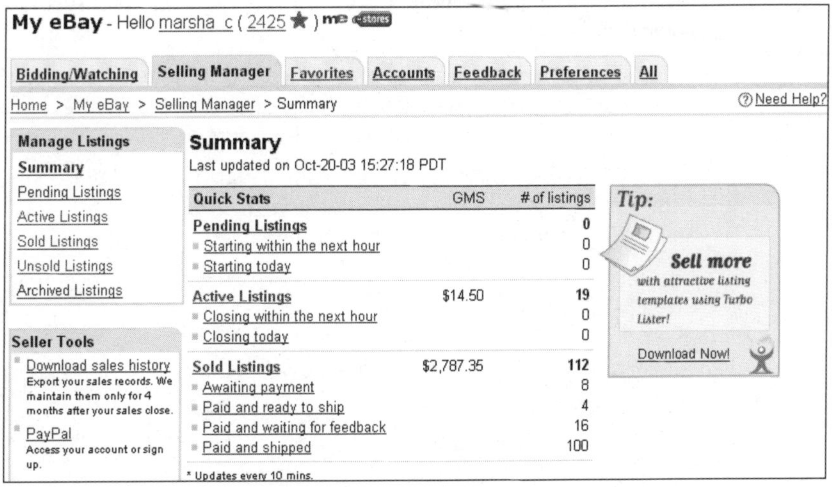

Figure 20-1: My Selling Manager home page.

Selling Manager is available from eBay for $4.99 a month. The Pro version, which adds inventory management and reporting features, is tailored to high-volume sellers, and it costs $15.99 a month. Both versions are available for a 30-day free trial at www.ebay.com/selling_manager/products.html.

eBay PowerSellers program

eBay offers an elite club for PowerSellers who fulfill the following requirements:

✔ Maintain a 98-percent positive feedback average with 100 or more feedback comments and an excellent sales performance record.

✔ List a minimum of four average monthly items for the past three months.

✔ Maintain minimum monthly gross sales of $1,000 of average gross monthly sales (Bronze level).

No, you don't need to wear an ugly tie. PowerSellers get a special icon next to their User IDs on the eBay site, thereby giving potential bidders the assurance that they're dealing with a seller of good repute who stands behind each sale. PowerSellers who meet or exceed eBay's requirements also get the following benefits:

✔ At the Bronze level and higher, you get a physical display sign for your place of business or for trade shows, identifying you as an eBay PowerSeller. Also, you get VIP admission to eBay events and access to 24/7 e-mail tech support with a very fast response time.

✔ $3,000 average in monthly gross sales (Silver level) gets you the benefits of the Bronze level, plus you can access a dedicated team of account specialists to handle your phone support in real time during eBay business hours.

✔ $10,000 average in monthly gross sales (Gold level) gets you the benefits of the Silver level, plus a dedicated account manager and a dedicated support hotline, 24 hours a day, 7 days a week!

✔ $25,000 average month in gross sales (Platinum) gets you Silver, Bronze, and Gold level benefits, plus I'll bet you get quicker callbacks from your account manager than at the Gold level.

✔ $150,000 average month in gross sales (Titanium) probably gets you a whole lot of special attention!

If you feel that you qualify for eBay's PowerSellers service (eBay knows who you are!), apply at pages.ebay.com/services/buyandsell/welcome.html.

Trading Assistant Program

For experienced eBay sellers who have a feedback rating of 97 percent or more, the Trading Assistant program is the place to be! This is the place where you can register to sell items for others who don't have the time or inclination to learn how to sell on eBay.

All the knowledge you've gained from reading this book will help you get items to sell. People with items to sell go to `pages.eBay.com/trading_assistants` and search for Trading Assistants by zip or area codes. After their search, they're presented with a list of sellers that are ready and willing to sell their goods (that's you, right?). Take a look at some of the sellers in your area that act as Trading Assistants to get an idea of what you should charge for your services.

For full information, go to `pages.ebay.com/tradingassistants/learnmore.html`.

Seller's Assistant Basic and Pro

Seller's Assistant software helps you design your auction-item pages, upload your images, fill in forms automatically, place your auctions, and track them. Its management forms keep you up-to-date on the progress of your transactions with the help of the Auto Fetch feature, which downloads auction information directly from eBay. Seller's Assistant became part of eBay in late 1999.

Seller's Assistant fees are paid on a monthly basis. The Basic version costs $9.99 and month and the Pro, $15.99. To check them out or to download the software, go to `pages.ebay.com/sellers_assistant`.

Appendix A

Answers for the Fanatic: Finding More Stuff to Sell

● ●

*A*fter you pick clean everything not nailed down in your house, you may want to broaden your horizons. The key to successfully selling items at eBay is to find things people actually want to buy at the right price. (Wow, what an incredible observation.) I know it seems obvious, but having stuff to *sell* isn't always the same as having things people *want to buy*. Using this concept, you can teach yourself all kinds of effective marketing strategies. Finding the item that may be "the next big thing" takes lots of work, timing, and sometimes a dose of good luck.

As an eBay seller, no doubt you'll receive tons of spam (unsolicited e-mails) guaranteeing that the sender has the hottest-selling items for you to sell on eBay. Think about this for a second. If you had the hot ticket, wouldn't you be selling it on eBay and making the fortune yourself? These people make money by preying on those who think there's a magic way to make money on eBay. There isn't. It takes old-fashioned elbow grease and research.

Knowing the Market

Just as successful stockbrokers know about individual companies, they also need to know about the marketplace as a whole. Sure, I know about the 300 Beanie Babies out there, and so does nearly everyone else. To get a leg up on your competition, you need to know the big picture as well. Here are some questions you should ask yourself as you contemplate making serious buckets of money (well, I hope) by selling items at eBay:

- ✔ **What items are currently hot?** If you see everyone around you rushing to the store to buy a particular item, chances are good that the item will become more valuable as stocks of it diminish. The simple rule of supply and demand says that whoever has something everyone else wants stands to gain major profits.

- ✔ **Do I see a growing interest in a specific item that might make it a big seller?** If you're starting to hear talk about a particular item, or even an era ('70s nostalgia? '60s aluminum Christmas trees? Who knew?), listen carefully and think of what you already own (or can get your hands on) that can help you catch a piece of the trend's action.

- ✔ **Should I hold on to this item and wait for its value to increase, or should I sell now?** Knowing when to sell an item that you think people may want is a tricky business. Sometimes, you can catch the trend too early and find out that you could have commanded a better price if only you waited. Other times, you may catch a fad that's already passé and find that no one's interested anymore. It's best to test the market with a small quantity of your hoard, dribbling items individually into the market until you've made back the money you spent to acquire them. When you have your cash back, the rest will be gravy.

- ✔ **Is a company discontinuing an item I should stockpile now and sell later?** Pay attention to items that are discontinued, especially toys and novelty items. If you find an item that a manufacturer has a limited supply of, you could make a tidy profit. If the manufacturer ends up reissuing the item, don't forget that the original run is still the most coveted — and valuable.

- ✔ **Was there a recall, an error, or a legal proceeding associated with my item?** If so, how will it affect the value of the item? For example, a toy recalled for safety reasons may no longer be appropriate for the kids, but it could be rare and collectible if intact.

Some people like to go with their gut feelings about when and what to buy for resale at eBay. By all means, if instinct has worked for you in the past, factor instinct in here, too. If you've done some research that looks optimistic but your gut says, "I'm not sure," listen to it; don't assume you're just hearing that lunchtime taco talking. Try testing the waters by purchasing *one* of the prospective items for resale at eBay. If that sale doesn't work out, you won't have a lot of money invested, and you can credit your gut with saving you some bucks.

Do You Have a Talent?

If you're talented in any way, you can sell your services on eBay. Home artisans, chefs, and even stay-at-home psychics are transacting business daily on the site. What a great way to make money on eBay — make your own product!

Many custom items do well on eBay. There's a demand for personalized invitations, cards, and announcements — and even return address labels (and you thought you had all you needed). Calligraphic work or computer-designed (customized with Fluffy and Fido's picture, awww) items are in big demand today, but no one seems to have the time to make them. Savvy sellers with talent can fill this market niche.

People go to trendy places (when they have the time) like Soho, the Grove, or the Village to find unique custom jewelry. They also go to eBay.

The world is your oyster on eBay, and the sky is the limit. Use your imagination, and you might be surprised at what your new business will be!

Catching Trends in the Media

Catching trends is all about listening and looking. You can find all kinds of inside information from newspapers, magazines, television, and of course, the Internet. Believe it or not, you can even find out what people are interested in these days by bribing a kid. Keep your eyes and ears open. When people say, "That Taco Bell Chihuahua is *everywhere* these days," instead of nodding your head vacantly, start getting ideas.

In newspapers

Newspapers are bombarded by press releases and inside information from companies the world over. Pay close attention to the various sections of the newspaper. Look for stories on celebrities and upcoming movies and see if any old fads are making a resurgence (you can sell items as "retro chic").

Read the stories about trade conventions, like the New York Toy Fair or the Consumer Electronics show. New products are introduced and given the thumbs up or down by journalists. This way you can start to think about the direction your area of expertise is going in.

On television

No matter what you think of television, it has an enormous impact on which trends come and go and which ones stick. Why else would advertisers sink billions of dollars into TV commercials? And look at the impact of Oprah's Book Club. Just one Oprah appearance for an author can turn a book into an overnight bestseller. More and more celebrities (even Homer Simpson) are talking about eBay. The buzz brings people to the site.

Tune in to morning news shows and afternoon talk shows. See what's being featured in the programs. The producers of these shows are on top of pop culture and move fast to be the first to bring you the next big thing. Take what they feature and think of a marketing angle. If you don't, you can be sure somebody else will.

Catch up with youth culture . . .

. . . or at least keep good tabs on it. There's no catching up with it, just as there's no way to say this without sounding over-the-hill: If you remember cranking up The Beatles, James Brown, or The Partridge Family (say what?) until your parents screamed, "Shut that awful noise off," you may be at that awkward time of life when you hardly see the appeal of what young people are doing or listening to. But if you want tips for hot auction items, tolerate the awful noise and listen to the kids around you. Children, especially pre-teens and teens, may be the best trend-spotters on the planet. See what kind of marketing tips you get when you ask a kid questions like these:

- ✔ **What's cool at the moment?** Or "rad" if you want to sound cool — whoops, that was '80s-speak, wasn't it?

- ✔ **What's totally uncool that was cool two months ago?** Their world moves at warp speed!

- ✔ **What music are you buying?** Christina Aguilera, The Neptunes, and Sum 41 — yup, all the hot bands with big hits — but maybe *ewww-that's-so-five-minutes-ago* by the time you read this.

- ✔ **What could I buy you that would make you really happy?** *Hint:* If the kid says, "A red BMW Z-3," or "Liposuction," look for a younger kid.

Check out eBay

The staff at eBay sends out reports regarding the up-and-coming items by category. Check out the "hot item" postings from the eBay staff by going to the Community hub page. In the Talk box, click the link for discussion boards. Scroll to the bottom, and you'll find the link for the Hot Items read-only discussion board.

Check out magazines

Magazines geared to the 18-to-34 age group (and sometimes to younger teens) can help you stay on top of what's hot. See what the big companies are pitching to this target audience (and whether they're succeeding). If a celebrity's suddenly visible in every other headline or magazine, be on the lookout for merchandise relating to that person. (Are we talking hysteria-plus-cash flow here, or just hysteria?)

The Hunt for eBay Inventory

If you're not sure what you want to sell for profit at eBay — but you're a shop-till-you-drop person by nature — then you've got an edge. Incorporate your advanced shopping techniques into your daily routine. If you find a bargain that interests you, chances are you have a knack for spotting stuff that other shoppers would love to get their hands on.

The goods are out there

When you shop to sell at eBay, don't rule out any shopping venue. From the trendiest boutique to the smallest junk shop, garage sales to Saks Outlet, keep your eye out for eBay inventory. The items people look for at eBay are out there; you just have to find them.

Check your favorite eBay category and see what the hot-selling item is. Better yet, go to your favorite store and make friends with the manager. Store managers are often privy to this type of information a couple of months in advance of a product release. If you ask, they'll tell you what's going to be the new hot item next month. After you're armed with the information you need, search out that item for the lowest price you can, and then you can give it a shot on eBay.

Keep these shopping locales in mind when you go on the eBay hunt:

✔ Upscale department stores, trendy boutiques, outlet stores, or flagship designer stores are good places to do some market research. Check out the newest items and then head to the clearance area or outlet store and scrutinize the bargain racks for brand-name items.

✔ Tour discount and dollar stores in your area. Many of the items these places carry are *overruns* (too many of something that didn't sell), *small runs* (too little of something that the big guys weren't interested in stocking), or out-of-date fad items that need a good home at eBay.

✔ Garage sales, tag sales, and moving sales offer some of the biggest bargains you'll ever come across. Check for vintage kitchen pieces and old toys, and make 'em an offer they can't refuse.

✔ Thrift stores are packed with used but usually good quality items. And you can feel good knowing that the money you spend in a nonprofit thrift shop is going to a good cause.

✔ Find going-out-of-business sales. You can pick up bargains if a shopkeeper just wants to empty the shelves so the store can close.

✔ Take advantage of any flea markets or swap meets in your area.

✔ Gift shops at museums, monuments, national parks, and theme parks can provide eBay inventory — but think about where to sell the items. Part of your selling success on eBay is *access*. People who can't get to Graceland may pay handsomely for an Elvis mini-guitar with the official logo on the box.

✔ Hang on to the freebies you get. If you receive handouts (lapel pins, pencils, pamphlets, books, interesting napkins, flashlights, towels, stuffed toys) from a sporting event, premiere, or historic event — or even a collectible freebie from a fast-food restaurant — they could be your ticket to some eBay sales.

Tips for the modest investor

If you're interested in making money in your eBay ventures but you're starting with limited cash, follow this list of eBay inventory Do's and Don'ts:

✔ **Don't** spend more than you can afford to lose. If you shop at boutiques and expensive department stores, buy things that you like to wear yourself (or give as gifts) in case they don't sell.

✔ **Do** try to find something local that's unavailable in a wider area. For example, if you live in an out-of-the-way place that has a local specialty, try selling that at eBay.

✔ **Don't** go overboard and buy something really cheap just because it's cheap. Figure out who would want the item first.

✔ **Do** consider buying in bulk, especially if you know the item sells well at eBay or if the item is inexpensive. Chances are good that if you buy one and it sells well at eBay, by the time you try to buy more, the item's sold out. If an item is inexpensive (say 99 cents), I always buy at least five of it. If no one bids on the item when you hold your auction, you're only out $5. (Anyone out there need any Bicentennial Commemorative coffee mugs?)

Appendix B

Ramping Up Your eBay Business

*B*oy, do I know the feeling! You started out slowly selling on eBay, and now you've sold quite a few things. You're thinking about devoting more time to your eBay business because you've begun to pull down some serious cash — and you think that you could make more. Now what?

It's time to get serious. You have the beginnings of a real-live e-business. Really and truly, you do! Yep, you may even become the next e-commerce tycoon. I don't want to burst your balloon, but you don't want to put the cart before the horse. You're going to need a few things before you can take over the Internet retail world and challenge those Shooting Star PowerSellers.

In this last part of the book, I give you a few pointers to steer you in the right direction to get your eBay business started. I highly recommend that you grab a copy of my other book, *Starting an eBay Business For Dummies* (Wiley Publishing, Inc.), which expands on all the ideas discussed in this chapter and more.

Professional Is as Professional Does

Ignore those silly, get-rich-quick-on-eBay e-mails. You're smarter than that. If you think a single class (daylong or otherwise) can make you an overnight success on eBay, you're sadly mistaken. Those who succeed on eBay have one of two things in common:

- ✔ They have a background in retailing and have a solid understanding of merchandising and marketing.
- ✔ They went to the school of hard knocks by observing and studying (like most of us) and applied what they learned — and succeeded.

In the next few sections, I profile two eBay users who have found success running eBay businesses. What do these two people have in common? They worked hard to get where they wanted to be. They didn't sit back and wait for magic flakes to fall from the sky and bless them with success. They knew what they wanted to do and pursued their goals. You can do that, too; no one is too old, too poor, or too busy. (Remember that you can run an eBay business part time.)

BornToDeal

There's nothing wrong with the school of hard knocks. Take the example of my friend Christopher Spencer, eBay user *BornToDeal*. Chris was definitely born to deal. When he was six, he was earning almost $50 a week recycling newspapers. In high school, rather than giving apples to teachers, he sold teachers home-baked cakes and cookies, making about $300 a month.

Chris's penchant for computers eventually led him to eBay, in 1999. He began by talking the owners of a local antiques store into letting him sell a few items on eBay on their behalf. He was quickly hooked. Christopher now runs close to 1,000 sales a week for those who want to sell items on eBay. He should be an inspiration for all Trading Assistants (see Chapter 20 on those who sell for others) on eBay.

Christopher's eBay business is big enough that he rents space in a commercial area and has people working full time to help him. By the way, Chris and I work together as instructors at eBay University.

PreservationPublishing

Jillian Cline is an author of note in an interesting field: She has written dog books — five to be exact. She has also trained and bred beautiful companion and show dogs. She's a real go-getter, forming her own publishing company and producing a line of cool dog gear to sell to pet lovers. Before eBay, Jillian sold her items though ads in magazines and through a slew of vendors at dog shows.

Jillian is also an expert on breed-specific legislation and has appeared on radio and television shows including *Oprah*. She opened her own e-commerce Web site and then gave eBay a try to expand her horizons. Despite her busy schedule, Jillian finds the time to sell items on eBay. Although it's not her entire business, she feels that it's an important addition to her commerce mix.

Organization Is Key

Organization is the key word for any retail business. Yes, your part- or full-time eBay business is an online retail business. I don't want you to think that getting organized is a big giant pain, but it will take some planning. You can compete successfully with the big guys. I do, and all serious eBay sellers can, too.

Setting up your eBay office

It's time to move the stuff out of the corner of your closet (or is it all over the dining room table?) and put it up on shelves. For starters, use any old shelves, but get the merchandise off the furniture and get organized! Here are a few organizational tips:

- **Bag and categorize all your items.** Use plastic sandwich baggies and boxes — the white boxes they sell at office supply stores to store old file folders. These boxes have lots of white space, so you have plenty of room for labeling the contents of each box. And the cutout holes in the boxes act as handles for easy toting.

  If you want to get fancy (and plan for the future), use the translucent plastic bins that you can find at stores like Wal-Mart or Target. They have secure-closing tops and easy-to-lift handles.

- **Set aside a separate work area.** You'll need this for packing and wrapping your items. It will also help when you need to assemble your items to ship.

- **Designate a place for storing your packing materials.** I used to have a spare bathroom off my office. It's still somewhat of a bathroom, but the shower has shelves loaded with different sizes of boxes and mailing envelopes.

Automating your shipping

Go back to Chapter 12 and take a look at my recommendations for your shipping setup. When you start your eBay business, it's time to sign up with a shipping service. UPS, FedEx, and the United States Postal Service (through Endicia.com or Stamps.com) all provide software that will shave considerable time off your paperwork. And don't forget the shipping insurance policy mentioned in Chapter 12 — it costs nothing until you use it.

Spring for a thermal label printer. It will cut an eternity off the packing time of each item. Think about what kind of gizmos the big guys have. With the advent of the Internet, handy gadgets like label printers are available to the little guys, too.

Getting legal

With success comes responsibility — responsibility to your local community (translation: You need a business license) and your country (your partner, Uncle Sam). Depending on where you live, you may have to get a business license — even if you work out of your house. Often the license fees are less for home-based businesses.

When you apply for your business license, be sure to tell the nice folks at the county office that giant trucks won't be making deliveries several times a day to your home. Also, note that you won't be transacting business at your home. Your business transactions will take place online and through the mail. This really makes a big difference to the county and to your neighbors. If you get to the point where the trucks *are* coming several times a day, it just might be time to move to a commercial location.

If you want to buy your merchandise wholesale — that's part of the idea: Buy low, sell high — you need to find out if your state requires a resale or vendor's license. Most do. Genuine wholesalers will require you to produce this license as proof of your business status. If they don't ask for it, they're probably not legitimate wholesalers. This license also allows you to purchase items for sale without paying sales tax. When you resell the items, you will charge sales tax (assuming you live in a state with sales tax). You have to report and pay the tax you've collected to the state within predefined time periods.

Keeping records like a pro

If you're in a business, whether full time or part time, you have to keep some serious records. Get a good accounting program to keep your records. This isn't playtime; it's time to put out a professional image. If you want to do things right, talk to the person who prepares your taxes or go to an enrolled agent to help you set up the books. My *Starting an eBay Business For Dummies* book gives you more information on how you can get started at home.

Considering a wireless home network

A wireless home network really helps you keep your sanity because you don't have to be tethered to your desk everyday. Wouldn't it be nice to be able to do some of your eBay business while sitting on the porch or in a hammock in the garden? Believe it or not, it can be done — without going to great expense. I'm writing this chapter on my laptop in my living room (with a wireless PC card), which is picking up a live Internet connection from my office. If I want to print something, it prints on the printer that's in another room. When I'm done, I'll beam this chapter to my editor in Indianapolis. Now, that's progress!

For details on choosing hardware, setting up a network, and keeping it secure, check out *Wireless Home Networking For Dummies,* by Danny Briere, Pat Hurley, and Walter Bruce (Wiley Publishing, Inc.).

Index

• S •